Cracknell's

Law Students' Companion

Constitutional and Administrative Law

Cracknell's
Law Students' Companion

Constitutional and Administrative Law

Fourth Edition

MICHAEL T MOLAN, BA, LLM (Lond), Barrister
Head of Law, South Bank University

Series Editor
D.G.Cracknell, LLB
of the Middle Temple, Barrister

OBP

OLD BAILEY PRESS

OLD BAILEY PRESS LIMITED
The Gatehouse, Ruck Lane, Horsmonden, Kent TN12 8EA

First published 1967
Fourth edition 1995

ISBN 1 85836 006 4

British Library Cataloguing-in-Publication.

A CIP Catalogue record for this book is available from the British Library.

Printed and bound in Great Britain.

Contents

Preface   vii

Cases   1

Statutes   89

    Magna Carta 1297 [209]   89

    Bill of Rights 1688 [210–221]   89–91

    Act of Settlement 1700 [222–225]   91–93

    Parliament Act 1911 [226–233]   93–95

    Official Secrets Act 1911 [234–235]   95–96

    Emergency Powers Act 1920 [236–237]   96–97

    Official Secrets Act 1920 [238–239]   98–99

    Statute of Westminster 1931 [240–244]   99–100

    Public Order Act 1936 [245–246]   100–101

    Statutory Instruments Act 1946 [247–254] 102–105

    Crown Proceedings Act 1947 [255–260]   105–108

    Life Peerages Act 1958 [261]   108–109

    Obscene Publications Act 1959 [262–265] 109–112

    Peerage Act 1963 [266–271]   112–114

    Police Act 1964 [272]   114

    Obscene Publications Act 1964 [273–274] 115–116

    War Damage Act 1965 [275]   116

    Parliamentary Commissioner Act 1967
      [276–291]   116–128

    Criminal Law Act 1967 [292]   128

    Immigration Act 1971 [293–304]   128–135

    European Communities Act 1972 [305–307] 135–138

    House of Commons Disqualification
      Act 1975 [308–313]   138–141

    Ministers of the Crown Act 1975 [314–317] 141–143

    Representation of the People Act 1981
      [318–319]   143

    Contempt of Court Act 1981 [320–334]   143–147

    Supreme Court Act 1981 [335–336]   148–149

Representation of the People Act 1983
[337–342]   149–151
Police and Criminal Evidence Act 1984
[343–417]   151–208
Interception of Communications Act 1985
[418–424]   208–212
Parliamentary Constituencies Act 1986
[425–429]   213–214
Public Order Act 1986 [430–447]   215–225
Crown Proceedings (Armed Forces)
Act 1987 [448–449]   225
Immigration Act 1988 [450–452]   226–227
Prevention of Terrorism (Temporary
Provisions) Act 1989 [453–475]   228–243
Official Secrets Act 1989 [476–487]   243–251
Tribunals and Inquiries Act 1992 [488–500] 252–260
Asylum and Immigration Appeals
Act 1993 [501–506]   260–263
European Communities (Amendment)
Act 1993 [507–513]   263–264
Criminal Justice and Public Order Act 1994
[514–529]   264–278
Treaties   279
European Convention for the Protection
of Human Rights and Fundamental
Freedoms 1950 [530–547]   279–283
Glossary   285
Index   297

Preface

During the period between the publication of the first edition of this work (previous editions also covered English Legal System) and the preparation of material for this fourth edition, the significance and relevance of constitutional and administrative law has increased perhaps more than that of any other area of legal studies. Two factors in particular have contributed to a reassessment of the subject. The first of these is the continued development of the principles of administrative law through judicial review. Within the past few years there have been decisions dealing with key issues such as the scope of judicial review (*ex parte Datafin, ex parte Equal Opportunities Commission*), the availability of coercive remedies against the executive (*M v Home Office*), and the concept of fair procedure (*ex parte Richmond-upon-Thames LBC, ex parte Doody, ex parte Institute of Dental Surgery*). These decisions all help to further define both the public law powers and the duties of executive agencies, and the rights of citizens unable to pray in aid a written constitution.

A second factor has been the continued assimilation of the principles and concepts of Community law as the impact of membership of the European Union on the British constitution has become ever more apparent. Decisions featured in this fourth edition, such as *Marleasing, Francovich* and *ex parte Rees-Mogg*, reflect not only the fact that there are very few areas of public law where issues of Community law are likely to be irrelevant, but also the complexities and subtleties to be encountered when attempting to discern the interplay between domestic and Community law.

Inevitably, given the breadth of material to be drawn on in compiling a collection of case summaries in the area of constitutional and administrative law, decisions have had to be made in terms of authorities to be included and those to be omitted. It is, however, the author's intention that this latest edition should provide an accurate, stimulating and helpful picture of current trends and developments in the subject.

I have stated the case law as of 6 April 1995. The statutory material extracted in this book incorporates amendments as of July 1994 together with provisions and amendments to existing legislation introduced by the Police and Magistrates' Court Act 1994 and the Criminal Justice and Public Order Act 1994.

Michael T Molan
South Bank University
April 1995

Cases

Abbassy v Commissioner of Police of the Metropolis [1]
[1990] 1 WLR 385 (Court of Appeal)

The plaintiff, an Iranian, was stopped by the police and asked four times about the ownership of the Mercedes car he was driving. He refused to provide the information requested and told the officers that British laws meant nothing to him. The plaintiff was then told that he was being arrested for 'unlawful possession' of the car and was subsequently held in custody for some two hours before being released. In an action for, inter alia, wrongful arrest and false imprisonment the judge ruled that the arrest had been unlawful as the constable's explanation of the reason for the arrest had been insufficient. The plaintiff was awarded £5,000 damages. The defendants appealed. *Held,* the judge had been wrong to withdraw from the jury the issue of whether or not the arresting constable had provided a sufficient explanation of the grounds for the arrest. The rules summarised in the speech of Viscount Simon in *Christie* v *Leachinsky* remained unqualified in any material respect by the Criminal Law Act 1967 or the Police and Criminal Evidence Act 1984 Act. The question of whether or not an arrested person was reasonably informed of the reasons for that arrest was ultimately a question for the jury.

Adams v War Office [1955] 3 All ER 245 [2]

The plaintiff's son, a soldier, was taking part in a military exercise when he was killed by the bursting of a shell. The Minister of Pensions issued a certificate certifying that the son's death would be treated as attributable to service for the purposes of entitlement to an award under the Royal Warrant, but subsequently decided no award should be made because the deceased left no dependants. The plaintiff brought an action against the defendants under the Law Reform (Miscellaneous Provisions) Act 1934. *Held,* by reason of s10(1) of the Crown Proceedings Act 1947, the defendants were exempt from liability in tort where a certificate, as in the present case, was issued by the Minister, irrespective of whether any pension was actually paid.

Agricultural, Horticultural and Forestry Industry [3]
Training Board v Aylesbury Mushrooms Ltd [1972] 1 WLR 190

The Minister of Labour proposed to set up a training board under the Industrial Training Act 1964. Section 1(4) of that Act imposed an obligation on the Minister to consult any organisation appearing to him to be representative of substantial numbers of employers engaging in relevant activities. A draft schedule was sent to the Mushroom Growers' Association (a specialist branch of the National Farmers' Union). It was never received. *Held,* that was merely an attempt to consult; the essence of consultation was the communication of a genuine invitation. Normally consultation with the parent body would constitute consultation with the parts (the NFU had been notified) but that general rule did not apply here because the Minister had intended to consult with the Mushroom Growers' Association as well as with the NFU. Accordingly the 1966 order which constituted the board had no application to mushroom growers.

1

Air Canada v Secretary of State for Trade [1983] 2 AC 394   **[4]**
(House of Lords)

The plaintiffs sought discovery of documents which they believed would show that the Secretary of State had exercised his powers, under the Airport Authorities Act 1975, unlawfully in directing the British Airports Authority (BAA) to increase the charges levied for the use of Heathrow Airport. The Secretary of State claimed public interest immunity. The documents in category A consisted of high-level ministerial papers relating to the formulation of government policy; those in category B consisted of inter-departmental communications between senior civil servants. At first instance the court held that it should inspect the documents in category A. The Court of Appeal allowed the appeal by the Secretary of State. The plaintiffs appealed. *Held*, dismissing the appeal, where the Crown objected to the production of a class of documents on the grounds of public interest immunity, the judge should not inspect the documents until he was satisfied that the documents contained material which would give substantial support to the contention of the party seeking disclosure, on an issue which arose in the case or which would assist any of the parties to the proceedings, and which was necessary for 'disposing fairly of the cause or matter' within RSC Ord 24 and 13(1). Only if the judge was so satisfied should he then examine the documents privately. Since it was improbable that the documents for which immunity was sought contained any material additional to what had already been published in a White Paper and in the House of Commons, those documents were unlikely to be of assistance, and accordingly they should not be inspected by the court. LORD FRASER expressed the view that the courts should not assist the litigant who wanted to go on a 'fishing' expedition in the hope that by inspecting the documents he might find something that would assist his case. (See also *Burmah Oil Co Ltd* v *Governor and Company of the Bank of England* and *Conway* v *Rimmer*.)

Allingham v Minister of Agriculture and Fisheries   **[5]**
[1948] 1 All ER 780

Under the Defence (General) Regulations 1939 the Minister of Agriculture and Fisheries delegated to the Bedfordshire Agricultural Executive Committee, as he was expressly empowered to do, his powers to give directions as to the cultivation and use of land for agricultural purposes. The committee decided that eight acres of sugar beet should be grown by the occupiers of certain land but delegated to its executive officer the selection of the particular field on which this crop should be cultivated, and he served a notice upon the occupiers specifying that field. The regulation required that the notice should specify not merely the use to be made but also the particular area affected. *Held*, this notice was bad because on the principle of delegatus non delegare the committee could not delegate its powers to some other person or body.

Anisminic Ltd v Foreign Compensation Commission   **[6]**
[1969] 2 AC 147 (House of Lords)

The Foreign Compensation Commission had the duty of determining (a) who could claim compensation under an Order in Council relating to money received from the Egyptian Government for expropriation of British-owned assets in Egypt after the Suez incident and (b) the amount to be awarded. By virtue of s4(4) of the Foreign Compensation Act 1950 no determination of the Commission was to be called in question in any court of law. Anisminic Ltd's claim was rejected and the company sought a declaration that the determination was a nullity in that the Commission had asked itself and answered the wrong question (about the status of the successor in title of Anisminic Ltd). *Held*, a declaration would be granted for the Commission had *exceeded its jurisdiction* in asking the wrong question. Its determination was, therefore, no determination at all. If the error which it made had been *within* the Commission's jurisdiction then the jurisdiction of the court to grant relief would have been ousted by the exclusionary formula. The difficult problem remains – when will the court consider that an error is so fundamental that it does go to jurisdiction? [See now s3 of the Foreign Compensation Act 1969 (appeals on question of law now lie to the Court of Appeal). The authority of the case in other areas is, of course, unaffected. Note, too, that in *Pearlman* v *Keepers and Governors of Harrow School* [1978] 3 WLR 736 LORD DENNING MR expressed the view that, following *Anisminic*, the distinction between an intra vires and ultra vires error of law was 'so fine ... that in truth the High Court has a choice before it whether to interfere with an inferior court on a point of law. If it chooses to interfere, it can formulate its decision in the words: "The court below had no jurisdiction to decide this point wrongly as it did." If it does not choose to interfere, it can say: "The court had jurisdiction to decide it wrongly, and did so." ... I would suggest that this distinction should now be discarded ... [T]he way to get things right is to hold thus: no court or tribunal has any jurisdiction to make an error of law on which the decision of the case depends. If it makes such an error, it goes outside its jurisdiction and certiorari will lie to correct it.' The House of Lords was later to reject this approach and endorse GEOFFREY LANE LJ's dissenting judgment in *Pearlman*; see *Re Racal Communications Ltd*.] (See also *R* v *Secretary of State for the Environment, ex parte Ostler*.)

Annamunthodo v Oilfield Workers' Trade Union   [7]
[1961] 3 All ER 621 (Privy Council)

The appellant was charged with four specific offences, each under a named different rule of the respondent trade union. He denied the charges at the initial hearing before the general council of the union but, owing to a previous engagement, did not attend the adjourned hearing. At this hearing he was convicted and expelled under another rule to which no reference had been made in the charges. *Held*, the appellant's expulsion should be set aside because to proceed under this other rule without adjourning to give him notice of the fresh charge was contrary to natural justice. 'If a domestic tribunal fails to act in accordance with natural justice, the person affected by their decision can always seek redress in the courts ... He will not, of course, be entitled to damages if he suffered none' (*per* LORD DENNING). (See also *Ridge* v *Baldwin*.)

Arrowsmith v Jenkins [1963] 2 QB 561   [8]

The defendant was the main speaker at a public meeting held at the junction between two main roads. The road was completely blocked for about five minutes when a path was cleared for vehicles by the police with the help of the defendant, using a loudspeaker. The road was partially blocked for the remainder of the defendant's speech, namely about 15 minutes. *Held*, the defendant was properly convicted of 'wilfully' obstructing free passage along the highway contrary to s12(1) of the Highways Act 1959.

Associated Provincial Picture Houses v Wednesbury   [9]
Corporation [1948] 1 KB 223 (Court of Appeal)

Acting under the Cinematograph Act 1909 and the Sunday Entertainments Act 1932, Wednesbury Corporation granted the plaintiffs' company a licence to give performances on Sundays, subject to the condition that no children under the age of 15 were to be admitted. The plaintiffs sought a declaration that the condition was ultra vires and unreasonable. The challenge failed at first instance and was renewed before the Court of Appeal. *Held,* the appeal would be dismissed. The condition was reasonable and hence intra vires. The Court of appeal regarded it as significant that it was being asked to review an executive, as opposed to a judicial, act; that the local authority had been granted a broad discretion by Parliament; and that the statute provided no appeal from the decision of the local authority. Provided that the authority acted within the four corners of its jurisdiction, its exercise of discretion could not be questioned in any court of law. To act within its jurisdiction the authority had to ensure that it had taken into account relevant considerations and ignored those that were irrelevant. Provided that it did so, it was not for the court to substitute its own opinion as regards the desirability of the condition in question for that of the authority. 'It is clear that the local authority are entrusted by Parliament with the decision on a matter which the knowledge and experience of that authority can best be trusted to deal with. The subject-matter with which the condition deals is one relevant for its consideration ... It is true to say that, if a decision on a competent matter is so unreasonable that no reasonable authority could ever have come to it, then the courts can interfere. That, I think, is quite right; but to prove a case of that kind would require something overwhelming, and, in this case, the facts do not come anywhere near anything of that kind ... The effect of the legislation is not to set up the court as an arbiter of the correctness of one view over another. It is the local authority that are set in that position ... The power of the court to interfere in each case is not as an appellate authority to override a decision of the local authority, but as a judicial authority which is concerned, and concerned only, to see whether the local authority have contravened the law by acting in excess of the powers which Parliament has confided in them' (*per* LORD GREENE MR).

Attorney-General v De Keyser's Royal Hotel Ltd [1920] AC 508   **[10]**
(House of Lords)

The Crown, relying on powers under the Defence of the Realm Regulations, requisitioned a certain hotel for use by the Royal Flying Corps for administrative purposes. The regulations provided for the payment of compensation as of right to persons whose land was compulsorily acquired. *Held,* the owners of the hotel were entitled to compensation. Even if the prerogative entitled the Crown to take the land without paying compensation (and it was held in *Burmah Oil Co (Burma Trading) Ltd v Lord Advocate* that the Crown had no such right at common law), the prerogative had been superseded by the statutory regulations and the Crown was not, in these circumstances, entitled to act under the prerogative. (But see *R v Secretary of State for the Home Department, ex parte Northumbria Police Authority.*)

Attorney-General v English [1983] 1 AC 116 (House of Lords)   **[11]**

The defendant, who was the editor of the *Daily Mail* newspaper, published an article in support of a candidate in a Parliamentary by-election. The candidate, who was severely physically handicapped, was running as a Pro-Life candidate, alleging that a practice had developed in some hospitals of killing newborn handicapped babies. The article was highly emotive in tone. Two days before the publication of the article, the trial had opened of Dr Leonard Arthur, a consultant paediatrician, on a charge of murdering a three-day-old child, suffering from Down's Syndrome, by giving instructions that a drug should be administered which caused the baby to die of starvation. The issues were whether the article, which was clearly a publication within s2(1) of the Contempt of Court Act 1981, but against which a deliberate intention to prejudice the trial was not alleged, was nevertheless subject to the strict liability rule because of the nature and circumstances of publication, and if so, whether the publication nevertheless escaped the operation of this rule by virtue of s5 of the 1981 Act, which protects a 'discussion in good faith of public affairs'. The Divisional Court held that the article created a substantial risk of seriously impeding Dr Arthur's trial, within the meaning of s2(2), with the consequence that the strict liability rule applied. The court further found that the onus of proving that s5 applied rested on the defence, and that it had not discharged this burden since the article contained accusations which were not necessary to a 'discussion' within the section. The defendants appealed. *Held*, the nature and circumstances of the publication satisfied s2(2), since the appearance of the article on the third day of Dr Arthur's trial involved a more than remote risk (which was all that the word 'substantial' meant to exclude) that the jury might be affected. However, the onus of proving that s5 was satisfied did not necessarily fall on the defendants, and in the present case the section did in fact apply. The newspaper had a duty to inform electors and discuss the programme of any candidate; to hold otherwise would prevent the discussion of mercy killings anywhere in the media during the progress of the trial, and seriously prejudice the candidate's ability to present her case to the electorate. In LORD DIPLOCK'S view the gagging of bona fide public discussion in the press of controversial matters of general public interest, merely because there are in existence contemporaneous legal proceedings in which some particular instance of those controversial matters may be in issue, was what s5 of the 1981 Act was intended to prevent.

Attorney-General v Fulham Corporation [1921] 1 Ch 440   **[12]**

The Metropolitan Borough of Fulham was a statutory body created under the London Government Act 1899. The corporation started a new scheme for washing clothes whereby it did not merely provide facilities for persons to do their own washing but did the washing itself and, for a small additional charge, collected and delivered it. *Held*, as this scheme was not authorised by the Baths and Wash-houses Acts 1846 to 1878, an injunction would be granted to restrain the corporation from carrying it out. [Note: Since 1963 local authorities have been empowered by statute to incur a small amount of expenditure for any purpose which in their opinion is in the interests of their area or its inhabitants.]

Attorney-General v Jonathan Cape Ltd [1976] QB 752   **[13]**

The Attorney-General sought an injunction to prevent the publication of the diaries of the late Richard Crossman, who had been a Cabinet minister between 1964 and 70. The diary contained detailed accounts of discussions at Cabinet meetings. Permission to publish accounts of Cabinet proceedings had been refused by the Secretary to the Cabinet. *Held*, the court had the power to restrain the improper publication of information acquired by a Minister in confidence, and the doctrine of collective responsibility justified the restriction, in the public interest, of confidential Cabinet discussions. To succeed in an application to suppress publication, the Attorney-General would have to show (inter alia) (a) that such publication would be a breach of confidence; (b) that the public interest required that the publication be restrained. The courts should only act, however, where the need for continuing confidentiality had been clearly shown, and on this basis publication in 1975 of Cabinet discussions during 1964–6 would not be restrained. LORD WIDGERY CJ also rejected the assertion that the publication would undermine ministerial responsibility if it revealed that the advice given to ministers by civil servants had been defective. He doubted that an individual civil servant had an enforceable right to have such advice treated as confidential for all time.

Attorney-General v Wilts United Dairies Ltd (1922) 91 LJKB 897   **[14]**
(House of Lords)

The Food Controller, purporting to act under statutory powers 'to regulate the supply and consumption of food in such manner as he thinks best for maintaining a proper supply of food, and to take such steps as he thinks best for encouraging the production of food', prohibited persons dealing in milk from buying milk in one area in England for export to another area except under licence, and imposed a charge of 2d per gallon as a condition of the granting of a licence, with a view to regulating the supply. *Held*, the imposition of such a charge was ultra vires the Food Controller. The charge was in reality 'a tax the levying of which can never be imposed upon subjects of this country by anything except plain and direct statutory means' (*per* LORD BUCKMASTER). (But see *China Navigation Co Ltd v Attorney-General*.)

Attorney-General of Hong Kong v Ng Yuen Shiu [1983] 2 AC 629   **[15]**
(Privy Council)

The applicant was an illegal immigrant to Hong Kong from Macau. The immigration authorities announced that if such persons made themselves known to the authorities, each case would be dealt with on its own merits before any determination was made. The applicant, who had been in Hong Kong for four years and had built up his own business, made himself known to the authorities who detained him whilst an order for his deportation was made. The applicant sought an order of certiorari to quash the deportation on the ground that he had been given no opportunity to make representations to the authorities as to why he should not be deported. The application was refused at first instance, but allowed on appeal. The Attorney-General now appealed to the Judicial Committee. *Held*, dismissing the appeal, the public undertaking to consider each case on its merits created a right on the part of each illegal immigrant that would not have otherwise existed. Good administration required that authorities should abide by such undertakings to the extent that they did not conflict with the authority's statutory duties. Where an applicant claimed to possess a legitimate expectation of being given a hearing, that expression should be interpreted as meaning 'reasonable' expectation. Thus 'legitimate expectations' were capable of including expectations which went beyond enforceable legal rights, provided that they had some reasonable basis. (See also *R v Criminal Injuries Compensation Board, ex parte Lain.*)

Attorney-General for New South Wales v Trethowan   **[16]**
[1932] AC 526 (Privy Council)

In 1929 the legislature of New South Wales had enacted that the Upper House should not be abolished except by a Bill which, before being presented to the Governor for the Royal Assent, should be approved by a referendum. Moreover, that requirement of a referendum could not itself be repealed except by referendum. In 1931 a new Government took office and secured the passage of two Bills: one purported to do away with the requirement of a referendum and the other abolished the Upper House. Two members of the Upper House sought a declaration that the proposed action was illegal and an injunction to restrain the Bills being presented for the Royal Assent. *Held*, the declaration and the injunction would be granted. New South Wales had a non-sovereign legislature and s5 of the Colonial Laws Validity Act 1865, which applied to New South Wales, provided that a 'colonial' legislature could make laws relating to its constitution, powers, etc, but those laws had to be 'in such manner and form as may ... be required' by existing law. The Act passed in 1929 required a referendum, and the Bills in question could not lawfully be presented unless and until they had been approved by a majority of the electors voting.

Barnard v National Dock Labour Board [1953] 2 QB 18 [17]
(Court of Appeal)

The Dock Workers (Regulation of Employment) Order 1947 required the National Dock Labour Board to delegate certain disciplinary functions to local dock boards. The plaintiffs, registered dock workers, refused to obey a lawful order, and the port manager, to whom the London Dock Labour Board had purported to delegate its disciplinary functions, suspended the plaintiffs from work. *Held*, the local board had no power to delegate its judicial or quasi-judicial function and for this reason the plaintiffs were entitled to a declaration that their suspension was wrongful and a nullity.

Beach v Freeson [1972] 1 QB 14 [18]

At the request of a constituent, G, the defendant, who was an MP, wrote to the Law Society with a complaint about the plaintiffs, who were solicitors in partnership. A copy of the letter was sent to the Lord Chancellor. The plaintiffs brought an action in libel. *Held*, the publication of both letters was protected by qualified privilege. Both the Law Society and the Lord Chancellor had sufficient interest in receiving the complaint.

Beatty v Gillbanks (1862) 9 QBD 308 [19]

The appellants, leaders of the Salvation Army in Weston-super-Mare, were convicted of unlawful assembly. The assembly, a procession through the streets of Weston-super-Mare, was not in itself unlawful, but, as on several previous occasions, it 'produced riots and disturbances of the peace and terror to the inhabitants'. The evidence showed that the disturbances were caused by people antagonistic to the Salvation Army and in particular by a body called the Skeleton Army. *Held*, the appellants had been wrongly convicted of the offence charged. 'The finding of the justices amounts to this, that a man may be convicted for doing a lawful act if he knows that his doing it may cause another to do an unlawful act. There is no authority for such a proposition' (*per* FIELD J).

Blackburn v Attorney-General [1971] 1 WLR 1037 [20]
(Court of Appeal)

The plaintiff sought declarations to the effect that by signing the Treaty of Rome the Government would surrender, in part, the sovereignty of the Crown in Parliament and that it would surrender it for ever. He alleged that that would be contrary to law. *Held* (on appeal from orders striking out the statement of claim and dismissing the actions as showing no reasonable cause of action), the appeal would be dismissed, because (1) the exercise of the treaty-making power was part of the prerogative which could not be called in question in the courts; (2) the question whether an Act implementing the signing of the Treaty was irrevocable should be left for decision until the question arose in concrete form. The court would not pronounce on hypothetical questions. (See also *R* v *Secretary of State for Foreign and Commonwealth Affairs, ex parte Rees-Mogg.*)

Board of Education v Rice [1911] AC 179 (House of Lords) [21]

A dispute concerning teachers' salaries arose between the Swansea Local Education Authority and the managers of some voluntary schools. The matter was referred to the Board of Education for determination but, in their decision, the Board failed to deal with the question (ie, the points in issue) submitted to them. *Held*, the Board's decision should be quashed by certiorari and a mandamus issued commanding the Board to determine the questions. 'I need not add that [the Board of Education] must act in good faith and fairly listen to both sides, for that is a duty lying upon every one who decides anything' (*per* LORD LOREBURN LC). (But see *Ceylon University* v *Fernando.*)

Bowman v Secular Society Ltd [1917] AC 406 (House of Lords)   [22]

The Secular Society Ltd was registered as a company limited by guarantee, the main object, as stated in its memorandum of association, being: 'To promote ... the principle that human conduct should be based on natural knowledge, and not upon supernatural belief, and that human welfare in this world is the proper end of all thought and action.' Was this blasphemous? *Held*, the propagation of anti-Christian doctrines, apart from scurrility or profanity, did not constitute blasphemy. It was for Parliament to alter the law so as to remove the special protection afforded by the law to the Christian religion if it was felt that public opinion was behind such a change. (See also *R* v *Lemon.*)

Bradlaugh v Clarke (1883) 8 App Cas 354 (House of Lords)   [23]

Bradlaugh voted and sat in the House of Commons during a debate without having made and subscribed the oath in accordance with the Parliamentary Oaths Act 1866. In view of this, under the provisions of that Act, a penalty of £500 was recoverable from Bradlaugh 'by action in one of Her Majesty's Superior Courts at Westminster'. The plaintiff, a common informer, sought to recover this penalty. *Held*, his action could not succeed as the penalty could be sued for only by the Crown.

Bradlaugh v Gosset (1884) 12 QBD 271   [24]

Bradlaugh was duly elected as a member for Northampton. The House of Commons resolved 'that the Serjeant-at-Arms do exclude Mr Bradlaugh from the House until he shall engage not further to disturb the proceedings of the House'. Bradlaugh sought an injunction to restrain the Serjeant-at-Arms from carrying out this resolution. *Held*, he would not succeed as this was a matter relating to the internal management of the procedure of the House: for this reason, the Court of Queen's Bench could not interfere.

Breen v Amalgamated Engineering Union [1971] 1 All ER 1148   [25]
(Court of Appeal)

The plaintiff was elected a shop steward of the union. One of the union rules required that the election be subject to approval by district committee. In this case the committee unanimously resolved that they were unable to approve the election. The plaintiff was not present and reasons for the decision were not given until the plaintiff complained. Reasons were then given by letter. One of those reasons was based on a false assumption. The plaintiff sought a declaration and damages. The judge at first instance dismissed the action on the grounds that it was not open to the court to review the committee's decision since they were merely exercising a discretion and were not obliged to act in accordance with natural justice. *Held*, a domestic body set up by the rules of a powerful association such as a trade union, which was given a discretion by those rules, must exercise the discretion *fairly* even though the functions were not judicial or quasi-judicial but were administrative. Therefore the committee must act in accordance with natural justice. (In the event it was found that the committee had not acted unfairly.) (See also *Gaiman* v *National Association for Mental Health.*)

Bribery Commissioner, The v Ranasinghe   [26]
[1965] AC 172 (Privy Council)

The appellant was the Bribery Commissioner of Ceylon who was under a duty to bring prosecutions before the Bribery Tribunal which was created by the Bribery Amendment Act 1958. The respondent, having been prosecuted for a bribery offence before that tribunal, was convicted and sentenced to a term of imprisonment and a fine. On appeal the Supreme Court declared the conviction and orders made against him null and inoperative on the ground that the persons composing the Bribery Tribunal which tried him were not lawfully appointed to the tribunal. The Supreme Court had taken the view that the method of appointing persons to the panel from which the tribunal was drawn offended against an important safeguard in the Constitution of Ceylon, contained in the Ceylon (Constitution) Orders in Council 1946 and 1947, and to the extent of that inconsistency purported to amend the constitution. There was no evidence that constitutional requirements relating to amendments (a two thirds majority in the House of Representatives, and the endorsement of a Speaker's certificate) had been complied with in respect of the 1958 Act. The question before the Privy Council, therefore, was whether the statutory provisions for the appointment of members of the panel of the Bribery Tribunal, otherwise than by the Judicial Service Commission, conflicted with s55 of the Constitution, and, if so, whether those provisions were valid. *Held*, the legislature of Ceylon was bound by the terms of the Constitution, and the courts would not uphold legislation that had not been enacted in accordance with that Constitution. When a constitution lays down that, in respect of compliance with procedures for constitutional amendment, a Speaker's certificate shall be conclusive for all purposes and shall not be questioned in any court of law, it is clearly intended that courts of law shall look to the certificate but shall look no further. The courts therefore have a duty to look for the certificate in order to ascertain whether the Constitution has been validly amended. Where the certificate is not apparent, there is lacking an essential part of the process necessary for amendment. Once it was shown that an Act conflicted with a provision in the Constitution, as was the case here, the certificate became an essential part of the legislative process. The case was to be distinguished from those that had concerned challenges to English statutes because, in the constitution of the United Kingdom, there was no governing instrument which prescribed the law-making powers and the forms which are essential to those powers. LORD PEARCE commented that a legislature has no power to ignore the conditions of law-making that are imposed by the instrument which itself regulates its power to make law.

Brind v Secretary of State for the Home Department. See R v Secretary of State for the Home Department, ex parte Brind

British Broadcasting Corporation v Johns   [27]
[1965] Ch 32 (Court of Appeal)

The BBC, a corporation established by Royal Charter, contended that it was entitled to Crown immunity from taxation. *Held*, the BBC was entitled to no such immunity since its activities were not a province of government, it being an independent body not exercising functions created and required by the government.

British Coal Corporation v R [1935] AC 500 (Privy Council)   [28]

The petitioners were convicted by the Canadian Court of King's Bench (Crown Side) on a charge of combining together with a view to unduly restraining the coal industry, and their appeal from the conviction was dismissed by the King's Bench (Appeal Side). On a petition for special leave to appeal to His Majesty in Council, objection was taken to the competency of the petition on the ground that appeals to His Majesty in Council in criminal cases from any judgment or order of any court in Canada had been effectively prohibited by a Canadian statute. Section 17 of this Act provided, inter alia: 'Notwithstanding any royal prerogative … no appeal shall be brought in any criminal case from any judgment or order of any court in Canada to any Court of Appeal or authority by which in the United Kingdom appeals or petitions to His Majesty in Council may be heard', and their lordships took the view that s91 of the British North America Act 1867 had invested the Dominion Parliament, in cases within its jurisdiction, with the power to regulate or prohibit the appeal to the King in Council. *Held*, the petition should be dismissed. 'No doubt the principle is clearly established that the King's prerogative cannot be restricted or qualified save by express words or necessary intendment. In connection with Dominion or Colonial matters that principle involves that if the limitation of the prerogative is by a Dominion or Colonial Act, not only must that Act itself deal with the prerogative either by express terms or by necessary intendment, but it must be the Act of a Dominion or Colonial Legislature which has been endowed with the requisite power by an Imperial Act likewise giving the power either by express terms or by necessary intendment' (*per* VISCOUNT SANKEY LC).

British Oxygen Ltd v Board of Trade   [29]
[1971] AC 610 (House of Lords)

The Board of Trade had a discretion to award investment grants in respect of 'plant' and adopted a policy of not awarding grants in respect of items of plant costing less than £25 each. British Oxygen had invested over £4m in gas cylinders which individually cost £20. The Board had declined to award an investment grant in respect of this expenditure, in accordance with its policy. At first instance a declaration was granted to the effect that the Board had not properly exercised its discretion. The Court of Appeal allowed an appeal; the company appealed. *Held*, the appeal would be dismissed. The Board was entitled to have a policy, especially where numerous applications were concerned, provided that it was prepared to listen to anyone with something to say. The evidence was that it had properly considered the present application and applied a lawful policy in rejecting it. 'There are two general grounds on which the exercise of an unqualified discretion can be attacked. It must not be exercised in bad faith, and it must not be so unreasonably exercised as to show that there cannot have been any real or genuine exercise of the discretion. But, apart from that, if the Minister thinks that policy or good administration requires the operation of some limiting rule, I find nothing to stop him … There may be cases where an officer or authority ought to listen to a substantial argument reasonably presented urging a change of policy. What the authority must not do is to refuse to listen at all. But a Ministry or large authority may have had to deal already with a multitude of similar applications and then they will almost certainly have evolved a policy so precise that it could well be called a rule. There can be no objection to that, provided the authority is always willing to listen to anyone with something new to say …' (*per* LORD REID).

Bromley London Borough Council v Greater London Council   [30]
[1983] 1 AC 768 (House of Lords)

In 1981 the Labour grouping won control of the Greater London Council (GLC). The new leadership set about implementing the 'Fares Fair' scheme, as they had promised they would in their election manifesto, resulting in a 25 per cent cut in

London Transport fares. The ratepayers were to pay increased rates as a means of helping to finance the scheme, and in due course a supplementary rate precept was issued to all 35 London boroughs. The decision to increase the level of rates also meant, under the relevant local government finance legislation then pertaining, that the GLC would lose some central government funding, a factor substantially increasing the burden on the ratepayers. The London Borough of Bromley challenged the validity of the whole procedure, and applied to the Divisional Court for an order of certiorari to quash the supplementary precept. Under the relevant legislation, the Transport (London) Act 1969, the GLC was under a general duty to develop policies and encourage measures which promoted '... the provision of integrated, efficient, and economic transport facilities and services for Greater London ...'. The responsibility for implementing those principles was, by s4 of the 1969 Act, conferred on the London Transport Executive (LTE). By s5(1) the LTE was under a general duty to provide public passenger transport facilities which best met the needs of Greater London, and to exercise and perform its functions in accordance with the principles laid down by the GLC and with due regard to '... efficiency, economy, and safety of operation ...'. By s7(3)(b), if at the end of an accounting period there was a deficit in the LTE's revenue account, the LTE was required, as far as practicable, to make up that deficit in the next accounting period, although under s7(6) the GLC was entitled to '... take such action as was necessary and appropriate to enable the LTE to comply with its duty under s7(3)(b) to balance its accounts'. The GLC was further empowered by s3(1) to make grants to the LTE ' ... for any purpose'. The application for certiorari was dismissed at first instance, but Bromley appealed successfully to the Court of Appeal. The GLC then appealed to the House of Lords. *Held*, in approving an arbitrary reduction in fares, the GLC had acted without due regard to ordinary business principles. The GLC had been empowered to make grants to London Transport in order to deal with situations such as the making good of unavoidable losses, not for the furtherance of a social policy. The burden placed on ratepayers as a result of the GLC's decision was excessive. Insufficient regard had been paid to their interests. The councillors forming the majority group had erred in regarding themselves as being irrevocably bound to carry out their manifesto promises regardless of the effect on the ratepayers. (Followed: *Prescott* v *Birmingham Corporation*; but see *Pickwell* v *Camden London Borough Council.*)

Burmah Oil Co (Burma Trading) Ltd v Lord Advocate [31]
[1965] AC 75 (House of Lords)

During the war of 1939–45 the GOC in Burma ordered the appellant's installations to be destroyed in order to deny resources to the enemy. The appellant sought reparation. *Held*, although the destruction was carried out lawfully under the Crown's prerogative at common law, there was no general rule that, even in time of war or imminent danger, such action could be taken without making payment for it. The Crown would only be immune for such payment in respect of 'battle damage' arising out of military operations. [Note: See now the War Damage Act 1965.] (See also *Attorney-General* v *De Keyser's Royal Hotel Ltd* and *Nissan* v *Attorney-General.*)

Burmah Oil Co Ltd v Governor and Company of the Bank of [32]
England [1980] AC 1090 (House of Lords)

In January 1965 the Bank of England, acting in conjunction with the Government, made an agreement with Burmah Oil to assist them in resolving their financial difficulties. The agreement involved, inter alia, the transfer of stock to the Bank. In October 1976 Burmah Oil claimed a declaration that the transfer of stock in 1975 was unconscionable, inequitable and unreasonable. They applied for an order for production of certain documents by the Bank. The Attorney-General intervened on behalf of the Crown, objecting to production. The certificate signed by the Chief Secretary to the Treasury stated that the specified documents fell into three categories, that the minister had personally read all the documents, and that he considered that their production would be injurious to the public interest. Category A comprised communications between government ministers and concerned the formulation of government policy. Category B consisted of communications between senior civil servants and the Bank relating to policy matters described in Category A documents. Category C comprised memoranda of telephone conversations and meetings between senior businessmen, ministers, civil servants and the Bank, and referred to information given in confidence by businessmen. The High Court judge upheld the Crown's claim, and the plaintiffs appealed. The Court of Appeal (LORD DENNING dissenting) dismissed the appeal, holding that it would be contrary to public policy to order discovery of documents, such as those in Categories A and B, which related to the formulation of government policy (*Conway* v *Rimmer* applied). Documents in Category C should also be protected, since it is in the interests of good government that it should be able to receive confidential information on business matters, and an order for discovery of these documents might impede the giving of confidential information in future. Burmah Oil appealed to the House of Lords but reduced their claim for discovery to ten of the documents in respect of which discovery had originally been sought. All ten documents were in Categories A and B. *Held*, (1) (LORD WILBERFORCE dissenting), the ten documents should be produced for inspection by the House, as the case was one where without inspection of the documents it was not possible to decide whether the balance of public interest lay for or against disclosure. The documents having been inspected, it was *held*, (2) (*per* LORD SALMON and LORD EDMUND-DAVIES, LORD KEITH OF KINKEL dubitante), that none of the documents contained matter of such evidential value as to make an order for their disclosure necessary for disposing fairly of the case; (*per* LORD SCARMAN) that the documents were relevant but their significance was not such as to override the public interest objections to their production; and (3) (*per* LORD KEITH and LORD SCARMAN), that where the court inspects a document and orders disclosure the Crown should have a right to appeal against the order before the document is disclosed. (See also *Air Canada* v *Secretary of State (for Trade)*.

Carltona Ltd v Commissioners of Works [1943] 2 All ER 560   **[33]**
(Court of Appeal)

The appellants were manufacturers of food products. On 4 November 1942 their factory was requisitioned by the Commissioners of Works under the provisions of the Defence (General) Regulations 1939, reg 51(1). The Regulations provided that such requisitioning could be authorised by a 'competent authority' a phrase encompassing the Commissioners of Works under the legislation. The appellants claimed a declaration that the Commissioners were not entitled to take possession on the ground that the order for requisition was invalid. Before the Court of Appeal the appellants contended, inter alia, that the invalidity arose because the 'competent authority' had never brought their minds to bear on the question of the propriety of the requisitioning since the decision had been taken by an Assistant Secretary (a civil servant) in the Ministry of Works. *Held*, the order was valid. By statute the functions and powers of the Commissioners of Works, were vested in the First Commissioner of Works, viz the Minister heading the Ministry of Works. It was wrong to contend that reg 51 meant that the minister in person should direct his mind to the matter, as this would clearly be a practical impossibility in the case of every requisition. In the administration of government so many functions are given to ministers that they could never attend to them all personally. Normally such functions are exercised under the authority of the minister by the officials in the department. Constitutionally, the decision of such an official is a decision of the minister, and constitutionally the minister is responsible to Parliament for the decision. (See also *R* v *Secretary of State for the Home Department, ex parte Oladehinde*.)

Ceylon University v Fernando [1960] 1 All ER 631 (Privy Council)   [34]

Miss Balasingham, a student of the University of Ceylon, alleged that the plaintiff, another student of the university, had fore-knowledge of the contents of the German passage in a zoology paper. The Vice-Chancellor appointed a commission of inquiry to assist him to inquire into the allegations, but when certain witnesses, including Miss Balasingham, were examined, the plaintiff was not present and two other witnesses were questioned by the Vice-Chancellor alone. The plaintiff was given no opportunity of questioning Miss Balasingham, but he did not ask to be allowed to do so. The board found the plaintiff guilty of an examination offence and suspended him indefinitely from all university examinations. The plaintiff sought a declaration that the board's decision was null and void on the ground that the inquiry was not conducted in accordance with principles of natural justice, and it was not disputed that the Vice-Chancellor's functions were quasi-judicial. *Held*, the procedure adopted by the Vice-Chancellor sufficiently complied with the requirements of natural justice. It might have been otherwise if the plaintiff had asked to examine the witnesses and had been refused. (But see *Board of Education* v *Rice*.)

Chandler v Director of Public Prosecutions [1964] AC 763   [35]
(House of Lords)

The appellants, as part of their campaign for nuclear disarmament, organised a demonstration at an airfield with the object of immobilising its aircraft. They were charged with conspiring and inciting to commit a breach of s1 of the Official Secrets Act 1911 in that their conduct was 'prejudicial to the safety or interest of the state'. The trial judge refused to allow the appellants to cross-examine or adduce evidence to the effect that the appellants' acts were not in fact so prejudicial. *Held*, the Home Secretary, having declared the airfield a 'prohibited area' within s3 of the Act, in that obstruction etc thereof 'would be useful to an enemy', the appellants were not entitled to say that their purposes were not prejudicial to the safety or interests of the State. The Crown alone was the judge of how the armed forces should be disposed and ordered, and the Crown's decision on such issue could not be questioned in any court of law. (But see *Council of Civil Service Unions* v *Minister for the Civil Service*.)

Chapman v Director of Public Prosecutions   [36]
(1989) 89 Cr App R 190

Constable Sneller was called to assist an officer who was being assaulted by a number of youths. Sneller saw a youth he suspected of being involved in the attack run into the flat occupied by the youth's father, the defendant. Sneller sought entry to the defendant's premises, but the defendant resisted, and was arrested for obstructing a constable in the execution of his duty. Sneller purported to be exercising his power of arrest under s24(6) of the Police and Criminal Evidence Act 1984 in relation to the defendant's son, in so far as he claimed to have had reasonable grounds for suspecting that an arrestable offence had been committed. The defendant's submission of no case to answer, in relation to the obstruction charge, was rejected by the justices, and he appealed by way of case stated, the question for the court being whether or not the justices were right to conclude that Sneller, at the time of the assault, was exercising a statutory power of entry and so was a constable acting in the execution of his duty. *Held*, allowing the appeal, a constable could only enter premises to arrest a person for an arrestable offence. The common assault on a fellow officer was not an arrestable offence. There was insufficient evidence to support Sneller's assertion that he had reasonable suspicion that an arrestable offence (eg actual bodily harm) had been committed by the defendant's son. BINGHAM LJ adopted the view of Lord Diplock, expressed in *Holgate-Mohammed* v *Duke* [1984] AC 437, to the effect that in a case where it is alleged that there has been an unlawful arrest, there are three questions to be answered. (1) Did the arresting officer suspect that the person who was arrested was guilty of the offence? The answer to this question will depend entirely on the findings of fact as to the officer's state of mind. (2) Assuming the officer had the necessary suspicion, was there reasonable cause for that suspicion? (3) Was there identification of the arrestable offence which the police constable could reasonably have suspected?

Cheney v Conn [1968] 1 WLR 242   [37]

A taxpayer contended that he was not liable to pay tax assessed against him on the basis that the assessments were invalid in that a substantial part of the tax revenue was allocated to the construction of nuclear weapons, the use of which was contrary, he alleged, to international law, part of which had been incorporated in the law of England by the Geneva Conventions Act 1957. *Held*, the assessments were not invalid. 'What the statute itself enacts cannot be unlawful because what the statute says and provides is itself the law and the highest form of law that is known to this country. It is the law which prevails over every other form of law and it is not for the court to say that a parliamentary enactment, the highest law in this country, is illegal' (*per* UNGOED-THOMAS J).

China Navigation Co Ltd v Attorney-General [1932] 2 KB 197   [38]
(Court of Appeal)

The plaintiffs, an English shipping company operating on the coast of China, desired protection against 'internal piracy', ie persons coming on board pretending to be passengers but with the intention of overpowering the ship's officers and robbing the ship in the course of the voyage. This danger was met by the provision of a small military guard of British soldiers in each ship. Could the Crown demand payment for supplying this protection against piracy? *Held*, it was entitled to do so as there was no obligation on the Crown to afford military protection to the plaintiffs in foreign parts. (But see *Attorney-General* v *Wilts United Dairies Ltd*.)

Christie v Leachinsky [1947] 1 All ER 567 (House of Lords)   [39]

The appellants, who had reasonable grounds for suspecting that the respondent had committed a felony of larceny, arrested him on a charge of unlawful possession, a statutory offence for which they had no power to arrest without warrant. The respondent was detained overnight in the police station. When the respondent was brought before the magistrate the charge of unlawful possession was withdrawn and he was directed to the cells by one of the appellants who told him that he was to be charged with larceny. The respondent claimed damages for false imprisonment. *Held*, he was entitled to damages in respect of his first night in custody: the appellants could not rely on their reasonable suspicion of larceny as the respondent had been told that he was being arrested for unlawful possession; but his claim for the period between the withdrawal of one charge and the making of the next would fail, as he knew for what alleged felony he had been detained. 'If a policeman arrests without warrant upon reasonable suspicion of felony, or of other crime of a sort which does not require a warrant, he must in ordinary circumstances inform the person arrested of the true ground of the arrest ... If the citizen is not so informed but is nevertheless seized, the policeman, apart from certain exceptions, is liable for false imprisonment' (*per* VISCOUNT SIMON). (See also *Abbassy* v *Commissioner of Police of the Metropolis.*)

Church of Scientology of California v Johnson-Smith   [40]
[1972] 1 QB 522

The plaintiffs brought an action in defamation arising out of a television interview given by the defendant, an MP. The defendant pleaded fair comment and privilege and in reply the plaintiffs sought to show that the defendant was actuated by malice. In order to establish that, it was necessary to refer to proceedings in Parliament. *Held*, it was not possible to refer to such proceedings for the purpose of supporting a cause of action even though the cause of action itself arose out of something done outside Parliament, and the evidence must be excluded. (Applied: *Dingle* v *Associated Newspapers Ltd*; see also *Rost* v *Edwards.*)

Churchward v R (1865) LR 1 QB 173   [41]

In 1854 the Admiralty Commissioners had entered into a contract with Churchward for the carriage of mails between Dover and Calais and Dover and Ostend. The contract was to continue until 26 April 1870. However, the Government refused to honour the contract from 1863 onwards, the House of Commons refused to authorise any expenditure on it, and expressly provided in the appropriate Acts of 1863–66 that no part of the sum granted by Parliament to meet expenditure on the mail service was to be paid to Churchward as regards the period subsequent to 20 June 1863. The contract had included an express term that Churchward was to be paid '... out of the monies provided by Parliament'. Churchward brought a petition of right against the Crown claiming £126,000 for breach of contract. *Held*, in the agreement there was only a covenant by the Commissioners on behalf of the Crown that, in consideration of Churchward performing his part of the contract, by having vessels always ready for the service, the Crown would pay him if Parliament provided the funds. Since Parliament had not provided the funds, there was no breach of contract on the part of the Crown. As SHEE J observed: 'In the case of a contract with commissioners on behalf of the Crown to make large payments of money during a series of years, I should have thought that the condition which clogs this covenant, though not expressed, must, on account of the notorious inability of the Crown to contract unconditionally for such money payments in consideration of such services, have been implied in favour of the Crown ...'

Cocks v Thanet District Council [1983] 2 AC 286 (House of Lords)   [42]

The plaintiff applied to the defendant council for re-housing under the Housing (Homeless Persons) Act 1977. Under the Act, the council's first duty was to enquire into the circumstances of the applicant's homelessness, and then to supply housing on the basis of that finding. The council found the applicant to be 'intentionally homeless' and thus entitled only to 'limited' accommodation rights. The plaintiff commenced proceedings in the county court. The question was whether or not it was an abuse of process for him to do so. *Held*, the proceedings should have been pursued by means of an application for judicial review. The housing authority's duty to enquire into the applicant's status, in order to determine whether or not there was a duty to house him, was a decision-making function falling within the sphere of public law. Once the authority accepted that it was under a duty to house the applicant, the discharge of that duty fell within the authority's executive functions, and rights in the sphere of private law would come into existence. (See also *Wandsworth London Borough Council* v *Winder.*)

Commissioners of Crown Lands v Page [1960] 2 QB 274   [43]
(Court of Appeal)

Premises were leased to Page by the Crown for 25 years. Eight years later the premises were requisitioned by the Minister of Works, acting under the Defence Regulations. Page argued that the Crown was in breach of an implied covenant guaranteeing his quiet enjoyment of the premises. *Held*, no covenant ensuring quiet enjoyment would be implied into the lease, as this would constitute a fetter on the freedom of the Crown to deal with the land and premises as might be necessitated by the national interest. The Crown does not, when making a private contract, undertake to fetter itself in the use of its powers. It would be ridiculous to suppose that it is making any promise about the way in which it will conduct the affairs of the nation. As DEVLIN LJ observed: 'No one can imagine, for example, that when the Crown makes a contract which could not be fulfilled in time of war, it is pledging itself not to declare war for so long as the contract lasts. Even if, therefore, there was an express covenant for quiet enjoyment, or an express promise by the Crown that it would not do any act which might hinder the other party to the contract in the performance of his obligations, the covenant or promise must by necessary implication be read to exclude those measures affecting the nation as a whole which the Crown takes for the public good.' (See further *Board of Trade* v *Temperley Steam Shipping Co Ltd* (1927) 27 Ll LR 230.)

Coney v Choyce [1975] 1 WLR 422   [44]

Regulation 2 of the County and Voluntary Schools (Notices) Regulations 1968, issued pursuant to s13 of the Education Act 1944, required the posting of notices in the vicinity of schools which were to be re-organised under a policy of comprehensivisation. In the case of two schools, the requisite notices had not been posted. The plaintiff claimed that the Secretary of State could not validly approve the comprehensivisation because of the failure to follow the required procedure. *Held*, the procedural requirement of giving notice had been substantially complied with, and there was no evidence of anyone suffering substantial prejudice as a result, hence the Secretary of State's action was lawful. Breach of procedural or formal rules is likely to be treated as a mere irregularity if the departure from the terms of the Act is of a trivial nature, or if no substantial prejudice has been suffered by those for whose benefit the requirements were introduced, or if serious public inconvenience would be caused by holding them to be mandatory, or if the court is for any reason disinclined to interfere with the act or decision that is impugned (*per* TEMPLEMAN J).

Congreve v Home Office [1976] 1 QB 629   [45]
(Court of Appeal)

The colour television licence was increased from £12 to £18 on 1 April 1975. Congreve, along with 20,000 others, applied for a new licence shortly before the date set for the increase, even though his own licence had not expired, because he would still make an overall saving. Contemplating a substantial loss of revenue if this practice was allowed, the Minister adopted a policy of revoking such licences after eight months if the extra £6 was not paid by the holder. The Minister purported to act under s1(2) of the Wireless Telegraphy Act 1949 which provided him with the discretion to issue licences subject to such terms (etc) as he thought fit, and s1(4) which provided that a licence could be revoked by notice being served on the holder. Congreve sought a declaration that the Minister's action was unlawful. He was unsuccessful at first instance and appealed to the Court of Appeal. *Held*, the appeal would be allowed. Discretion must be exercised in accordance with the law, taking all relevant considerations into account, omitting irrelevant ones, and not being influenced by any ulterior motives. The Minister was acting unlawfully in using his statutory power of revocation for a purpose for which it was never intended, namely, preventing a large-scale loss of revenue. There was nothing in the regulations to stop citizens taking out 'overlapping' licences. The Minister's dislike of it could not afford a good reason for revoking them. (See also *Wheeler* v *Leicester City Council*.)

Conway v Rimmer [1968] AC 910 (House of Lords) [46]

The plaintiff, a former police officer, sued his former superintendent for malicious prosecution. The defendant disclosed the existence of certain reports which he had made about the plaintiff which were admittedly relevant to the plaintiff's claim. The Home Secretary objected to the production of these reports on the ground that each fell within a class of document the production of which would be injurious to the public interest. *Held*, the Minister's objection was not conclusive. When it was claimed that a document belonged to such a class the court could itself inspect the document and, if it thought desirable, order production. Before ordering production the court must balance the public interest in the proper administration of justice against the likely prejudice to the proper functioning of the public service and must give full weight to the minister's reasons for objecting to production. It is a mater of some debate how far the House of Lords overruled its own decision in *Duncan* v *Cammell Laird & Co Ltd*. This was the first case in which it had an opportunity so to do, following the statement of the Lord Chancellor in 1966 that the House would no longer regard itself as bound by past decisions. (See also *Air Canada* v *Secretary of State for Trade*.)

Cook v Alexander [1974] QB 279 (Court of Appeal) [47]

The plaintiff, a teacher at an approved school, had criticised the way in which the school was run in letters to a newspaper. The Home Secretary ordered an inquiry. The school was ordered to be closed. There was a debate in the House of Lords on the closure of the school. In the debate a bishop strongly criticised the plaintiff. The next day the *Daily Telegraph* published on its back page a short 'Parliamentary sketch' which consisted of a commentary describing the reporter's impression of the salient aspects of the debate. This sketch emphasised the bishop's attack and referred to a rebuttal of the attack and to a full report of the debate on an inside page. The plaintiff claimed damages for libel in respect of the sketch against the defendants (the writer, editor and publishers concerned). *Held*, the reporter of a sketch of parliamentary proceedings is entitled to select that part of a debate which appears to him to be of special public interest and such a sketch was protected by qualified privilege if made fairly and honestly and without malice. Since this sketch had been made without malice and was a fair report of the proceedings, it was protected by qualified privilege. Given the length of debates in Parliament no newspaper could possibly report them in full, give the names of all the speakers, or even summarise the main speeches.

Cooper v Board of Works for the Wandsworth District [48]
(1863) 14 CBNS 180

Statute empowered the district board to alter or demolish a house where the builder had neglected to give notice of his intention to build seven days before proceeding to lay or dig the foundations. The plaintiff was employed to build a house in Wandsworth, and had already reached the second storey, when the defendant district board, without giving him any notice, sent its surveyor and a number of workmen, at a late hour in the evening, and razed it to the ground. It did this because it said that it had not received notice of intention to build. *Held*, the plaintiff was entitled to damages as the powers granted by statute to the defendant district board were subject to the qualification 'that no man is to be deprived of his property without his having an opportunity of being heard ... I think the board ought to have given notice to the plaintiff, and to have allowed him to be heard' (*per* ERLE CJ).

Costa v ENEL [1964] ECR 585 (European Court of Justice) [49]

Italy had nationalised the production and distribution of electricity, and transferred the assets of the private undertakings to a new State body, ENEL. Costa, as a shareholder in one of the private undertakings which had been nationalised, and also as a consumer, claimed before an Italian court that the 1962 nationalisation legislation infringed provisions of the EEC Treaty. The matter went to the European Court, where the Italian government argued that it was obliged to apply its national legislation in preference to EC legislation. *Held*, Member States were obliged to give precedence to Community law in the event of a conflict with domestic law. The application of Community law could not vary from one State to another dependent upon subsequent domestic laws without undermining the attainment of the objectives of the Treaty of Rome. In the view of the court '... by creating a Community of unlimited duration, having its own institutions, its own personality, its own legal capacity and capacity of representation on the international plane and, more particularly, real powers stemming from a limitation of sovereignty or a transfer of powers from the States to the Community, the Member States have limited their sovereign rights albeit within limited fields and have thus created a body of law which binds both their nationals and themselves.'

Council of Civil Service Unions v Minister for the Civil [50]
Service [1984] 3 WLR 1174 (House of Lords)

Acting pursuant to delegated prerogative power, Article 4 of the Civil Service Order in Council 1982, the Minister for the Civil Service (the Prime Minister) issued an oral instruction to the unions representing those civil servants employed at Government Communications Headquarters (GCHQ), altering the conditions of service so as to prohibit membership of trade unions by the civil servants employed there. Past practice had been for the Prime Minister to consult the unions at GCHQ before making such changes. The reason for not doing so on this occasion was a fear that the proposed changes might prompt industrial action at GCHQ, which would have a deleterious effect on national security. Two questions fell to be considered: firstly, whether the exercise of prerogative power by the Prime Minister was reviewable, and secondly, if it was, whether the use of such power had been contrary to the rules of natural justice due to lack of prior consultation. *Held*: (1) Delegated prerogative power was not immune from judicial review; the scope of such powers could be ascertained by reference to their object, to the procedure by which they were to be exercised. The justiciability of the matter in dispute was a more relevant factor than the source of the power being exercised. (2) The previous course of conduct that had been followed in consulting the trade unions prior to any changes in terms and conditions of employment created a legitimate expectation of consultation prior to any changes being made in the future. On the facts, however, the demands of national security superseded the need to comply with natural justice, hence the declaration sought would be refused. LORD DIPLOCK observed: 'I find it difficult to envisage in any of the various fields in which the prerogative remains the only source of the relevant decision-making power a decision of a kind that would be open to attack through the judicial process on [the basis of irrationality] ... Such decisions will generally involve the application of government policy. The reasons for the decision-maker taking one course rather than another do not normally involve questions to which, if disputed, the judicial process is adapted to provide the right answer, by which I mean that the kind of evidence that is admissible under judicial procedures and the way in which it has to be adduced tend to exclude from the attention of the court competing policy considerations which, if the executive discretion is to be wisely exercised, need to be weighed against one another, a balancing exercise which judges by their upbringing and experience are ill-qualified to perform.' (See also *R* v *Home Secretary, ex parte Bentley*; but see *Chandler* v *Director of Public Prosecutions, R* v *Criminal Injuries Compensation Board, ex parte Lain* and *The Case of Proclamations.*)

Customs and Excise Commissioners v Cure and Deeley Ltd [51]
[1962] 1 QB 340

The Finance (No 2) Act 1940, which introduced purchase tax, gave power to the Commissioners to make regulations for 'any matters for which provision appears to them to be necessary' to give effect to the Act. One such regulation provided that if no return or an incomplete return were submitted the Commissioners were empowered to determine the amount due and that amount would stand unless the person in question, within a certain time, proved to the satisfaction of the Commissioners the actual amount due. *Held*, that regulation was ultra vires because (1) the Commissioners had taken upon themselves the powers of the High Court judge to decide issues of fact and law; (2) the subject was liable to pay whatever the Commissioners assessed whereas the only liability was to pay the amount due; (3) it was capable of excluding access to the courts. The court regarded the regulation as an arbitrary and unreasonable exercise of the power conferred.

Davy v Spelthorne Borough Council [1984] AC 262 [52]
(House of Lords)

In September 1977 the plaintiff, the owner of premises used to produce concrete, applied to the council for permission to continue using his site for this purpose for another ten years. His application was rejected, but as a result of further negotiations with council officers an agreement was reached in November 1979, under which the council would issue an enforcement notice directing him to cease his user of the land, with the operation of his notice being suspended for three years. In exchange the plaintiff promised not to exercise his statutory right of appeal against the notice, which had to be exercised within 35 days of its being issued. In October 1980 the notice was issued in accordance with the agreement. In August 1982 the plaintiff issued a writ against the Council seeking an injunction to stop the notice taking effect, damages for negligent advice, and the setting aside of the notice. The plaintiff argued that the agreement had been ultra vires the council and therefore void. By the time the litigation reached the House of Lords only the claim for damages remained, the council contending that it should be struck out as an abuse of process. *Held*, to proceed by way of writ in order to recover damages was not an abuse of process in this case. The plaintiff was no longer contesting the validity of the enforcement notice, but the nature of the advice that led to his failing to challenge it. If the case still had a public law element it was no more than collateral to the main action and this came within the exceptions envisaged by LORD DIPLOCK in *O'Reilly* v *Mackman*. The court had no power to transfer the action to proceed as if it had been commenced under Order 53, with the result that if the writ was struck out, the plaintiff would have to start afresh with an application under Order 53. This might prejudice the plaintiff as he would be out of time; at the very least such a course of action would be uncertain. [Note the observation of LORD WILBERFORCE: 'The expressions "private law" and "public law" have recently been imported into the law of England from countries which, unlike our own, have separate systems concerning public law and private law. No doubt they are convenient expressions for descriptive purposes. In this country they must be used with caution, for, typically, English law fastens not on principles but on remedies. The principle remains intact that public authorities and public servants are, unless clearly exempted, answerable in the ordinary courts for wrongs done to individuals.'] (See also *Wandsworth London Borough Council* v *Winder.*)

Derbyshire County Council v Times Newspapers Ltd   [53]
[1993] 2 WLR 449 (House of Lords)

The defendant newspaper published articles which were severe in their criticism of the plaintiff local authority's management of its pension funds. The local authority sought to bring proceedings for libel against the defendants, who responded by applying to have the proceedings struck out as disclosing no known cause of action. At first instance the application to strike out was dismissed. The Court of Appeal allowed the appeal on the basis that, while a trading corporation could, in certain circumstances, sue for defamation, a local authority could not do so as regards its reputation in respect of administrative or governmental functions. The local authority appealed to the House of Lords. *Held*, the appeal would be dismissed. It was not in the public interest to permit democratically elected local government bodies to bring actions for defamation. The threat of a civil action might inhibit legitimate public comment on, or criticism of, the activities of a local authority. LORD KEITH OF KINKEL indicated, obiter, that this prohibition on the right to sue for defamation would extend equally to central government bodies. Any individual councillor who felt that his reputation had been damaged by a publication that allegedly defamed the council of which he was a member would still be able to maintain an action for defamation in his own right. Note that LORD KEITH, although reaching the same conclusion as the Court of Appeal, did so without reliance on the European Convention on Human Rights. While BALCOMBE LJ, in the Court of Appeal, had felt that domestic law was uncertain on the point, LORD KEITH said: 'I have reached my conclusion based on the common law of England ... and can only add that ... the common law of England is consistent with obligations assumed by the Crown under the Treaty in this particular field.'

Dimes v Grand Junction Canal Proprietors (1852) 3 HL Cas 759   [54]
(House of Lords)

A public company filed a bill in equity against a landowner and the cause was heard before the Vice-Chancellor who granted the relief sought by the company. On appeal, this order was affirmed by the Lord Chancellor, Lord Cottenham, who, unknown to the defendant landowner, held shares in the company to the amount of several thousand pounds. *Held*, the Lord Chancellor's decree was voidable and should be reversed, though it was not suggested that LORD

COTTENHAM was influenced by the interest he had in the company. (See also *R* v *Sussex Justices, ex parte McCarthy.*)

Dingle v Associated Newspapers Ltd [1960] 1 All ER 294   **[55]**

In an action for damages for libel, counsel for the plaintiff seemed to indicate that it was intended to attack the report of a select committee of the House of Commons, perhaps to the extent of impugning the validity of the report, on the ground of some defect of procedure. *Held*, to impugn the validity of such a report outside Parliament would be contrary to s1, Article 9, of the Bill of Rights 1688. [Note: The case went on appeal to the House of Lords, [1962] 2 All ER 737, but this point was not discussed.] (Applied in *Church of Scientology of California* v *Johnson-Smith.*)

Director of Public Prosecutions v Luft [1977] AC 962   **[56]**
(House of Lords)

At the General Election held in October 1974 candidates representing a political party known as the National Front stood for election, alongside candidates from the major political parties, in three Lancashire constituencies, Blackley, Bolton East and Bolton West. The respondents were members of various 'anti-fascist' associations, strongly opposed to the policies advocated by the National Front. In the course of the election campaign, the respondents distributed pamphlets urging voters not to vote for the National Front candidates, and accusing members of that political party of being liars and fascists. Each of the respondents was charged (inter alia) under s63 of the Representation of the People Act 1949 with the offence of incurring, without authorisation in writing of an election agent, the expense of issuing publications with a view to promoting or procuring the election of a candidate at the parliamentary election in the constituency in which that respondent had distributed pamphlets. The question certified for consideration by the House of Lords was whether, on a prosecution under s63 of the Representation of the People Act 1949, it is necessary to prove that expense was incurred with a view to promoting or procuring the election of a particular candidate and insufficient to establish that the view or motive of the person incurring the expense was to prevent the election of a particular candidate. *Held*, the restrictions upon unauthorised expenditure related not only to expenditure aimed at ensuring election but also to expenditure designed to prevent the election of opposing candidates. Where there are more than two candidates for a constituency, to persuade electors not to vote for one of those candidates in order to prevent his being elected must have the effect of improving the collective prospects of success of the other candidates though it may be uncertain which one of them will benefit most.

Donnelly v Jackman [1970] 1 All ER 987   **[57]**

A police officer approached Donnelly in order to make enquiries about an offence. Donnelly ignored the officer's repeated instructions to stop and speak to him. The officer touched Donnelly on the shoulder to stop him (he had no intention of arresting him), whereupon Donnelly struck the officer with some force. Donnelly was charged with and convicted of assaulting a police officer in execution of his duty. *Held*, the officer was in execution of duty. The touching of the man's shoulder was a trivial interference with his liberty and was not sufficient to take the conduct outside the execution of duty. [Note: It would seem that, although trivial, the touching was, in fact, technically a battery.] (Distinguished: *Kenlin* v *Gardiner.*)

Doody v Secretary of State for the Home Department. See **R v Secretary of State for the Home Department, ex parte Doody**

Duke v GEC Reliance Ltd [1988] AC 618 (House of Lords)   [58]

The complainant was a female employee dismissed by her employer shortly after her 60th birthday. Male employees were retired at 65. The complainant claimed that despite s6(4) of the Sex Discrimination Act 1975, which appeared to permit employers to discriminate on the grounds of sex as regards retirement, she was entitled to equal treatment as a result of an EEC Directive (76/207). Her complaint was dismissed by an industrial tribunal, the Employment Appeal Tribunal, and the Court of Appeal. She appealed to the House of Lords. *Held*, dismissing the appeal, the 1976 Act permitted employers to discriminate as regards retirement arrangements, and the operation of the legislation was unaffected by the Directive as it was not of direct effect between individuals. Hence the complainant could not sue her employer for non-compliance. LORD TEMPLEMAN expressed the view that s2(4) of the European Communities Act 1972 did not enable or constrain a British court to distort the meaning of a British statute in order to enforce against an individual a Community directive which has no direct effect between individuals. (See also *Marleasing SA v La Comercial Internacional de Alimentacion SA*.)

Duncan v Cammell Laird & Co Ltd [1942] AC 624 (House of Lords) [59]

While undergoing her submergence tests the submarine *Thetis*, which had been built by the respondents under contract with the Admiralty, sank to the bottom and failed to return to the surface. Ninety-nine men lost their lives, and actions for damages for negligence were brought by those representing, or dependent upon, some of the deceased against, inter alia, the respondents. The Admiralty directed the respondents not to produce certain documents, including reports as to the condition of the *Thetis* when raised, and to object to production thereof except under order of the court, on the ground of Crown privilege. *Held*, although a decision ruling out documents is the decision of the judge, the respondents should not be compelled to give inspection of the documents, as an objection by a minister validly taken to production, on the ground that it would be injurious to the public interest, is conclusive. However, a minister 'ought not to take the responsibility of withholding production except in cases where the public interest would otherwise be damnified, for example, where disclosure would be injurious to national defence, or to good diplomatic relations, or where the practice of keeping a class of documents secret is necessary for the proper functioning of the public service' (*per* VISCOUNT SIMON LC). (But see *Conway v Rimmer*.)

Duncan v Jones [1936] 1 KB 218   [60]

The appellant was about to hold a meeting in a certain street when the respondent police officer forbade her to do so. The appellant said 'I'm going to hold it', stepped on to a box and started to address the people who were present. The respondent immediately took her into custody and she was fined 40s for the statutory offence under the Prevention of Crimes Acts 1871–1885 of unlawfully and wilfully obstructing the respondent when in the execution of his duty. There was a finding of fact that the appellant must have known of the probable consequences of her holding the meeting – namely, a disturbance and possibly a breach of the peace – and was not unwilling that such consequences should ensue. *Held*, the conviction was right. 'It does not require authority to emphasise the statement that it is the duty of a police officer to prevent apprehended breaches of the peace. Here it is found as a fact that the respondent reasonably apprehended a breach of the peace. It then ... became his duty to prevent anything which in his view would cause that breach of the peace. While he was taking steps so to do he was wilfully obstructed by the appellant. I can conceive no clearer case within the statutes than that' (*per* HUMPHREYS J).

Dunlop v Woollahra Municipal Council [1982] AC 158   [61]
(Privy Council)

In 1974, in a purported exercise of their powers under ss308 and 309 respectively in Part XI of the Local Government Act 1919, the defendant council resolved to fix a building line for the plaintiff's property, and to regulate the number of storeys which might be contained in any residential flat building erected on that property. The plaintiff claimed to recover from the council damages in respect of the financial loss he alleged he had sustained during the time taken to establish the invalidity of the planning restrictions. *Held*, even if any duty of care was owed in the exercise of statutory powers, which contention was doubted, there was insufficient evidence of negligence on the part of the council. Judicial review remained the appropriate way in which to challenge the validity of action taken by administrative authorities. (See also *Rowling* v *Takaro Properties Ltd.*)

Dunn v Macdonald [1897] 1 QB 555   [62]

Having unsuccessfully brought a petition of right against the Crown (see *Dunn* v *R*), the plaintiff alleged, inter alia, that the defendant (Her Majesty's Commissioner and Consul-General for the Niger Protectorate) had untruly represented and warranted to the plaintiff that he was duly authorised and empowered to engage the plaintiff for three years certain. The plaintiff claimed damages for breach of the alleged warranty. *Held*, the defendant was entitled to judgment as the doctrine of an implied warranty of authority is not applicable to a public servant acting on behalf of the Crown.

Dunn v R [1896] 1 QB 116   [63]

The suppliant was engaged in the service of the Crown as a consular agent in the Niger Protectorate for a period of three years certain, and he claimed damages for having been dismissed before the expiration of that period. *Held*, his petition would fail as 'there must be imported into the contract for the employment of the petitioner the term which is applicable to civil servants in general, namely, that the Crown may put an end to the employment at its pleasure' (*per* LORD HERSCHELL).

Durayappah v Fernando [1967] 2 All ER 152 (Privy Council)   [64]

The Minister of Local Government of Ceylon was given a statutory power to dissolve a municipal council if it appeared to him that such council was incompetent or otherwise neglectful in the performance of its duties. The Minister sent a commissioner to enquire into certain complaints and to make a report. The commissioner made his report having seen the minutes of the council but without having seen any of the Members of the council or given them any opportunity of expressing their views in the matter. The Minister ordered the dissolution of the council. The appellant, the mayor at the time of the dissolution, sought mandates in the nature of certiorari and quo warranto to quash the order and a declaration that he was entitled to act as mayor. *Held*, (a) as to the application of the principle audi alteram partem: 'In their Lordships' opinion there are three matters which must always be borne in mind in considering whether the principle should be applied or not ... first, what is the nature of the property, the office held, status enjoyed or services to be performed by the complainant of injustice. Secondly, in what circumstances or upon what occasions is the person claiming to be entitled to exercise the measure of control entitled to intervene. Thirdly, when a right to intervene is proved what sanctions in fact is the latter entitled to impose upon the other ...' (*per* LORD UPJOHN); (b) applying such principles, the council should have been given the opportunity to be heard because firstly, there was a wide measure of independence given to it by statute; secondly, the charge of incompetence was a serious one; thirdly, since the council owned its property the effect of a dissolution was the deprivation of such property; (c) the Minister's order was not however a nullity but was voidable only at the election of the council and not on the initiative of the appellant acting personally, unless for some reason it was impracticable for the council to take its own initiative.

Dyson v Attorney-General [1911] 1 KB 410 [65]
(Court of Appeal)

Having received a form from the Commissioners of Inland Revenue making certain inquiries and threatening him with a penalty unless the inquiries were answered by a certain date, the plaintiff sought to test the legality of the procedure by bringing an action against the Attorney-General for a declaration that he was under no obligation to comply. *Held*, the court had jurisdiction to entertain such an action. [Note: This was the starting-point of the rise of the declaratory judgment as a remedy in administrative law.]

Edwards v Director of Public Prosecutions [66]
(1993) 97 Cr App R 301

Two men, Fox and Sumner, were observed by police officers who believed them to be using cannabis. When challenged, the men appeared to try to dispose of certain substances. They were informed that they were being arrested for obstructing the officers in the execution of their duties under the Misuse of Drugs Act 1971. A woman named Prendergast intervened to prevent the arrest of Fox and was arrested for obstruction contrary to s51(3) Police Act 1964. Edwards intervened to prevent the arrest of Prendergast and was similarly arrested for obstruction contrary to s51(3). The defendants submitted that there was no case to answer since there was no power to arrest without warrant for obstruction under the Misuse of Drugs Act 1971. Under s25 of the Police and Criminal Evidence Act 1984, where a constable has reasonable grounds for suspecting that any offence which is not an arrestable offence has been committed or attempted or is being committed or attempted, he may arrest the relevant person if it appears to him that service of a summons is impracticable or inappropriate because any of the general arrest conditions (see s25(3)) is satisfied. The magistrates found that in the circumstances there was a power to arrest under s25 of the 1984 Act as, on the facts now known, the arresting officer would have every reason to doubt the truth of any name he was given by the suspect; hence the arrests were lawful. On appeal by way of case stated, the Divisional Court considered the question of whether or not the arresting officer, in the circumstances of the case, had had the power to arrest Fox under s25(3)(a) and (b) and /or s25(3)(d)(i) of the 1984 Act. *Held*, the appeal would be allowed. As the power to arrest without warrant for obstruction of a police officer in the execution of his duty contrary to the Misuse of Drugs Act 1971 had been abolished by s26 of the Police and Criminal Evidence Act 1984, the only power to arrest for such obstruction would be that now arising under s25 of the 1984 Act – power of summary arrest in relation to a non-arrestable offence. By simply telling Fox that he was '... nicked for obstruction ...', the officer had failed to give s25(1) of the 1984 Act or any of the general arrest conditions detailed in s25(3) as justification. By virtue of s28(5) of the 1984 Act, an arrest is not lawful unless the arrestee is informed of the grounds of arrest.

There were no circumstances in the present case that precluded the giving of that information; it was obviously practicable for the officer to give reasons for the arrest, because that is precisely what he did. Unfortunately they were invalid. It may be the case that the arrest would have been valid if the general arrest conditions under s25 had been given as the reason for arrest, but the arrest could not be retrospectively validated. As EVANS LJ observed: 'It may seem unrealistic that the court should be concerned after the event with the precise words that were used ... Nevertheless, it has to be borne in mind that giving correct information as to the reasons for an arrest is a matter of the utmost constitutional significance in a case where a reason can be and is given at the time.'

Ellen Street Estates Ltd v Minister of Health [1934] 1 KB 590   [67]
(Court of Appeal)

The court approved *Vauxhall Estates Ltd* v *Liverpool Corporation* [1932] 1 KB 733 and confirmed that Parliament cannot bind itself as to the form of future legislation or effectively enact that a provision in one statute shall not be altered by a later Act except by express words. 'The Legislature cannot, according to our constitution, bind itself as to the form of subsequent legislation and it is impossible for Parliament to enact that in a subsequent statute dealing with the same subject-matter there can be no implied repeal' (*per* MAUGHAM LJ).

Ellis v Dubowski [1921] 3 KB 621   [68]

The Licensing Committee of the Middlesex County Council granted a licence under the Cinematograph Act 1909 in respect of the Gaiety Cinema, Twickenham. The licence was granted subject to the condition 'that no film be shown which has not been certified for public exhibition by the British Board of Film Censors', a body appointed by traders in the film industry for censorship purposes. *Held*, this condition was unreasonable and ultra vires as 'a condition putting the matter into the hands of a third person or body not possessed of statutory or constitutional authority is ultra vires the committee' (*per* LAWRENCE CJ). (See also *Lavender (H) & Son Ltd* v *Minister of Housing and Local Government.*)

Enderby Town Football Club Ltd v Football Association Ltd   [69]
[1971] Ch 591 (Court of Appeal)

The Football Association (FA) controlled the game of association football. The second defendant, a county football association affiliated to the FA, appointed a commission to enquire into the activities of the plaintiff club. Following a finding of gross negligence the club was censured. The club appealed on certain points of law to the FA and requested permission to be legally represented. That was refused because of a rule of the FA. The club sought an injunction to stop the hearing in the absence of legal representation. *Held*, the club was not entitled to representation before the FA. An action for a declaration would be the most appropriate way of dealing with the points raised. If the club chose instead to bring the points of law before the FA it must abide by its rules which excluded legal representation. '... is it lawful for a body to stipulate in its rules that its domestic tribunal shall not permit legal representation? Such a stipulation is ... clearly valid so long as it is construed as directory and not imperative: for that leaves it open to the tribunal to permit legal representation in an exceptional case when the justice of the case so requires' (*per* LORD DENNING MR). (See also *R* v *Secretary of State for the Home Department, ex parte Tarrant.*)

Entick v Carrington (1765) 19 St Tr 1030   **[70]**

A warrant of the Secretary of State ordered the defendants, who were King's Messengers, to search for the plaintiff and bring him, together with his books and papers, in safe custody before the Secretary of State to be examined. The plaintiff brought an action of trespass for breaking and entering his house and seizing his papers. *Held*, he was entitled to succeed as 'a warrant to seize and carry away the party's papers in the case of a seditious libel, is illegal and void and with respect to the argument of state necessity or a distinction that has been aimed at between state offences and others, the common law does not understand that kind of reasoning ... If the King himself has no power to declare when the law ought to be violated for reason of state, I am sure we his judges have no such prerogative' (*per* LORD CAMDEN CJ). (See also *Malone* v *Metropolitan Police Commissioner.*)

Errington v Minister of Health [1935] 1 KB 249 (Court of Appeal)   **[71]**

Under the Housing Act 1930, Jarrow Corporation made a clearance order in respect of certain buildings and submitted it to the Minister of Health for confirmation. After notice of objection to the clearance order had been given, the Minister caused a public local inquiry to be held, but the town clerk of Jarrow later submitted additional evidence and arranged a meeting between members of the council and officials of the Ministry, including the person who had held the inquiry. The objectors knew nothing of the evidence or meeting. *Held*, the confirming order should be quashed. Although the act of confirming a clearance order was an administrative act, in holding the inquiry the Minister was exercising a quasi-judicial function and, for this reason, he was required to act in accordance with the rules of natural justice; that is, he should have heard both sides, not one side (Jarrow Corporation) in the absence of the other (the objectors).

Fisher v Oldham Corporation [1930] 2 KB 364   **[72]**

By mistake, Oldham police caused an innocent man, whom they suspected of obtaining by false pretences, to be taken into custody. The man afterwards laid a claim against Oldham Corporation for damages for false imprisonment. *Held*, he could not succeed as the police were not the servants or agents of the corporation. [Note: See now the Police Act 1964, s48.]

Fox v Stirk [1970] 3 All ER 7 (Court of Appeal)   **[73]**

By s1(1) of the Representation of the People Act 1949, the persons entitled to vote at a parliamentary election were those 'resident' in a constituency on the qualifying date, ie 10 October. Students at Bristol and Cambridge Universities who were living in halls of residence appealed against decisions of electoral registration officers that they were not entitled to be registered. *Held*, they were entitled to be put on the register – there was a sufficient degree of permanence of residence for them to be considered as residents.

Francovich v Italian Republic [1992] IRLR 84   **[74]**
(European Court of Justice)

The plaintiffs were employees of private Italian companies that had become insolvent. Following the employers' inability to meet the plaintiffs' outstanding claims under their contracts of employment, the plaintiffs commenced proceedings in the Italian courts against the Italian Republic, requesting a finding that the State, despite its failure to implement Directive 80/987 containing measures to protect employees wishing to make claims against insolvent employers, was liable to compensate the plaintiffs in respect of their outstanding claims for arrears of pay. The following questions were referred for consideration by the European Court of Justice: (1) Under Community law in force, can an individual who has suffered as a result of the failure by the State to implement Directive 80/987, which failure has been established by a judgment of the Court of Justice, require that State to comply with those provisions contained in it which are sufficiently precise and unconditional by relying directly on the Community rules against the Member State in order to obtain the guarantees which that Member State was to ensure, and, in any event, is he entitled to claim damages suffered in respect of provisions which do not have that status? (2) Must the combined provisions of Articles 3 and 4 of Council Directive 80/987 be interpreted as meaning that where a State has not exercised its option to introduce the limitations provided for in Article 4, that State is bound to pay employees their entitlement in the amount laid down in Article 3? (3) If the answer to question 2 is in the negative, would the Court establish what is the minimum guarantee which the State must ensure pursuant to Directive 80/987 to an employee entitled so that part of the payment due to him can be considered payable under the Directive itself? *Held*, the provisions of the Insolvency Directive 80/987 were not sufficiently unconditional and precise to have direct effect, and thus the rights created thereunder could not be asserted in proceedings against a Member State in national courts in the absence of implementing measures adopted within the prescribed period. Within the context of the law of a Member State relating to liability, damages could be recovered from a Member State that had failed to implement a Community Directive as required, provided that the directive in question attributed identifiable rights to individuals, and provided that there was a chain of causation between the loss suffered and the State's failure to comply with the requirements of implementation. Given the answer to the first question, the court did not consider it necessary to answer the second and third questions posed.

Franklin v Minister for Town and Country Planning   [75]
[1947] 2 All ER 289 (House of Lords)

In a speech made at a public meeting in Stevenage Town Hall, the Minister of Town and Country Planning said, in relation to the Stevenage New Town scheme: 'The project will go forward because it must go forward.' Some weeks after this the New Towns Bill received the Royal Assent and under this the Stevenage New Town Designation Order 1946 was made by which Stevenage was designated a 'new town' within the Act. Pursuant to the Act a public inquiry was held to hear objections, but no evidence in support of the order was adduced by the Minister and having considered the objections and the inspector's report he rejected such objections as were made. *Held*, the Minister had no judicial or quasi-judicial duties imposed on him, his statutory duties being of an administrative nature, so that considerations of bias were irrelevant, the sole question being whether or not he genuinely considered the report and the objections. Further, there was no need for the Minister to call evidence in support of the order since the object of the inquiry was to inform his mind and not to consider any issue between him and the objectors. In all the circumstances, the order would be upheld.

Gaiman v National Association for Mental Health   [76]
[1970] 2 All ER 362

The Association, a company limited by guarantee, was a charitable body concerned with the preservation and development of mental health. The Articles of Association provided, inter alia, in Article 7 that a member should cease to be a member if requested by resolution of the Council of Management to resign. There was a right of appeal. The Council acting under Article 7 expelled 302 members of the Association who were suspected of being Scientologists (between which group and the Association there existed a state of hostility). The plaintiffs sought a mandatory injunction requiring the Association to afford plaintiffs all rights of membership until the trial of the action. *Held*, inter alia, the principles of natural justice did not apply to the expulsion of members because (a) there was a duty owed by the Council to the corporation to exercise their powers bona fide and that duty might involve acting with speed whereas natural justice would involve delay; (b) a person who joined the Association did so accepting the existence of Article 7; (c) the wording gave unrestricted power and this militated against natural justice; (d) membership of the Association involved no real interest in property and no question of livelihood or reputation. MEGARRY J: 'If the discretion conferred is absolute and unfettered, and no charge is made, then I find it difficult to see how there can be any requirement to provide what Lord Hodson in *Ridge* v *Baldwin* regarded as two of the three outstanding features of natural justice, namely "the right to have notice of charges of misconduct" and "the right to be heard in answer to those charges".' Later MEGARRY J said: 'A further point put before me was whether there is any rule of public policy which prevents the principles of natural justice from being ousted by an express term which excludes them.' He refused to express a view on this matter, although for the purposes of the present case he was prepared to assume that such a term would be invalid. [Note: On scope of control, see also LORD DENNING MR in *Breen* v *Amalgamated Engineering Union* referring to domestic bodies (eg trade unions, Jockey Club, etc): 'Often their rules are framed so as to give them a discretion. They then claim that it is an "unfettered" discretion with which the courts have no right to interfere. They go too far. They claim too much. The Minister made the same claim in [*Padfield* v *Minister of Agriculture, Fisheries and Food*] and was roundly rebuked by the House of Lords for his impudence.']

Garland v British Rail Engineering Ltd [1983] 2 AC 751   [77]
(European Court of Justice and House of Lords)

The appellant was a female employee of the respondent company, whose employees enjoyed (ex gratia) free travel on British Rail. Upon retirement male employees continued to enjoy this benefit for themselves and their families. In the case of retiring female employees, the benefit did not extend to their families. The appellant contended that this discrimination was not permitted by s6(4) of the Sex Discrimination Act 1964 and was in breach of Article 119 of the EEC Treaty. The appellant's case was dismissed by an industrial tribunal, but she was successful before the Employment Appeal Tribunal. The respondent employers appealed successfully to the Court of Appeal. On appeal to the House of Lords, the issue was referred to the European Court of Justice, which held that the discrimination was in breach of Article 119, which was directly applicable where a domestic court found such discrimination to exist. The case was referred back to the House of Lords. *Held*, the decision of the Employment Appeal Tribunal would be restored. Domestic legislation was to be construed so as to ensure compliance with international obligations as evidenced in international treaties, a fortiori where the treaty obligation arose under one of the Community treaties to which section 2 of the European Communities Act 1972 applied. The instant case was not one that required the court to consider whether, having regard to the express direction as to the construction of enactments 'to be passed' contained in section 2(4) of the 1972 Act, anything short of an express positive statement in an Act of Parliament passed after 1 January 1973 (ie that a particular provision was intended to be made in breach of an obligation assumed by the United Kingdom under a Community treaty) would justify an English court in construing that provision in a manner inconsistent with a Community treaty obligation of the United Kingdom. In the absence of such a provision, the courts should seek to give effect to

Community law obligations, no matter how wide a departure from the prima facie meaning of the language of the domestic legislation might be needed in order to achieve consistency.

General Council of Medical Education and Registration of the   [78]
United Kingdom v Spackman [1943] 2 All ER 337 (House of Lords)

Under s29 of the Medical Act 1858, if after 'due inquiry' a doctor is found guilty of infamous conduct in any professional respect his name may be deleted from the register of medical practitioners. In certain divorce proceedings it was found that a doctor had committed adultery with a person with whom he stood in a professional relationship. In view of this, the General Medical Council fixed a meeting to decide whether or not his name should be removed from the Medical Register, and at this meeting the doctor desired to call evidence challenging the finding of adultery which was available at the time of, but was not adduced in, the proceedings for divorce. The Council decided that they would not receive this evidence and directed that the doctor's name should be erased from the Medical Register. *Held*, the Council's refusal to hear this evidence prevented there being a 'due inquiry' as required by s29 of the Act of 1858 and an order of certiorari should be granted.

Gilmore's Application, Re. See R v Medical Appeal Tribunal,   [79]
ex parte Gilmore Glynn v Keele University [1971] 2 All ER 89

In the exercise of power conferred upon him by the statutes of the University, the Vice-Chancellor of Keele wrote to the plaintiff informing him that following an incident at the University in which he was said to have been involved, he would be excluded from residence on the campus. Notification of the date of the appeal from that decision was sent to him but he was abroad at the time and missed the hearing. The plaintiff sought an injunction. *Held*, the Vice-Chancellor was acting in a quasi-judicial capacity and thus had not complied with the rules of natural justice, because he had not sent for the student but had merely written to him informing the student of his decision. However, an injunction would be refused because the plaintiff had suffered no injustice – he had merely been deprived of the right to make a plea in mitigation (the facts not being in dispute).

Hall & Co Ltd v Shoreham-by-Sea Urban District Council   [80]
[1964] 1 All ER 1 (Court of Appeal)

The plaintiffs sought planning permission to develop for industrial purposes land adjoining a busy main road. The planning authority granted permission subject to the condition that the plaintiffs would at their own expense construct an ancillary road providing a right of passage for persons proceeding to and from other adjoining properties. *Held*, although the planning authority's object was reasonable, since in effect the condition amounted to a requirement that the plaintiffs should dedicate the road to the public without any right to compensation (there being a more regular course under the Highways Act 1959), the condition was so unreasonable as to be ultra vires.

Harper v Secretary of State for the Home Department   [81]
[1955] 1 Ch 238 (Court of Appeal)

The Boundary Commission submitted a report to the Home Secretary recommending certain changes in constituency boundaries. Pursuant to s2(5) of the House of Commons (Redistribution of Seats) Act 1949, the Home Secretary laid the report before Parliament together with certain draft Orders in Council.

These Orders in Council were approved by Parliament, and the Home Secretary was proposing to submit them to the Queen in Council. *Held*, even if the report departed from the rules laid down by the 1949 Act, if the method was one which Parliament did not like, Parliament could have modified or rejected it. The matter was entirely within Parliament's discretion, it not being contemplated that it could be competent for a court to decide whether a particular course adopted by the commissioner was right.

Harris v Minister for the Interior 1952 (2) SA 428 (A)   **[82]**
(Appellate Division of the Supreme Court of South Africa)

The question arose as to whether the Separate Representation of Voters Act 1951, which provided for the separate representation of European and non-European voters in the Province of the Cape of Good Hope, was enforceable in a court of law. It was common ground that the Act of 1951 had not been passed in conformity with the South Africa Act 1909, which provided, inter alia, that no person should be removed from the register of voters because of his race or colour and that this provision could be repealed or amended only by a Bill passed by not less than two-thirds of the total number of members of both South African Houses of Parliament sitting together. The 1951 Act had been passed by the House of Assembly and the Senate sitting separately. *Held*, the Act of 1951 was invalid, null and void and of no legal force and effect. The Statute of Westminster left the relevant clauses of the South Africa Act intact and it followed that the courts had power to declare an Act invalid on the ground that it was not passed in conformity with them.

HK (an infant), Re [1967] 2 QB 617   **[83]**

AR was a Commonwealth citizen ordinarily resident in the United Kingdom within the meaning of s2(2)(a) of the Commonwealth Immigrants Act 1962. He arrived from Pakistan accompanied by HK, an infant, claiming that HK was his son who, being under 16 years of age, had a right of entry under s2(2)(b) of the Act. The immigration authorities, suspecting that the infant was over 16, refused entry to the UK. AR sought habeas corpus and certiorari to quash the immigration officer's decision. *Held*, refusing the relief, (a) whether or not the immigration officer was acting in a judicial or quasi-judicial capacity, the rules of natural justice applied to the extent that, within the legislative framework of the Act, the officer was required to act fairly and dispassionately, giving the immigrant an opportunity of satisfying him of the relevant matters; (b) the burden was on the immigrant, and since both father and son knew that they had to satisfy the officer and had an opportunity to do so, the officer's decision was arrived at fairly; (c) even if there might have been further enquiry, the decisions were unimpeachable when made and the only possible remedy might have been mandamus. (See also *R v Birmingham City Justices, ex parte Chris Foreign Foods (Wholesalers) Ltd* and *R v Gaming Board for Great Britain, ex parte Benaim and Khaida*.)

Home Office v Dorset Yacht Company Limited [1970] AC 1004   **[84]**
(House of Lords)

Borstal trainees escaped while working in the custody of three officers, and damage was caused to a yacht. There arose a preliminary issue as to duty of care. *Held*, there was a duty of care. There was no ground in public policy for granting complete immunity from liability in negligence to the Home Office or its officers. But see LORD DIPLOCK: 'Neither the *intentional release* of a borstal trainee under supervision, nor the *unintended* escape of a borstal trainee still under detention which was the *consequence of the application of a system of relaxed control* intentionally adopted by the Home Office ... can have been intended by Parliament to give rise to any cause of action ...'

Howard v Boddington (1877) 2 PD 203   [85]

Section 9 of the Public Worship Act 1874 stated that a bishop who intended to act upon a complaint against an incumbent within his diocese had to give that incumbent a copy of the complaint within 21 days of receiving it. In this case, some seven weeks elapsed before this was done. The question for the court was whether the requirement was directory or mandatory. *Held*, the statutory time limit was mandatory, and failure to observe it was fatal to the legality of any subsequent proceedings. To determine whether or not a provision was mandatory it was necessary to look to the subject-matter dealt with by the legislation, to consider the importance of the provision that had been disregarded, and the relation of that provision to the general object intended to be secured by the Act.

Impositions Case, Attorney-General v Bates (1606) 2 St Tr 371   [86]

Mr Bates, the defendant, paid the statutory duty of 2s 6d a hundred on currants imported from Venice but refused to pay a duty of 5s a hundred on such currants imposed by a mere act of the Crown. *Held*, the King could impose by prerogative duty on imports and exports. The impost was 'not upon a subject, but ... upon Bates, as upon a merchant, who imports goods within this land, charged before by the King; and at the time when the impost was imposed upon them, then were the goods of the Venetians, and not the goods of a subject, nor within the land, but only upon those which shall be after imported; and so all the arguments, which were made for the subject, fail' (*per* FLEMMING CB).

Inland Revenue Commissioners v National Federation of   [87]
Self-Employed and Small Businesses Ltd [1981] 2 WLR 722
(House of Lords)

In an effort to prevent large-scale tax evasion by casual workers in Fleet Street, the Inland Revenue came to an agreement with the unions whereby the Inland Revenue would agree to an 'amnesty' as regards the investigation of unpaid tax in previous years, in return for the casual workers now providing accurate information when they registered for work so that tax could be collected. The Federation, which felt that its members were often unfairly harassed by the Inland Revenue with regard to the collection of tax, sought a declaration that the 'amnesty' was ultra vires the Inland Revenue, and an order of mandamus to compel it to recover the tax due. The Divisional Court, at the full hearing, held that the Federation lacked locus standi under Order 53, 5.3(5). The Court of Appeal, by a majority, allowed the Federation's appeal. The Inland Revenue appealed. *Held*, allowing the appeal, (1) the existence of locus standi was a matter of fact and law to be decided on legal principles; (2) in many cases the issue of standing would need to be addressed at the application for leave stage, and subsequently at the full hearing of the application for review when both sides of the argument could be advanced; (3) factors to be considered in assessing standing included the powers or the duties in law of those against whom the relief was being sought, the position of the applicant in relation to those powers or duties, and the nature and extent of the ultra vires action alleged; (4) the fact that the words 'sufficient interest' were used to cover all the forms of remedy allowed by the rule did not mean that the test would be the same in all cases. Unlike the relationship between ratepayers and local authorities, dealings between taxpayers and the Inland Revenue were confidential. No taxpayer had any right to know the amount of tax paid by any other taxpayer. 'The total confidentiality of assessments and of negotiations between individuals and the revenue is a vital element in the working of the system. As a matter of general principle I would hold that one taxpayer has no sufficient interest in asking the court to investigate the tax affairs of another taxpayer or to complain that the latter has been under-assessed or over-assessed: indeed, there is a strong public interest that he should not. And this principle applies equally to groups of taxpayers: an aggregate of individuals each of whom has no interest cannot of itself have an interest' (*per* LORD WILBERFORCE). (See also *R v Secretary of State for Foreign Affairs, ex parte World Development Movement Ltd.*)

Jeffs v New Zealand Dairy Production and Marketing Board [88]
[1966] 3 All ER 863 (Privy Council)

The Board (established by statute) had power to define areas from which factories could get cream and milk. The Board had a financial interest in R Company (to which it had made loans). Notwithstanding that the Board made a zoning order covering, inter alia, R Company. A committee appointed by the Board to investigate supply held a public inquiry at which the appellants gave evidence. The committee made a report recommending, inter alia, that compensation be paid to R Company for loss of supply. The Board affirmed the committee's decision without seeing the written statements made; its members, other than the members of the committee, were not informed of the evidence given. The appellants sought certiorari to quash the decision and an injunction to prevent payment to R Company. *Held*, the Act setting up the Board had intended to make an exception to the rule that no one should be judge in his own cause and the Board had a duty to determine the question despite its financial interest, *but* the Board was under a duty to act judicially in determining zoning questions affecting the rights of individuals and it had not done so here. In reaching its decision without consideration of, and in ignorance of, the evidence presented it had failed to hear the interested parties. [Note: The Board had no power to delegate its functions.] (But see *R v Local Government Board, ex parte Arlidge.*)

Johnstone v Pedlar [1921] 2 AC 262 (House of Lords) [89]

The plaintiff was a naturalised American citizen (born in Ireland). He returned to Ireland and took part in the rebellion of 1916 in Dublin. On 1 May 1918 he was arrested on a charge of illegal drilling. He was convicted and served a six-month prison sentence in a Belfast gaol. When he was arrested he had with him some money and a cheque which were seized and detained by the police. The seizure and detention were subsequently ratified by the Chief Secretary of Ireland. The plaintiff brought an action against the Chief Commissioner of the Police for the recovery of the money and cheque. The Chief Commissioner pleaded that the plaintiff was an alien and that the money was detained by direction of the Crown as an act of state. *Held*, the defence of act of state could not be used against the plaintiff as a friendly alien on British territory. Whilst on British territory the friendly alien owes temporary allegiance to the British Crown and is entitled to the protection of British law, otherwise aliens present on British territory would be at the mercy of any department entitled to use the name of the Crown for an 'Act of State'. (Distinguished in *Nissan v Attorney-General.*)

Jones v Department of Employment [1988] 2 WLR 493 [90]
(Court of Appeal)

The plaintiff applied for unemployment benefit in 1984. His claim was rejected by the adjudication officer. He later appealed successfully to the Social Security Appeal Tribunal. Nevertheless, the plaintiff commenced an action for negligence against the defendant Department claiming damages in respect of the loss caused by the giving of the negligent advice. In the County Court, the Department applied to have the action struck out as disclosing no cause of action. This contention was based on the arguments that the statutory framework provided the only remedies available; that the adjudication officer did not owe the plaintiff a duty of care; that in any event, the officer had been discharging duties of a judicial nature, and the Department could, therefore, rely on s2(5) of the Crown Proceedings Act 1947. The County Court judge refused to strike out the action, and the Department appealed to the Court of Appeal. *Held*, allowing the appeal, whilst the adjudication officer could not be described as falling within the scope of the 'judicial immunity' referred to in s2(5) of the 1947 Act, it would be wrong to impose upon him any common law duty of care regarding negligent advice. The only private law action that might be sustainable in such circumstances was an action for misfeasance. Further, to allow an action for negligence to proceed would be to offend the object of the relevant legislation which had established a framework of appeals from decisions of adjudication officers, appeal lying ultimately to the Social Security Commissioner whose decision was to be regarded as 'final' on all matters other than questions of law.

Kenlin v Gardiner [1966] 3 All ER 931   [91]

Two schoolboys, who were in fact on an innocent mission, were thought by police officers (who were in plain clothes) to be acting suspiciously. On being approached the boys, who did not realise that the men were police officers, ran away, whereupon they were grasped by the officers (but not with a view to arrest). They then struck the officers and were charged with assaulting them in execution of duty contrary to s51(1) of the Police Act 1964. *Held*, a plea of self-defence was open to the boys since the taking hold of the boys was an assault as it was not an integral part of the arrest procedure, but in order to detain them for questioning (which they had no right to do). For a conviction under s51 it is not necessary to prove that the accused was aware that he was assaulting a police officer, but if the accused had made a genuine and reasonable mistake, eg that the person was a thug and not a police officer, that would be relevant in judging the reasonableness of the resistance exerted (*per* WINN LJ). (Distinguished in *Donnelly v Jackman*.)

Kruse v Johnson [1898] 2 QB 91   [92]

A by-law made by the Kent County Council provided: 'No person shall sound or play upon any musical or noisy instrument or sing in any public place or highway within fifty yards of any dwellinghouse after being required by any constable, or by an inmate of such home personally, or by his or her servant, to desist.' *Held*, the by-law was valid as it was reasonable. LORD RUSSELL CJ thought that the courts ought to be slow to condemn as invalid any by-law on the ground of supposed unreasonableness unless it were found to be partial and unequal in its operation as between different classes, manifestly unjust, disclosed bad faith or involved such oppressive or gratuitous interference with the rights of those subject to them as could find no justification in the minds of reasonable men.

Lavender (H) & Son Ltd v Minister of Housing and Local   [93]
Government [1970] 3 All ER 871

The applicants sought planning permission to extract minerals from an agricultural holding. Permission was refused on the ground that the Minister of Agriculture, Fisheries and Food objected, whereupon the applicants appealed to the Minister of Housing and Local Government under s23 of the Town and County Planning

Act 1962. The appeal was dismissed and the Minister gave as one of his reasons that it was his policy not to grant permission if the Minister of Agriculture, Fisheries and Food was opposed to it. An application was made under s179 of the 1962 Act for an order to quash the decision. *Held*, the Minister of Housing and Local Government had failed in the exercise of his discretion by acting solely in accordance with stated policy thereby disabling himself from exercising his discretion, and he had improperly delegated his duties in relation to the appeal to the Minister of Agriculture, etc (who had no status in the matter, save in a consultative capacity). (See also *Ellis* v *Dubowski*.)

Lee v Showmen's Guild of Great Britain [1952] 1 All ER 1175   [94]
(Court of Appeal)

A dispute arose between two showmen, the plaintiff and one Shaw, both of whom were members of the Showmen's Guild, as to whose Noah's Ark should occupy a certain site at Bradford Fair Ground. The plaintiff occupied the site but on a complaint by Shaw a committee of the Guild, acting in accordance with one of the Guild's rules, fined the plaintiff £100 for 'unfair competition'. The plaintiff failed to pay the fine and, under powers conferred by the same rule, the committee resolved that he was deemed to have ceased to be a member of the Guild. *Held*, in finding that the plaintiff was guilty of 'unfair competition', the committee had misconstrued the relevant rule and, for this reason, the fine and expulsion were ultra vires and void. The fact that the Guild was a domestic rather than a statutory tribunal did not exclude the courts from enquiring whether that tribunal had properly applied the relevant rule or observed the rules of natural justice.

Lever Finance Ltd v Westminster City London Borough   [95]
Council [1971] 1 QB 222 (Court of Appeal)

Developers who were seeking planning permission attached a plan of the work to the application. Permission was granted. Later the plans were changed and those were submitted. The local authority's planning officer (who had mislaid the first plan) erroneously assumed that the variation was not material and informed the architect that no further consent was necessary. The developers acted on that representation. Local residents objected when they found that the building was much nearer to their properties than was first anticipated. The local authority suggested that the developers apply for further permission, which they did, but the application was refused. The developers brought an action for a declaration and an injunction restraining the authority from taking down the house. *Held*, there was valid planning permission because a planning permission covered work specified in the plans and minor variations. It was the practice of local authorities to allow officers to decide on the materiality of changes in plans, and the representation made by the officer in this situation was within the officer's ostensible authority and was binding on the authority (*per* LORD DENNING MR and MEGAW LJ). (But see *Western Fish Products Ltd* v *Penwith District Council*.)

Lewis v Cattle [1938] 2 KB 454   [96]

The question arose as to whether a police officer is a 'person who holds office under His Majesty' within the meaning of the Official Secrets Act. *Held*, he is, because 'every police officer in England and Wales, whether he be a member of the Metropolitan Police Force or a member of the police force of a county, city, or borough, holds the office of constable, and within his constablewick he has all the duties and rights conferred by common law or statute on the holders of that office. He is required to take an oath of office and his primary duty is to preserve the King's peace' (*per* LORD HEWART CJ). His Lordship added that there 'are many offices which are held under His Majesty the holders whereof are not in any proper sense of the words in the service of His Majesty. So also there are many persons in the service of His Majesty who do not in any proper sense of the words hold office under His Majesty.'

Lewis v Chief Constable of the South Wales Constabulary   [97]
[1991] 1 All ER 206 (Court of Appeal)

The plaintiffs had been arrested on suspicion of burglary and taken to a police station. One had been told the reason for the arrest ten minutes after it had occurred, the other some 23 minutes after arrest. They were detained for about five hours and then released. In an action for false arrest and wrongful imprisonment, they were awarded damages for unlawful detention of only ten and 23 minutes respectively. They appealed, contending that, in view of s28(3) of the Police and Criminal Evidence Act 1984, they were entitled to compensation for the whole period of their detention. *Held*, dismissing the appeals, arrest is a situation. It is a matter of fact. Whether a person has been arrested depends not on the legality of his arrest but on whether he has been deprived of his liberty to go where he pleases. There was no doubt that, on the facts of this case, the appellants had been deprived of their liberty at the moment that they were arrested. Arrest is a continuing act and is the process of being kept in custody or deprived of liberty. It would not be inconsistent with the wording of the Police and Criminal Evidence Act 1984 s28(3) to say that from the moment when reasons were given the arrest became lawful, or the continued deprivation of liberty became lawful, or the continued custody became lawful. Hence the trial judge's direction as to the time to be taken into account for the calculation of damages had been correct.

Liversidge v Anderson [1942] AC 206 (House of Lords)   [98]

The plaintiff was detained in prison under certain defence regulations. The defendant, the Home Secretary, had power to order his detention if he had reasonable cause to believe the plaintiff to be a person of hostile origin or associations. The plaintiff sought particulars of the grounds on which the defendant entertained this belief. *Held*, he was not entitled to them as the matter was one of executive discretion: the Minister was not acting judicially. 'Not only is the belief to be his (ie the Minister's), but the estimate of the reasonableness of the causes which have induced such belief is also to be his, and his alone' (*per* LORD ROMER). (But see *Roberts* v *Hopwood*.)

Lloyd v McMahon [1987] 2 WLR 812 (House of Lords)   [99]

The appellants were councillors serving on Liverpool City Council, who had been surcharged for wilful misconduct by the district auditor, following their delay in setting a lawful rate for Liverpool for the year 1985–86. The councillors were notified by the district auditor that they could make representations in writing before he reached a final decision, and they responded collectively with documentary evidence explaining that they had delayed setting a rate pending any decision by central government to increase its grant support for the council. On 6 September 1985 the district auditor issued a certificate, pursuant to s20(1) of the Local Government Finance Act 1982, certifying that a sum of £106,103 was due from the appellant councillors as being the loss directly attributable to their delay in setting a rate. The councillors appealed against the certification to the Divisional Court, and were invited to give oral evidence in support of their case by that court but declined to do so. The Divisional Court dismissed the appeals, and this decision was upheld by the Court of Appeal. The councillors appealed.

Held, dismissing the appeals, there was evidence of wilful misconduct by the councillors, and the district auditor had not acted unfairly in refusing to allow them an oral hearing prior to his issuing of the certificate under the 1982 Act. There was no evidence that an oral hearing would have supplied a defence which was lacking from the written representations of the appellants or could have validated or reinforced possible defences foreshadowed in their written representations. 'An oral hearing could not detract from the force of the documentary evidence or supplement the written defence of the appellants in any material respects.' (*per* LORD TEMPLEMAN). 'It is easy to envisage cases where an oral hearing would clearly be essential in the interests of fairness, for example where an objector states that he has personal knowledge of some facts indicative of wilful misconduct on the part of a councillor. In that situation justice would demand that the councillor be given an opportunity to depone to his own version of the facts ... If the appellants had attended an oral hearing they would no doubt have reiterated the sincerity of their motives from the point of view of advancing the interests of the inhabitants of Liverpool. It seems unlikely, having regard to the position adopted by their counsel on this matter before the Divisional Court, that they would have been willing to reveal or answer questions about the proceedings of their political caucus' (*per* LORD KEITH OF KINKEL).

M v Home Office [1993] 3 WLR 433 (House of Lords)   [100]

M had arrived in the United Kingdom from Zaire seeking political asylum, but was not granted permission to remain following the finding of Kenneth Baker, the then Home Secretary, that M had not established the required 'well grounded fear of persecution' in Zaire. M was due to be returned to Zaire on 1 May 1991, the flight leaving London at 6.30pm. An application for judicial review to challenge the Secretary of State's decision on asylum was heard on 1 May, and at 5.55pm GARLAND J indicated that, as in his view there was an arguable case to be considered, M should not be removed from the country until there had been a full hearing of the case. Counsel for the Home Office indicated that the Home Office would seek to prevent M's removal from the country, although he had not been instructed to give an undertaking that M's removal would be prevented. M did depart on the flight to Zaire, and later that evening the judge granted a mandatory order compelling the Home Office to ensure the return of M to the United Kingdom. The Home Secretary declined to obey the order, and instead challenged its validity in the courts. During these proceedings GARLAND J accepted that he did not have the power to issue what amounted to a mandatory injunction against the Minister, but suggested that he had been seeking to ensure compliance with the earlier undertaking given by counsel for the Secretary of State to the effect that the judicial review proceedings would not be rendered otiose by M's removal from the jurisdiction. M brought proceedings for contempt against the Secretary of State based on his failure to comply with the court's order while it had been in force. At first instance, SIMON BROWN J refused to accept that such contempt proceedings were possible as regards the Crown or government departments, since coercive orders could not in any event be enforced. M appealed against this dismissal of his application. A majority of the Court of Appeal held that, while the Crown and government departments could not be guilty of contempt of court, proceedings could be maintained in respect of ministers and civil servants, and that on the facts of this case the Home Secretary had personally been in contempt of court. The Home Secretary appealed to the House of Lords. M cross-appealed. *Held,* the appeal and cross-appeal would be dismissed, subject to the Court of Appeal's order being varied so that it should be addressed to the 'Secretary of State for Home Affairs' and not 'Kenneth William Baker'. Under s31 of the Supreme Court Act 1981 the courts had the power to grant coercive orders against a minister of the Crown acting in an official capacity. In particular, RSC Ord 53 r3(10) empowered the court to grant an interim injunction against a minister. LORD WOOLF expressed the view that s21 of the Crown Proceedings Act 1947 had not been intended to affect the right of an individual to seek injunctive relief against an individual Crown servant, acting in his official capacity, to prevent the commission of a tort. He explained further that as the prerogative orders have never been available against the Crown, when s31(2) of the Supreme Court Act 1981 extended the prerogative jurisdiction to include the granting of injunctions, including interim injunctions, by way of judicial review proceedings, it was not creating a conflict with s21 of the 1947 Act (that is, it did not create the possibility of injunctions being granted against the Crown as such). The provision merely created a procedure by which an injunction could be obtained against a minister exercising statutory power in his official capacity. Prior to 1947, prerogative orders had been available in respect of a minister of the Crown acting in an official capacity; hence the effect of s31(2) was to make injunctive relief available in such cases although, in LORD WOOLF'S view, the power to do so should be exercised sparingly. Although no finding of contempt could be made against the Crown, if a minister flouted a coercive order contempt proceedings could be maintained against the minister, in his official capacity, and his department. It followed that although the sanctions for such contempt could not be personal or punitive, the court's finding of contempt would be an indication that the minister had acted improperly, an appropriate order as to costs could be made, and there would in all likelihood be repercussions for the minister in terms of parliamentary scrutiny. On the facts of the instant case the judge hearing the application had had jurisdiction to grant an order restraining the Home Secretary from proceeding with M's deportation, and the Home Secretary had been in contempt of court in failing to take adequate steps in order to ensure compliance. (See also *R* v *Secretary of State for Transport, ex parte Factortame Ltd.*)

Macarthys Ltd v Smith [1979] 3 All ER 325; [1981] QB 180   **[101]**
(Court of Appeal, European Court of Justice)

Macarthys Ltd employed a man to manage their stockroom at £60 per week. Four and a half months after he had left their employment, they took on a woman stockroom manager at £50 per week. She claimed that she was entitled to equal pay by virtue of s1(2)(a)(i) of the Equal Pay Act 1970. Before an industrial tribunal the employers contended, unsuccessfully, that that section only applied where men and women were employed on like work at the same time. The Employment Appeal Tribunal dismissed the employer's appeal on the grounds that s1(2)(a)(i) was to be construed so as to give effect to the principle contained in Article 119 of the EEC Treaty which clearly related to successive as well as contemporaneous employment. On appeal to the Court of Appeal. *Held*, (1) (LORD DENNING MR dissenting), the 1970 Act was to be construed according to the ordinary canons of construction which did not include reference to the Treaty of Rome; (2) (LORD DENNING MR dissenting), it was not clear whether Article 119 related to successive as well as concurrent employment; (3) (LORD DENNING MR concurring), as there was doubt as to the ambit of Article 119 and as the court was bound by s2 of the European Communities Act to give priority to the provisions of the EEC Treaty, the question of the true interpretation would be referred to the European Court under Article 177. 'In construing our statute, we are entitled to look to the Treaty as an aid to its construction; but not only as an aid but as an overriding force. If on close investigation it should appear that our legislation is deficient or is inconsistent with Community law by some oversight of our draftsmen then it is our bounden duty to give priority to Community law. Such is the result of s2(1) and (4) of the European Communities Act 1972. I pause here, however, to make one observation on a constitutional point. Thus far I have assumed that our

Parliament, whenever it passes legislation, intends to fulfil its obligations under the Treaty. If the time should come when our Parliament deliberately passes an Act with the intention of repudiating the Treaty or any provision in it or intentionally of acting inconsistently with it and says so in express terms then I should have thought that it would be the duty of our courts to follow the statute of our Parliament' (*per* LORD DENNING MR).

Following the reference under Article 177, the European Court of Justice ruled that Article 119 did not require contemporaneous employment for the application of equal pay provisions, and that the right to equal pay enshrined in that Article was directly applicable in the national courts of each country. When the case was remitted to the Court of Appeal for implementation, LORD DENNING MR observed: 'It is important now to declare – and it must be made plain – that the provisions of Article 119 of the EEC Treaty take priority over anything in our English statute on equal pay which is inconsistent with Article 119. That priority is given by our own law. It is given by the European Communities Act 1972 itself. Community law is now part of our law: and, whenever there is any inconsistency, Community law has priority. It is not supplanting English law. It is part of our law which overrides any other part which is inconsistent with it.'

McEldowney v Forde [1971] AC 632 (House of Lords)   [102]

Under the Civil Authorities (Special Powers) Act (NI) 1922 certain powers were vested in the Minister of Home Affairs in Northern Ireland including powers to '… take all such steps and issue all such orders as may be necessary for preserving the peace and maintaining order … provided that the ordinary course of law and avocations of life and enjoyment of property are to be interfered with as little as possible' (s1(1)). By s1(3) there was power to make regulations for the preservation of peace and the maintenance of order. In 1922 such a regulation was made dealing with 'unlawful associations' and a list was added. In 1967 'Republican Clubs' were added to that list. *Held* (LORD PEARCE and LORD DIPLOCK dissenting), the regulation was not ultra vires because (1) the regulation to be valid need not be shown to be *necessary* for preserving the peace and maintaining order nor to comply with the proviso to s1(1) since the limitations contained in s1(1) on the exercise of executive powers did not apply to the exercise of legislative powers; (2) the courts would not interfere with the exercise of the power to make regulations since there was no question that bad faith arose, and there was no apparent misconstruction of the enabling Act; (3) the regulation of 1967 mentioned 'Republican Clubs or any like organisation howsoever described'. That phrase did not render the regulation invalid on the basis of its being too vague or ambiguous.

McInnes v Onslow-Fane [1978] 1 WLR 1520   [103]

The plaintiff had applied to the Western Area Council of the British Board of Boxing Control for a boxing manager's licence, but his application was refused. The plaintiff now sought a declaration that the Board had acted in breach of natural justice, in not informing him of the case against him, and not granting him an oral hearing. *Held*, refusing the declaration, the applicant merely had the right to have his application considered fairly, which it had been. In application cases nothing is being taken away, and in all normal circumstances there are no charges, and therefore no requirement of providing an opportunity of being heard in answer to the charges. Similarly there is no general obligation to give reasons for such decisions. More may be required in terms of procedural safeguards in 'expectation cases', which differ from the application cases only in that the applicant has some legitimate expectation from what has already happened that his application will be granted, for example where an existing licence-holder applies for a renewal of his licence, because a refusal may involve the question of what it is that has happened to make the applicant unsuitable for the membership or licence for which he was previously thought suitable. In forfeiture cases, where some existing right or position is taken away, the individual has a right to an unbiased tribunal, the right to notice of the charges and the right to be heard in answer to the charges. 'If one accepts that "natural justice" is a flexible term which imposes different requirements in different cases, it is capable of applying appropriately to the whole range of situations indicated by terms such as "judicial", "quasi-judicial" and "administrative". Nevertheless, the further the situation is away from anything that resembles a judicial or quasi-judicial situation, and the further the question is removed from what may reasonably be called a justiciable question, the more appropriate it is to reject an expression which includes the word "justice" and to use instead terms such as "fairness" or "the duty to act fairly" ...' (*per* SIR ROBERT MEGARRY V-C).

Madzimbamuto v Lardner-Burke [1969] 1 AC 645 (Privy Council) [104]

The Privy Council was required to assess the legality of acts of the Smith Government following the Unilateral Declaration of Independence in 1965, to the effect that Southern Rhodesia was no longer a Crown colony but an independent sovereign state. By the Southern Rhodesia Act 1965 the Parliament of the UK declared that it alone had responsibility for Southern Rhodesia. Under that Act an Order in Council was made stating that any instrument made or act done except as authorised by an Act of the UK Parliament was void. The usurping government proceeded on the basis that its new constitution had superseded the old. Under the new constitution an order was made for the detention of the appellant's husband. *Held*, the regulations made in Rhodesia after UDI had no legal validity. The usurping government could not be said to be the lawful government whilst the legitimate government was trying to regain control. The usurping government had neither de jure nor de facto authority.

Malone v Metropolitan Police Commissioner [1979] Ch 344   [105]

The plaintiff was an antiques dealer who had been acquitted of handling stolen goods. During the course of his trial evidence was given indicating that his telephone lines had been tapped by the police. He sought declarations to the effect (inter alia) that any interception, monitoring or recording of conversations on his telephone lines without his consent, or the disclosure of the contents thereof to third parties, the defendant, or police officers, was unlawful, even if done pursuant to a warrant of the Home Secretary; that he had a right of property, privacy and confidentiality in respect of telephone conversations on his telephone lines, and that the interception, monitoring and disclosures thereof constituted unlawful interference with those rights; that the interception, monitoring (etc) of conversations on his telephone lines violated Article 8 of the European Convention for the Protection of Human Rights and Fundamental Freedoms (right to respect for his private and family life, home and correspondence). *Held*, the applications would be refused. It was not for the courts to usurp the role of the legislature by creating a right to privacy where previously none had existed in English law. The European Convention on Human Rights was not part of the domestic law, hence no declaration could be granted as to its application to the instant case. If any declaration were to be granted on the basis of the Convention it would have no legal effect at all. 'No new right in the law, fully-fledged with all the appropriate safeguards, can spring from the head of a judge deciding a particular case: only Parliament can create such a right ... Where there is some major gap in the law, no doubt a judge would be capable of framing what he considered to be a proper code to fill it; and sometimes he may be tempted. But he has to remember that his function is judicial, not legislative, and that he ought not to use his office to legislate in the guise of exercising his judicial powers' (*per* SIR ROBERT MEGARRY V-C). (See also *Entick* v *Carrington*.)

Manuel v Attorney-General [1983] Ch 77 (Court of Appeal)   [106]

The Canada Act 1982 had the effect (inter alia) of empowering the Canadian legislature to amend the Canadian constitution without, in future, having to seek the approval of Parliament at Westminster. The plaintiff represented a number of Canadian Indians who sought declarations to the effect that the United Kingdom Parliament, under the terms of the Statute of Westminster 1931 and the British North America Acts 1867 to 1964, had not had the power to amend the constitution of Canada so as to prejudice the Canadian Indian nations without their consent. Such consent not having been obtained, the plaintiffs sought declarations to the effect that the Canada Act 1982 was ultra vires. *Held*, the declarations would not be granted. The Canada Act 1982 had been duly enacted and the courts could not question its validity. The existence of a convention that Parliament would not legislate for the Dominion without consent would not prevent the courts from nevertheless giving effect to any such legislation so enacted, regardless of consent. To the extent that the Statute of Westminster 1931 purported to create preconditions for any future legislation affecting Canada, s4 did not provide that no Act of the United Kingdom Parliament could extend to a Dominion as part of the law of that Dominion unless the Dominion had in fact requested and consented to the enactment thereof. The condition that had to be satisfied was that it should be 'expressly declared in that Act that that Dominion has requested, and consented to, the enactment thereof'. It was not possible to read into this a requirement that this meant a declaration of a independently ascertainable consent. The legislature had thus reserved to itself the sole function of deciding whether the requisite request and consent have been made and given. That it had been so satisfied was indicated in the preamble of the Canada Act 1982 which stated 'Whereas Canada has requested and consented to the enactment of an Act of the Parliament of the United Kingdom to give effect to the provisions hereinafter set forth ...'. In the light of this, the proposition that the 1982 Act was ultra vires was unarguable. (Followed: *Pickin* v *British Railways Board*.)

Marleasing SA v La Comercial Internacional de   [107]
Alimentacion SA [1992] 1 CMLR 305 (European Court of Justice)

The plaintiff company had sought the nullification, in the Spanish courts, of the creation of the defendant company, on the basis that it had been formed with the sole purpose of defrauding creditors. The plaintiff's legal challenge was based on the provisions of Spanish law (sections 1261 and 1275 of the Civil Code) which rendered invalid contracts which were without legal purpose or caused unlawful consequences. The defendants called in aid Article 11 of the Council Directive 68/151 claiming that it listed exhaustively the circumstances in which the nullity of a company could be declared, and that the ground relied upon by the plaintiff was not listed in the Directive. The Directive had not, at the time this case came before the Spanish courts, been incorporated into the domestic law of Spain. The question referred to the European Court of Justice was whether or not Article 11 was directly applicable so as to preclude a declaration of nullity of a public limited company on a ground other than those set out in the said Article. *Held*, a national court, hearing a case falling within the scope of Council Directive 68/151 on co-ordination of safeguards which, for the protection of the interests of members and others, are required by Member States of companies within the meaning of the second paragraph of Article 58 EEC with a view to making such safeguards equivalent throughout the Community, is required to interpret its national law in the light of the wording of the purpose of that directive in order to preclude a declaration of nullity of a public limited company on a ground other than those listed in Article 11 of the directive. The Member States' obligation arising from a directive to achieve the result envisaged by the directive and the duty under Article 5 EEC to take all appropriate measures, whether general or particular, to ensure the fulfilment of that obligation, is binding on all the authorities of Member States including, for matters within their jurisdiction, the courts. In applying national law, therefore, whether the provisions in question were adopted before or after the directive, the national court called upon to interpret it is required to do so, so far as possible, in the light of the wording and the purpose of the directive in order to achieve the result pursued by the latter. (See also *Duke* v *GEC Reliance Ltd.*)

Metropolitan Asylum District Managers v Hill   [108]
(1881) 6 App Cas 193 (House of Lords)

A statute authorised the building of hospitals by the appellants, and one was erected at Hampstead for the reception of persons suffering from small-pox and other infectious or contagious diseases. The respondents resided near to the hospital and it was established that it constituted a nuisance to them. *Held*, an injunction restraining the use of the building as a hospital receiving patients of this kind would be granted and damages would be awarded against the appellants because the statute was permissive and not imperative. 'Where the terms of the statute are not imperative, but permissive, when it is left to the discretion of the persons empowered to determine whether the general powers committed to them shall be put into execution or not, I think the fair inference is that the legislature intended that discretion to be exercised in strict conformity with private rights, and did not intend to confer licence to commit nuisance in any place which might be selected for the purpose' (*per* LORD WATSON).

Mills v London County Council [1925] 1 KB 213   [109]

London County Council (LCC), acting under the Cinematograph Act 1909, granted a licence to Mr Mills, a cinema owner, subject to a condition that no film which had not been passed for universal exhibition by the British Board of Film Censors could be exhibited in the premises without the express consent of the Council. Mills complained that by this condition the LCC had unlawfully delegated its certifying powers. *Held*, the condition was valid, as the LCC had not completely divested itself of the power to decide whether or not a particular film should be shown. The condition provided an exception where the express consent of the Council was given, effectively providing an appeal in the matter from the decision of the British Board of Film Censors to the Council itself.

Minister of Health v R, ex parte Yaffe [1931] AC 494   [110]
(House of Lords)

Liverpool Corporation submitted an improvement scheme under the Housing Act 1925 to the Ministry of Health for confirmation, and the Minister made an order modifying the scheme and confirming it as modified. The owner of two houses which were to be acquired compulsorily under the scheme sought a writ of certiorari to quash the Minister's order as being made without jurisdiction, on the ground that the scheme which the order purported to confirm was not an improvement scheme within the meaning of the Act of 1925. *Held*, the scheme was such an improvement scheme because it contained the minimum statutory essentials. The fact that the Act provided that 'the order of the Minister when made shall have effect as if enacted in this Act' did not preclude the court from calling in question the order of the Minister where the scheme presented to him for confirmation was inconsistent with the provisions of the Act. 'If one can find that the scheme is inconsistent with the provisions of the Act which authorises the scheme, the scheme will be bad, and that can only be gone into by way of proceedings in certiorari' (*per* VISCOUNT DUNEDIN).

New South Wales (State of) v Bardolph (1934) 52 CLR 455   [111]

The plaintiff owned a publication in which the regional tourist board for New South Wales (acting on the authority of the State Premier) contracted for the insertion of a series of advertisements over a two-year period for a sum of £1,114. Shortly after this agreement was made, there was a change in the political control of the administration, and the Government now refused to pay for the advertisements. The plaintiff nevertheless continued to run them, and at the end of the contract period claimed the sum due. *Held*, dismissing the appeal by the State, although the contract had not been expressly authorised by the State Legislature, the relevant Appropriation Acts had made sums available for 'Government advertising', and the amount available far exceeded that now sought by the plaintiff. The plaintiff was therefore entitled to succeed in his action for damages. In the absence of some controlling statutory provision, contracts were enforceable against the Crown if: (a) the contract is entered into in the ordinary or necessary course of Government administration; (b) it is authorised by the responsible Ministers of the Crown; and (c) the payments which the contractor is seeking to recover are covered by or referable to a parliamentary grant for the class of service to which the contract relates. 'The failure of the plaintiff to prove (c) does not affect the validity of the contract in the sense that the Crown is regarded as stripped of its authority or capacity to enter into the contract ... The enforcement of such contracts is to be distinguished from their inherent validity' (*per* EVATT J at first instance, affirmed on appeal). '... the prior provision of funds by Parliament is not a condition preliminary to the obligation of the contract. If it were so, performance on the part of the subject could not be exacted nor could there be, if he did perform, established a disputed claim to an amount of money under his contract until actual disbursement of the money in dispute was authorised by Parliament' (*per* DIXON J on appeal).

Nissan v Attorney-General [1970] AC 179 (House of Lords)   [112]

The plaintiff, a British subject, ran an hotel in Cyprus. During a period of civil strife United Kingdom troops were brought in at the invitation of the Cyprus Government in order to help restore peace. The hotel was occupied by the UK contingent as its headquarters. Subsequently the contingent was incorporated into a United Nations Force. The plaintiff sought compensation from the Crown in respect of alleged loss suffered to his property on the ground, inter alia, that the seizure and occupation of the hotel were acts under the royal prerogative. The parties agreed that an order should be made for the decision of questions of law as a preliminary issue. *Held*, the actions of the British forces were not of such a character that the court had no jurisdiction to entertain the action since the acts did not amount to acts of state. 'The respondent asserts that possession of his hotel was taken under prerogative powers and that there should be payment ... He *does not found* his claim on the existence of a treaty between Her Majesty and the Republic of Cyprus ... I agree with Winn LJ that the act of occupying the hotel ought not to be regarded as an act necessary for the implementing of an act of state' (*per* LORD MORRIS). LORD REID adopted a different approach: the respondent, being a British subject, could not be deprived of his legal right to redress by any assertion that the acts complained of were acts of state. Just because the British troops became part of the UN force did not mean that the respondent could have no cause of action and so liability might continue until the period when Finnish troops took over (as part of the UN Force). (See also *Burmah Oil Co (Burma Trading) Ltd* v *Lord Advocate*.)

NV Algemene Transport-en Expeditie Onderneming van   [113] Gend en Loos v Nederlandse Administratie der Belastingen (Case 26/62) [1963] ECR 1 (European Court of Justice)

Van Gend imported into the Netherlands a quantity of ureaformaldehyde on which he was required to pay an import duty of 8 per cent. He claimed that when the Treaty of Rome came into force (on 1 January 1958) in the Netherlands, ureaformaldehyde was reclassified and made subject to a lower level of import duty. The essence of his claim was that, by increasing the duty to 8 per cent, the Netherlands government had infringed Article 12 of the Treaty. At first instance the Netherlands Revenue Administration (Nederlandse Administratie der Belastingen) denied that there had been any increase. On appeal the Revenue Tribunal (Tariefcommissie), without determining the level of duty payable, referred to the European Court of Justice the question of whether or not Article 12 was directly applicable and of direct effect. *Held*, Article 12 produced direct effects and gave rise to individual rights in the domestic law of Member States. The objective of the EEC Treaty, to establish a Common Market, suggests that it is more than an agreement which merely creates mutual obligations between the contracting States. Community law constitutes a new legal order of international law for the benefit of which the Member States have limited their sovereign rights, albeit within limited fields, and the subjects of which comprise not only Member States but also their nationals. Independently of the legislation of Member States, Community law imposes obligations on individuals and creates rights, these rights arising not only where they are expressly granted by the Treaty but also by reason of obligations which the Treaty imposes in a clearly defined way upon individuals as well as upon the Member States and upon the institutions of the Community. The wording of Article 12, containing a clear and unconditional prohibition, unqualified by any reservation on the part of States which would make its implementation conditional upon a positive legislative measure enacted under national law, made it ideally adapted to produce direct effects in the legal relationship between Member States and their subjects, without any legislative intervention on the part of Member States.

O'Reilly v Mackman [1983] 2 AC 237 (House of Lords)   [114]

The plaintiffs were all prisoners who had been disciplined by the Hull Prison Board of Visitors. Each prisoner sought, by way of action, to challenge the validity of the proceedings on the basis that they had been vitiated by breaches of natural justice. The Board contended that any such challenges should have been brought by way of an application for judicial review, and that the actions should be struck out as an abuse of process. *Held*, the only rights that the plaintiffs possessed as against the Board of Visitors arose in public law, and fell to be protected by public law, hence it constituted an abuse of process to proceed other than by way of an application for judicial review. By proceeding by way of action, the plaintiffs evaded the safeguards imposed in the public interest against groundless, unmeritorious or tardy attacks upon the validity of decisions made by public authorities in the field of public law. Those safeguards included the requirement of leave to apply for judicial review, and the short time limits for such applications. Procedural handicaps, such as unavailability of discovery or the unavailability of prerogative orders and private law remedies in respect of the same application, that had led litigants before 1977 to proceed by way of writ rather than applying for one of the prerogative orders, had now been removed with the introduction of the new RSC Order 53. 'Now that those disadvantages to applicants have been removed and all remedies for infringements of rights protected by public law can be obtained upon an application for judicial review, as can also remedies for infringements of rights under private law if such infringements should also be involved, it would in my view as a general rule be contrary to public policy, and as such an abuse of the process of the court, to permit a person seeking to establish that a decision of a public authority infringed rights to which he was entitled to protection under public law to proceed by way of an ordinary action and by this means to evade the provisions of Order 53 for the protection of such authorities ... I have described this as a general rule; for though it may normally be appropriate to apply it by the summary process of striking out the action, there may be exceptions, particularly where the invalidity of the decision arises as a collateral issue in a claim for infringement of a right of the plaintiff arising under private law, or where none of the parties objects to the adoption of the procedure by writ or originating summons. Whether there should be other exceptions should, in my view, at this stage in the development of procedural public law, be left to be decided on a case to case basis ...' (*per* LORD DIPLOCK). (See also *Cocks v Thanet District Council* and *Roy v Kensington and Chelsea and Westminster Family Practitioner Committee.*)

Padfield v Minister of Agriculture, Fisheries and Food   **[115]**
[1968] AC 997 (House of Lords)

The appellants, who were members of a regional committee of the Milk Marketing Board, made a complaint to the Minister pursuant to s19(3) of the Agriculture Marketing Act 1958 asking that the complaint (about differentials in prices) be referred to the committee of investigation established under the Act. The Minister declined to refer the complaint on the ground, inter alia, that the complaint raised wide issues. The appellants sought mandamus. (Note: Section 19 provided for the Minister appointing, inter alia, a committee of investigation which under subs(3)(b) shall 'be charged with the duty if the Minister in any case so directs of considering and reporting to the minister on ... any complaint made to the Minister'.) *Held*, the words 'if the Minister in any case so directs' did not confer an absolute discretion on the Minister (*per* LORD REID and LORD PEARCE). Parliament must have conferred the discretion with the intention that it should be used to promote the policy and objects of the Act which had to be determined by construing the Act as a whole: and construction was always a matter of law for the court. As the Minister's discretion had never been properly exercised according to law the appeal would be allowed and the matter remitted to the Queen's Bench Division with a direction to require the Minister to reconsider the application. (See also *Gaiman v National Association for Mental Health.*)

Parlement Belge, The (1880) 5 PD 197 (Court of Appeal)   **[116]**

The *Parlement Belge*, a mail packet the property of the King of the Belgians, manned by officers of the Royal Belgian navy, running between Ostend and Dover, collided with the *Daring*. Besides carrying letters the *Parlement Belge* carried merchandise and passengers and their luggage for hire. *Held*, the *Parlement Belge* was not liable to be seized in a suit in rem to recover redress for the collision. 'As a consequence of the absolute independence of every sovereign authority and of the international comity which induces every sovereign state to respect the independence of every other sovereign state, each and every one declines to exercise by means of any of its courts, any of its territorial jurisdiction over the person of any sovereign or ambassador of any other state, or over the public property of any state which is destined to its public use, or over the property of any ambassador, though such sovereign, ambassador or property be within its territory, and therefore, but for the common agreement, subject to its jurisdiction' (*per* BRETT LJ).

Parliamentary Election for Bristol South-East, Re   [117]
[1964] 2 QB 257

The House of Commons, confirming the report of its Committee of Privileges, resolved that the respondent had ceased to be a member of that House on succeeding to the Viscountcy of Stansgate. The respondent was a candidate at the consequent by-election and received a majority of votes and was returned as the duly elected Member of Parliament. The respondent's incapacity was known to the electors before they cast their votes. *Held*, the petitioner, the only other candidate at the by-election, was duly elected as the Member of Parliament for the constituency.

Parliamentary Privilege Act 1770, In the Matter of the   [118]
[1958] 2 All ER 329 (Privy Council)

The Rt Hon G R Strauss, a member of the House of Commons, wrote a letter to the Paymaster-General in which he called his attention to certain conduct of the London Electricity Board. The Board's solicitors wrote to Mr Strauss demanding a withdrawal and an apology and stating that, if these were not forthcoming, they were instructed to issue a writ for libel against him. The House of Commons resolved to refer the matter to its Committee of Privileges which decided that the London Electricity Board and their solicitors had acted in breach of the privilege of Parliament. However, they also concluded that the opinion of the Privy Council should be sought on the question whether the House would be acting contrary to the Parliamentary Privilege Act 1770 if it treated the issue of a writ against a Member of Parliament in respect of a speech or proceeding by him in Parliament as a breach of its privileges. *Held*, it would not be so acting as s1 of the Act of 1770 applied only to proceedings against Members of Parliament in respect of their duties and actions as individuals, and not in respect of their conduct in Parliament as Members of Parliament, and did not abridge or affect the ancient and essential privilege of freedom of speech in Parliament secured by Article 9 of the Bill of Rights 1688.

Pasmore v Oswaldtwistle Urban District Council [1898] AC 387   [119]
(House of Lords)

The plaintiff alleged that the sewers within the urban district of Oswaldtwistle were insufficient for the purpose of draining the Whiteash Paper Mill of which he was owner and occupier. The Public Health Act 1875 required the defendants to make such sewers as might be necessary for effectually draining their district and the plaintiff sought a writ of mandamus commanding the defendants to comply with this obligation. *Held*, as the Act of 1875 provided a specific remedy by way of a complaint to the Local Government Board, the plaintiff's claim for a writ of mandamus would fail.

Pett v Greyhound Racing Association Ltd [1968] 2 All ER 545   [120]
(Court of Appeal)

An inquiry was to be held by track stewards of a greyhound racing stadium about the withdrawal of a dog. The rules of the National Greyhound Racing Club, to which the trainer had agreed when he obtained his licence, did not prescribe the procedure to be followed by stewards at inquiries, and they did not exclude legal representation. The trainer sought legal representation but the stewards decided against. An interlocutory injunction was granted restraining the inquiry from being held. *Held*, prima facie, the trainer was entitled to an oral hearing and, the inquiry being of serious importance to him, to be legally represented. Therefore a sufficient prima facie case had been made out. (But see sequel, below.)

Pett v Greyhound Racing Association Ltd (No 2)   [121]
[1969] 2 All ER 221

This was an action for, inter alia, a declaration that the defendants were acting ultra vires in refusing to allow legal representation. *Held*, the plaintiff did not have a right to be legally represented because in the absence of express requirements in the instrument conferring quasi-judicial powers on a domestic tribunal the tribunal was required only to comply with those elementary and essential principles of 'fairness' which must as a matter of necessary implication be treated as applicable in the exercise of those powers, that is, the principles of natural justice, and in the present case legal representation was not essential. Whether legal representation will be regarded as an essential ingredient of natural justice must depend on the level of sophistication of the tribunal in question (*per* LYELL J). (Eventually the Greyhound Racing Association Ltd allowed legal representation.)

Pickin v British Railways Board [1974] AC 765 (House of Lords)   [122]

The Bristol and Exeter Railway, to which the defendants were successors, was set up by private Act in 1836, and the statute provided that if the line ceased to be used the land should revert to the ownership of the landowners on either side of the track. The defendant Board in 1968 secured a private Act which (inter alia) took away those rights, and proposed to close the line. The plaintiff, an objector to the principle of closing branch lines, bought land alongside the track and claimed a declaration that he was entitled to the land on which the abandoned line lay. He claimed that the 1968 Act had been secured fraudulently, because the preamble recited that lists of owners and plans had been deposited in Somerset County Record Office, which they had not. *Held*, the court would not question the validity of an enrolled Bill. No distinction was to be drawn in this regard between private and public Acts of Parliament. The law was correctly stated by Lord Campbell in *Edinburgh and Dalkeith Railway Co* v *Wauchope* (1842) 8 Cl & F 710. The function of the court is to construe and apply the enactments of Parliament. It is not concerned with the manner in which Parliament or its officers carrying out its standing orders perform those functions. Any examination of those matters would necessarily involve problems of parliamentary privilege. (See also *Manuel* v *Attorney-General*.)

Pickstone v Freemans plc [1989] 1 AC 66 (House of Lords)   [123]

The Equal Pay (Amendment) Regulations 1983 sought to amend the Equal Pay Act 1970 so as to ensure compliance with Article 119 of the EEC Treaty which provides: 'Each Member State shall ... ensure and subsequently maintain the application of the principle that men and women should receive equal pay for equal work ...' Under the 1970 Act, as amended, female employees were entitled to the same level of pay as male colleagues carrying out work of equal value. Mrs Pickstone received £77.66 per week as a warehouse operative, while a male colleague ('a checker warehouse operative') carrying out work of the same value was paid £81.88 per week. The employers contended that there was no discrimination because, although the applicant was one of five women paid £77.66 per week, there was also a male warehouse operative paid the same amount. The industrial tribunal and Employment Appeal Tribunal both dismissed the applicant's claim of discrimination on the basis that, as there was a male employee being paid the same amount for the work carried out by the applicant, the equal pay provisions could not be invoked. The Court of Appeal allowed the employee's appeal, and the employers now appealed. *Held*, dismissing the appeal, where Parliament has amended the law so as to comply with Community law, the courts should strive to adopt a purposive approach to interpretation if at all possible, rather than succumb to the conclusion that Parliament has simply failed in its purpose. '... a construction which permits the section to operate as a proper fulfilment of the United Kingdom's obligation under the Treaty involves not so much doing violence to the language of the section as filling a gap by an implication which arises, not from the words used, but from the manifest purpose of the Act and the mischief it was intended to remedy. The question is whether that can be justified by the necessity – indeed the obligation – to apply a purposive construction which will implement the United Kingdom's obligations under the Treaty ... It must, I think, be recognised that so to construe a provision which, on its face, is unambiguous involves a departure from a number of well-established rules of construction. The intention of Parliament has, it is said, to be ascertained from the words which it has used and those words are to be construed according to their plain and ordinary meaning. The fact that a statute is passed to give effect to an international treaty does not, of itself, enable the treaty to be referred to in order to construe the words used other than in their plain and unambiguous sense ... I think, however, that it has also to be recognised that a statute which is passed in order to give effect to the United Kingdom's obligations under the EEC Treaty falls into a special category and it does so because, unlike other treaty obligations, those obligations have, in effect, been incorporated into English law by the European Communities Act 1972' (*per* LORD OLIVER OF AYLMERTON).

Pickwell v Camden London Borough Council [1983] 2 WLR 583   **[124]**

Manual workers employed by Camden London Borough Council ('the council') went on indefinite strike in February 1979. The council negotiated a pay deal with their employees, in order to persuade them to return to work, which was more generous than that achieved by local authority manual workers elsewhere in the country. At the next round of national pay negotiations for such workers an agreement was reached that they should have a £5–£7 pay increase. The council agreed to pay this to its own workers even though they were already earning more than their counterparts elsewhere in the country. Mr Pickwell, the district auditor, acting under s161(1) Local Government Act 1972, applied to the court for a declaration that this payment was contrary to law. *Held*, for the district auditor to succeed in his application he had to establish that the council had acted in excess of its statutory powers. Such illegality could be established by showing that the decision was not, in reality, a decision made in the exercise of the council's statutory power to fix wage rates, but for some other extraneous, irrelevant, or collateral purpose, for example, to undermine the incomes policy, or to sabotage, for political purposes, the national negotiations which were proceeding simultaneously, or to achieve some other social or political objective. On the facts, the evidence showed that the council had been motivated by a desire to prevent further disruption to the borough's residents. Alternatively, the district auditor could satisfy the court that no reasonable local authority would have made such a decision in the circumstances. The court was satisfied that the decision on levels of pay could not be impugned on *Wednesbury* grounds. If the ratepayers felt that the council had acted unwisely in reaching its pay settlement with the refuse workers they could express this view through the ballot box at the next local elections. The application would be dismissed. (But see *Bromley London Borough Council* v *Greater London Council.*)

Prebble v Television New Zealand Ltd [1994] 3 WLR 970   [125]
(Privy Council)

Television New Zealand broadcast a programme in which allegations were made of impropriety on the part of the Labour government. The plaintiff, the minister for state-owned enterprises, alleged that the programme had defamed him by implying, inter alia, that he had misled the House of Representatives concerning the government's policy on the sale of state-owned industries. The defence contended that either the programme had not conveyed any defamatory meaning, or to the extent that it had its contents were true. At first instance those elements of the defence statements that sought to rely on statements made in proceedings in Parliament in order to refute the plaintiff's claim were struck out, on the basis that reliance on them infringed Article 9 of the Bill of Rights 1689. The decision was upheld by the Court of Appeal, but in addition a majority of the court held that the plaintiff's action should be stayed unless and until privilege in respect of the statements relied upon was waived by the House of Representatives. The Privileges Committee of the House of Representatives had concluded that it did not have the power to waive the privilege. The plaintiff appealed to the Board against the stay of his action, and the defendants sought to appeal against the upholding of the first instance decision to strike out parts of the defence submission. *Held,* the plaintiff's appeal would be successful and the action allowed to proceed. The defendant's appeal would be dismissed. The fact that the person making the impugned statement in Parliament was also the initiator of the legal proceedings did not justify any departure from the principle enshrined in Article 9 of the Bill of Rights 1689. The privilege in question belonged to Parliament, not to individual members. Whether or not a member has misled Parliament was a matter to be dealt with by Parliament and fell outside the jurisdiction of the courts. If the defendant had intended to adduce evidence of proceedings in Parliament simply to prove what had been said or decided, there would have been no objection. In the instant case, however, the defendant sought to adduce the evidence in order to prove that the House had been misled. The Privy Council accepted that there might be cases where justice demanded a stay of proceedings, where, eg, the majority of the evidence relied upon by the defendant was protected by privilege and it would be impossible from him to defend a libel action unless that privilege was waived. Failure to grant a stay in such cases could result in a significant restriction on the freedom of the press to comment on political affairs. The present case did not fall within that category, however. The majority of the statements relied upon by the defence were not protected by privilege and it was not unjust in circumstances to allow the action to proceed. (Doubted: *Rost* v *Edwards.*)

Prescott v Birmingham Corporation [1954] 3 All ER 698   [126]
(Court of Appeal)

Birmingham Corporation provided free travelling facilities on trams and omnibuses within their district for women aged 65 and over and men aged 70 and over between 10am and 4pm, excluding Saturdays. A ratepayer sought, inter alia, a declaration that the scheme was illegal as being ultra vires the corporation. *Held,* he was entitled to a declaration in these terms as the corporation had no power to make a gift in money's worth to a particular section of the local community at the expense of the general body of ratepayers. (Distinguished in *Pickwell* v *Camden London Borough Council;* followed in *Bromley London Borough Council* v *Greater London Council.*)

## Proclamations, The Case of (1611) 12 Co Rep 74							[127]

The question arose as to whether the King by his proclamation could prohibit new buildings in and about London and the making of starch out of wheat. The two Chief Justices, the Chief Baron, and Baron Altham, upon conference with the Lords of the Privy Council, resolved 'that the King by his proclamation cannot create any offence which was not an offence before ... for if he may create an offence where none is, upon that ensues fine and imprisonment ... Also it was resolved, that the King hath no prerogative, but that which the law of the land allows him. But the King for prevention of offences may by proclamation admonish his subjects that they keep the laws, and do not offend them ... Lastly, if the offence be not punishable in the Star-chamber, the prohibition of it by proclamation cannot make it punishable there.' (See also *Council of Civil Service Unions* v *Minister for the Civil Service*.)

## Prohibitions del Roy (1607) 12 Co Rep 63							[128]

COKE LCJ, in the presence, and with the clear consent of all the judges of England, and Barons of the Exchequer, decided 'that the King in his own person cannot adjudge any case, either criminal, as treason, felony, etc, or betwixt party and party, concerning his inheritance, chattels, or goods, etc, but this ought to be determined and adjudged in some court of justice, according to the law and custom of England; and always judgments are given, ideo consideratum est per curiam, so that the court gives the judgment ... God had endowed his Majesty with excellent science, and great endowments of nature; but His Majesty was not learned in the laws of his realm of England, and causes which concern the life, or inheritance, or goods, or fortunes of his subjects, are not to be decided by natural reason but by the artificial reason and judgment of law, which law is an act which requires long study and experience, before that a man can attain to the cognisance of it.' (See also *The Case of Proclamations*.)

## Puhlhofer v Hillingdon London Borough Council							[129]
[1986] 2 WLR 259 (House of Lords)

The applicants were a married couple with two children who, at the time of the application, were living in bed and breakfast accommodation. They applied to the local authority, under s4(5) of the Housing (Homeless Persons) Act 1977, for appropriate accommodation. This request was rejected on the ground that the applicants were not 'homeless' for the purposes of the 1977 Act, as understood by the local authority. The Divisional Court held that the accommodation was not appropriate for the applicants and as a result they were to be deemed 'homeless'. This finding was reversed by the Court of Appeal, which felt that although the accommodation might be less than ideal, it was nevertheless 'accommodation'. The applicants appealed. *Held*, even though the accommodation occupied by an applicant might be overcrowded and unfit for human habitation, a local housing authority was nevertheless justified in concluding that the applicant for housing was not homeless within the meaning of the 1977 Act. Under the legislation the question: 'What is properly to be regarded as accommodation?' is a question of fact to be decided by the local authority. The function of the courts is to review the legality of the decisions of inferior bodies such as housing authorities, not to provide an appeal from their findings of facts. 'Although the action or inaction of a local authority is clearly susceptible to judicial review where they have misconstrued the Act, or abused their powers or otherwise acted perversely, I think that great restraint should be exercised in giving leave to proceed by judicial review. The plight of the homeless is a desperate one, and the plight of the applicants in the present case commands the deepest sympathy. But it is not, in my opinion, appropriate that the remedy of judicial review, which is a discretionary remedy, should be made use of to monitor the actions of local authorities under the Act save in the exceptional case. The ground on which the courts will review the exercise of an administrative discretion is abuse of power, eg bad faith, a mistake in construing the limits of the power, a procedural irregularity or unreasonableness in the *Wednesbury* sense ... Where the existence or non-existence of a fact is left to the judgment and discretion of a public body and that fact involves a broad spectrum ranging from the obvious to the debatable to the just conceivable, it is the duty of the court to leave the decision of that fact to the public body to whom Parliament had entrusted the decision-making power save in a case where it is obvious that the public body, consciously or unconsciously, are acting perversely' (*per* LORD BRIGHTMAN).

R v Aston University Senate, ex parte Roffey [1969] 2 All ER 964   [130]

Two students at the University were sent down for failure in examinations, after the examiners' meeting had considered their academic performance and a wide range of personal factors. The students were not given the opportunity to make representations to the meeting. They applied for certiorari and mandamus. *Held*, the examiners, who had the sole discretion whether to allow a re-sit of the examination or to ask the student to withdraw from the course, had to observe the rules of natural justice and they had not done so here since common fairness demanded that the students be given the right to be heard. However, because of the delay (over seven months) in seeking the remedies, and given that the remedies were discretionary, they would be refused. BLAIN J: 'I share Donaldson J's view that the right to be heard is often an example of and an integral part of the concept of natural justice, and also his view that it is not always a necessary ingredient of that concept.'

R v Barnet and Camden Rent Tribunal, ex parte Frey   [131]
Investments Ltd [1972] 1 All ER 1185 (Court of Appeal)

A housing action group tried to persuade the local authority to exercise its powers under s72 of the Rent Act 1968 ('either the lessor or the lessee under a Part VI contract or the local authority may refer the contract to the rent tribunal') to refer contracts of tenancy made by a landlord to the local rent tribunal. After much discussion (and opposition from the landlord) the authority decided to refer certain of the lettings (22 in all) to the tribunal, whereupon the landlord applied for an order of prohibition to prevent the tribunal from proceeding, contending, inter alia, that the references were invalid because the authority's decision had been influenced by irrelevant or improper considerations. *Held*, unless it could be shown that the council had acted with mala fides or frivolously or vexatiously it was impossible to say that the matter was ultra vires. The council's power to refer the contracts could not be inhibited by the fact that the tenants themselves did not want the references to be made. Since the council's decision to refer did not affect the basic rights of landlords the decision would not necessarily be vitiated by reason of the fact that some irrelevant matter had been considered or that it had failed to consider a relevant fact. The crucial decision was that of the tribunal itself. SALMON J stated that the decision in *R v Paddington and St Marylebone Rent Tribunal, ex parte Bell London and Provincial Properties Ltd* turned on its own special facts (a 'block reference') with no consideration of facts of individual tenancies.

R v Birmingham City Justices, ex parte Chris Foreign Foods   [132]
(Wholesalers) Ltd [1970] 3 All ER 945

Under the Food and Drugs Act 1955 a quantity of food was brought before a justice (to determine whether it should be destroyed), the meeting being attended by the senior food inspector and the chief veterinary officer. After an inspection of the food, notice was given to the appellants and the hearing was adjourned. At the next meeting the applicants made submissions and called evidence. At the end of the hearing the justice retired with the public analyst and the chief veterinary officer stating that he wished to take their advice. All three returned and the justice came to a conclusion unfavourable to the applicant, who sought an order of certiorari. *Held,* the justice was under a duty to act openly, impartially and fairly. The retirement of the justice in the company of the officials amounted to a breach of natural justice since he did not give notice to the applicants of the advice received and so they had no chance to meet the case against them. Certiorari would be granted. 'Much argument has been adduced in this present case as to the exact position of the justice under this procedure. Was his a judicial function ... Was he throughout an administrator? ... I find it quite unnecessary to come to any decision in the matter, any more than I did ... in *Re H K (an infant)* ... even though he was acting in an administrative ... capacity the justice had to bring qualities of impartiality and fairness to bear on the problem' (*per* LORD PARKER CJ).

R v Boundary Commission for England, ex parte Foot   [133]
[1983] QB 600 (Court of Appeal)

The leader of the Labour Party, Michael Foot, applied for judicial review and an order of prohibition or an injunction to prevent the Boundary Commission from laying before Parliament its report on the redrawing of constituency boundaries. The grounds for the application were that in drawing up its report the Commission had failed to pay sufficient regard to its duty to produce substantially equal constituencies, and had not exercised its discretion to propose constituencies that crossed London borough boundaries. The application was rejected at first instance and renewed on appeal. *Held,* dismissing the application, the Commission's discretion in carrying out its functions was a very wide one. Although not above the law, the Commission differed from many other public authorities in that, even at the very end of its deliberations, it made no final decision, but merely made recommendations to the Secretary of State, the recommendations eventually having to be approved by Parliament. The concept of unreasonableness, as enunciated by Lord Greene MR in *Associated Provincial Picture Houses Ltd* v *Wednesbury Corporation,* could be applied to govern and limit the activities of the Commission; it would not, however, entitle judges to intervene merely because they considered that they might (or indeed would) have made different recommendations on the merits. The onus falling upon any litigant seeking to show that the conclusions of the Commission were such that no reasonable Commission could have arrived at them was a heavy one, which by its very nature would be difficult to discharge. 'There are many Acts of Parliament which give ministers and local authorities extensive powers to take action which affects the citizenry of this country, but give no right of appeal to the courts. In such cases, the courts are not concerned or involved so long as ministers and local authorities do not exceed the powers given to them by Parliament. Those powers may give them a wide range of choice on what action to take or to refrain from taking and so long as they confine themselves to making choices within that range, the courts will have no wish or power to intervene. But if ministers or local authorities exceed their powers – if they choose to do something or to refrain from doing something in circumstances in which this is not one of the options given to them by Parliament – the courts can and will intervene in defence of the ordinary citizen' (*per* LORD DONALDSON MR).

R v Chief Constable of Lancashire, ex parte Parker   [134]
[1993] 2 WLR 428

The applicants' premises were entered by police offices purporting to act under search warrants, and items were seized. The officers carrying out the searches provided the occupiers with warrants comprising photocopies of the authorisations unaccompanied by the schedules that would have detailed the articles sought. The applicants now sought judicial review, seeking orders of certiorari to quash the warrants and a declaration to the effect that the entries and searches had been unlawful. *Held,* the application would succeed in so far as the declarations sought would be granted. A search warrant comprised two documents, the authorisation and the schedule of articles to be seized. Subsections 15(7) and (8) of the Police and Criminal Evidence Act 1984 require that two certified copies should be made of any warrant, so that one may be given to the occupier, or left at the premises. The certification is so that the occupier does not have to rely on the word of the police as to the warrant's validity. Showing the occupier a copy of the warrant would not suffice. As NOLAN LJ observed: 'It seems to us clear beyond argument that when the Act refers to a warrant issued by a judge it means the whole of the original document seen and approved and put forth by him ... It would be wholly contrary to the purpose of the legislation if a judge could authorise the police to replace the whole or a part of the original warrant, for the purposes of its execution, by an uncertified photocopy which he has not seen.' Hence the original warrant had been valid, and certiorari would not be granted to quash it, but the subsequent searches were unlawful, given the failure to comply with the statutory requirements concerning authentication and completeness of copies.

R v Chief Constable of the West Midlands Police, ex parte [135] Wiley: R v Chief Constable of the Nottinghamshire Police, ex parte Sunderland [1994] 3 WLR 433 (House of Lords)

In two separate trials the applicants were acquitted following the decision of the prosecution to offer no evidence. Both applicants instituted complaints to the Police Complaints Authority and civil actions for damages. Given the state of the law at the time, neither applicant would have been allowed access to the complaints file in order to prepare for the civil action, hence solicitors for the applicants had sought undertakings from the respondents to the effect that they would not rely on, or make use of, any information provided by the applicants in the course of their complaints to the Police Complaints Authority. The undertakings were refused, and the applicants sought judicial review of these refusals; the second applicant also sought an injunction to prevent the Chief Constable from using the material in question. At first instance POPPLEWELL J granted the relief sought and the Chief Constables' appeals to the Court of Appeal were dismissed. On appeal to the House of Lords it was argued by both sides that public interest immunity did not attach to the documents collated in the course of an investigation into complaints against the police under Part IX of the Police and Criminal Evidence Act 1984. *Held,* the appeals would be allowed. LORD BROWNE-WILKINSON explained that the difficulties in this area had arisen from the earlier decision of the Court of Appeal in *Neilson* v *Laugharne* [1981] QB 736. In that case OLIVER LJ had relied upon a number of arguments for upholding public interest, inter alia, that evidence collected during a police complaints investigation should be subject to public interest immunity because police officers and other witnesses would be inhibited by the fear that their statements might subsequently be used in civil proceedings; and that the need to check statements individually to see if they should be the subject of a contents claim placed too heavy a burden on the police. Rejecting these arguments, LORD BROWNE-WILKINSON pointed out that the Police Complaints Authority itself no longer supported the automatic 'class' immunity that followed from the *Neilson* decision, and added that the recognition of a new class-based public interest immunity required clear and compelling evidence that it was necessary in the public interest. Despite Lord Hailsham's comments in *D* v *National Society for the Prevention of Cruelty to Children* [1978]

AC 171, to the effect that the categories of public interest were not closed and must alter from time to time as social changes required, no sufficient case had been made out to justify the class of public interest immunity created by the *Neilson* decision. (Overruled: the previous line of authority based on *Neilson* and promulgated via *Hehir* v *Commissioner of Police of the Metropolis* [1982] 1 WLR 715, *Makanjuola* v *Commissioner of Police of the Metropolis* [1992] 3 All ER 617 and *Halford* v *Sharples* [1992] 1 WLR 736.)

R v Commissioner of Police of the Metropolis, ex parte   [136]
Blackburn [1968] 2 QB 118 (Court of Appeal)

Raymond Blackburn sought an order of mandamus (inter alia) compelling the Commissioner to enforce the law against illegal gambling. *Held*, whilst there might be extreme cases where the courts would issue orders of mandamus directed at the Commissioner, as a general rule day to day policing policies were a matter for the police alone.

R v Criminal Injuries Compensation Board, ex parte Lain   [137]
[1967] 2 All ER 770

A scheme was promulgated under prerogative powers to compensate victims of crimes of violence by way of ex gratia payments. The scheme provided for the appointment of a Board to hear claims and that its decision would 'not be subject to appeal or to ministerial review'. The scheme also set out basic principles by which compensation should be assessed. The plaintiff, being dissatisfied with a decision of the Board, sought certiorari on the grounds that there were errors on the face of the record. *Held*, (a) the Board was amenable to the supervisory jurisdiction of the High Court since it was a body of a public rather than a private character, having a power to determine matters affecting subjects and a duty to act judicially; (b) the facts that the Board was created by prerogative rather than statute and that its decisions gave rise to no legally enforceable rights did not oust the court's jurisdiction. (But see *Council of Civil Service Unions* v *Minister for the Civil Service*.)

R v Disciplinary Committee of the Jockey Club, ex parte   [138]
the Aga Khan [1993] 1 WLR 909 Court of Appeal

The applicant was the owner of the filly 'Aliysa', the winner of the Epsom Oaks in 1989. Following a routine test after the race, the horse's urine was found to contain traces of a banned substance. The Jockey Club fined the trainer £200, and disqualified the horse. There was no allegation of wrongdoing on the part of the applicant, but he alleged that his reputation had been injured, and the value of the horse adversely affected. On a trial of a preliminary issue, the Court of Appeal was asked to rule upon the susceptibility of the Jockey Club to judicial review. *Held*, the Jockey Club was not a public body whose decisions were challengeable by way of judicial review. SIR THOMAS BINGHAM MR accepted that the Jockey Club enjoyed a virtual monopoly over the regulation of a significant national activity, exercised powers that affected the public, recognised that if the Jockey Club did not carry out its functions the government would probably have created a public body for the purpose, and admitted that those submitting to the Club's jurisdiction did so voluntarily. He was nevertheless unable to accept that the Club met the requirements of a public body for the purposes of review, because: '[It] has not been woven into any system of governmental control of horse-racing ... while the ... Club's powers may be described as, in many ways, public, they are in no sense governmental ...' Similar views were expressed by HOFFMANN LJ. FARQUHARSON LJ felt that the Club fell outside the scope of public law because its members agreed to be bound by its rules and was thus a '... domestic body acting by consent'. As regards the question of whether or not the Jockey Club could ever be regarded as a public body for the purposes of review, the Master of the Rolls observed: 'Cases where the applicant ... has no contract on which to rely may raise different considerations and the existence or non-existence of alternative remedies may then be material.'

R v East Berkshire Health Authority, ex parte Walsh   [139]
[1984] 3 WLR 818 (Court of Appeal)

Walsh had been a Senior Nursing Officer at Wrexham Park Hospital. He was dismissed as a result of alleged misconduct, after an unsuccessful appeal against the decision of a disciplinary body established pursuant to statute. He applied for judicial review of the dismissal. The authority argued that as the relationship between the parties arose out of contract it was a private law matter and an application under Order 53 was an abuse of the court process – Walsh should have proceeded by way of writ. At first instance the application was allowed to proceed. The authority appealed. *Held*, allowing the appeal, simply because Walsh was employed in a public service did not make his dismissal from it a matter of public law. The only rights under consideration in the instant case arose from Walsh's contract of employment, a matter which did not arise within the sphere of public law. 'Parliament can underpin the position of public authority employees by directly restricting the freedom of the public authority to dismiss, thus giving the employee "public law" rights and at least making him a potential candidate for administrative law remedies. Alternatively it can require the authority to contract with its employees on specified terms with a view to the employee acquiring "private law" rights under the terms of the contract of employment. If the authority fails or refuses to thus create "private law" rights for the employee, the employee will have "public law" rights to compel compliance, the remedy being mandamus requiring the authority so to contract or a declaration that the employee has those rights. If, however, the authority gives the employee the required contractual protection, a breach of that contract is not a matter of "public law" and gives rise to no administrative law remedies' (*per* LORD DONALDSON MR). (Distinguished in *R v Secretary of State for the Home Department, ex parte Benwell.*)

R v Electricity Commissioners, ex parte London Electricity   [140]
Joint Committee Co (1920) Ltd [1924] 1 KB 171 (Court of Appeal)

A number of electricity companies sought orders of prohibition and certiorari in respect of a scheme for the supply of electricity contained in a draft order made by the Electricity Commissioners. *Held*, the scheme was ultra vires. As to the scope and availability of certiorari and prohibition: 'Prohibition restrains the tribunal from proceeding further in excess of jurisdiction; certiorari requires the record or the order of the court to be sent up to the King's Bench Division, to have its legality inquired into, and, if necessary, to have the order quashed. It is to be noted that both writs deal with questions of excessive jurisdiction, and doubtless in their origin dealt almost exclusively with the jurisdiction of what is described in ordinary parlance as a Court of Justice. But the operation of the writs has extended to control the proceedings of bodies which do not claim to be, and would not be recognised as, Courts of Justice. Wherever any body of persons having legal authority to determine questions affecting the rights of subjects, and having the duty to act judicially, act in excess of their legal authority they are subject to the controlling jurisdiction of the King's Bench Division exercised in these writs ... I can see no difference in principle between certiorari and prohibition, except that the latter may be invoked at an earlier stage' (*per* ATKIN LJ).

R v Gaming Board for Great Britain, ex parte Benaim and [141] Khaida [1970] 2 QB 417 (Court of Appeal)

Under the Gaming Act 1968 premises used for gaming must be licensed. Before a licence may be applied for it is necessary to obtain a certificate of consent (showing that the applicant is a suitable person) from the Gaming Board. The Board refused to give such a certificate to the applicants who sought an order of certiorari, alleging that the Board had failed to observe the rules of natural justice. *Held*, the application would be dismissed. 'It is not possible to lay down rigid rules as to when the principles of natural justice are to apply: nor as to their scope and extent. Everything depends on the subject matter ... [In this situation] the best guidance is to be found by reference to the cases of immigrants. They have no right to come in (by analogy the applicants have no right to carry on gambling) but they have a right to be heard ... It follows that the Board has a duty to act *fairly*. They must let the applicant know what their impressions are so that he can disabuse them.' The Board had no need to reveal the source of the information in their possession. LORD DENNING MR went on to say that there was no need to give reasons for their decision. The court found that the Board had acted with complete fairness: 'They kept their sources secret but disclosed all the information' (per LORD DENNING MR). (See also *Re H K (an infant)*.)

R v Gough [1993] 2 WLR 883 (House of Lords) [142]

The appellant and his brother were charged with conspiracy to rob. The case against the appellant's brother was dropped before it reached the trial stage, but the appellant was tried and convicted. When the verdict was announced, the appellant's brother caused a disturbance in the courtroom, whereupon one of the members of the jury recognised him as her nextdoor neighbour. The trial judge declined to act on this new evidence, on the basis that he was functus officio. The appellant appealed unsuccessfully to the Court of Appeal and now renewed his appeal before the House of Lords. *Held*, the appeal would be dismissed. Allegations of bias would normally fall within one of three categories. Where actual bias was alleged, the proceedings would be invalidated upon proof of bias. Where the allegation of bias rested upon a pecuniary or proprietary interest, the proceedings would be invalidated upon proof of the pecuniary or proprietary interest. In cases of apparent bias, where there was no pecuniary or proprietary interest, the correct test was that propounded by the Court of Appeal in the instant case, namely that of whether or not there was a real danger of bias. The 'real danger' test was equally applicable to arbitrators and members of inferior tribunals. Where an allegation of apparent bias was made in relation to a justices' clerk, the court should go further and consider whether or not the clerk had advised the justices, and if so, whether or not it should infer that this advice had adversely affected their evaluation of the defendant's case. LORD GOFF OF CHIEVELEY criticised the emergence of the 'reasonable suspicion' test in judicial cases as being a misinterpretation of the decision in *R v Sussex Justices, ex parte McCarthy*. He preferred the approach adopted in *R v Camborne Justices, ex parte Pearce* [1954] 2 All ER 850, which rejected 'reasonable suspicion' on the grounds that it presented too low a threshold for challenge, opening up the possibility of appeal on the flimsiest of pretexts.

R v Graham-Campbell, ex parte Herbert [1935] 1 KB 594 [143]

Drinks were served in various bars of the Houses of Parliament, while Parliament was sitting, without reference to the ordinary licensing laws, and this action was an attempt to prosecute members of the House Kitchen Committee for breaches of the ordinary law. *Held*, the action would fail because the House had exclusive jurisdiction to regulate its own affairs as it wished and the courts could not interfere. 'Here, as it seems to me, the magistrate was entitled to say, on the materials before him, that in the matters complained of the House of Commons was acting collectively in a matter which fell within the area of the internal affairs of the House, and, that being so, any tribunal might well feel, on the authorities, an invincible reluctance to interfere. To take the opposite course might conceivably be, in proceedings of a somewhat different character from these, after the various stages of those proceedings had been passed, to make the House of Lords the arbiter of the privileges of the House of Commons' (*per* LORD HEWART CJ).

R v Home Secretary, ex parte Bentley [1994] 2 WLR 101   **[144]**

The applicant's brother, Derek Bentley, was convicted of the murder of a police officer in 1952. Despite the jury's recommendation, and the advice of Home Office officials, to the effect that the death penalty should not be enforced in this case, Bentley was executed in 1953. In 1992 the Home Secretary, while indicating that he had some sympathy for the view that Bentley should not have been hanged, refused to grant him a posthumous pardon, on the ground that it was not Home Office policy to do so unless the defendant concerned had been proved to be both technically and morally innocent of any crime. The Home Secretary was satisfied that, following a review of the case, Bentley's innocence had not been established. An application was made for judicial review of the Home Secretary's refusal. *Held*, the court would decline to make any order, but would invite the Home Secretary to look again at the range of options that might permit some formal recognition to be given to the generally accepted view that Bentley should not have been hanged. There was no reason why, in the light of the House of Lords' decision in *Council of Civil Service Unions* v *Minister for the Civil Service*, the exercise of the prerogative of mercy should not be susceptible to review. While the formulation of policy relating to the granting of pardons might not be justiciable, the failure by a Home Secretary to consider the variety of ways in which that prerogative might be exercised could be reviewed. In the instant case the Home Secretary should have considered whether or not the grant of a conditional posthumous pardon was appropriate as recognition that the State had made a mistake, and that Bentley should have had his sentence commuted.

R v Higher Education Funding Council, ex parte Institute   **[145]**
of Dental Surgery [1994] 1 WLR 242

The respondent statutory body was empowered, by the Education Reform Act 1988, to appoint a panel to assess the quality of research undertaken at universities. Research was rated on a scale of 0–5, and in a previous assessment the applicant institution's research had been rated at 3.0. In 1992 the respondent's panel assessed the applicant institution's research and rated it at 2.0. Research ratings were linked to funding, and the lower rating resulted in a cut of £270,000 in the applicant's research grant. The Chief Executive of the HEFC refused to give reasons for the lower rating, and refused to entertain an appeal unless the applicant institution could show that the rating had been based on erroneous information. The applicant institution applied for judicial review of the 2.0 rating and the refusal to give reasons. *Held*, the application would be dismissed. SEDLEY J, summarised the law relating to the duty to give reasons thus: '1. There is no general duty to give reasons for a decision, but there are classes of case where there is such a duty. 2. One such class is where the subject matter is an interest so highly regarded by the law – for example personal liberty – that fairness requires that reasons, at least for particular decisions, be given as of right. 3.(a) Another such class is where the decision appears aberrant. Here fairness may require reasons so that the recipient may know whether the aberration is in the legal sense real (and so challengeable) or apparent. (b) It follows that this class does not include decisions which are in themselves challengeable by reference only to the reasons for them. A pure exercise of academic judgment is such a decision. (c) Procedurally, the grant of leave in such cases will depend upon prima facie evidence that something has gone wrong. The respondent may then seek to demonstrate that it is not so and that the decision is an unalloyed exercise of an intrinsically unchallengeable judgment. If the respondent succeeds, the application fails. If the respondent fails, relief may take the form of an order of mandamus to give reasons, or (if a justiciable flaw has been established) other appropriate relief.'

R v Inspectorate of Pollution, ex parte Greenpeace Ltd (No 2)   [146]
[1994] 4 All ER 329

British Nuclear Fuels (BNFL) was authorised to discharge radioactive waste resulting from its undertakings by virtue of permission granted by the Inspectorate of Pollution and the Ministry of Agriculture, acting pursuant to the Radioactive Substances Act 1960. In 1992 BNFL sought further authorisation to discharge waste resulting from the operation of its thermal oxide reprocessing plant. Prior to the granting of these new authorisations BNFL sought variations to its existing authorisations in order to test its new plant before it came into operation. The applicants applied for judicial review, seeking an order of certiorari to quash the respondents' decision to grant the variation, and an injunction to prevent the new authorisations from taking effect. Leave to apply for review was granted but the court refused to grant a stay on the implementation of the authorisations. On the hearing of the application for review the respondents contended (inter alia) that the applicants lacked locus standi to challenge the variations. *Held*, although the applicants did have locus standi the application would be dismissed on its merits. In determining the issue of locus standi the court would take into account the nature of the applicant body, the extent of its interest, the remedies sought, the extent to which the applicant was a responsible body, its consultative status if any, the extent of its membership and support and whether the applicant body would have any other viable means of challenging the matter in question. The court was also mindful of the fact that if the objections to the authorisations had not been consolidated and organised by a pressure group such as Greenpeace the proceedings could have been far lengthier and more expensive. Although this was a decision of the High Court OTTON J felt at liberty not to follow the decision of the Court of Appeal in *R v Secretary of State for the Environment, ex parte Rose Theatre Trust Co* [1990] 1 QB 504 on the ground that in that case '... the circumstances were different, the interest group had been formed for the exclusive purpose of saving the Rose Theatre site and no individual member could show any personal interest in the outcome'. (Applied in *R v Secretary of State for Foreign Affairs, ex parte World Development Movement Ltd*.)

R v Lemon, R v Gay News Ltd [1979] 2 WLR 281 (House of Lords)   [147]

The appellants, who were editor and publishers of a newspaper for homosexuals, published a poem purporting to describe acts of sodomy and fellatio with the body of Christ immediately after His death and to ascribe homosexual activities during His lifetime. They were charged with blasphemous libel. The following point of law was certified by the Court of Appeal as of general public importance: 'Was the learned trial judge correct (as the Court of Appeal held) first in ruling and then in directing the jury that in order to secure the conviction of the appellants for publishing a blasphemous libel: (1) it was sufficient if the jury took the view that the publication complained of vilified Christ in His life and crucifixion and (2) it was not necessary for the Crown to establish any further intention on the part of the appellants beyond an intention to publish that which in the jury's view was a blasphemous libel.' *Held* (LORDS DIPLOCK and EDMUND-DAVIES dissenting), the offence of blasphemous libel only requires the prosecution to prove the intention to publish material which was in fact blasphemous. 'The movement of the law is illustrated by recent statutes. The Obscene Publications Act 1959 focuses attention upon the words or article published, not the intention of the author or publisher. The test of obscenity depends on the article itself. Section 5 of the Public Order Act 1936 has been significantly amended by the addition of a new section, 5A. The Race Relations Act 1976, s70(2), by providing that section 5A be added, has made it unnecessary to prove an intention to provoke a breach of the peace in order to secure a conviction for incitement to racial hatred. All this makes legal sense in a plural society which recognises the human rights and fundamental freedoms of the European Convention. Article 9 provides that everyone has the right to freedom of religion, and the right to manifest his religion in worship, teaching, practice, and observance. By necessary implication the Article imposes a duty on all of us to refrain from insulting or outraging the religious feelings of others. Article 10 provides that every one shall have the right to freedom of expression. The exercise of this freedom "carries with it duties and responsibilities" and may be subject to such restrictions as are presented by law and are necessary "for the prevention of disorder or crime, for the protection of health or morals, for the protection of the reputations or rights of others". It would be intolerable if by allowing an author or publisher to plead the excellence of his motives and the right of free speech he could evade the penalties of the law even though his words were blasphemous in the sense of constituting an outrage upon the religious feelings of his fellow citizens. This is no way forward for a successful plural society. Accordingly, the test of obscenity by concentrating attention on the words complained of is, in my judgment, equally valuable as a test of blasphemy' (*per* LORD SCARMAN). (See also *Bowman* v *Secular Society Ltd.*)

R v Local Government Board, ex parte Arlidge [1915] AC 120   **[148]**
(House of Lords)

The Hampstead Borough Council made a closing order in respect of the respondent's house. The respondent made an unsuccessful application for the order to be determined, and he appealed to the appellants who appointed an inspector to hold a public local inquiry. At the inquiry evidence was adduced on behalf of the respondent and, after receiving the report of the inspector and the shorthand notes of the proceedings, the appellants ordered the appeal to be dismissed. The respondent contended that this order should be quashed as it did not disclose by which officer the appeal had been decided, the respondent had not been heard orally by the appellants and he had not seen the report of the appellants' inspector. *Held*, the order should not be disturbed. 'Such a body as the Local Government Board has the duty of enforcing obligations on the individual which are imposed in the interests of the community. Its character is that of an organisation with executive functions. In this it resembles other great departments of the State. When, therefore, Parliament entrusts it with judicial duties. Parliament must be taken, in the absence of any declaration to the contrary, to have intended it to follow the procedure which is its own, and is necessary if it is to be capable of doing its work efficiently ... Provided the work is done judicially and fairly in the sense indicated by Lord Loreburn [in *Board of Education* v *Rice*], the only authority that can review what has been done is the Parliament to which the Minister in charge is responsible ... I do not think that the Board was bound to hear the respondent orally, provided it gave him the opportunities he actually had' (per VISCOUNT HALDANE LC). (But see *Jeffs* v *New Zealand Dairy Production and Marketing Board.*)

R v Medical Appeal Tribunal, ex parte Gilmore [1957] 1 QB 574 **[149]**
(Court of Appeal)

Because they failed to apply reg 2(5) of the National Insurance (Industrial Injuries) (Benefit) Regulations 1948, a medical appeal tribunal wrongly assessed the extent of the applicant's disablement. Reference to a specialist's report in their written adjudication made that report a part of the record and, as the medical appeal tribunal conceded, it disclosed an error of law. The National Insurance (Industrial Injuries) Act 1946 stipulated that any decision of a medical appeal tribunal of a question arising under that Act 'shall be final'. *Held*, notwithstanding that the decision of the medical appeal tribunal was by statute made 'final', certiorari could still issue for excess of jurisdiction or for error of law on the face of the record. DENNING LJ found it 'very well settled that the remedy of certiorari is never to be taken away by any statute except by the most clear and explicit words'.

R v Northumberland Compensation Appeal Tribunal,   **[150]**
ex parte Shaw [1952] 1 KB 338 (Court of Appeal)

By the passing of the National Health Service Act 1946, the applicant, Thomas Shaw, lost his employment as clerk to the West Northumberland Joint Hospital Board. Aggrieved by the amount of compensation awarded to him by the compensating authority, the Gosforth Urban District Council, he referred the matter to the tribunal designated by the National Health Service (Transfer of Offices and Compensation) Regulations 1948. It became the duty of the tribunal to consider the matter so referred 'in accordance with the provisions' of the regulations and 'to determine accordingly whether any and, if so, what compensation ought to be awarded to the claimant' (reg 12). The tribunal therefore were bound by the definition of 'service' contained in the regulations. The order of the tribunal set out the period of the applicant's service with the hospital board as being from 7 October 1936 to 31 March 1949. It set out the contention of the compensating authority that the compensation payable should be based on that period of service with the hospital board, and the tribunal stated that they agreed that this service was the only service to be taken into account. The decision did not set out the contention of the applicant, who was clerk to the Gosforth Urban District Council, that the whole of his local government service should be taken into account. And the tribunal dismissed the appeal from the decision of the compensating authority. Thereupon the applicant applied to the Divisional Court for an order of certiorari to remove the decision of the tribunal into the King's Bench Division that it might be quashed. Before the Divisional Court it was admitted by counsel for the tribunal that there was error on the face of the decision given by the tribunal, but he contended that certiorari would lie to such a statutory tribunal only in the case of want or excess of jurisdiction. The Divisional Court granted the order for certiorari and the tribunal appealed. The Gosforth Urban District Council did not appeal. *Held*, the tribunal's decision could be reviewed and quashed by the High Court on the ground that there was an error of law on the face of the record. The record for these purposes comprises the document which initiates the proceedings, any pleadings, and the adjudication. It does not include the evidence, or the reasons, unless the tribunal choose to incorporate them. If reasons are stated, and they reveal an error of law, certiorari lies to quash the decision. 'The Court of King's Bench has an inherent jurisdiction to control all inferior tribunals, not in an appellate capacity, but in a supervisory capacity. This control extends not only to seeing that the inferior tribunals keep within their jurisdiction, but also to seeing that they observe the law. The control is exercised by means of a power to quash any determination by the tribunal which, on the face of it, offends against the law. The King's Bench does not substitute its own views for those of the tribunal ... It leaves it to the tribunal to hear the case again ...' (*per* DENNING LJ). (But see *O'Reilly* v *Mackman*.)

R v Paddington and St Marylebone Rent Tribunal,   [151]
ex parte Bell London and Provincial Properties Ltd
[1949] 1 All ER 720

Following reductions made by a rent tribunal in respect of two of their flats, the landlords and owners of a block of flats were notified that an application had been made to a rent tribunal by the local authority under the Furnished Houses (Rent Control) Act 1946 for consideration of the rents of all the flats in that particular block. The application was made by the local authority pursuant to their policy that where two or more reductions of rent had been made by the tribunal in respect of any property, all other contracts of letting to which the Act applied relating to such property should be referred to the tribunal. The tribunal made orders reducing the rents of another eight of the landlords' furnished flats. *Held*, the act of the local authority in referring all other contracts of letting to the tribunal was not a genuine exercise of the power conferred on them by the Act and the tribunal would be prohibited from proceeding with the application in respect of the remaining flats. An order of certiorari would be granted to bring up and quash the eight orders already made. (But see *R* v *Barnet and Camden Rent Tribunal, ex parte Frey Investments Ltd*.)

R v Paddington Valuation Officer, ex parte Peachy Property   [152]
Corporation Ltd [1965] 2 All ER 836 (Court of Appeal)

A ratepayer who owned a number of flats sought mandamus and certiorari to quash a valuation list, primarily because of under-valuation of other types of property. *Held*, (a) the ratepayer was not barred from seeking these orders merely because a statutory remedy existed; (b) the ratepayer was a party aggrieved (even though any change would only make a negligible difference to his rates) and since he was challenging the validity of the whole or a substantial part of the list, the prerogative orders were a proper remedy; (c) the prerogative orders could issue to the valuation officer for he was a public officer dealing with questions affecting the rights of the subject and had a corresponding duty to act 'judicially', ie fairly and justly; (d) mandamus could issue forthwith with certiorari being postponed until a new list had been compiled.

R v Panel on Take-overs and Mergers, ex parte Datafin plc   [153]
[1987] 2 WLR 699 (Court of Appeal)

The Panel on Take-overs and Mergers operated as a self-regulating unincorporated association supervising a code of conduct to be observed in the take-overs of listed public companies. The Panel had no direct statutory, prerogative or common law powers but its functions were supported by certain statutory powers and penalties introduced after the creation of the Panel. The applicants sought leave to apply for judicial review of a decision of the Panel but leave was refused on the ground that the court had no jurisdiction to hear the application. The applicants appealed. The Panel argued, inter alia, that the supervisory jurisdiction of the court was confined to bodies whose powers derived solely from legislation or the exercise of the prerogative, and that therefore judicial review did not extend to the Panel. *Held*, despite lacking any direct statutory, prerogative or common law powers, the Panel was subject to judicial review. In determining whether a body was amenable to review, and in particular the order of certiorari, regard was to be had to the functions of the body and not simply the source of its power. The Panel was amenable to certiorari because it was exercising public law functions, and in the absence of any other means of control, such as might be exerted by the threat of private law proceedings in contract or tort, it was in the public interest for the court to extend its supervisory function.

R v Parliamentary Commissioner, ex parte Dyer   [154]
[1994] 1 All ER 375

The applicant had complained to the Parliamentary Commissioner for Administration (PCA) in relation to the alleged mishandling of her claim for invalidity benefit and other related welfare benefits. Subsequent to the PCA's investigation the Department of Social Security agreed to offer the applicant an apology and an ex gratia payment of £500 plus her expenses. The PCA reported to the applicant's MP and the department that he considered this a satisfactory outcome. The applicant now sought judicial review of the PCA' s alleged failure to investigate all of her complaints, his failure to seek her comments on the settlement, and his view that he was precluded from re-opening the complaint. The PCA contended that either his decisions were unreviewable as he was answerable to Parliament for the discharge of his functions, or, alternatively, his decisions could only be reviewed in the exceptional case where he had abused his discretion. *Held*, the application would be refused. While in theory the PCA's decisions were reviewable, in practice, given the wide discretion vested in him by the Parliamentary Commissioner Act 1967 (as amended), the court would be reluctant to intervene. Consequently the PCA's decision only to select certain of the applicant's complaints for investigation would not be overturned. His practice of submitting a draft report to the department being investigated, but not to the complainant, was not contrary to natural justice, given that it was the department that would have to defend its actions if it was found to have been guilty of maladministration. Having submitted his report to the relevant government department, and to the relevant MP, the PCA had no remaining power to re-open the complaint as he was functus officio.

R v Paty (1705) 2 Ld Rayd 1105   [155]

The defendants, Paty and four others, were committed by the Speaker of the House of Commons by virtue of an order of that House. The cause for committal stated in the return to a writ of habeas corpus was insufficient in law. HOLT CJ took the view that the defendants should be released, as if the House of Commons 'declare themselves to have privileges, which they have no legal claim to, the people of England will not be estopped by that declaration'.

R v Port of London Authority, ex parte Kynoch Ltd   [156]
[1919] 1 KB 176 (Court of Appeal)

Kynoch Ltd sought to challenge a decision of the authority refusing them a licence to construct a deep-water wharf on the Thames. The decision was a result of a policy adopted by the authority of not granting licences for the type of work that it carried out itself. The Divisional Court refused Kynoch Ltd mandamus; the company appealed. *Held*, dismissing the appeal, the authority had properly considered the application before refusing it in accordance with its policy. The court would intervene if there was evidence that, in an over-rigid adherence to the adopted policy, the decision-making body had closed its ears to the application and refused to consider any distinguishing evidence that the applicant sought to adduce. 'There are on the one hand cases where a tribunal in the honest exercise of its discretion has adopted a policy, and, without refusing to hear an applicant, intimates to him what its policy is, and that after hearing him it will in accordance with its policy decide against him, unless there is something exceptional in his case. I think counsel for the applicants would admit that, if the policy has been adopted for reasons which the tribunal may legitimately entertain, no objection could be taken to such a course. On the other hand there are cases where a tribunal has passed a rule, or come to a determination, not to hear any application of a particular character by whomsoever made. There is a wide distinction to be drawn between these two cases ...' (*per* BANKS LJ).

R v Rand (1866) LR 1 QB 230   [157]

Two justices were trustees of a hospital and a friendly society respectively, and both of these bodies invested part of their funds in bonds of Bradford Corporation. The West Riding of Yorkshire Justices, including the two in question, granted a certificate applied for by Bradford Corporation in respect of the filling of a reservoir. This application had been opposed by certain mill-owners who now contended that the certificate should be quashed on the ground that the justices, or some of them, were interested in the subject-matter. *Held*, the certificate would not be quashed as the justices, who had acted perfectly bona fide, were not disqualified from acting in the matter.

R v Samuel [1988] 2 WLR 920 (Court of Appeal)   [158]

The appellant was interviewed by the police on four occasions about a robbery and two burglaries. The appellant denied any involvement. During the second interview he asked for access to a solicitor, but his request was refused on the ground of the likelihood of other suspects involved in the robbery being inadvertently warned. At the fourth interview the appellant confessed to the two burglaries and he was charged with those offences at 4.30pm. At 4.45pm a solicitor was informed of the charges, but denied access. Shortly afterwards the appellant confessed to the robbery and the solicitor was allowed to see him one hour later. At the trial, the appellant contended that evidence of the latter confession should be excluded, but it was admitted and he was convicted of robbery. *Held*, the conviction would be quashed. In the circumstances, the refusal of access to a solicitor had been unjustified and the interview in question should not have taken place. An officer dealing with a detainee's request for a solicitor can only deny the request if he believes that allowing consultation with a solicitor *will* lead to one or more of the things set out in paras (a) to (c) of s58(8) of the 1984 Act (interference with witnesses, alerting accomplices, disposing of proceeds, etc). 'Therefore, inadvertent or unwitting conduct apart, the officer must believe that a solicitor will, if allowed to consult with a detained person, thereafter commit a criminal offence (assisting an offender following the commission of an offence). Solicitors are officers of the court. We think that the number of times that a police officer could genuinely be in that state of belief will be rare. Moreover it is our view that, to sustain such a basis for refusal, the grounds put forward would have to have reference to a specific solicitor. We do not think they could ever be successfully advanced in relation to solicitors generally ...' (*per* HODGSON J).

R v Sang [1980] AC 402 (House of Lords)   [159]

The appellant pleaded not guilty to a charge that he conspired with others to utter forged United States banknotes. Requesting a trial within a trial, his counsel said that he hoped to establish that the appellant had been induced to commit the offence by an informer acting on the instructions of the police and that but for such persuasion the appellant would not have committed the offence. Counsel then hoped that the judge would rule, in the exercise of his discretion, that no evidence of the offence so incited should be admitted and that he would direct the entry of a not guilty verdict. The judge ruled that he had no discretion to exclude the evidence. *Held*, although a judge always had a discretion to refuse to admit evidence if he thought its prejudicial effect outweighed its probative value, here the evidence should not have been excluded, whether or not it had been obtained as a result of the activities of an agent provocateur. English law did not recognise a defence of entrapment.

R v Secretary of State for Employment, ex parte Equal [160] Opportunities Commission [1994] 2 WLR 409 (House of Lords)

The Equal Opportunities Commission (EOC) made representations to the Secretary of State to the effect that existing domestic law relating to redundancy and unfair dismissal was contrary to EC law as it indirectly discriminated against female employees by offering reduced protection to part-time workers. The Secretary of State rejected these assertions. The EOC thereupon applied for judicial review (seeking a declaration and an order of mandamus) of the Secretary of State's decision not to act in this matter, with a view to challenging the differential in the qualifying dates for redundancy compensation. It was joined in its application by D, a part-time worker, who had been made redundant shortly before the day on which she would have become eligible for a redundancy payment. The EOC also made an application for judicial review (seeking a declaration and an order of mandamus) of the Secretary of State's failure to amend the law to take into account an earlier period of full-time employment in calculating the amount of redundancy payment due. At first instance the application was refused. The EOC and D appealed unsuccessfully to the Court of Appeal, where it was held, inter alia, that D's application did not have a sufficient public law element to warrant consideration by way of judicial review, and should be pursued before an industrial tribunal. Furthermore (DILLON LJ dissenting), there were other means by which questions as to the extent to which domestic law was compatible with EC law could be resolved. The Secretary of State could not be compelled by the courts to introduce amending legislation. The Secretary of State's letter did not, in any event, raise any justiciable issues, as it did not affect any individual's legal rights or duties, and in the light of these points the EOC lacked locus standi to pursue its applications. D and the EOC appealed to the House of Lords. *Held*, (1) D's appeal would be dismissed, as it did not raise a matter suitable for determination by way of judicial review, and ought not to have been advanced against the Secretary of State as he was not her employer, and would not be liable to compensate her in the event of her case succeeding. (2) The Commission's appeal would be allowed, as the Secretary of State had not discharged the burden of showing that the indirect discrimination against women resulting from the threshold provisions of the 1978 Act was objectively justified, and not an infringement of Article 119 of the EEC treaty. (3) Even though the case was not one where the court would have been empowered to grant a prerogative order, as there was no 'decision' of the Secretary of State to quash, reference to the *Factortame* series of cases (see [1989] 2 WLR 997, [1990] 3 WLR 818 and [1992] 2 WLR 239) confirmed that the Commission was entitled to apply for a declaration as to the extent to which the provisions of the 1978 Act relating to redundancy and compensation for unfair dismissal were compatible with Community law. Such an application would not involve a declaration that the United Kingdom or the Secretary of State was in breach of Community obligations, as the Commission's purpose could be served simply by a declaration confirming the incompatibility of domestic law and Community law.(4) (LORD JAUNCEY OF TULLICHETTLE dissenting) The Commission did have locus standi, as the litigation concerned the extent to which the legislation ensured equality of treatment of employees. LORD KEITH OF KINKEL observed: '... it would be a very retrograde step now to hold that the EOC has no locus standi to agitate in judicial review proceedings questions related to sex discrimination which are of public importance and affect a large section of the population. The determination of this issue turns essentially upon a consideration of the statutory duties and public law role of the EOC as regards which no helpful guidance is to be gathered from decided cases ...' (See also *R v Secretary of State for Transport, ex parte Factortame Ltd.*)

R v Secretary of State for Foreign Affairs, ex parte   [161] World Development Movement Ltd [1995] 1 All ER 611

In July 1991 the Foreign Secretary, in the exercise of his discretion under s1(1) of the Overseas and Development Act 1980, made a grant to the Malaysian government for the building of the Pergau Dam. In April 1994, despite concerns about the funding of the project, the Foreign Secretary refused to withhold outstanding payments. The applicants, a pressure group concerned with abuses of overseas aid, sought to challenge the legality of both the original decision to grant aid, and the later decision not to withhold outstanding payments, on the ground that the Foreign Secretary had known that the aid was not being granted for a sound economic development. *Held*, the application would be allowed and a declaration granted to the effect that the Foreign Secretary's decision of July 1991 had been unlawful. On the issue of locus standi, ROSE LJ, in concluding that the applicants did have sufficient interest, recognised that, whilst the dominant factor was the merit of the application itself, other significant matters included the need to uphold the rule of the law, the fact that no other organisation was likely to launch such a challenge, and the key role played by the applicants in giving advice, guidance and assistance regarding aid. In particular it was felt that if the applicant in *R v Secretary of State for Foreign and Commonwealth Affairs, ex parte Rees-Mogg* was properly regarded as having had locus standi on the basis of his '... sincere concerns for constitutional issues...', then a fortiori the applicants in the present case should have standing, given their track record in promoting aid for under-developed nations. Regarding the substantive issue of vires, his Lordship accepted that the discretion to grant aid under s1(1) of the 1980 Act had to be exercised for a proper purpose, in particular for promoting development of a recipient country's economy. The affidavit evidence of the respondent indicated that the contemplated development, in the form of the Pergau Dam project, was so economically unsound that no economic argument in its favour could be contructed. The fact that Parliament had not limited power under the 1980 Act by expressly specifying that it had to be exercised for a sound development purpose did not mean that it could, therefore, be used to promote unsound development. The court recognised that the respondent would have to take into account wider political and diplomatic considerations when deciding whether or not to honour a pledge to grant overseas aid, but those factors only became relevant once a proper purpose for granting aid arose under the 1980 Act. It could not be left to the respondent himself to determine whether or not a grant of aid under the 1980 Act would be lawful. (Applied: *R v Inspectorate of Pollution, ex parte Greenpeace Ltd (No 2).*)

R v Secretary of State for Foreign and Commonwealth   [162] Affairs, ex parte Everett [1989] 2 WLR 224 (Court of Appeal)

The applicant lived in Spain and his British passport was endorsed by the Spanish for residence there. He applied for a new passport on the expiry of the old one, but the Consul in Malaga refused it. There was a warrant out for the applicant's arrest in the UK, and it was Foreign Office policy not to renew passports for anyone in that situation. The applicant sought judicial review of the decision. MANN J granted the relief sought and the Secretary of State appealed. *Held*, allowing the appeal, although passports are issued under the royal prerogative in the discretion of the Secretary of State, if an application for a passport is wrongly refused for a bad reason, the court would inquire into the refusal by way of judicial review. The Secretary of State, in the fair exercise of his discretion, was entitled to refuse the passport, but was required to give his reason for so doing. On the facts of the instant case, the applicant had suffered no injustice, hence there were no grounds for granting relief.

R v Secretary of State for Foreign and Commonwealth Affairs, [163] ex parte Rees-Mogg [1994] 1 All ER 457

The applicant was opposed to the ratification by the United Kingdom of the Maastricht Treaty on European Union, as evidenced by the European Community (Amendment) Act 1993. He brought proceedings against the Foreign Secretary seeking a declaration (inter alia) that ratification of the treaty's Protocol on Social Policy (that Protocol being specifically excluded from the operation of the European Communities Act 1972 by the 1993 Act) would be an unlawful exercise of prerogative power as it would involve an alteration to Community law without parliamentary approval, and that the establishment of a common foreign policy (under Title V of the Maastricht Treaty) would involve a loss of prerogative power, which could only be achieved by way of statutory enactment. *Held*, (inter alia) when Parliament intends to limit the scope of prerogative power it does so by express words. An intention to limit the prerogative power of Her Majesty's ministers to amend the Treaty of Rome could not be discerned from a reading of s2(1) of the European Communities Act 1972. In any event, the Protocol did not fall within the definition of 'the Treaties' in s2(1) of the 1972 Act, being specifically excluded by s1(1) of that Act; thus any argument based on s2(1) of the 1972 was without foundation. On the second issue, it had not been the intention of Parliament, by way of the 1972 Act, to curtail the treaty-making powers of the Crown under the prerogative. On the facts, the ratification of Title V of the Maastricht Treaty did not involve a diminution of prerogative power; it was an exercise of that power. As a last resort, it was presumed, it would be open to the United Kingdom to renege on its obligations under the treaty, and reassert the prerogative power to formulate and execute foreign policy in the areas affected. (See also *Blackburn* v *Attorney-General*; but see *R* v *Secretary of State for the Home Department, ex parte Fire Brigades Union*.)

R v Secretary of State for the Environment, ex parte Ostler [164]
[1977] 1 QB 122 (Court of Appeal)

Proposals for a road widening scheme in Boston were published in 1972. The applicant, who had business premises in the town centre there, made no objection to the proposals as, from the published plans, they did not appear to affect his property. After these first orders were confirmed supplementary proposals were put forward, which could affect the applicant's property. He objected to the supplementary proposals at the subsequent public inquiry, but was not allowed to raise objections to the first proposals on the ground that they had become final. The applicant alleged that there had been a secret agreement between the government department and a firm of local wine merchants whereby, if they raised no objection to the original proposals, the department would make the supplementary proposals under which they would be provided with better access to their premises by the widening of Craythorne Lane, where Mr Ostler's premises were situated. Mr Ostler now sought to challenge the orders on the ground that they were procured in bad faith and in breach of natural justice. The Secretary of State raised a preliminary objection to the proceedings on the ground that any challenge was barred by para 2, Schedule 2, to the Highways Act 1959, which prohibited the questioning of such an order in any legal proceedings whatsoever, apart from in the six weeks immediately following the making of the order. *Held*, decisions such as those in question were administrative in nature, and it was in the public interest that once taken, they should soon become unchallengeable in the courts. As the time limit for challenging these decisions had expired, this application for certiorari could not be allowed to proceed on any grounds. The decision in *Anisminic Ltd* v *Foreign Compensation Commission* had not altered the law as stated in *Smith* v *East Elloe Rural District Council*, first because in the *Anisminic* case the Act ousted the jurisdiction of the court altogether, whereas in the *East Elloe* case the court had been concerned with a partial ouster clause. Secondly, the *Anisminic* case concerned a determination by a truly judicial body, the Foreign Compensation Commission, whereas the *East Elloe* case was concerned with an administrative decision. Thirdly, the *Anisminic* case was concerned with the actual determination of a tribunal, whereas in *East Elloe* the court had been concerned with the validity of the process by which the decision was reached. 'Looking at it broadly, it seems to me that the policy underlying the statute is that when a compulsory purchase order has been made, then if it has been wrongly obtained or made, a person aggrieved should have a remedy. But he must come promptly. He must come within six weeks. If he does so, the court can and will entertain his complaint. But if the six weeks expire without any application being made, the court cannot entertain it afterwards. The reason is because, as soon as that time has elapsed, the authority will take steps to acquire property, demolish it and so forth. The public interest demands that they should be safe in doing so' (*per* LORD DENNING MR).

R v Secretary of State for the Home Department,   **[165]**
ex parte Benwell [1984] 3 WLR 843

The applicant sought an order of certiorari to quash the decision of the Secretary of State confirming his dismissal from the prison service on the ground that the procedure before the disciplinary bodies concerned had been in breach of natural justice. *Held*, the applicant was entitled to use judicial review to challenge the decision of the Home Secretary. As a prison officer he had no contract of employment that could be enforced in civil proceedings. The Home Secretary's power to deal with the disciplinary proceedings arose under statutory provisions, and was therefore within the sphere of public law. (Distinguished: *R v East Berkshire Health Authority, ex parte Walsh*.)

R v Secretary of State for the Home Department,   **[166]**
ex parte Brind [1991] 2 WLR 588 (House of Lords)

The Home Secretary, acting pursuant to powers conferred upon him by s29(3) of the Broadcasting Act 1981 in regard to the IBA, and clause 13(4) of the licence and agreement with the BBC, ordered both organisations to refrain from broadcasting interviews with members and representatives of certain named terrorist organisations. The applicants were journalists who sought a declaration that the restrictions were ultra vires the minister's powers, and an order of certiorari to quash the restrictions. They contended that the restrictions were ultra vires on the grounds that Parliament could not have intended to empower the Minister to issue restrictions that were in breach of Article 10 of the European Convention on Human Rights; that the restrictions were out of all proportion to the problem that the minister sought to deal with; that the restrictions would conflict with the terms of the BBC's Charter, under which it had to report on news items impartially; and that the restrictions were absurd and perverse. The Divisional Court dismissed the application, holding that the 1981 Act appeared to provide the Minister with a very wide power to censor the output of the IBA, without any formal parliamentary control. WATKINS LJ expressly rejected the notion that the courts should intervene on the grounds of proportionality. His Lordship contended that this would result in the court substituting its own view for that of the Minister. The applicants, having appealed unsuccessfully to the Court of Appeal, appealed to the House of Lords. *Held*, dismissing the appeal, the restrictions were not ultra vires. LORDS ACKNER and LOWRY rejected the concept of proportionality as not yet part of English law, though they said it might become part of English law if the European Convention on Human Rights were incorporated into English law. Until such time neither the executive nor the judges were bound to take it into account when performing their respective functions. LORDS ACKNER and LOWRY expressed concern that the test of proportionality went much further than the test of irrationality (or total unreasonableness) by transforming judicial review into a merits-based appellate jurisdiction. Their lordships felt that judges were not equipped by training, experience or expert knowledge to determine whether a minister had struck a proper balance in the exercise of his powers, unless the decision was so out of balance (eg imposition of excessive penalties) as to become irrational or totally unreasonable. LORDS ROSKILL and BRIDGE OF HARWICH left open the possibility of development of the doctrine of proportionality as part of English common law but considered it was not applicable to the facts (in their view the restrictions on broadcasting were not excessive in their interference with free speech). '... where Parliament has conferred on the executive an administrative discretion without indicating the precise limits within which it must be exercised, to presume that it must be exercised within Convention limits would be to go far beyond the resolution of an ambiguity. It would be to impute to Parliament an intention not only that the executive should exercise the discretion in conformity with the Convention, but also that the domestic courts should enforce that conformity by the importation into domestic administrative law of the text of the Convention and the jurisprudence of the European Court of Human Rights in the interpretation and application of it. If such a presumption is to apply to the statutory discretion exercised by the Secretary of State under section 29(3) of the [Broadcasting Act 1981] in the instant case, it must also apply to any other statutory discretion exercised by the executive which is capable of involving an infringement of Convention rights. When Parliament has been content for so long to leave those who complain that their Convention rights have been infringed to seek their remedy in Strasbourg, it would be surprising suddenly to find that the judiciary had, without Parliament's aid, the means to incorporate the Convention into such an important area of domestic law and I cannot escape the conclusion that this would be a judicial usurpation of the legislative function' (*per* LORD BRIDGE).

R v Secretary of State for the Home Department,   [167]
ex parte Doody [1993] 3 WLR 154 (House of Lords)

The applicants were all prisoners serving life sentences following convictions for murder. The Minister, acting under s61 of the Criminal Justice Act 1967, had the power to determine the first date upon which such prisoners might be considered for release (ie the point at which the 'penal element' of the sentence would expire). The procedure adopted was that the Minister would consult the views of the trial judge and the Lord Chief Justice prior to informing a prisoner of the first date for review of his continued detention. The effect was that a prisoner would then be aware of his minimum period of imprisonment. Each of the applicants, in respect of his own conviction, sought to challenge the decision of the Minister in respect of the date set for review. The applicants, in challenging the legality of the procedure adopted by the Minister, sought declarations to the effect that: (i) in setting the minimum period for detention the Minister could not exceed the period recommended by the judiciary; (ii) the Minister was required to inform a prisoner of the judicial recommendation; (iii) the Minister should inform a prisoner of his reasons for departing from the judicial recommendation, if this was what he intended to do; (iv) a prisoner should be given the opportunity to make representations prior to the Minister's determination of the period to be served; (v) a prisoner should be informed of any information of which he was not already appraised upon which the Minister intended to act. The Divisional Court dismissed the applications. The Court of Appeal allowed the prisoners' appeals in part, holding that a prisoner receiving a mandatory life sentence was entitled to know what the judicial recommendation had been as to the penal element of the sentence to be served, and had the right to make written representations to the Home Secretary prior to the minister's decision. The Minister, however, was entitled to depart from the judicial recommendation, without informing the prisoner of the reasons for so doing. The Secretary of State appealed and the prisoners cross-appealed. *Held*, the Secretary of State's appeal would be dismissed and the cross-appeal allowed in part. The declarations granted by the Court of Appeal would be confirmed, subject to the addition of a further declaration to the effect that the Secretary of State was obliged to give reasons for departing from the period recommended by the judiciary as regards the 'penal element' of the sentence. The Secretary of State was not bound to follow the judicial recommendation as to the minimum period of detention, as he would have to take into account broader public policy issues in making such decisions. LORD MUSTILL, in addressing the issue of the right to make representations in public law, commented as follows: 'What does fairness require in the present case? My Lords, I think it unnecessary to refer by name to or to quote from, any of the oft-cited authorities in which the courts have explained what is essentially an intuitive judgment. They are far too well known. From them, I derive the following. (1) Where an Act of Parliament confers an administrative power there is a presumption that it will be exercised in a manner which is fair in all the circumstances. (2) The standards of fairness are not immutable. They may change with the passage of time, both in the general and in their application to decisions of a particular type. (3) The principles of fairness are not to be applied identically by rote in every situation. What fairness demands is dependent on the context of the decision, and this is to be taken into account in all its aspects. (4) An essential feature of the context is the statute which creates the discretion, as regards both its language and the shape of the legal and administrative system within which the decision is taken. (5) Fairness will very often require that a person who may be adversely affected by the decision will have an opportunity to make representations on his own behalf either before the decision is taken, with a view to producing a favourable result, or after it is taken, with a view to procuring its modification, or both. (6) Since the person affected cannot usually make worthwhile representations without knowing what factors may weigh against his interests, fairness will very often require that he is informed of the gist of the case that he has to answer.' While confirming that there was no general legal duty to give reasons for an administrative decision, LORD MUSTILL went on to observe that it was important that there should be '... an effective means of detecting the kind of error which would entitle the court to intervene ...' should a decision as to sentencing be wrong in law. In his Lordship's view, a requirement that reasons be given for departing from a judicial recommendation as to the minimum term could provide evidence of any such errors. [Note: This decision overruled *Payne* v *Lord Harris of Greenwich* [1981] 2 All ER 842, which LORD MUSTILL regarded as reflecting an outmoded view of the duty to give reasons. In particular he felt that in the thirteen years since that decision the perception of society's obligation towards persons serving prison sentences had changed noticeably, and that the trend in administrative law was now firmly towards openness in decision-making.]

R v Secretary of State for the Home Department, ex parte [168]
Fire Brigades Union [1995] 2 All ER 244 (House of Lords)

A scheme existed for allocating public funds by way of compensation for the victims of crime. The scheme, which was administered by the Criminal Injuries Compensation Board, was created under the prerogative. Sections 108–117 of the Criminal Justice Act 1988 sought to codify this scheme and place it on a statutory basis, leaving the quantum of any funds awarded to be determined by application of the common law principles. Section 171(1) empowered the Secretary of State to bring the scheme into effect on a day to be announced. In November 1993, in the exercise of his prerogative powers, the Secretary of State announced a new tariff scheme under which set amounts would be payable to the victims of crime, depending upon how their claims were categorised. The effect of this new tariff scheme was that much lower awards would be made in the future, resulting in a halving of the cost of the criminal injuries compensation scheme by the year 2000. The applicants applied for judicial review of (i) the Secretary of State's failure to implement the statutory scheme under the 1988 Act and (ii) his exercise of prerogative power in introducing the revised tariff for awards. The application was dismissed at first instance, and on appeal to the Court of Appeal held that, whilst the Secretary of State was under no duty to introduce the statutory scheme, it was an abuse of his common law prerogative powers to introduce a compensation scheme other than that contained in the 1988 Act. The Secretary of State appealed to the House of Lords and the applicants cross-appealed. *Held* (Lords Mustill and Keith dissenting), the appeal and cross-appeals would be dismissed. The Secretary of State had a discretion under s171(1) of the 1988 Act to bring the scheme into effect at some future date. If the applicant's contention, to the effect that the Secretary of State had to bring the scheme into effect at some time, was correct it would mean the courts being able to grant an order of mandamus to this effect. LORD KEITH observed that it would be undesirable for the courts to be seen to be intervening in the legislative process to this extent. The section was to be read as conferring a discretion upon the Secretary of State that had to be exercised (or not) according to law. In the instant case the Secretary of State had acted unlawfully in determining that he would never exercise his powers under s171(1). Further, the Secretary of State could not rely on his own act of introducing a revised scheme for compensation under the prerogative as a ground for not exericsing his discretion under s171(1). Hence the introduction of the revised scheme under the prerogative, given the pre-existing statutory scheme, constituted an abuse of power and was thus ultra vires. LORD KEITH (dissenting) viewed the decision as to whether or not to implement the legislation as one that was essentially administrative or political, in respect of which the Secretary of State owed a duty to Parliament, not the public at large. Hence it would be inappropriate for the courts to intervene. (But see *R v Secretary of State for Foreign and Commonwealth Affairs, ex parte Rees-Mogg*.)

R v Secretary of State for the Home Department, [169]
ex parte Northumbria Police Authority
[1988] 2 WLR 590 (Court of Appeal)

The Home Secretary issued a circular to all chief constables informing them that the Home Office maintained a central store of riot equipment, such as CS gas. It went on to state that if chief constables experienced difficulties in persuading their respective police authorities to sanction the supply of such equipment, it would be made directly available on request to the Home Office. The Home Secretary claimed that either the power to supply such equipment was provided by s41 of the Police Act 1964, or that he was exercising his prerogative power to maintain law and order. The police authority maintained that it alone was responsible for sanctioning the provision of such equipment to a chief constable, and that the exercise of any prerogative power by the Home Secretary was inconsistent with its own power under s4(4) of the 1964 Act. At first instance the Divisional Court held that, although the Home Secretary did not have the power to supply such equipment under s41 of the Act, he could do so in the exercise of his prerogative power to maintain law and order. This had not been replaced by s4(4) of the Act. The police authority now appealed to the Court of Appeal. *Held,* the Home Secretary was empowered to supply such equipment by s41 of the 1964 Act. Further, even if he was not, he could still do so in the exercise of his prerogative power to maintain law and order. This power had not been replaced by statute, because s4(4) did not provide the police authority with monopoly control over the supply of equipment. 'By its very nature, the subject of maintaining the Queen's peace and keeping law and order has over the years inevitably been dealt with by statute much more than the war prerogative has been. Instances of the way in which such a prerogative may be used are more readily provided by example than by being placed in categories, but I have no doubt that the Crown does have a prerogative power to keep the peace, which is bound up with its undoubted right to see that crime is prevented and justice administered' (*per* CROOM-JOHNSON LJ). (But see *Attorney-General v De Keyser's Royal Hotel Ltd.*)

R v Secretary of State for the Home Department,   [170]
ex parte Oladehinde [1990] 3 WLR 797 (House of Lords)

The applicants had been served with notices of intention to deport by immigration officers. The officers had been acting under the instructions of immigration inspectors to whom the function of making decisions to deport had been delegated by the Secretary of State. After appealing unsuccessfully to the adjudicator and the Immigration Appeal Tribunal, the applicants sought judicial review of the deportation decisions on the ground (inter alia) that the Secretary of State acted unlawfully in delegating his power of deportation under s3(5)(a) of the Immigration Act 1971 to immigration inspectors. The Divisional Court granted the application for review, quashing the deportation orders, on the grounds that it had been the intention of Parliament that the immigration officers should have had a distinct function, that of controlling entry to the country, whilst the Secretary of State was to be concerned with decisions relating to the right to remain and deportation. The Court of Appeal allowed the Secretary of State's appeal, and the applicants appealed further to the House of Lords. *Held,* dismissing the appeals, there was nothing in the wording of s3(5)(a) which appeared expressly or impliedly to limit the Secretary of State's power to delegate his function to order deportation. In the absence of any such statutory restrictions, the factors to which the court would have regard were the seniority of the officers to whom the power had been delegated, the possibility of any conflict with their other statutory duties, and whether they had fully considered the applicants' cases. In all these respects it was established that the Secretary of State had acted lawfully. 'The immigration service is comprised of Home Office civil servants for whom the Secretary of State is responsible and I can for myself see no reason why he should not authorise members of that service to take decisions under the *Carltona Ltd v Commissioners of Works* principle providing they do not conflict with or embarrass them in the discharge of their specific statutory duties under the Act and that the decisions are suitable to their grading and experience' (*per* LORD GRIFFITHS).

R v Secretary of State for the Home Department,   [171]
ex parte Tarrant [1985] QB 251

The applicants were all prisoners. Two had been charged with mutiny contrary to the prison rules, and on a finding of guilt had incurred considerable loss of remission. The application for judicial review challenged the validity of the disciplinary hearings on the ground that the board of visitors had wrongfully denied them legal representation. *Held*, although legal representation was not available to prisoners as of right, the board, in exercising its discretion to permit such representation, was required to act within the bounds of reasonableness. To deny legal representation when the consequences of a finding of guilt carried the risk of substantial penalties could be an unreasonable decision that rendered unfair any subsequent proceedings. (See also *Enderby Town Football Club Ltd* v *Football Association Ltd.*)

R v Secretary of State for Transport, ex parte Factortame Ltd   [172]
[1990] 3 CMLR 867; R v Secretary of State for Transport,
ex parte Factortame Ltd (No 2) [1991] 1 AC 603
(European Court of Justice and House of Lords)

Fishing quotas were introduced by the EEC to prevent over-fishing. The United Kingdom Parliament enacted the Merchant Shipping Act 1988 (Part II) to protect British fishing interests by restricting the number of vessels whose catch could be counted against the British quota. The Secretary of State issued regulations under the Act that required any vessel wishing to fish as part of the British fleet to be registered under the 1988 Act. Registration was contingent upon a vessel's owner being a British citizen or domiciled in Britain. In the case of companies, the shareholders would have to meet these requirements. The applicants were British-registered companies operating fishing vessels in British waters. These companies now found it impossible to obtain registration because their shareholders and directors were Spanish. The applicants contended that the regulations effectively prevented them from exercising their rights under Community law to fish as part of the British fleet. The Secretary of State contended that Community law did not prevent the United Kingdom from introducing domestic legislation determining which companies were 'British nationals' and which were not. The applicants sought judicial review of the Minister's decision that their registration should cease; of the Minister's determination that they were no longer 'British' ships; and of the relevant parts of the Act and Regulations which would have the effect of preventing them from fishing. By way of remedies they sought: a declaration that the Minister's decision should not take effect because of its inconsistency with Community law; an order of prohibition to prevent the Minister from regarding the ships as de-registered; damages under s35 of the Supreme Court Act 1981; and an interim injunction suspending the operation of the legislation pending the ruling of the European Court of Justice. Regarding the interpretation of Community law, the Divisional Court requested a preliminary ruling under Article 177 of the Treaty of Rome so that the questions relating to the applicant's rights could be resolved. Pending that ruling, the court granted the applicants interim relief in the form of an injunction to suspend the operation of the legislation by restraining the Minister from enforcing it, thus enabling the applicants to continue fishing. The Secretary of State successfully challenged the order for interim relief in the Court of Appeal, and the applicants appealed to the House of Lords. *Held*, the appeal would be dismissed. English courts had no power to grant interim relief to prevent the operation of a statute passed by Parliament. If the ultimate decision of the European Court went against the applicants they would have enjoyed approximately two years' (the length of time it would take for the European Court to resolve the matter) unjust enrichment by being allowed to continue fishing. Further, the courts had no power to grant an interim injunction against the Crown. Sections 21(2) and 23(2)(b) of the Crown Proceedings Act 1947 preserved what had been the common law position, ie that such relief was not available in judicial review proceedings on the Crown side. On this basis there was no way that the interim relief could be obtained. The question of whether or not there was an overriding principle of Community law to the effect that Member States must provide some form of relief to litigants who claim that their rights are being interfered with, pending a decision of the European Court of Justice, was referred to the European Court of Justice under Article 177 by the House of Lords. *Held*, Community law required the courts of Member States to give effect to the directly enforceable provision of Community law. Such Community laws rendered any conflicting national law inapplicable. A court which would grant interim relief but for a rule of domestic law should set aside that rule of domestic law in favour of observing Community obligations. On the reference back to the House of Lords: *Held*, in determining whether interim relief by way of an injunction should be granted, the determining factor should not be the availability of damages as a remedy, but the balance of convenience, taking into account the importance of upholding duly enacted laws. Damages are not available against a public body exercising its powers in good faith. The court should not restrain a public authority from enforcing an apparently valid law unless it is satisfied, having regard to all the circumstances, that the challenge to the validity of the law is prima facie so firmly based as to justify so exceptional a course being taken. 'If the supremacy within the European Community of Community law over the national law of Member States was not always inherent in the EEC Treaty (Cmnd 5179–11) it was certainly well established in the jurisprudence of the European Court of Justice long before the United Kingdom joined the Community. Thus, whatever limitation of its sovereignty Parliament accepted when it enacted the European Communities Act 1972 was entirely voluntary. Under the terms of the Act of 1972 it has always been clear that it was the duty of a United Kingdom court, when delivering final judgment, to override any rule of national law found to be in conflict with any directly enforceable rule of Community law. Similarly, when decisions of the European Court of Justice have exposed areas of United Kingdom statute law which failed to implement Council directives, Parliament has always loyally accepted the obligation to make appropriate and prompt amendments. Thus there is nothing in any way novel in according supremacy to rules of Community law in those areas to which they apply, and to insist that, in the protection of rights under Community law, national courts must not be inhibited by rules of national law from granting interim relief in appropriate cases is no more than a logical recognition of that supremacy' (*per* LORD BRIDGE OF HARWICH). (See also *M* v *Home Office*.)

R v Secretary of State for Transport, ex parte Richmond-   [173]
Upon-Thames London Borough Council [1994] 1 All ER 577

Acting pursuant to s78(3)(b) of the Civil Aviation Act 1982, the Secretary of State for Transport purported to alter the regulations relating to night-flying restrictions affecting London's airports. Under the proposed scheme, instead of there being a fixed maximum number of aircraft movements at each airport, each airport would be given a number of quota points. Each aircraft movement at night would result in points being deducted. Each type of aircraft would be classified according to its 'quota count' based on the noise levels it produced. Hence an airport could choose to permit more movements by quieter aircraft as against a lesser number of movements by noisier aircraft. A number of local authorities sought judicial review of the Minister's proposals. *Held*, the application would be allowed. The 1982 Act required the Minister to specify the maximum number of aircraft movements permitted. Note that one of the arguments put forward on behalf of the applicants related to their legitimate expectation that the new scheme would not result in any increase in noise from night flights. Mr Justice Laws recognised that the expression 'legitimate expectation' could be used in two situations. First, in relation to what he described as the 'procedural expectation', where a public authority provides that it will give certain persons a hearing before arriving at a decision on a particular matter. Secondly, there was the situation where a public body had adopted a policy and by promise or past practice indicated that this would be its *continuing* policy. In such cases the court may intervene where it considers the public body to be acting unfairly where it changes the policy without giving those affected a hearing. Some commentators had described such cases as involving 'substantive expectations', but LAWS J expressed the view that '... the putative distinction between procedural and substantive rights in this context has little, if any, utility; the question is always whether the discipline of fairness, imposed by the common law, ought to prevent the public authority ... from acting as it proposes.' Significantly, LAWS J rejected any contention that there could be, in public law, a legitimate expectation that a particular policy would not be changed even though those affected had been consulted. Such a contention, he said, '... would impose an obvious and unacceptable fetter upon the power, and duty, of a responsible public authority to change its policy when it considered that that was required in fulfilment of its public responsibilities'. He further added that in his view '... the law of legitimate expectation, where it is invoked in situations other than one where the expectation relied on is distinctly one of consultation, only goes so far as to say that there may arise conditions in which, if policy is to be changed, a specific person or class of persons affected must first be notified and given the right to be heard.'

R v Self [1992] 1 WLR 476 (Court of Appeal)   [174]

The appellant, who was believed to have stolen a bar of chocolate, was arrested by a store detective and another member of the public. During the course of the arrest the appellant assaulted those trying to apprehend him. The appellant was ultimately acquitted of theft but convicted of assault with intent to resist or prevent lawful apprehension, contrary to s38 of the Offences Against the Person Act 1861. On appeal, the appellant contended that as he had been acquitted on the theft charge, neither the store detective nor any other member of the public could have been empowered to arrest him under s24(5) of the Police and Criminal Evidence Act 1984, since this required proof that an arrestable offence had been committed. It followed, therefore, that the detention had not been lawful, and thus he should not have been convicted under s38. *Held*, allowing the appeal, a condition precedent to the exercise of the citizen's power of arrest under s24(5) was that an arrestable offence had already been committed. Given that the appellant had not committed an arrestable offence he had been entitled to resist his apprehension, and could not be convicted under the 1861 Act. 'The power to arrest [under s24(5)] is confined to the person guilty of the offence or anyone who the person making the arrest has reasonable grounds for suspecting to be guilty of it. But of course if he is not guilty there can be no valid suspicion ...' (*per* GARLAND J). (See also *Walters v W H Smith & Son Ltd*.)

R v Sheer Metalcraft Ltd [1954] 1 All ER 542   [175]

The accused were charged on an indictment containing 14 counts of infringements of the Iron and Steel Prices Order 1951. It was contended on behalf of the accused that this was not a valid statutory instrument in that the schedules thereto, which were an integral part of it and contained the maximum prices for different commodities of steel, had not been printed with the instrument when it was printed by the Queen's Printer, although the Minister had not certified that such printing was unnecessary. *Held*, this contention should be rejected. The statutory instrument was valid after it had been made by the Minister concerned and laid before Parliament, and the Crown had discharged the burden of proving that at the date of the alleged contraventions reasonable steps had been taken for bringing the instrument to the notice of the public or persons likely to be affected by it.

R v Sussex Justices, ex parte McCarthy [1924] 1 KB 256   [176]

McCarthy was involved in a motorcycle accident which resulted in his being sued by the victim, Whitworth, for damages, and being prosecuted for dangerous driving. At his trial for the criminal offence, the clerk to the magistrates was a partner in the firm of solicitors acting for Whitworth in his civil action against McCarthy. Further, the clerk retired with the magistrates when they came to consider their verdict which, in the event, was one of guilty. McCarthy applied for an order of certiorari to quash the conviction. *Held*, the conviction would be quashed. Actual bias was not necessary; a reasonable suspicion of bias would be sufficient to vitiate proceedings. '... a long line of cases shows that it is not merely of some importance but is of fundamental importance that justice should not only be done, but should manifestly and undoubtedly be seen to be done. The question therefore is not whether in this case the deputy clerk made any observation or offered any criticism which he might not properly have made or offered; the question is whether he was so related to the case in its civil aspect as to be unfit to act as clerk to the justices in the criminal matter. The answer to that question depends not upon what actually was done but upon what might appear to be done. Nothing is to be done which creates even a suspicion that there has been an improper interference with the course of justice' (*per* LORD HEWART CJ). (See also *Dimes* v *Grand Junction Canal Proprietors* and *R* v *Gough.*)

Racal Communications Ltd, Re [1981] AC 374 (House of Lords)   [177]

The Director of Public Prosecutions applied to Vinelott J in the High Court for an order allowing his department to inspect the books of Racal Communications on the ground that there was reasonable cause to believe that an officer of the company had committed offences in connection with the conduct of the company's affairs. VINELOTT J dismissed the application on the ground that the evidence did not disclose misconduct which would enable him to exercise his power under s441 of the Companies Act 1948 to grant the order sought. Section 441(3) of the Act declared any such decision of a High Court judge to be not appealable. Despite this, VINELOTT J granted leave to appeal against his own decision to the Court of Appeal. The Court of Appeal applied *Pearlman* v *Keepers and Governors of Harrow School* [1979] QB 56, holding that the judge had made an error going to jurisdiction, which meant that s441(3) was ineffective. The company appealed. *Held*, allowing the appeal, the jurisdiction of the Court of Appeal was wholly statutory. It had no common law power to exercise a function as a reviewing court. The doctrine of judicial review could only apply to bodies of limited jurisdiction, not High Court judges acting in a judicial capacity. The only way in which such a decision could be challenged was by way of appeal, if statute so provided. In this case s441(3) clearly removed any right of appeal. The courts would be more likely to invoke the *Anisminic* doctrine where a decision had been made on a point of law by an administrative body, as these were necessarily less expert in such matters than judicial bodies. 'The break-through made by *Anisminic* was that, as respects administrative tribunals and authorities, the old distinction between errors of law that went to jurisdiction and errors of law that did not, was for practical purposes abolished. Any error of law that could be shown to have been made by them in the course of reaching their decision on matters of fact or of administrative policy would result in their having asked themselves the wrong question with the result that the decision they reached would be a nullity ... But there is no similar presumption ... where a decision-making power is conferred by statute upon a court of law ... where the decision of the court is made final and conclusive by the statute, this may involve the survival of those subtle distinctions formerly drawn between errors of law which go to jurisdiction and errors of law which do not that did so much to confuse

English administrative law before *Anisminic*. ... Judicial review is available as a remedy for mistakes of law made by inferior courts and tribunals only. Mistakes of law made by judges of the High Court acting in their capacity as such can be corrected only by means of appeal to an appellate court; and if, as in the instant case, the statute provides that the judge's decision shall not be appealable, they cannot be corrected at all ...' (*per* LORD DIPLOCK).

Rantzen v Mirror Group Newspapers (1986) Ltd   [178]
[1993] 3 WLR 953 (Court of Appeal)

The plaintiff, a well known television presenter, brought an action for defamation against the defendant in respect of an article published in its *People* newspaper. The article claimed that the plaintiff had protected the identity of a schoolteacher, known to her to be a child molester, in return for his assistance in the preparation of a television programme on child abuse. The plaintiff claimed that the article suggested that she was thus insincere and hypocritical in her public espousal of the need for help to be given to the victims of child abuse. The plaintiff succeeded in her action for defamation and was awarded £250,000 in damages by the jury. The defendants appealed on the ground (inter alia) that to permit such an excessive award of damages to stand would amount to an infringement of the right to freedom of expression enshrined in Article 10 of the European Convention on Human Rights. *Held,* the appeal would be allowed. Section 8(2) of the Courts and Legal Services Act 1990 empowered the Court of Appeal to reduce a jury's award of damages where it considered the award to be excessive. Article 10 of the European Convention on Human Rights was relevant since, although it did not form part of domestic law, it reflected the rules of the common law in relation to freedom of expression. The right of a jury in a libel action to award unlimited damages was difficult to reconcile with the wording of Article 10, in the sense that it required any limitation on freedom of expression, such as the law of defamation, to be necessary in a democratic society. The court doubted whether such large awards were necessary to protect the reputation of plaintiffs. In order to show that the award of damages was a restriction on free speech 'prescribed by law', it was essential that the jury be given guidance on the basis of previous decisions. The award in the instant case would be reduced to £110,000.

Rederiaktiebolaget Amphitrite v R [1921] 3 KB 500   [179]

The owners of the vessel *Amphitrite* were given assurances by the British Government, acting through diplomatic channels, that if the ship docked at a British port she would not be detained in the way that similar vessels were under wartime measures. While being docked at Hull the ship was detained by the United Kingdom Government, and eventually had to be sold by the owners. After the war, the owners sued the United Kingdom Government for damages for breach of contract. *Held,* even if there was a contract in this case (which was dubious) the petition would fail, on the ground that the Government had to remain free to take what action was necessary in the national interest, and could not be hampered by the restraints of contract in this respect. 'No doubt the Government can bind itself through its officers by a commercial contract, and if it does so it must perform it like anybody else or pay damages for the breach. But this was not a commercial contract; it was an arrangement whereby the Government purported to give an assurance as to what its executive action would be in the future in relation to a particular ship in the event of her coming to this country with a particular kind of cargo. And that is, to my mind, not a contract for the breach of which damages can be sued for in a court of law. It was merely an expression of intention to act in a particular way in a certain event' (*per* ROWLATT J).

Reference re Amendment of the Constitution of Canada [180]
(1982) 125 DLR (3rd) 1

The Canadian Government had submitted to the United Kingdom proposals for a draft constitution which would effectively give Canada complete control over its own constitution. Provinces opposed to the changes sought, by way of a declaration, the view of the Supreme Court of Canada in relation to the following question: 'Is it a constitutional convention that the House of Commons and Senate of Canada will not request Her Majesty the Queen to lay before the Parliament of the United Kingdom of Great Britain and Northern Ireland a measure to amend the Constitution of Canada affecting federal-provincial relationships or the powers, rights or privileges granted or secured by the Constitution of Canada to the provinces, their legislatures or governments without first obtaining the agreement of the provinces? *Held* (by a majority of six to three), the convention was part of the Canadian constitution. The majority were guided by the views of Sir Ivor Jennings (*The Law and the Constitution* 5th ed p136) to the effect that, when considering the question of whether or not a convention was established, three questions required consideration: What are the precedents? Do the actors in the precedents believe that they are bound by a rule? Is there a reason for the rule? A single precedent with a good reason may be enough to establish the rule. A whole string of precedents without such a reason will be of no avail, unless it is perfectly certain that the persons concerned regarded themselves as bound by it.

Rhondda's (Viscountess) Claim [1922] 2 AC 339 (House of Lords) [181]

The Sex Disqualification (Removal) Act 1919 provided that a person should not be disqualified by sex or marriage from the exercise of any public function or any civil or judicial office or post. By virtue of this Act, Viscountess Rhondda, a peeress of the United Kingdom in her own right, claimed to be entitled to receive a writ of summons to Parliament. *Held*, she was not so entitled because (1) although the Act of 1919 removed a general disability it did not create a right, and the dignity of peerage was not one that gave to the holder, being a woman, the right to sit in the House of Lords; (2) in any event Parliament cannot have intended to make such an important change merely by implication.

Rice v Connolly [1966] 2 All ER 649 [182]

The defendant was thought by a police constable to be acting suspiciously and was asked several times for his name and address. He refused to give them, and when asked to accompany the police constable to a police box he refused to do so unless arrested. *Held*, the defendant's conviction of wilfully obstructing a police constable in the execution of his duty contrary to s51(1) of the Police Act 1964 should be quashed. 'It seems to me quite clear that though every citizen has a moral duty or, if some like, a social duty to assist the police, there is no legal duty to that effect, and indeed the whole basis of the common law is the right of the individual to refuse to answer questions put to him by persons in authority, and to refuse to accompany those in authority to any particular place; short, of course, of arrest' (*per* LORD PARKER CJ).

Ridge v Baldwin [1964] AC 40 (House of Lords) [183]

The defendants were the watch committee of Brighton and the plaintiff sought a declaration that their purported termination of his appointment as chief constable of Brighton was illegal, ultra vires and void. He also claimed payment of salary and pension, or, alternatively, damages. The question arose as to whether the defendants had power to dismiss the plaintiff under the Municipal Corporations

Act 1882, whereby they had a public duty to remove any constable 'whom they think negligent in the discharge of his duty, or otherwise unfit for the same'; and, if they had such power, whether they were bound to exercise it in accordance with natural justice. *Held*, assuming the defendants had such a power, they were bound to exercise it in accordance with the principles of natural justice and the terms of the Police (Discipline) Regulations 1952 which were held to be applicable to the case, by informing the plaintiff of what was alleged against him and by hearing his defence or explanation; further, the failure of the defendants to adhere to these rules rendered their decision a nullity and not merely voidable. (See also *Annamunthodo* v *Oilfield Workers' Trade Union* and *Gaiman* v *National Association for Mental Health*.)

Roberts v Hopwood [1925] AC 578 (House of Lords)   [184]

The Metropolis Management Act 1925 empowered Poplar Corporation to employ such servants as might be necessary and to allow them such wages as they (the Council) 'may think fit'. In the year ending 31 March 1922, as in the previous year, the corporation paid its lowest grade of workers, whether man or woman, a minimum wage of £4 per week as they thought that this was the lowest wage which they, as a public authority which should be a model employer, ought to pay for adult labour. During this period the cost of living was falling rapidly but the corporation said that it did not think that wages should be exclusively related to the cost of living. *Held*, the corporation had not exercised its statutory discretion reasonably and, as excessive expenditure on a lawful object may be illegal, the district auditor had rightly surcharged the aldermen and councillors in respect of the amount of the excess paid to their employees. (But see *Liversidge* v *Anderson*.)

Rodwell v Thomas [1944] 1 KB 596   [185]

The plaintiff, a civil servant, was dismissed following an inquiry as to his conduct. He brought an action for damages for wrongful dismissal and contended that the procedure adopted for hearing his case was contrary to that expressly agreed at a meeting of the National (Whitley) Council between representatives of the Crown, the Treasury and the Civil Service and impliedly incorporated in his contract of service. *Held*, his action could not succeed as the procedure adopted at the hearing was not a breach of his contract of service. Further, as a Crown servant may be dismissed at pleasure, any contract providing for his employment for a specified time or that the employment can only be terminated in certain ways is a clog upon the power of the Crown to dismiss at pleasure, and of no effect.

Rost v Edwards [1990] 2 WLR 1280   [186]

The plaintiff, an MP, sued the defendants for libel. He had been the subject of an article in the *Guardian* newspaper which allegedly implied that he had used his membership of the House of Commons Select Committee on Energy to acquire information, which he in turn sold to companies overseas. The plaintiff alleged that, as a result of this, he had been de-selected from membership of the Standing Committee of the Electricity Privatisation Bill and had not been appointed as Chair of the Energy Select Committee. To support these claims the plaintiff sought to adduce evidence of the appointment procedures of the House of Commons committees. In relation to his failure to register his business interests, the plaintiff further sought to adduce evidence as to the criteria for registration in the Register of Members' Interests and his reasons for non-registration. The question arose during the trial as to whether the evidence the plaintiff sought to adduce was inadmissible on the ground that it was protected by parliamentary privilege as it related to proceedings in Parliament. *Held*, the evidence relating to appointments to committees could not be adduced, the reason for the de-selection would involve discussing and examining the proceedings of the House because the appointment and de-selection of members of a committee of the House forms part of the proceedings of that House. The evidence relating to the Register of Members' Interests could be adduced. 'There are clearly cases where Parliament is to be the sole judge of its affairs. Equally there are clear cases where the courts are to have exclusive jurisdiction. In a case which may be described as a grey area a court, while giving full attention to the necessity for comity between the courts and Parliament, should not be astute to find a reason for ousting the jurisdiction of the court and for limiting or even defeating a proper claim by a party to litigation before it. If Parliament wishes to cover a particular area with privilege it has the ability to do so by passing an Act of Parliament giving itself the right to exclusive jurisdiction' (*per* POPPLEWELL J). (See also *Church of Scientology of California* v *Johnson-Smith* and *Prebble* v *Television New Zealand Ltd*.)

Rowling v Takaro Properties Ltd [1988] 2 WLR 419   [187]
(Privy Council)

The plaintiff had, since 1969, tried to make a commercial success of the development of a tourist lodge in New Zealand. In 1973, following several unsuccessful years' trading, a financial rescue package was put together for the lodge which involved, inter alia, the sale of shares to a Japanese company. This transaction required the consent of the New Zealand Minister of Finance, the respondent. The Minister had always made it known that he did not think that the land on which the lodge was built should ever have been sold to the plaintiff. After referring the matter to a Cabinet committee, he refused to give the consent that was needed in order for the rescue plan to go ahead. The regulations requiring the Minister's consent required him to act with reference to, inter alia, '... the public interest ... the credit, overseas resources, or development of New Zealand'. The plaintiff was successful in 1975 in obtaining judicial review of the Minister's refusal to give his consent, on the basis that he had been motivated by an irrelevant consideration, namely the desire to see the land resort to New Zealand ownership. This decision was too late to save the financial package set up to aid the lodge, however, and a receiver was appointed. The plaintiff then launched a civil action against the Minister alleging that he had negligently failed to take into account a relevant consideration when construing his powers, and had caused the plaintiff's financial loss as a result. At first instance, QUILLIAM J dismissed the case on the basis that there had been no breach of the duty of care owed. On appeal, it was held that the Minister had been in breach of the duty of care owed to the plaintiff. The Minister appealed to the Privy Council. *Held*, even assuming that a duty of care was owed by the Minister, it had not been established that it had been breached. The Minister's decision not to grant his consent to the financial arrangements was not one arrived at unreasonably or negligently, despite the judicial review proceedings. In any event, he had referred the matter to a Cabinet committee. On the broader issue of when a private law duty of care would arise in relation to the exercise of public law powers, the distinction between policy and operational decisions was not the only relevant factor. The question should be approached pragmatically, with reference to the availability of judicial review in respect of the action, the likelihood of negligence actually being established, and the danger of inducing undue caution amongst administrators. Arguably, the only private law action that should be allowed to succeed in these circumstances was an action for malicious abuse of power. There were further difficulties in identifying those situations where a minister could be said to be under a duty to obtain legal advice. (See also *Dunlop* v *Woollahra Municipal Council*.)

Roy v Kensington and Chelsea and Westminster Family   **[188]**
Practitioner Committee [1992] 2 WLR 239 (House of Lords)

The plaintiff was a general practitioner who sought payment from the defendant committee of part of his basic practice allowance. The committee had decided to withhold payment, having concluded that the plaintiff had failed to devote a substantial amount of his time to general practice. The committee derived its jurisdiction in this matter from the National Health Service (General Medical and Pharmaceutical) Regulations 1974, and the 'Statement of Fees and Allowances' published thereunder. The committee applied successfully to have the plaintiff's claim struck out as an abuse of process on the basis that he was seeking to challenge a public law decision, but this was reversed by the Court of Appeal. The committee now appealed to the House of Lords. *Held*, dismissing the appeal, regardless of whether or not there was a contract between the parties, the applicant was pursuing the issue of non-payment for work done, which was clearly a private law right, and as such the claim did not constitute an abuse of process. 'Roy's printed case contained detailed arguments in favour of a contract between him and the committee, but before your Lordships [counsel for Roy] argued that the doctor had a private law right, whether contractual or statutory. With regard to *O'Reilly* v *Mackman* he argued in the alternative. The "broad approach" was that "the rule in *O'Reilly* v *Mackman*" did not apply generally against bringing actions to vindicate private rights in all circumstances in which those actions involved a challenge to a public law act or decision, but that it merely required the aggrieved person to proceed by judicial review only when private law rights were not at stake. The "narrow approach" assumed that the rule applied generally to all proceedings in which public law acts or decisions were challenged, subject to some exceptions when private law rights were involved. There was no need in *O'Reilly* v *Mackman* to choose between these approaches, but it seems clear that Lord Diplock considered himself to be stating a general rule with exceptions. For my part, I much prefer the broad approach' (*per* LORD LOWRY).

Schmidt v Secretary of State for Home Affairs   **[189]**
[1969] 1 All ER 904 (Court of Appeal)

The plaintiffs, Scientologists, who were aliens, were granted permits for a limited stay at an educational establishment in the United Kingdom. They later applied for an extension, but in the meantime it had been announced in a Government statement that it was recognised that Scientology was socially harmful, and that Scientology establishments would no longer be recognised as 'educational establishments' for the purposes of Home Office policy. Accordingly the extension was refused. The plaintiffs sought a declaration that the decision was void in that the rules of natural justice had not been observed. *Held*, the statement of claim would be struck out because (1) the Secretary of State for Home Affairs had power under the Aliens Order 1953 to refuse admission to aliens or to refuse extension and he had exercised that power fairly and validly; (2) an alien had no right to enter the United Kingdom without leave and his stay could be terminated without reasons being given. Accordingly no question of natural justice arose. As to whether the Home Secretary had fettered his discretion by his laying down a general policy about Scientology: 'The Home Secretary may in the honest exercise of his discretion adopt a policy and announce it to those concerned so long as in exceptional cases he will listen to reasons why it should not apply' (*per* LORD DENNING MR). (But see *Attorney-General of Hong Kong* v *Ng Yuen Shiu.*)

Secretary of State for Education and Science v Tameside   **[190]**
Metropolitan Borough Council [1976] 3 WLR 641
(House of Lords)

In November 1975 the Secretary of State for Education and Science ('the Minister') approved a scheme submitted by Tameside Metropolitan Borough Council ('the

Council') for the comprehensivisation of the schools within its area. The scheme was to come into effect in September 1976. In May 1976 local elections were held in Tameside, and political control of the Council passed from the Labour party to the Conservatives. The Conservatives had campaigned on a policy of reversing the proposed change-over to comprehensive education. Section 68 of the Education Act 1944 provided: 'If the Secretary of State is satisfied, either on complaint by any person or otherwise, that any local education authority or the managers or governors of any county or voluntary school have acted or are proposing to act unreasonably with respect to the exercise of any power conferred or the performance of any duty imposed by or under this Act, he may, notwithstanding any enactment rendering the exercise of the power or the performance of the duty contingent upon the opinion of the authority or of the managers or governors, give such directions as to the exercise of the power or the performance of the duty as appear to him to be expedient ...' In June 1976 the Minister, acting under s68, directed the Council to give effect to the scheme approved in 1975. The Council refused to comply with this directive, and the Minister applied for an order of mandamus, ordering the Council to comply. The Divisional Court felt that there was evidence before the Minister that the Council was proposing to act unreasonably and granted the order sought. This decision was reversed by the Court of Appeal which considered fresh evidence indicating that schools could be changed back to the selective system before September 1976 without too much disruption. The Minister appealed. *Held*, the appeal would be dismissed. There was insufficient evidence for the Minister's view that the Council was proposing to act unreasonably, in the sense that the change of educational policy at such a late stage would cause chaos and confusion. Although the Minister's power was drafted in subjective terms, the existence or otherwise of these facts, constituting as they did a precondition to the exercise of the power, was a matter the court could have regard to. In any event, the parents must have been mindful of such possibilities when they voted for the policy. Simply because the Minister disagreed with the Council's policy did not mean that it was necessarily unreasonable. 'Local education authorities are entitled under the Act to have a policy, and this section does not enable the Secretary of State to require them to abandon or reverse a policy just because the Secretary of State disagrees with it. Specifically, the Secretary of State cannot use power under this section to impose a general policy of comprehensive education on a local authority which does not agree with the policy. He cannot direct it to bring in a scheme for total comprehensive education in its area. If it has done so he cannot direct it to implement it. If he tries to use a direction under s68 for this purpose, his direction would be clearly invalid' (*per* LORD WILBERFORCE).

Sheriff of Middlesex, Case of (1840) 11 Ad & E 273   **[191]**

Under the hand of the Speaker, the following warrant was issued and addressed to the Serjeant-at-arms: 'Whereas the House of Commons have this day resolved that [two men], having been guilty of a contempt and breach of the privileges of this House, be committed to the custody of the Serjeant-at-arms attending this House: These are therefore to require you to take into your custody the bodies of the said [two men] and them safety to keep during the pleasure of this House; for which this shall be your sufficient warrant.' *Held*, although the warrant did not state the real cause of commitment, it was good on the face of it and the court could not inquire further into the matter. However, if the grounds of commitment had been stated, the court could have examined their validity.

Ship Money, Case of (R v Hampden) (1673) 3 State Tr 826   **[192]**

In 1634, because of the encroachments of the Dutch and 'the growing insolence of the Turkish and Algerine pirates', it was sought to fit out a Navy sufficient to guard the seas by imposing upon every sea-port and place of merchandise the finding of a certain number of ships and men, in proportion to their wealth and trade, or an equivalent sum of money. In the follow year writs for 'ship money' were issued to inland counties also and John Hampden, of Buckinghamshire, was assessed to pay 20s, which sum he refused to pay. The question arose as to whether the writs were legal. *Held*, when the good and safety of the kingdom in general is concerned, and the whole kingdom is in danger, the King may, by writ, under the Great Seal of England, command all the subjects, at their charge, to provide and furnish such number of ships, with men, munition, and victuals, and for such time as the King shall think fit, for the defence and safeguard of the kingdom from such danger and peril. In such a case the King is the sole judge, both of the danger, and when and how the same is to be prevented and avoided.

Smith v East Elloe Rural District Council [1956] AC 736   **[193]**
(House of Lords)

In 1948 a compulsory purchase order was made and confirmed in respect of the appellant's land, and in 1954 she commenced an action claiming, inter alia, a declaration that the compulsory purchase order was made or confirmed wrongfully and in bad faith. The Acquisition of Land (Authorisation Procedure) Act 1946 stipulated that a compulsory purchase order must be challenged within six weeks of its making or confirmation and, subject to this, could not 'be questioned in any legal proceedings whatsoever'. *Held*, the court could not entertain the action so far as it impugned the validity of the compulsory purchase order. (See also *R* v *Secretary of State for the Environment, ex parte Ostler.*)

Stockdale v Hansard (1839) 9 Ad & E 1; 112 ER 1112   **[194]**

The Inspectors of Prisons reported to the Secretary of State that improper books published by the plaintiff had been permitted in Newgate Prison. This report was printed and published by the defendant under orders from the House of Commons. *Held*, nevertheless, the plaintiff was entitled to damages for libel. The resolution of one House alone cannot alter the law. It was for the courts to determine the existence and extent of parliamentary privilege. For the sequel see *Case of the Sheriff of Middlesex*. [Note: The Parliamentary Papers Act 1840 finally resolved the conflict. That Act conferred absolute privilege on statements in parliamentary papers.]

Stourton v Stourton [1963] 1 All ER 606   **[195]**

A wife judicially separated from her husband sought to have her husband arrested for contempt of court for failing to comply with an order made under the Married Women's Property Act 1882. The husband was a peer entitled to sit in the House of Lords. *Held*, on his claim of privilege, in regard to the existence, scope and effect of a claim of privilege, the court looked to the common law as declared in decided cases rather than to parliamentary practice; the privilege from arrest enjoyed by MPs existed only where the arrest was a civil rather than a criminal process; and since the wife was seeking to compel performance of a civil obligation, he was protected by privilege. Semble, a peer entitled to sit in the House of Lords is entitled to claim privilege whether Parliament is sitting or not.

Sydney Municipal Council v Campbell [1925] AC 338   **[196]**
(Privy Council)

The Municipal Council of Sydney had statutory powers to acquire compulsorily land required for specified purposes. The council purported to exercise this power to acquire some land for one of the specified purposes but it was found that it really wanted the land because of its probable increase in value. *Held*, it would be restrained from acquiring the land because it was exercising its powers for a purpose differing from those specified by the statute. 'A body such as the Municipal Council of Sydney, authorised to take land compulsorily for specified purposes, will not be permitted to exercise its powers for different purposes, and if it attempts to do so, the courts will interfere' (*per* DUFF J).

Thomas v Sawkins [1935] 2 KB 249   [197]

The appellant was one of the conveners of a meeting held in a private hall, which the public were invited to attend. Although they were refused admission, the respondent police sergeant and other police officers insisted on entering the hall and remaining there during the meeting. The respondent and the other officers had reasonable grounds for believing that, if they were not present, seditious speeches would be made or a breach of the peace would take place, or both. *Held*, to prevent any such offence or a breach of the peace the police were entitled to enter and to remain on the premises. 'If a constable in the execution of his duty to preserve the peace is entitled to commit an assault, it appears to me that he is equally entitled to commit a trespass' (*per* LAWRENCE J).

Town Investments Ltd v Department of the Environment   [198]
[1978] AC 359 (House of Lords)

A lease on an office block was granted to the Secretary of State for the Environment 'for and on behalf of Her Majesty'. The block was occupied by civil servants. One of the questions was to determine who the tenant was, the Secretary of State or Her Majesty. *Held*, the use of premises by government servants for government purposes constituted occupation of the premises by the Crown as tenant. The civil servants were servants of the Crown. 'Where ... we are concerned with the legal nature of the exercise of executive powers of government, I believe that some of the more Athanasian-like features of the debate in your Lordships' House could have been eliminated if instead of speaking of "the Crown" we were to speak of "the Government" a term appropriate to embrace both collectively and individually all of the ministers of the Crown and parliamentary secretaries under whose direction the administrative work of government is carried on by the civil servants employed in the various Government departments. It is through them that the executive powers of Her Majesty's Government in the United Kingdom are exercised, sometimes in the more important administrative matters in Her Majesty's name, but most often under their own official designation. Executive acts of Government that are done by any of them are acts done by "the Crown" in the fictional sense in which that expression is now used in English public law' (*per* LORD DIPLOCK).

University of Ceylon v Fernando. See Ceylon University v Fernando

Van Duyn v Home Office (Case 41/74) [1974] ECR 1337   [199]
(European Court of Justice)

The United Kingdom Government allowed the Church of Scientology to operate in England, but sought to limit its activities by not granting work permits to foreign nationals seeking to take up employment with the church in England. Ms Van Duyn, a Dutch national offered employment by the church in England, was refused a work permit by the Home Office. She sought a declaration that the Minister's prohibition was in contravention of Article 48 of the Treaty of Rome, and was not permitted under Council Directive No 64/221. Pursuant to Article 177, PENNYCUICK V-C referred three questions to the European Court of Justice: (1) Was Article 48 of the EEC Treaty directly applicable so as to confer on individuals rights enforceable by them in the courts of a Member State? (2) Was Council Directive No 64/221 of 25 February 1964, on the co-ordination of special measures concerning the movement and residence of foreign nationals which are justified on grounds of public policy, public security or public health, directly applicable so as to confer on individuals rights enforceable by them in the courts of a Member State? (3) Were Article 48 of the Treaty and Article 3 of Directive No 64/221 to be interpreted as meaning that a Member State, in the performance of its duty to base a measure taken on grounds of public policy exclusively on the personal conduct of the individual concerned, was entitled to take into account as matters of personal conduct (a) the fact that the individual is or has been associated with some body or organisation the activities of which the Member State considers contrary to the public good but which are not unlawful in that state; (b) the fact that the individual intends to take employment in the Member State with such a body or organisation, it being the case that no restrictions are placed upon nationals of the Member State who wish to take similar employment with such a body or organisation? *Held*, (1) Article 48 imposed on Member States a precise obligation which did not require the adoption of any further measure on the part either of the Community institutions or of the Member States, leaving them, in relation to its implementation, no discretionary power. (2) The Council Directive conferred on individuals rights which were enforceable by them in the courts of a Member State and which the national courts were required to protect. Where the Community authorities have, by directive, imposed on Member States the obligation to pursue a particular course of conduct, the useful effect of such an act would be weakened if individuals were prevented from relying on it before their national courts and if the latter were prevented from taking it into consideration as an element of Community law. (3) A Member State, for reasons of public policy, can, where it deems it necessary, refuse a national of another Member State the benefit of the principle of freedom of movement for workers in a case where such a national proposes to make up a particular offer of employment even though the Member State does not place a similar restriction upon its own nationals. A Member State, in imposing restrictions justified on grounds of public policy, is entitled to take into account, as a matter of personal conduct of the individual concerned, the fact that the individual is associated with some body or organisation the activities of which the Member State considers socially harmful but which are not unlawful in that State, despite the fact that no restriction is placed upon nationals of the said Member State who wish to take similar employment with these same bodies or organisations.

Walker v Baird [1892] AC 491 (Privy Council) [200]

The Admiralty ordered the defendant, a senior naval officer, to enforce a treaty relating to lobster fishing entered into with the French government. In obedience to this order, the defendant took and retained possession of a lobster factory owned by the plaintiffs, who were British subjects, and situated on British territory (Newfoundland). *Held*, the defence of act of state was no answer to the plaintiffs' claim for damages for trespass.

Walters v WH Smith & Son Ltd [1914] 1 KB 595 [201]

The plaintiff was employed by the defendants at a bookstall in King's Cross station; he also owned a newsagent's shop (which was a breach of his contract of employment). Over a period of several months the bookstall suffered a series of thefts of money and books and, consequently, the defendants set a trap for the thief by secretly marking some of the stock, including a book entitled *Traffic*. When they later sent an agent round to the newsagent's shop to buy a copy of the book it was found to bear the secret mark. On being interviewed by the defendants the plaintiff admitted taking the book but said that he had intended to pay for it. The defendant was arrested and he was subsequently prosecuted for theft. On being found not guilty the plaintiff sued the defendants for false imprisonment. *Held*, he had been falsely imprisoned since the plaintiffs were wrong in believing that he had committed a crime. 'The felony for which they gave the plaintiff into custody had not in fact been committed, and, therefore, the very basis upon which they must rest any defence of lawful excuse for the wrongful arrest of another fails them in this case ... they have failed in law to justify the arrest and there must therefore ... be judgment for the plaintiff' (*per* ISAACS CJ). (See also *R* v *Self*.)

Wandsworth London Borough Council v Winder   [202]
[1984] 3 WLR 1254 (House of Lords)

Wandsworth London Borough Council ('the Council') let one of its, flats to the respondent on a weekly tenancy. In 1981, in pursuance of its statutory obligation under the Housing Act 1957, it resolved to increase the rent and served the respondent with a notice of increase. The respondent considered it excessive and continued to pay the original rent. The following year there was a further resolution by the Council and a further notice of increase of rent was served on the respondent, who again refused to pay the increase. A notice seeking possession was served on him followed by a claim for possession in the county court on the ground of failure to pay rent. The respondent denied that he owed any sums to the Council, contending that the Council's decisions to make the increases were ultra vires and void, and each of the notices was likewise ultra vires and void. The Council, relying on *O'Reilly* v *Mackman*, applied to strike out the defence on the ground that it constituted an abuse of process, in so far as it raised public law issues by way of a defence to a private law action. The respondent contended that the decision in *O'Reilly* v *Mackman* only dealt with the initiation of proceedings, and the rule of public policy which it declared did not apply to a defendant wishing to raise a defence. The county court judge, on the Council's appeal from the registrar's decision, held that there was no distinction to be drawn between the raising of an issue of public law by way of a claim or by way of defence, and allowed the appeal. This decision was reversed by the Court of Appeal, and the Council appealed to the House of Lords. *Held*, dismissing the appeal, although the case did not fall within the exceptions formulated by Lord Diplock in *O'Reilly* v *Mackman*, it was to be distinguished from both *O'Reilly* v *Mackman* and *Cocks* v *Thanet District Council* in so far as in both of those cases the individual had instigated the proceedings against the public authority. The arguments, set out in both decisions for protecting public authorities against unmeritorious or dilatory challenges to their decisions had to be set against the arguments for preserving the ordinary rights of private citizens to defend themselves against unfounded claims. These rights had not been swept away by Order 53, which was directed to introducing a procedural reform. 'If the public interest requires that persons should not be entitled to defend actions brought against them by public authorities, where the defence rests on a challenge to a decision by the public authority, then it is for Parliament to change the law' (*per* LORD FRASER OF TULLYBELTON). (See also *Davy* v *Spelthorne Borough Council.*)

Western Fish Products Ltd v Penwith District Council   [203]
[1981] 2 All ER 204 (Court of Appeal)

The plaintiffs purchased a factory for processing fish products and inquired of the local planning authority whether or not existing use rights were in force in respect of such activities. The planning officer, Mr Giddens, replied by letter that the proposed use of the factory was within existing use rights, and in reliance on this the plaintiff company commenced use of the factory. At a later date the planning authority wrote to the plaintiffs requesting them to apply for planning permission for their use of the factory. The subsequent application was refused and an enforcement notice was issued. The plaintiffs sought a declaration claiming, inter alia, that the planning authority was estopped from denying the existing user rights by Mr Giddens's letter. The application was unsuccessful at first instance, and the plaintiffs appealed to the Court of Appeal. *Held*, dismissing the appeal, the planning officer could not make a decision that had been entrusted by Parliament to the planning authority. The situation might be different had the power to grant planning permission been delegated to the officer under s101(1) of the Local Government Act 1972. An estoppel might arise where an officer acted within the scope of his ostensible authority and there was evidence over and above his mere holding of an office to justify the person dealing with him in believing that the officer had the power to make the decision in question. Further, estoppel might be allowed where all that was involved was the waiving of a mere technicality. The extension of estoppel beyond these two exceptions could not be justified. (But see *Lever Finance Ltd* v *Westminster City London Borough Council.*)

Westminster Corporation v London and North-Western Railway Co [1905] AC 426 (House of Lords)   **[204]**

Acting under the Public Health (London) Act 1891, Westminster Corporation constructed public lavatories under the ground in the middle of Parliament Street and access to them was obtained by means of a subway with an entrance on both sides of the street. It was contended that the statutory powers were exercised improperly as the corporation's real objective was to construct a subway. *Held*, this contention could not be accepted as there was no evidence that the corporation had acted otherwise than reasonably and in good faith. 'In order to make out a case of bad faith it must be shewn that the corporation constructed this subway as a means of crossing the street under colour and pretence of providing public conveniences which were not really wanted at that particular place' (*per* LORD MACNAGHTEN).

Wheeler v Leicester City Council [1985] 1 AC 1054 (House of Lords)   **[205]**

Leicester City Council ('the Council') had for a number of years allowed Leicester Rugby Football Club ('the club') the use of one of its recreation grounds for training and matches. The Council was committed to an anti-apartheid policy, and when an English Rugby Union tour to South Africa, for which three members of the club were selected, was announced in March 1984 the Council questioned the club over its attitude to the tour. The Council asked the club whether: it supported the Government opposition to the tour; it agreed that the tour was an insult to a large proportion of the local population; it would condemn the tour and press for its cancellation; it would press the players not to participate in the tour. The club explained that whilst it deplored the apartheid system, it could not order players not to go. The Council, in August 1984, passed the following resolution: 'Resolved that the Leicester Football Club be suspended from using the Welford Road recreation ground for a period of 12 months and that the situation be reviewed at the end of that period in the light of the club's attitude to sporting links with South Africa.' The Council relied (inter alia) upon s71 of the Race Relations Act 1976 as justification for its actions. Section 71 states: 'Without prejudice to their obligation to comply with any other provision of this Act, it shall be the duty of every local authority to make appropriate arrangements with a view to securing that the various functions are carried out with due regard to the need: (a) to eliminate unlawful racial discrimination and (b) to promote equality of opportunity, and good relations, between persons of different racial groups.' Six club members sought judicial review of the Council's action, but were unsuccessful before both the Divisional Court and the Court of Appeal. They renewed their appeal before the House of Lords. *Held*, allowing the appeal, as the club had been guilty of no misconduct it was unreasonable for the Council to penalise it for non-compliance with its anti-apartheid policy. The Council could not use its statutory powers of management or any other statutory powers for the purposes of punishing the club when the club had done no wrong. The Council had not acted fairly towards the club. (See also *Associated Provincial Picture Houses Ltd* v *Wednesbury Corporation* and *Congreve* v *Home Office*.)

White and Collins v Minister of Health [1939] 2 KB 838 [206]
(Court of Appeal)

Ripon Borough Council exercised powers of compulsory purchase over land owned by the appellants. By s75 of the Housing Act 1936, these powers were not to be exercised over land forming part of any park, garden, or pleasure ground required for the amenity or convenience of any house. The appellants contended that some of the land over which the Council had exercised its powers fell within the protection of s75 and thus could not be acquired in this way. A public inquiry was held into objections to the scheme, but the Minister confirmed the compulsory purchase order. The landowners applied to the High Court to quash the Minister's confirmation, but CHARLES J held the question arising under s75 to be one of fact and ruled that it was not open to the court to reconsider the decision. The landowners appealed. *Held*, the order would be quashed. Given that the jurisdiction to make the order was dependent on a finding of fact, it was self-evident that the court which had to consider whether there was jurisdiction to make or confirm the order must have been entitled to review the vital finding, on which the existence of the jurisdiction relied upon depended, if the right to apply to the court was not to be illusory. There was no evidence before the inspector in the instant case sufficient to entitle the local authority or the Minister to come to a conclusion that the land in question was not part of the park in question.

Wise v Dunning [1902] 1 KB 167 [207]

The appellant called himself a Protestant 'crusader'. He went about carrying a crucifix and, on his own admission, made use of expressions very insulting to the faith of the Roman Catholic population among whom he went. Riots and disturbances had resulted from his conduct previously and, on the occasion in question, the magistrate found that the language of the appellant was provocative so that disturbances were likely to occur again. Large crowds had assembled in the streets, and a serious riot was only prevented by the interference of the police. The appellant was taken before the magistrate and bound over to keep the peace and be of good behaviour for twelve months (recognisance in the sum of £100 with two sureties of £50 each). He appealed against this order. *Held*, dismissing the appeal, the magistrate was entitled to bind the appellant over to be of good behaviour since he had previously used language and conduct the natural consequence of which was that breaches of the peace occurred and intended to do the same again in the future.

Zamora, The [1916] 2 AC 77 (Privy Council) [208]

In the course of his judgment LORD PARKER OF WADDINGTON said: 'The idea that the King in Council, or indeed any branch of the executive, has power to prescribe or alter the law to be administered by courts of law in this country is out of harmony with the principles of our constitution. It is true that under a number of modern statutes, various branches of the executive have power to make rules having the force of statutes, but all such rules derive their validity from the statute which creates the power, and not from the executive body by which they are made.' (But see *Council of Civil Service Unions* v *Minister of the Civil Service*.)

Statutes

MAGNA CARTA 1297
(25 Edw 1)

29 Imprisonment, etc, contrary to law   [209]

No freeman shall be taken or imprisoned, or be disseised of his freehold, or liberties, or free customs, or be outlawed, or exiled, or any other wise destroyed; nor will we not pass upon him, nor condemn him, but by lawful judgment of his peers, or by the law of the land. We will sell to no man, we will not deny or defer to any man either justice or right.

BILL OF RIGHTS 1688
(1 Will & Mar sess 2 c 2)
[210]

Whereas the lords spirituall and temporall and comons assembled at Westminster lawfully fully and freely representing all the estates of the people of this realme did upon the thirteenth day of February in the yeare of our Lord one thousand six hundred and eighty eight present unto their Majesties then called and known by the names and stile of William and Mary Prince and Princess of Orange being present in their proper persons a certaine declaration in writeing made by the said lords and comons in the words following viz

Whereas the late King James the Second by the assistance of diverse evill councillors judges and ministers imployed by him did endeavour to subvert and extirpate the Protestant religion and the lawes and liberties of this kingdome

By assumeing and exerciseing a power of dispensing with and suspending of lawes and the execution of lawes without consent of Parlyament.

By committing and prosecuting diverse worthy prelates for humbly petitioning to be excused from concurring to the said assumed power.

By issueing and causeing to be executed a commission under the great seale for erecting a court called the court of commissioners for ecclesiasticall causes.

By levying money for and to the use of the Crowne by pretence of prerogative for other time and in other manner then the same was granted by Parlyament.

By raising and keeping a standing army within this kingdome in time of peace without consent of Parlyament and quartering soldiers contrary to law.

By causing severall good subjects being protestants to be disarmed at the same time when papists were both armed and imployed contrary to law.

By vilating the freedome of election of members to serve in Parlyament.

By prosecutions in the Court of King's Bench for matters and causes cognizable onely in Parlyament and by diverse other arbitrary and illegall courses.

And whereas of late yeares partiall corrupt and unqualifyed persons have beene returned and served on juryes in tryalls and particularly diverse jurors in tryalls for high treason which were not freeholders.

And excessive baile hath beene required of persons committed in criminall cases to elude the benefitt of the lawes made for the liberty of the subjects.

And excessive fines have been imposed.

And illegall and cruell punishments inflicted.

And severall grants and promises made of fines and forfeitures before any conviction or judgement against the persons upon whome the same were to be levyed.

All which are utterly and directly contrary to the knowne lawes and statutes and freedom of this realme.

And whereas the said late King James the Second haveing abdicated the government and the throne being thereby vacant his Hignesse the Prince of Orange (whome it hath pleased Almighty God to make the glorious instrument of delivering this kingdome from popery and arbitrary power) did (by the advice of the lords spirituall and temporall and diverse principall persons of the commons) cause letters to be written to the lords spirituall and temporall being protestants and other letters to the several countyes cityes universities boroughs and cinque ports for the choosing of such persons to represent them as were of right to be sent to Parlyament to meete and sitt at Westminster upon the two and twentyeth day of January in this yeare one thousand six hundred eighty and eight in order to such an establishment as that their religion lawes and liberties might not againe be in danger of being subverted, upon which letters elections haveing beene accordingly made.

And thereupon the said lords spirituall and temporall and commons pursuant to their respective letters and elections being now assembled in a full and free representative of this nation takeing into their most serious consideration the best means for attaining the ends aforesaid doe in the first place (as their auncestors in like case have usually done) for the vindicating and asserting their auntient rights and liberties, declare

1 Suspending power   [211]

That the pretended power of suspending of laws or the execution of laws by regall authority without consent of Parlyament is illegall.

2 Late dispensing power   [212]

That the pretended power of dispensing with laws or the execution of laws by regall authoritie as it hath been assumed and exercised of late is illegall.

3 Ecclesiastical courts illegal   [213]

That the commission for erecting the late court of commissioners for ecclesiastical causes and all other commissions and courts of like nature are illegal and pernicious.

4 Levying money   [214]

That levying money for or to the use of the Crowne by pretence of prerogative without grant of Parlyament for longer time or in other manner then the same is or shall be granted is illegal.

5 Right to petition [215]

That it is the right of the subjects to petition the King and all commitments and prosecutions for such petitioning are illegal.

6 Standing army [216]

That the raising or keeping a standing army within the kingdome in time of peace unlesse it be with consent of Parlyament is against law.

7 Subjects' arms [217]

That the subjects which are protestants may have arms for their defence suitable to their conditions and as allowed by law.

8 Freedom of election [218]

That election of members of Parlyament ought to be free.

9 Freedom of speech [219]

That the freedome of speech and debates or proceedings in Parlyament ought not to be impeached or questioned in any court or place out of Parlyament.

10 Excessive bail [220]

That excessive baile ought not to be required nor excessive fines imposed nor cruell and unusuall punishments inflicted.

11 Juries [221]

That jurors ought to be duly impannelled and returned ...

[As amended by the Juries Act 1825, s62; Statute Law Revision Act 1950.]

ACT OF SETTLEMENT 1700
(12 & 13 Will 3 c 2)

1 The Princess Sophia, Electress and Duchess dowager [222] of Hanover, daughter of the late Queen of Bohemia, daughter of King James the First, to inherit after the King and the Princess Anne, in default of issue of the said princess and his Majesty, respectively: and the heirs of her body, being protestants

The most excellent Princess Sophia Electress and Duchess dowager of Hanover daughter of the most excellent Princess Elizabeth late Queen of Bohemia daughter of our late sovereign lord king James the First of happy memory be and is hereby declared to be the next in succession in the protestant line to the imperiall crown and dignity of the said realms of England France and Ireland with the dominions and territories thereunto belonging after his Majesty and the Princess Ann of Denmark and in default of issue of the said Princess Ann and of his Majesty respectively and that from and after the deceases of his said Majesty our now sovereign lord and of her royall Highness the Princess Ann of Denmark and for default of issue of the said Princess Ann and of his Majesty respectively the crown

91

and regall government of the said kingdoms of England France and Ireland and of the dominions thereunto belonging with the royall state and dignity of the said realms and all honours stiles titles regalities prerogatives powers jurisdictions and authorities to the same belonging and appertaining shall be remain and continue to the said most excellent Princess Sophia and the heirs of her body being protestants. And thereunto the said lords spirituall and temporall and commons shall and will in the name of all the people of this realm most humbly and faithfully submitt themselves their heirs and posterities and do faithfully promise that after the deceases of his Majesty and her royall Highness and the failure of the heirs of their respective bodies to stand to maintain and defend the said Princess Sophia and the heirs of her body being protestants according to the limitation and succession of the crown in this Act specified and contained to the utmost of their powers with their lives and estates against all persons whatsoever that shall attempt any thing to the contrary.

2 The persons inheritable by this Act, holding   [223] communion with the church of Rome, incapacitated as by the former Act, to take the oath at their coronation, according to Stat 1 W & M c 6

Provided always and it is hereby enacted that all and every person and persons who shall or may take or inherit the said crown by vertue of the limitation of this present Act and is are or shall be reconciled to or shall hold communion with the see or church of Rome or shall profess the popish religion or shall marry a papist shall be subject to such incapacities as in such case or cases are by the said recited Act provided enacted and established. And that every King and Queen of this realm who shall come to and succeed in the imperiall crown of this kingdom by vertue of this Act shall have the coronation oath administered to him her or them at their respective coronations according to the Act of Parliament made in the first year of the reign of his Majesty and the said late Queen Mary intituled An Act for establishing the coronation oath and shall make subscribe and repeat the declaration in the Act first above recited mentioned or referred to in the manner and form thereby prescribed.

3 Further provisions for securing the religion, laws,   [224] and liberties of these realms

And whereas it is requisite and necessary that some further provision be made for securing our religion laws and liberties from and after the death of his Majesty and the Princess Ann of Denmark and in default of issue of the body of the said princess and of his Majesty respectively. Be it enacted by the Kings most excellent Majesty by and with the advice and consent of the lords spirituall and temporall and commons in Parliament assembled and by the authority of the same.

That whosoever shall hereafter come to the possession of this crown shall joyn in communion with the Church of England as by law established.

That in case the crown and imperiall dignity of this realm shall hereafter come to any person not being a native of this kingdom of England this nation be not obliged to ingage in any warr for the defence of any dominions or territories which do not belong to the crown of England without the consent of Parliament.

That after the said limitation shall take effect as aforesaid no person born out of the kingdoms of England Scotland or Ireland or the dominions thereunto belonging (although he be made a denizen[)] (except such as are born of English parents) shall be capable to be of the privy council or a member of either House of Parliament or to enjoy any office or place of trust either civill or military or to have any grant of land tenements or hereditaments from the Crown to himself or to any other or others in trust for him.

That no pardon under the great seal of England be pleadable to an impeachment by the commons in Parliament.

4 The laws and statutes of the realm confirmed [225]

And whereas the laws of England are the birthright of the people thereof and all the Kings and Queens who shall ascend the throne of this realm ought to administer the government of the same according to the said laws and all their officers and ministers ought to serve them respectively according to the same. The said lords spirituall and temporall and commons do therefore further humbly pray that all the laws and statutes of this realm for securing the established religion and the rights and liberties of the people thereof and all other laws and statutes of the same now in force may be ratified and confirmed. And the same are by his Majesty by and with the advice and consent of the said lords spirituall and temporall and commons and by authority of the same ratified and confirmed accordingly.

[As amended by 4 & 5 Anne c 20, ss27, 28; 1 Geo 1 stat 2 c 51; Status of Aliens Act 1914, s28, Schedule 3.]

PARLIAMENT ACT 1911
(1 & 2 Geo 5 c 13)

[226]

Whereas it is expedient that provision should be made for regulating the relations between the two Houses of Parliament:

And whereas it is intended to substitute for the House of Lords as it at present exists a Second Chamber constituted on a popular instead of hereditary basis, but such substitution cannot be immediately brought into operation:

And whereas provision will require hereafter to be made by Parliament in a measure effecting such substitution for limiting and defining the powers of the new Second Chamber, but it is expedient to make such provision as in this Act appears for restricting the existing powers of the House of Lords.

1 Powers of House of Lords as to Money Bills [227]

(1) If a Money Bill, having been passed by the House of Commons, and sent up to the House of Lords at least one month before the end of the session, is not passed by the House of Lords without amendment within one month after it is so sent up to that House, the Bill shall, unless the House of Commons direct to the contrary, be presented to His Majesty and become an Act of Parliament on the Royal Assent being signified, notwithstanding that the House of Lords have not consented to the Bill.

(2) A Money Bill means a Public Bill which in the opinion of the Speaker of the House of Commons contains only provisions dealing with all or any of the following subjects, namely, the imposition, repeal, remission, alteration, or regulation of taxation; the imposition for the payment of debt or other financial purposes of charges on the Consolidated Fund, the National Loans Fund or on money provided by Parliament, or the variation or repeal of any such charges; supply; the appropriation, receipt, custody, issue or audit of accounts of public money; the raising or guarantee of any loan or the repayment thereof; or

subordinate matters incidental to those subjects or any of them. In this subsection the expressions 'taxation', 'public money', and 'loan' respectively do not include any taxation, money, or loan raised by local authorities or bodies for local purposes.

(3) There shall be endorsed on every Money Bill when it is sent up to the House of Lords and when it is presented to His Majesty for assent the certificate of the Speaker of the House of Commons signed by him that it is a Money Bill. Before giving his certificate, the Speaker shall consult, if practicable, two members to be appointed from the Chairmen's Panel at the beginning of each Session by the Committee of Selection.

2 Restriction of the powers of the House of Lords as [228] to Bills other than Money Bills

(1) If any Public Bill (other than a Money Bill or a Bill containing any provision to extend the maximum duration of Parliament beyond five years) is passed by the House of Commons in two successive sessions (whether of the same Parliament or not), and, having been sent up to the House of Lords at least one month before the end of the session, is rejected by the House of Lords in each of those sessions, that Bill shall, on its rejection for the second time by the House of Lords, unless the House of Commons direct to the contrary, be presented to His Majesty and become an Act of Parliament on the Royal Assent being signified thereto, notwithstanding that the House of Lords have not consented to the Bill: Provided that this provision shall not take effect unless one year has elapsed between the date of the second reading in the first of those sessions of the Bill in the House of Commons and the date on which it passes the House of Commons in the second of those sessions.

(2) When a Bill is presented to His Majesty for assent in pursuance of the provisions of this section, there shall be endorsed on the Bill the certificate of the Speaker of the House of Commons signed by him that the provisions of this section have been duly complied with.

(3) A Bill shall be deemed to be rejected by the House of Lords if it is not passed by the House of Lords either without amendment or with such amendments only as may be agreed to by both Houses.

(4) A Bill shall be deemed to be the same Bill as a former Bill sent up to the House of Lords in the preceding session if, when it is sent up to the House of Lords, it is identical with the former Bill or contains only such alterations as are certified by the Speaker of the House of Commons to be necessary owing to the time which has elapsed since the date of the former Bill, or to represent any amendments which have been made by the House of Lords in the former Bill in the preceding session, and any amendments which are certified by the Speaker to have been made by the House of Lords in the second session and agreed to by the House of Commons shall be inserted in the Bill as presented for Royal Assent in pursuance of this section: Provided that the House of Commons may, if they think fit, on the passage of such a Bill through the House in the second session, suggest any further amendments without inserting the amendments in the Bill, and any such suggested amendments shall be considered by the House of Lords, and, if agreed to by that House, shall be treated as amendments made by the House of Lords and agreed to by the House of Commons; but the exercise of this power by the House of Commons shall not affect the operation of this section in the event of the Bill being rejected by the House of Lords.

3 Certificate of Speaker [229]

Any certificate of the Speaker of the House of Commons given under this Act shall be conclusive for all purposes, and shall not be questioned in any court of law.

4 Enacting words [230]

(1) In every Bill presented to His Majesty under the preceding provisions of this Act, the words of enactment shall be as follows, that is to say:

'Be it enacted by the King's most Excellent Majesty, by and with the advice and consent of the Commons in this present Parliament assembled, in accordance with the provisions of the Parliament Acts 1911 and 1949 and by authority of the same, as follows.'

(2) Any alteration of a Bill necessary to give effect to this section shall not be deemed to be an amendment of the Bill.

5 Provisional Order Bills excluded [231]

In this Act the expression 'Public Bill' does not include any Bill for confirming a Provisional Order.

6 Saving for existing rights and privileges of the [232]
House of Commons

Nothing in this Act shall diminish or qualify the existing rights and privileges of the House of Commons.

7 Duration of Parliament [233]

Five years shall be substituted for seven years as the time fixed for the maximum duration of Parliament under the Septennial Act 1715.

[As amended by the Parliament Act 1949, s2(2); National Loans Act 1968, s1(5).]

OFFICIAL SECRETS ACT 1911
(1 & 2 Geo 5 c 28)

1 Penalties for spying [234]

(1) If any person for any purpose prejudicial to the safety or interests of the State –

(a) approaches, inspects, passes over, or is in the neighbourhood of, or enters any prohibited place within the meaning of this Act; or

(b) makes any sketch, plan, model, or note which is calculated to be or might be or is intended to be directly or indirectly useful to an enemy; or

(c) obtains, collects, records, or publishes, or communicates to any other person any secret official code word, or pass word, or any sketch, plan, model, article, or note, or other document or information which is calculated to be or might be or is intended to be directly or indirectly useful to an enemy;

he shall be guilty of [an offence]

(2) On a prosecution under this section, it shall not be necessary to show that the accused person was guilty of any particular act tending to show a purpose prejudicial to the safety or interests of the State, and, notwithstanding that no such act is proved against him, he may be convicted if, from the circumstances of the case, or his conduct, or his known character as proved, it appears that his

purpose was a purpose prejudicial to the safety or interests of the State; and if any sketch, plan, model, article, note, document, or information relating to or used in any prohibited place within the meaning of this Act, or anything in such a place or any secret official code word or pass word, is made, obtained, collected, recorded, published, or communicated by any person other than a person acting under lawful authority, it shall be deemed to have been made, obtained, collected, recorded, published or communicated for a purpose prejudicial to the safety or interests of the State unless the contrary is proved.

3 Definition of prohibited place   [235]

For the purposes of this Act, the expression 'prohibited place' means –

(a) Any work of defence, arsenal, naval or air force establishment or station, factory, dockyard, mine, minefield, camp, ship, or aircraft belonging to or occupied by or on behalf of His Majesty, or any telegraph, telephone, wireless or signal station, or office so belonging or occupied, and any place belonging to or occupied by or on behalf of His Majesty and used for the purpose of building, repairing, making or storing any munitions of war, or any sketches, plans, models, or documents relating thereto, or for the purpose of getting any metals, oil, or minerals of use in time of war; and

(b) any place not belonging to His Majesty where any munitions of war, or any sketches, models, plans or documents relating thereto, are being made, repaired, gotten, or stored under contract with, or with any person on behalf of, His Majesty, or otherwise on behalf of His Majesty; and

(c) any place belonging to or used for the purposes of His Majesty which is for the time being declared by order of a Secretary of State to be a prohibited place for the purposes of this section on the ground that information with respect thereto, or damage thereto, would be useful to an enemy; and

(d) any railway, road, way, or channel, or other means of communication by land or water (including any works or structures being part thereof or connected therewith), or any place used for gas, water, or electricity works or other works for purposes of a public character, or any place where any munitions of war, or any sketches, models, plans or documents relating thereto, are being made, repaired, or stored otherwise than on behalf of His Majesty, which is for the time being declared by order of a Secretary of State to be a prohibited place for the purposes of this section, on the ground that information with respect thereto, or the destruction or obstruction thereof, or interference therewith, would be useful to an enemy.

[As amended by the Official Secrets Act 1920, ss10, 11, Schedules 1, 2.]

EMERGENCY POWERS ACT 1920
(10 & 11 Geo 5 c 55)

1 Issue of proclamations of emergency   [236]

(1) If at any time it appears to His Majesty that there have occurred, or are about to occur, events of such a nature as to be calculated, by interfering with the supply and distribution of food, water, fuel, or light, or with the means of locomotion, to deprive the community, or any substantial portion of the community, of the essentials of life, His Majesty may, by proclamation (hereinafter referred to as a proclamation of emergency), declare that a state of emergency exists. No such proclamation shall be in force for more than one month, without prejudice to the issue of another proclamation at or before the end of that period.

(2) Where a proclamation of emergency has been made the occasion thereof shall forthwith be communicated to Parliament, and, if Parliament is then separated by such adjournment or prorogation as will not expire within five days, a proclamation shall be issued for the meeting of Parliament within five days, and Parliament shall accordingly meet and sit upon the day appointed by that proclamation, and shall continue to sit and act in like manner as if it had stood adjourned or prorogued to the same day.

2 Emergency regulations [237]

(1) Where a proclamation of emergency has been made, and so long as the proclamation is in force, it shall be lawful for His Majesty in Council, by Order, to make regulations for securing the essentials of life to the community, and those regulations may confer or impose on a Secretary of State or other Government department, or any other persons in His Majesty's service or acting on His Majesty's behalf, such powers and duties as His Majesty may deem necessary for the preservation of the peace, for securing and regulating the supply and distribution of food, water, fuel, light, and other necessities, for maintaining the means of transit or locomotion, and for any other purposes essential to the public safety and the life of the community, and may make such provisions incidental to the powers aforesaid as may appear to His Majesty to be required for making the exercise of those powers effective: Provided that nothing in this Act shall be construed to authorise the making of any regulations imposing any form of compulsory military service or industrial conscription: Provided also that no such regulation shall make it an offence for any person or persons to take part in a strike, or peacefully to persuade any other person or persons to take part in a strike.

(2) Any regulations so made shall be laid before Parliament as soon as may be after they are made, and shall not continue in force after the expiration of seven days from the time when they are so laid unless a resolution is passed by both Houses providing for the continuance thereof.

(3) The regulations may provide for the trial, by courts of summary jurisdiction, of persons guilty of offences against the regulations; so, however, that the maximum penalty which may be inflicted for any offence against any such regulations shall be imprisonment with or without hard labour for a term of three months, or a fine not exceeding level 5 on the standard scale, or not exceeding a lesser amount, or both such imprisonment and fine, together with the forfeiture of any goods or money in respect of which the offence has been committed: Provided that no such regulations shall alter any existing procedure in criminal cases, or confer any right to punish by fine or imprisonment without trial.

(4) The regulations so made may be added to, altered, or revoked by resolution of both Houses of Parliament or by regulations made in like manner and subject to the like provisions as the original regulations.

(5) The expiry or revocation of any regulations so made shall not be deemed to have affected the previous operation thereof, or the validity of any action taken thereunder, or any penalty or punishment incurred in respect of any contravention or failure to comply therewith, or any proceeding or remedy in respect of any such punishment or penalty.

[As amended by the Statute Law Revision Act 1963; Emergency Powers Act 1964, s1; Criminal Justice Act 1982, s41; Statute Law (Repeals) Act 1986; Statute Law (Repeals) Act 1993, s1(1), Schedule 1, Part XIV.]

OFFICIAL SECRETS ACT 1920
(10 & 11 Geo 5 c 75)

1 Unauthorised use of uniforms; falsification of reports,   **[238]**
forgery, personation, and false documents

(1) If any person for the purpose of gaining admission, or of assisting any other person to gain admission, to a prohibited place, within the meaning of the Official Secrets Act 1911 (hereinafter referred to as 'the principal Act'), or for any other purpose prejudicial to the safety or interests of the State within the meaning of the said Act –

(a) uses or wears, without lawful authority, any naval, military, air-force, police, or other official uniform, or any uniform so nearly resembling the same as to be calculated to deceive, or falsely represents himself to be a person who is or has been entitled to use or wear any such uniform; or

(b) orally, or in writing in any declaration or application, or in any document signed by him or on his behalf, knowingly makes or connives at the making of any false statement or any omission; or

(c) tampers with any passport or any naval, military, air-force, police, or official pass, permit, certificate, licence, or other document of a similar character (hereinafter in this section referred to as an official document), or has in his possession any forged, altered, or irregular official document; or

(d) personates, or falsely represents himself to be a person holding, or in the employment of a person holding office under His Majesty, or to be or not to be a person to whom an official document or secret official code word, or pass word, has been duly issued or communicated, or with intent to obtain an official document, secret official code word or pass word, whether for himself or any other person, knowingly makes any false statement; or

(e) uses, or has in his possession, or under his control, without the authority of the Government Department or the authority concerned, any die, seal, or stamp of or belonging to, or used, made or provided by any Government Department, or by any diplomatic, naval, military, or air force authority appointed by or acting under the authority of His Majesty, or any die, seal or stamp so nearly resembling any such die, seal or stamp as to be calculated to deceive, or counterfeits any such die, seal or stamp, or uses, or has in his possession, or under his control, any such counterfeited die, seal or stamp;

he shall be guilty of [an offence] ...

(3) In the case of any prosecution under this section involving the proof of a purpose prejudicial to the safety or interests of the State, subsection (2) of section one of the principal Act shall apply in like manner as it applies to prosecutions under that section.

6 Duty of giving information as to commission   **[239]**
of offences

(1) Where a chief officer of police is satisfied that there is reasonable ground for suspecting that an offence under section 1 of the principal Act has been committed and for believing that any person is able to furnish information as to the offence or suspected offence, he may apply to a Secretary of State for permission to exercise the powers conferred by this subsection and, if such permission is granted, he may authorise a superintendent of police, or any police officer not below the rank of inspector, to require the person believed to be able to furnish information to give any information in his power relating to the offence or suspected offence, and, if so required and on tender of his reasonable

expenses, to attend at such reasonable time and place as may be specified by the superintendent or other officer; and if a person required in pursuance of such an authorisation to give information, or to attend as aforesaid, fails to comply with any such requirement or knowingly gives false information, he shall be guilty of [an offence].

(2) Where a chief officer of police has reasonable grounds to believe that the case is one of great emergency and that in the interest of the State immediate action is necessary, he may exercise the powers conferred by the last foregoing subsection without applying for or being granted the permission of a Secretary of State, but if he does so shall forthwith report the circumstances to the Secretary of State.

(3) References in this section to a chief officer of police shall be construed as including references to any other officer of police expressly authorised by a chief officer of police to act on his behalf for the purposes of this section when by reason of illness, absence, or other cause he is inable to do so.

[As amended by the Official Secrets Act 1939, s1; Forgery and Counterfeiting Act 1981, s30, Schedule, Pt I.]

STATUTE OF WESTMINSTER 1931
(22 & 23 Geo 5 c 4)

Preamble   [240]

Whereas the delegates of His Majesty's Governments in the United Kingdom, the Dominion of Canada, the Commonwealth of Australia, the Dominion of New Zealand, the Union of South Africa, the Irish Free State and Newfoundland, at Imperial Conferences holden at Westminster in the years of our Lord nineteen hundred and twenty-six and nineteen hundred and thirty did concur in making the declarations and resolutions set forth in the Reports of the said Conferences:

And whereas it is meet and proper to set out by way of preamble to this Act that, inasmuch as the Crown is the symbol of the free association of the members of the British Commonwealth of Nations, and as they are united by a common allegiance to the Crown, it would be in accord with the established constitutional position of all the members of the Commonwealth in relation to one another that any alteration in the law touching the Succession to the Throne or the Royal Style and Titles shall hereafter require the assent as well of the Parliaments of all the Dominions as of the Parliament of the United Kingdom:

And whereas it is in accord with the established constitutional position that no law hereafter made by the Parliament of the United Kingdom shall extend to any of the said Dominions as part of the law of that Dominion otherwise than at the request and with the consent of that Dominion:

And whereas it is necessary for the ratifying, confirming and establishing of certain of the said declarations and resolutions of the said Conferences that a law be made and enacted in due form by authority of the Parliament of the United Kingdom:

And whereas the Dominion of Canada, the Commonwealth of Australia, the Dominion of New Zealand, the Union of South Africa, the Irish Free State and Newfoundland have severally requested and consented to the submission of a measure to the Parliament of the United Kingdom for making such provision with regard to the matters aforesaid as is hereafter in that Act contained:

Now, therefore, be it enacted by the King's most Excellent Majesty by and with the advice and consent of the Lords Spiritual and Temporal, and Commons, in this present Parliament assembled, and by the authority of the same, as follows –

1 Meaning of 'Dominion' in this Act   [241]

In this Act the expression 'Dominion' means any of the following Dominions, that is to say, the Dominion of Canada, the Commonwealth of Australia, the Dominion of New Zealand, the Irish Free State and Newfoundland.

2 Validity of laws made by Parliament of a Dominion   [242]

(1) The Colonial Laws Validity Act 1865, shall not apply to any law made after the commencement of this Act by the Parliament of a Dominion.

(2) No law and no provision of any law made after the commencement of this Act by the Parliament of a Dominion shall be void or inoperative on the ground that it is repugnant to the law of England, or to the provisions of any existing or future Act of Parliament of the United Kingdom, or to any order, rule or regulation made under any such Act, and the powers of the Parliament of a Dominion shall include the power to repeal or amend any such Act, order, rule or regulation in so far as the same is part of the law of the Dominion.

3 Power of Parliament of Dominion to legislate extra-territorially   [243]

It is hereby declared and enacted that the Parliament of a Dominion has full power to make laws having extra-territorial operation.

4 Parliament of United Kingdom not to legislate for Dominion except by consent   [244]

No Act of Parliament of the United Kingdom passed after the commencement of this Act shall extend, or be deemed to extend, to a Dominion as part of the law of that Dominion unless it is expressly declared in that Act that that Dominion has requested, and consented to, the enactment thereof.

NB. In so far as s4, above, applies to Canada and Australia, it was repealed by the Canada Act 1982 and Australia Act 1986 respectively. By virtue of the Ireland Act 1949, the Irish Free State (now Republic of Ireland) ceased to be part of Her Majesty's dominions.

[As amended by the South Africa Act 1962, s2(3), Schedule 5.]

PUBLIC ORDER ACT 1936
(1 Edw 8 & 1 Geo 6 c 6)

1 Prohibition of uniforms in connection with political objects   [245]

(1) Subject as hereinafter provided, any person who in any public place or at any public meeting wears uniform signifying his association with any political organisation or with the promotion of any political object shall be guilty of an offence: Provided that, if the chief officer of police is satisfied that the wearing of any such uniform as aforesaid on any ceremonial, anniversary, or other special occasion will not be likely to involve risk of public disorder, he may, with the consent of a Secretary of State, by order permit the wearing of such uniform on that occasion either absolutely or subject to such conditions as may be specified in the order.

(2) Where any person is charged before any court with an offence under this section, no further proceedings in respect thereof shall be taken against him

without the consent of the Attorney-General except such as are authorised by section 6 of the Prosecution of Offences Act 1979 so, however, that if that person is remanded in custody he shall, after the expiration of a period of eight days from the date on which he was so remanded, be entitled to be released on bail without sureties unless within that period the Attorney-General has consented to such further proceedings as aforesaid.

2 Prohibition of quasi-military organisations [246]

(1) If the members or adherents of any association of persons, whether incorporated or not, are –

(a) organised or trained or equipped for the purpose of enabling them to be employed in usurping the functions of the police or of the armed forces of the Crown; or

(b) organised and trained or organised and equipped either for the purpose of enabling them to be employed for the use or display of physical force in promoting any political object, or in such manner as to arouse reasonable apprehension that they are organised and either trained or equipped for that purpose;

then any person who takes part in the control or management of the association, or in so organising or training as aforesaid any members or adherents thereof, shall be guilty of an offence under this section: Provided that in any proceedings against a person charged with the offence of taking part in the control or management of such an association as aforesaid it shall be a defence to that charge to prove that he neither consented to nor connived at the organisation, training, or equipment of members or adherents of the association in contravention of the provisions of this section.

(2) No prosecution shall be instituted under this section without the consent of the Attorney-General ...

(5) If a judge of the High Court is satisfied by information on oath that there is reasonable ground for suspecting that an offence under this section has been committed, and that evidence of the commission thereof is to be found at any premises or place specified in the information, he may, on an application made by an officer of police of a rank not lower than that of inspector, grant a search warrant authorising any such officer as aforesaid named in the warrant together with any other persons named in the warrant and any other officers of police to enter the premises or place at any time within one month from the date of the warrant, if necessary by force, and to search the premises or place and every person found therein, and to seize anything found on the premises or place or on any such person which the officer has reasonable ground for suspecting to be evidence of the commission of such an offence as aforesaid: Provided that no woman shall, in pursuance of a warrant issued under this subsection, be searched except by a woman.

(6) Nothing in this section shall be construed as prohibiting the employment of a reasonable number of persons as stewards to assist in the preservation of order at any public meeting held upon private premises, or the making of arrangements for that purpose or the instruction of the persons to be so employed in their lawful duties as such stewards, or their being furnished with badges or other distinguishing signs.

[As amended by the Criminal Jurisdiction Act 1975, s14(4), Schedule 5, para 1; Bail Act 1976, s12, Schedule 2, para 10; Prosecution of Offences Act 1979, s11(1), Schedule 1.]

STATUTORY INSTRUMENTS ACT 1946
(9 & 10 Geo 6 c 36)

1 Definition of 'Statutory Instrument' [247]

(1) Where by this Act or any Act passed after the commencement of this Act power to make, confirm or approve orders, rules, regulations or other subordinate legislation is conferred on His Majesty in Council or on any Minister of the Crown then, if the power is expressed –

(a) in the case of a power conferred on His Majesty, to be exercisable by Order in Council;

(b) in the case of a power conferred on a Minister of the Crown, to be exercisable by statutory instrument,

any document by which that power is exercised shall be known as a 'statutory instrument' and the provisions of this Act shall apply thereto accordingly.

(2) Where by any Act passed before the commencement of this Act power to make statutory rules within the meaning of the Rules Publication Act 1893 was conferred on any rule-making authority within the meaning of that Act, any document by which that power is exercised after the commencement of this Act shall, save as is otherwise provided by regulations made under this Act, be known as a 'statutory instrument' and the provisions of this Act shall apply thereto accordingly.

2 Numbering, printing, publication and citation [248]

(1) Immediately after the making of any statutory instrument, it shall be sent to the King's printer of Acts of Parliament and numbered in accordance with regulations made under this Act, and except in such cases as may be provided by any Act passed after the commencement of this Act or prescribed by regulations made under this Act, copies thereof shall as soon as possible be printed and sold by the King's printer of Acts of Parliament.

(2) Any statutory instrument may, without prejudice to any other mode of citation, be cited by the number given to it in accordance with the provisions of this section, and the calendar year.

3 Supplementary provisions as to publication [249]

(1) Regulations made for the purposes of this Act shall make provision for the publication by His Majesty's Stationery Office of lists showing the date upon which every statutory instrument printed and sold by the King's printer of Acts of Parliament was first issued by that office; and in any legal proceedings a copy of any list so published purporting to be the imprint of the King's printer shall be received in evidence as a true copy, and an entry therein shall be conclusive evidence of the date on which any statutory instrument was first issued by His Majesty's Stationery Office.

(2) In any proceedings against any person for an offence consisting of a contravention of any such statutory instrument, it shall be a defence to prove that the instrument had not been issued by His Majesty's Stationery Office at the date of the alleged contravention unless it is proved that at that date reasonable steps had been taken for the purpose of bringing the purport of the instrument to the notice of the public, or of persons likely to be affected by it, or of the person charged.

(3) Save as therein otherwise expressly provided, nothing in this section shall affect any enactment or rule of law relating to the time at which any statutory instrument comes into operation.

4 Statutory instruments which are required to be laid [250]
before Parliament

(1) Where by this Act or any Act passed after the commencement of this Act any statutory instrument is required to be laid before Parliament after being made, a copy of the instrument shall be laid before each House of Parliament and, subject as hereinafter provided, shall be so laid before the instrument comes into operation: Provided that if it is essential that any such instrument should come into operation before copies thereof can be so laid as aforesaid, the instrument may be made so as to come into operation before it has been so laid; and where any statutory instrument comes into operation before it is laid before Parliament, notification shall forthwith be sent to the Lord Chancellor and to the Speaker of the House of Commons drawing attention to the fact that copies of the instrument have yet to be laid before Parliament and explaining why such copies were not so laid before the instrument came into operation.

(2) Every copy of any such statutory instrument sold by the King's printer of Acts of Parliament shall bear on the face thereof –

(a) a statement showing the date on which the statutory instrument came or will come into operation; and
(b) either a statement showing the date on which copies thereof were laid before Parliament or a statement that such copies are to be laid before Parliament.

5 Statutory instruments which are subject to annulment [251]
by resolution of either House of Parliament

(1) Where by this Act or any Act passed after the commencement of this Act, it is provided that any statutory instrument shall be subject to annulment in pursuance of resolution of either House of Parliament, the instrument shall be laid before Parliament after being made and the provisions of the last foregoing section shall apply thereto accordingly, and if either House, within the period of forty days beginning with the day on which a copy thereof is laid before it, resolves that an Address be presented to His Majesty praying that the instrument be annulled, no further proceedings shall be taken thereunder after the date of the resolution, and His Majesty may by Order in Council revoke the instrument, so, however, that any such resolution and revocation shall be without prejudice to the validity of anything previously done under the instrument or to the making of a new statutory instrument ...

6 Statutory instruments of which drafts are to be [252]
laid before Parliament

(1) Where by this Act or any Act passed after the commencement of this Act it is provided that a draft of any statutory instrument shall be laid before Parliament, but the Act does not prohibit the making of the instrument without the approval of Parliament, then, in the case of an Order in Council the draft shall not be submitted to His Majesty in Council, and in any other case the statutory instrument shall not be made, until after the expiration of a period of forty days beginning with the day on which a copy of the draft is laid before each House of Parliament,

or, if such copies are laid on different days, with the later of the two days, and if within that period either House resolves that the draft be not submitted to His Majesty or that the statutory instrument be not made, as the case may be, no further proceedings shall be taken thereon, but without prejudice to the laying before Parliament of a new draft ...

7 Supplementary provisions as to sections 4, 5 and 6   [253]

(1) In reckoning for the purposes of either of the last two foregoing sections any period of forty days, no account shall be taken of any time during which Parliament is dissolved or prorogued or during which both Houses are adjourned for more than four days.

(2) In relation to any instrument required by any Act, whether passed before or after the commencement of this Act, to be laid before the House of Commons only, the provisions of the last three foregoing sections shall have effect as if references to that House were therein substituted for references to Parliament and for references to either House and each House thereof.

(3) The provisions of sections four and five of this Act shall not apply to any statutory instrument being an order which is subject to special Parliamentary procedure, or to any other instrument which is required to be laid before Parliament, or before the House of Commons, for any period before it comes into operation.

8 Regulations   [254]

(1) The Treasury may, with the concurrence of the Lord Chancellor and the Speaker of the House of Commons, by statutory instrument make regulations for the purposes of this Act, and such regulations may, in particular –

(a) provide for the different treatment of instruments which are of the nature of a public Act, and of those which are of the nature of a local and personal or private Act;

(b) make provisions as to the numbering, printing, and publication of statutory instruments including provision for postponing the numbering of any such instrument which does not take effect until it has been approved by Parliament, or by the House of Commons, until the instrument has been so approved;

(c) provide with respect to any classes or descriptions of statutory instrument that they shall be exempt, either altogether or to such extent as may be determined by or under the regulations, from the requirement of being printed and of being sold by the King's printer of Acts of Parliament, or from either of those requirements;

(d) determine the classes of cases in which the exercise of a statutory power by any rule-making authority constitutes or does not constitute the making of such a statutory rule as is referred to in subsection (2) of section one of this Act, and provide for the exclusion from that subsection of any such classes;

(e) provide for the determination by a person or persons nominated by the Lord Chancellor and the Speaker of the House of Commons of any question –

(i) as to the numbering, printing, or publication of any statutory instrument or class or description of such instruments:

(ii) whether or to what extent any statutory instrument or class or description of such instruments is, under the regulations, exempt from any such requirement as is mentioned in paragraph (c) of this subsection:

(iii) whether any statutory instrument or class or description of such instruments is in the nature of a public Act or of a local and personal or private Act:

(iv) whether the exercise of any power conferred by an Act passed before the commencement of this Act is or is not the exercise of a power to make a statutory rule.

(2) Every statutory instrument made under this section shall be subject to annulment in pursuance of resolution of either House of Parliament.

CROWN PROCEEDINGS ACT 1947
(10 & 11 Geo 6 c 44)

PART I

SUBSTANTIVE LAW

1 Right to sue the Crown [255]

Where any person has a claim against the Crown after the commencement of this Act, and, if this Act had not been passed, the claim might have been enforced, subject to the grant of His Majesty's fiat, by petition of right, or might have been enforced by a proceeding provided by any statutory provision repealed by this Act, then, subject to the provisions of this Act, the claim may be enforced as of right, and without the fiat of His Majesty, by proceedings taken against the Crown for that purpose in accordance with the provisions of this Act.

2 Liability of the Crown in tort [256]

(1) Subject to the provisions of this Act, the Crown shall be subject to all those liabilities in tort to which, if it were a private person of full age and capacity, it would be subject –

(a) in respect of torts committed by its servants or agents;

(b) in respect of any breach of those duties which a person owes to his servants or agents at common law by reason of being their employer; and

(c) in respect of any breach of the duties attaching at common law to the ownership, occupation, possession or control of property:

Provided that no proceedings shall lie against the Crown by virtue of paragraph (a) of this subsection in respect of any act or omission of a servant or agent of the Crown unless the act or omission would apart from the provisions of this Act have given rise to a cause of action in tort against that servant or agent or his estate.

(2) Where the Crown is bound by a statutory duty which is binding also upon persons other than the Crown and its officers, then, subject to the provisions of this Act, the Crown shall, in respect of a failure to comply with that duty, be subject to all those liabilities in tort (if any) to which it would be so subject if it were a private person of full age and capacity.

(3) Where any functions are conferred or imposed upon an officer of the Crown as such either by any rule of the common law or by statute, and that officer commits a tort while performing or purporting to perform those functions, the liabilities of the Crown in respect of the tort shall be such as they would have been if those functions had been conferred or imposed solely by virtue of instructions lawfully given by the Crown.

(4) Any enactment which negatives or limits the amount of the liability of any Government department or officer of the Crown in respect of any tort committed

by that department or officer shall, in the case of proceedings against the Crown under this section in respect of a tort committed by that department or officer, apply in relation to the Crown as it would have applied in relation to that department or officer if the proceedings against the Crown had been proceedings against that department or officer.

(5) No proceedings shall lie against the Crown by virtue of this section in respect of anything done or omitted to be done by any person while discharging or purporting to discharge any responsibilities of a judicial nature vested in him, or any responsibilities which he has in connection with the execution of judicial process.

(6) No proceedings shall lie against the Crown by virtue of this section in respect of any act, neglect or default of any officer of the Crown, unless that officer has been directly or indirectly appointed by the Crown and was at the material time paid in respect of his duties as an officer of the Crown wholly out of the Consolidated Fund of the United Kingdom, moneys provided by Parliament, or any other Fund certified by the Treasury for the purposes of this subsection or was at the material time holding an office in respect of which the Treasury certify that the holder thereof would normally be so paid.

10 Provisions relating to the armed forces [257]

(1) Nothing done or omitted to be done by a member of the armed forces of the Crown while on duty as such shall subject either him or the Crown to liability in tort for causing the death of another person, or for causing personal injury to another person, in so far as the death or personal injury is due to anything suffered by that other person while he is a member of the armed forces of the Crown if –

(a) at the time when that thing is suffered by that other person, he is either on duty as a member of the armed forces of the Crown or is, though not on duty as such, on any land, premises, ship, aircraft or vehicle for the time being used for the purposes of the armed forces of the Crown; and

(b) the Secretary of State certifies that his suffering that thing has been or will be treated as attributable to service for the purposes of entitlement to an award under the Royal Warrant, Order in Council or Order of His Majesty relating to the disablement or death of members of the force of which he is a member:

Provided that this subsection shall not exempt a member of the said forces from liability in tort in any case in which the court is satisfied that the act or omission was not connected with the execution of his duties as a member of those forces.

(2) No proceedings in tort shall lie against the Crown for death or personal injury due to anything suffered by a member of the armed forces of the Crown if –

(a) that thing is suffered by him in consequence of the nature or condition of any such land, premises, ship, aircraft or vehicle as aforesaid, or in consequence of the nature or condition of any equipment or supplies used for the purposes of those forces; and

(b) the Secretary of State certifies as mentioned in the preceding subsection;

nor shall any act or omission of an officer of the Crown subject him to liability in tort for death or personal injury, in so far as the death or personal injury is due to anything suffered by a member of the armed forces of the Crown being a thing as to which the conditions aforesaid are satisfied.

(3) A Secretary of State, if satisfied that it is the fact –

(a) that a person was or was not on any particular occasion on duty as a member of the armed forces of the Crown; or

(b) that at any particular time any land, premises, ship, aircraft, vehicle, equipment or supplies was or was not, or were or were not, used for the purposes of the said forces;

may issue a certificate certifying that to be the fact; and any such certificate shall, for the purposes of this section, be conclusive as to the facts which it certifies.

PART II

JURISDICTION AND PROCEDURE

21 Nature of relief   [258]

(1) In any civil proceedings by or against the Crown the court shall, subject to the provisions of this Act, have power to make all such orders as it has power to make in proceedings between subjects, and otherwise to give such appropriate relief as the case may require: Provided that –

(a) where in any proceedings against the Crown any such relief is sought as might in proceedings between subjects be granted by way of injunction or specific performance, the court shall not grant an injunction or make an order for specific performance, but may in lieu thereof make an order declaratory of the rights of the parties; and

(b) in any proceedings against the Crown for the recovery of land or other property the court shall not make an order for the recovery of the land or the delivery of the property, but may in lieu thereof make an order declaring that the plaintiff is entitled as against the Crown to the land or property or to the possession thereof.

(2) The court shall not in any civil proceedings grant any injunction or make any order against an officer of the Crown if the effect of granting the injunction or making the order would be to give any relief against the Crown which could not have been obtained in proceedings against the Crown.

PART III

JUDGMENTS AND EXECUTION

25 Satisfaction of orders against the Crown   [259]

(1) Where in any civil proceedings by or against the Crown, or in any proceedings on the Crown side of the King's Bench Division, or in connection with any arbitration to which the Crown is a party, any order (including an order for costs) is made by any court in favour of any person against the Crown or against a Government department or against an officer of the Crown as such, the proper officer of the court shall, on an application in that behalf made by or on behalf of that person at any time after the expiration of twenty-one days from the date of the order or, in case the order provides for the payment of costs and the costs require to be taxed, at any time after the costs have been taxed, whichever is the later, issue to that person a certificate in the prescribed form containing particulars of the order: Provided that, if the court so directs, a separate certificate shall be issued with respect to the costs (if any) ordered to be paid to the applicant.

(2) A copy of any certificate issued under this section may be served by the person in whose favour the order is made upon the person for the time being named in the record as the solicitor, or as the person acting as solicitor, for the Crown or for the Government department or officer concerned.

(3) If the order provides for the payment of any money by way of damages or otherwise, or of any costs, the certificate shall state the amount so payable, and the appropriate Government department shall, subject as hereinafter provided, pay to the person entitled or to his solicitor the amount appearing by the certificate to be due to him together with the interest, if any, lawfully due thereon: Provided that the court by which any such order as aforesaid is made or any court to which an appeal against the order lies may direct that, pending an appeal or otherwise, payment of the whole of any amount so payable, or any part thereof, shall be suspended, and if the certificate has not been issued may order any such directions to be inserted therein.

(4) Save as aforesaid no execution or attachment or process in the nature thereof shall be issued out of any court for enforcing payment by the Crown of any such money or costs as aforesaid, and no person shall be individually liable under any order for the payment by the Crown, or any Government department, or any officer of the Crown as such, of any such money or costs.

PART IV

MISCELLANEOUS AND SUPPLEMENTAL

28 Discovery   [260]

(1) Subject to and in accordance with rules of court and county court rules –

(a) in any civil proceedings in the High Court or a county court to which the Crown is a party, the Crown may be required by the court to make discovery of documents and produce documents for inspection; and

(b) in any such proceedings as aforesaid, the Crown may be required by the court to answer interrogatories:

Provided that this section shall be without prejudice to any rule of law which authorises or requires the withholding of any document or the refusal to answer any question on the ground that the disclosure of the document or the answering of the question would be injurious to the public interest. Any order of the court made under the powers conferred by paragraph (b) of this subsection shall direct by what officer of the Crown the interrogatories are to be answered.

(2) Without prejudice to the proviso to the preceding subsection, any rules made for the purposes of this section shall be such as to secure that the existence of a document will not be disclosed if, in the opinion of a Minister of the Crown, it would be injurious to the public interest to disclose the existence thereof.

NB Section 10, above, was repealed by the Crown Proceedings (Armed Forces) Act 1987, s1, save that it may be revived by order of the Secretary of State at any time.

[As amended by the Defence (Transfer of Functions) Order 1964; Statute Law (Repeals) Act 1981; Statute Law (Repeals) Act 1993, s1(1), Schedule 1, Part I.]

LIFE PEERAGES ACT 1958
(6 & 7 Eliz 2 c 21)

1 Power to create life peerages carrying right to sit in the   [261]
House of Lords

(1) Without prejudice to Her Majesty's powers as to the appointment of Lords of Appeal in Ordinary, Her Majesty shall have power by letters patent to confer on

any person a peerage for life having the incidents specified in subsection (2) of this section.

(2) A peerage conferred under this section shall, during the life of the person on whom it is conferred, entitled him –

(a) to rank as a baron under such style as may be appointed by the letters patent; and
(b) subject to subsection (4) of this section, to receive writs of summons to attend the House of Lords and sit and vote therein accordingly,

and shall expire on his death.

(3) A life peerage may be conferred under this section on a woman.

(4) Nothing in this section shall enable any person to receive a writ of summons to attend the House of Lords, or to sit and vote in that House, at any time when disqualified therefor by law.

OBSCENE PUBLICATIONS ACT 1959
(7 & 8 Eliz 2 c 66)

1 Test of obscenity [262]

(1) For the purposes of this Act an article shall be deemed to be obscene if its effect or (where the article comprises two or more distinct items) the effect of any one of its items, is, if taken as a whole, such as to tend to deprave and corrupt persons who are likely, having regard to all relevant circumstances, to read, see or hear the matter contained or embodied in it.

(2) In this Act 'article' means any description of article containing or embodying matter to be read or looked at or both, any sound record, and any film or other record of a picture or pictures.

(3) For the purposes of this Act a person publishes an article who –

(a) distributes, circulates, sells, lets on hire, gives, or lends it or who offers it for sale or for letting on hire; or
(b) in the case of an article containing or embodying matter to be looked at or a record, shows, plays or projects it.

(4) For the purposes of this Act a person also publishes an article to the extent that any matter recorded on it is included by him in a programme included in a programme service.

(5) Where the inclusion of any matter in a programme so included would, if that matter were recorded matter, constitute the publication of an obscene article for the purposes of this Act by virtue of subsection (4) above, this Act shall have effect in relation to the inclusion of that matter in that programme as if it were recorded matter.

(6) In this section 'programme' and 'programme service' have the same meaning as in the Broadcasting Act 1990.

2 Prohibition of publication of obscene matter [263]

(1) Subject as hereinafter provided, any person who, whether for gain or not, publishes an obscene article or who has an obscene article for publication for gain (whether gain to himself or gain to another) shall be liable –

(a) on summary conviction to a fine not exceeding the prescribed sum or to imprisonment for a term not exceeding six months;

(b) on conviction on indictment to a fine or to imprisonment for a term not exceeding three years or both.

(3) A prosecution for an offence against this section shall not be commenced more than two years after the commission of the offence.

(3A) Proceedings for an offence under this section shall not be instituted except by or with the consent of the Director of Public Prosecutions in any case where the article in question is a moving picture film of a width of not less than sixteen millimetres and the relevant publication or the only other publication which followed or could reasonably have been expected to follow from the relevant publication took place or (as the case may be) was to take place in the course of a film exhibition; and in this subsection 'the relevant publication' means –

(a) in the case of any proceedings under this section for publishing an obscene article, the publication in respect of which the defendant would be charged if the proceedings were brought; and

(b) in the case of any proceedings under this section for having an obscene article for publication for gain, the publication which, if the proceedings were brought, the defendant would be alleged to have had in contemplation.

(4) A person publishing an article shall not be proceeded against for an offence at common law consisting of the publication of any matter contained or embodied in the article where it is of the essence of the offence that the matter is obscene.

(4A) Without prejudice to subsection (4) above, a person shall not be proceeded against for an offence at common law –

(a) in respect of a film exhibition or anything said or done in the course of a film exhibition, where it is of the essence of the common law offence that the exhibition or, as the case may be, what was said or done was obscene, indecent, offensive, disgusting or injurious to morality; or

(b) in respect of an agreement to give a film exhibition or to cause anything to be said or done in the course of such an exhibition where the common law offence consists of conspiring to corrupt public morals or to do any act contrary to public morals or decency.

(5) A person shall not be convicted of an offence against this section if he proves that he had not examined the article in respect of which he is charged and had no reasonable cause to suspect that it was such that his publication of it would make him liable to be convicted of an offence against this section.

(6) In any proceedings against a person under this section the question whether an article is obscene shall be determined without regard to any publication by another person unless it could reasonably have been expected that the publication by the other person would follow from publication by the person charged.

(7) In this section 'film exhibition' has the same meaning as in the Cinemas Act 1985.

3 Powers of search and seizure   [264]

(1) If a justice of the peace is satisfied by information on oath that there is reasonable ground for suspecting that, in any premises in the petty sessions area for which he acts, or on any stall or vehicle in that area, being premises or a stall or vehicle specified in the information, obscene articles are, or are from time to time, kept for publication for gain, the justice may issue a warrant under his hand empowering any constable to enter (if need be by force) and search the premises, or to search the stall or vehicle, and to seize and remove any articles found therein or thereon which the constable has reason to believe to be obscene articles and to be kept for publication for gain.

(2) A warrant under the foregoing subsection shall, if any obscene articles are seized under the warrant, also empower the seizure and removal of any documents found in the premises or, as the case may be, on the stall or vehicle which relate to a trade or business carried on at the premises or from the stall or vehicle.

(3) Subject to subsection 3A of this section any articles seized under subsection (1) of this section shall be brought before a justice of the peace acting for the same petty sessions area as the justice who issued the warrant, and the justice before whom the articles are brought may thereupon issue a summons to the occupier of the premises or, as the case may be, the user of the stall or vehicle to appear on a day specified in the summons before a magistrates' court for that petty sessions area to show cause why the articles or any of them should not be forfeited; and if the court is satisfied, as respects any of the articles, that at the time when they were seized they were obscene articles kept for publication for gain, the court shall order those articles to be forfeited: Provided that if the person summoned does not appear, the court shall not make an order unless service of the summons is proved. Provided also that this subsection does not apply in relation to any article seized under subsection (1) of this section which is returned to the occupier of the premises or, as the case may be, to the user of the stall or vehicle in or on which it was found.

(3A) Without prejudice to the duty of a court to make an order for the forfeiture of an article where section 1(4) of the Obscene Publications Act 1964 applies (orders made on conviction), in a case where by virtue of subsection (3A) of section 2 of this Act proceedings under the said section 2 for having an article for publication for gain could not be instituted except by or with the consent of the Director of Public Prosecutions, no order for the forfeiture of the article shall be made under this section unless the warrant under which the article was seized was issued on an information laid by or on behalf of the Director of Public Prosecutions.

(4) In addition to the person summoned, any other person being the owner, author or maker of any of the articles brought before the court, or any other person through whose hands they had passed before being seized, shall be entitled to appear before the court on the day specified in the summons to show cause why they should not be forfeited.

(5) Where an order is made under this section for the forfeiture of any articles, any person who appeared, or was entitled to appear, to show cause against the making of the order may appeal to the Crown Court; and no such order shall take effect until the expiration of the period within which the notice of appeal to the Crown Court may be given against the order or, if before the expiration thereof notice of appeal is duly given or application is made for the statement of a case for the opinion of the High Court, until the final determination or abandonment of the proceedings on the appeal or case.

(6) If as respects any articles brought before it the court does not order forfeiture, the court may if it thinks fit order the person on whose information the warrant for the seizure of the articles was issued to pay such costs as the court thinks reasonable to any person who has appeared before the court to show cause why those articles should not be forfeited; and costs ordered to be paid under this subsection shall be enforceable as a civil debt.

(7) For the purposes of this section the question whether an article is obscene shall be determined on the assumption that copies of it would be published in any manner likely having regard to the circumstances in which it was found, but in no other manner …

4 Defence of public good [265]

(1) Subject to subsection 1A of this section a person shall not be convicted of an offence against section 2 of this Act, and an order for forfeiture shall not be made under the foregoing section, if it is proved that publication of the article in question is justified as being for the public good on the ground that it is in the interests of science, literature, art or learning, or of other objects of general concern.

(1A) Subsection (1) of this section shall not apply where the article in question is a moving picture film or soundtrack, but –

(a) a person shall not be convicted of an offence against section 2 of this Act in relation to any such film or soundtrack, and
(b) an order for forfeiture of any such film or soundtrack shall not be made under section 3 of this Act,

if it is proved that publication of the film or soundtrack is justified as being for the public good on the ground that it is in the interests of drama, opera, ballet or any other art, or of literature or learning.

(2) It is hereby declared that the opinion of experts as to the literary, artistic, scientific or other merits of an article may be admitted in any proceedings under this Act either to establish or to negative the said ground.

(3) In this section 'moving picture soundtrack' means any sound record designed for playing with a moving picture film, whether incorporated with the film or not.

[As amended by the Obscene Publications Act 1964, s1(1); Courts Act 1971, s56(2), Schedule 8, para 37, Schedule 9, Part I; Criminal Law Act 1977, ss53(1), (5), (6), (7), 65(4), (5), Schedules 12, 13; Magistrates' Courts Act 1980, s32(2); Police and Criminal Evidence Act 1984, s119(2), Schedule 7, Part I; Cinemas Act 1985, s24(1), Schedule 2, para 6; Broadcasting Act 1990, ss162(1), 203(3), Schedule 21.]

PEERAGE ACT 1963
(1963 c 48)

1 Disclaimer of certain hereditary peerages [266]

(1) Subject to the provisions of this section, any person who, after the commencement of this Act, succeeds to a peerage in the peerage of England, Scotland, Great Britain or the United Kingdom may, by an instrument of disclaimer delivered to the Lord Chancellor within the period prescribed by this Act, disclaim that peerage for his life.

(2) Any instrument of disclaimer to be delivered under this section in respect of a peerage shall be delivered within the period of twelve months beginning with the day on which the person disclaiming succeeds to that peerage or, if he is under the age of twenty-one when he so succeeds, the period of twelve months beginning with the day on which he attains that age; and no such instrument shall be delivered in respect of a peerage by a person who has applied for a writ of summons to attend the House of Lords in right of that peerage ...

(4) In reckoning any period prescribed by this section for the delivery of an instrument of disclaimer by any person no account shall be taken of any time during which that person is shown to the satisfaction of the Lord Chancellor to have been subject to any infirmity of body or mind rendering him incapable of exercising or determining whether to exercise his rights under this section.

(5) The provisions of Schedule 1 to this Act shall have effect with respect to the form of instruments of disclaimer under this section, and the delivery, certification and registration of such instruments.

2 Disclaimer by members of the House of Commons [267]
and parliamentary candidates

(1) Where a person who succeeds to a peerage to which section 1 of this Act applies is a member of the House of Commons when he so succeeds, any instrument of disclaimer to be delivered by him under that section in respect of that peerage shall be delivered within the period of one month beginning with the date of his succession, and not later; and until the expiration of that period he shall not, by virtue of that peerage, be disqualified for membership of the House of Commons whether or not he has delivered such an instrument: Provided that –

(a) a person who is exempt from disqualification for membership of the House of Commons by virtue only of this subsection shall not sit or vote in that House while so exempt; and

(b) if any such person applies for a writ of summons to attend the House of Lords in right of the peerage in question, this subsection shall cease to apply to him.

(2) Where a person who succeeds to such a peerage as aforesaid has been or is nominated as a candidate at a parliamentary election held in pursuance of a writ issued before his succession, he shall not (unless he applies for such a writ of summons as aforesaid) be disqualified by virtue of that peerage for election to the House of Commons at that election, and if he is so elected subsection (1) of this section shall apply to him as if he had succeeded to the peerage immediately after the declaration of the result of the election.

(3) Where an instrument of disclaimer is delivered under this Act by a person to whom this section applies, a copy of that instrument shall be delivered to the Speaker of the House of Commons.

(4) In reckoning any period prescribed by this section in relation to any person no account shall be taken –

(a) of any time during which proceedings are pending on any parliamentary election petition in which the right of that person to be elected or returned to the House of Commons is in issue;

(b) of any time during which that person is shown to the satisfaction of the Speaker of the House of Commons to have been subject to any such infirmity as is mentioned in subsection (4) of section 1 of this Act; or

(c) of any time during which Parliament is prorogued or both Houses of Parliament are adjourned for more than four days;

and if Parliament is dissolved during that period the foregoing provisions of this section shall cease to apply to that person in respect of the peerage in question.

3 Effects of disclaimer [268]

(1) The disclaimer of a peerage by any person under this Act shall be irrevocable and shall operate, from the date on which the instrument of disclaimer is delivered –

(a) to divest that person (and, if he is married, his wife) of all right or interest to or in the peerage, and all titles, rights, offices, privileges and precedence attaching thereto; and

(b) to relieve him of all obligations and disabilities (including any disqualification in respect of membership of the House of Commons and elections to that House) arising therefrom,

but shall not accelerate the succession to that peerage nor affect its devolution on his death.

(2) Where a peerage is disclaimed under this Act, no other hereditary peerage

shall be conferred upon the person by whom it is disclaimed, and no writ in acceleration shall be issued in respect of that peerage to the person entitled thereto on his death.

(3) The disclaimer of a peerage under this Act shall not affect any right, interest or power (whether arising before or after the disclaimer) of the person by whom the peerage is disclaimed, or of any other person, to, in or over any estates or other property limited or settled to devolve with that peerage.

(4) The reference in the foregoing subsection to estates or other property limited or settled to devolve with a peerage shall, for the purposes of the application of this Act to Scotland, be construed as including a reference to estates or other land devolving as aforesaid under an entail or special destination, or the beneficial interest in which so devolves under a trust.

4 Scottish peerages [269]

The holder of a peerage in the peerage of Scotland shall have the same right to receive writs of summons to attend the House of Lords, and to sit and vote in that House, as the holder of a peerage in the peerage of the United Kingdom; and the enactments relating to the election of Scottish representative peers shall cease to have effect.

5 Irish peerages [270]

The holder of a peerage in the peerage of Ireland shall not by virtue of that peerage be disqualified –

(a) for being or being elected as a member of the House of Commons for any constituency in the United Kingdom; or

(b) for voting at elections for that House whether or not he is a member of that House.

6 Peeresses in own right [271]

A woman who is the holder of a hereditary peerage in the peerage of England, Scotland, Great Britain or the United Kingdom shall (whatever the terms of the letters patent or other instrument, if any, creating that peerage) have the same right to receive writs of summons to attend the House of Lords, or to sit and vote in that House, and shall be subject to the same disqualifications in respect of membership of the House of Commons and elections to that House, as a man holding that peerage.

POLICE ACT 1964
(1964 c 48)

51 Assaults on constables [272]

(1) Any person who assaults a constable in the execution of his duty, or a person assisting a constable in the execution of his duty, shall be guilty of an offence ...

(3) Any person who resists or wilfully obstructs a constable in the execution of his duty, or a person assisting a constable in the execution of his duty, shall be guilty of an offence ...

OBSCENE PUBLICATIONS ACT 1964
(1964 c 74)

1 Obscene articles intended for publication for gain [273]

(2) For the purpose of any proceedings for an offence against ... section 2 [of the Obscene Publications Act 1959] a person shall be deemed to have an article for publication for gain if with a view to such publication he had the article in his ownership, possession or control.

(3) In proceedings brought against a person under the said section 2 for having an obscene article for publication for gain the following provisions shall apply in place of subsections (5) and (6) of that section, that is to say –

(a) he shall not be convicted of that offence if he proves that he had not examined the article and had no reasonable cause to suspect that it was such that his having it would make him liable to be convicted of an offence against that section; and

(b) the question whether the article is obscene shall be determined by reference to such publication for gain of the article as in the circumstances it may reasonably be inferred he had in contemplation and to any further publication that could reasonably be expected to follow from it, but not to any other publication.

(4) Where articles are seized under section 3 of the Obscene Publications Act 1959 (which provides for the seizure and forfeiture of obscene articles kept for publication for gain), and a person is convicted under section 2 of that Act of having them for publication for gain, the Court on his conviction shall order the forfeiture of those articles: Provided that an order made by virtue of this subsection (including an order so made on appeal) shall not take effect until the expiration of the ordinary time within which an appeal in the matter of the proceedings in which the order was made may be instituted or, where such an appeal is duly instituted, until the appeal is finally decided or abandoned; and for this purpose –

(a) an application for a case to be stated or for leave to appeal shall be treated as the institution of an appeal; and

(b) where a decision on appeal is subject to a further appeal, the appeal shall not be deemed to be finally decided until the expiration of the ordinary time within which a further appeal may be instituted or, where a further appeal is duly instituted, until the further appeal is finally decided or abandoned.

(5) References in section 3 of the Obscene Publications Act 1959 and this section to publication for gain shall apply to any publication with a view to gain, whether the gain is to accrue by way of consideration for the publication or in any other way.

2 Negatives etc for production of obscene articles [274]

(1) The Obscene Publications Act 1959 (as amended by this Act) shall apply in relation to anything which is intended to be used, either alone or as one of a set, for the reproduction or manufacture therefrom of articles containing or embodying matter to be read, looked at or listened to, as if it were an article containing or embodying that matter so far as that matter is to be derived from it or from the set.

(2) For the purposes of the Obscene Publications Act 1959 (as so amended) an article shall be deemed to be had or kept for publication if it is had or kept for the reproduction or manufacture therefrom of articles for publication; and the question whether an article so had or kept is obscene shall –

(a) for purposes of section 2 of the Act be determined in accordance with section 1(3)(b) above as if any reference there to publication of the article were a reference to publication of articles reproduced or manufactured from it; and
(b) for purposes of section 3 of the Act be determined on the assumption that articles reproduced or manufactured from it would be published in any manner likely having regard to the circumstances in which it was found, but in no other manner.

WAR DAMAGE ACT 1965
(1965 c 18)

1 Abolition of rights at common law to compensation [275]
for certain damage to or destruction of property

(1) No person shall be entitled at common law to receive from the Crown compensation in respect of damage to, or destruction of, property caused (whether before or after the passing of this Act, within or outside the United Kingdom) by Acts lawfully done by, or on the authority of, the Crown during, or in contemplation of the outbreak of, a war in which the Sovereign was, or is, engaged.

(2) Where any proceedings to recover at common law compensation in respect of such damage or destruction have been instituted before the passing of this Act, the court shall, on the application of any party, forthwith set aside or dismiss the proceedings, subject only to the determination of any question arising as to costs or expenses.

PARLIAMENTARY COMMISSIONER ACT 1967
(1967 c 13)

1 Appointment and tenure of office [276]

(1) For the purpose of conducting investigations in accordance with the following provisions of this Act there shall be appointed a Commissioner, to be known as the Parliamentary Commissioner for Administration.

(2) Her Majesty may by Letters Patent from time to time appoint a person to be the Commissioner, and any person so appointed shall (subject to subsections (3) and (3A) of this section) hold office during good behaviour.

(3) A person appointed to be the Commissioner may be relieved of office by Her Majesty at his own request, or may be removed from office by Her Majesty in consequence of Addresses from both Houses of Parliament, and shall in any case vacate office on completing the year of service in which he attains the age of sixty-five years.

(3A) Her majesty may declare the office of Commissioner to have been vacated if satisfied that the person appointed to be the Commissioner is incapable for medical reasons –

(a) of performing the duties of his office; and
(b) of requesting to be relieved of it.

3 Administrative provisions [277]

(1) The Commissioner may appoint such officers as he may determine with the approval of the Treasury as to numbers and conditions of service.

(2) Any function of the Commissioner under this Act may be performed by any officer of the Commissioner authorised for that purpose by the Commissioner or may be performed by any officer so authorised –

(a) of the Health Service Commissioner for England;
(b) of the Health Service Commissioner for Scotland; or
(c) of the Health Service Commissioner for Wales.

3A Appointment of acting Commissioner [278]

(1) Where the office of Commissioner becomes vacant, Her Majesty may, pending the appointment of a new Commissioner, appoint a person under this section to act as the Commissioner at any time during the period of twelve months beginning with the date on which the vacancy arose.

(2) A person appointed under this section shall hold office during Her Majesty's pleasure and, subject to that, shall hold office –

(a) until the appointment of a new Commissioner or the expiry of the period of twelve months beginning with the date on which the vacancy arose, whichever occurs first; and

(b) in other respects, in accordance with the terms and conditions of his appointment which shall be such as the Treasury may determine.

(3) A person appointed under this section shall, while he holds office, be treated for all purposes, except those of section 2 of this Act, as the Commissioner.

(4) Any salary, pension or other benefit payable by virtue of this section shall be charged on and issued out of the Consolidated Fund.

4 Departments etc subject to investigation [279]

(1) Subject to the provisions of this section and to the notes contained in Schedule 2 to this Act, this Act applies to the government departments, corporations and unincorporated bodies listed in that Schedule; and references in this Act to an authority to which this Act applies are references to any such corporation or body.

(2) Her Majesty may by Order in Council amend Schedule 2 to this Act by the alteration of any entry or note, the removal of any entry or note or the insertion of any additional entry or note.

(3) An Order in Council may only insert an entry if –

(a) it relates –

(i) to a government department; or
(ii) to a corporation or body whose functions are exercised on behalf of the Crown; or

(b) it relates to a corporation or body –

(i) which is established by virtue of Her Majesty's prerogative or by an Act of Parliament or an Order in Council or order made under an Act of Parliament or which is established in any other way by a Minister of the Crown in his capacity as a Minister or by a government department;

(ii) at least half of whose revenues derive directly from money provided by Parliament, a levy authorised by an enactment, a fee or charge of any other description so authorised or more than one of those sources; and

(iii) which is wholly or partly constituted by appointment made by Her Majesty or a Minister of the Crown or government department.

(4) No entry shall be made in respect of a corporation or body whose sole activity is, or whose main activities are, included among the activities specified in subsection (5) below.

(5) The activities mentioned in subsection (4) above are –

(a) the provision of education, or the provision of training otherwise than under the Industrial Training Act 1982;
(b) the development of curricula, the conduct of examinations or the validation of educational courses;
(c) the control of entry to any profession or the regulation of the conduct of members of any profession;
(d) the investigation of complaints by members of the public regarding the actions of any person or body, or the supervision or review or such investigations or of steps taken following them.

(6) No entry shall be made in respect of a corporation or body operating in an exclusively or predominantly commercial manner or a corporation carrying on under national ownership an industry or undertaking or part of an industry or undertaking.

(7) Any statutory instrument made by virtue of this section shall be subject to annulment in pursuance of a resolution of either House of Parliament.

(8) In this Act –

(a) any reference to a government department to which this Act applies includes a reference to any of the Ministers or officers of such a department; and
(b) any reference to an authority to which this Act applies includes a reference to any members or officers of such an authority.

5 Matters subject to investigation   [280]

(1) Subject to the provisions of this section, the Commissioner may investigate any action taken by or on behalf of a government department or other authority to which this Act applies, being action taken in the exercise of administrative functions of that department or authority, in any case where –

(a) a written complaint is duly made to a member of the House of Commons by a member of the public who claims to have sustained injustice in consequence of maladministration in connection with the action so taken; and
(b) the complaint is referred to the Commissioner, with the consent of the person who made it, by a member of that House with a request to conduct an investigation thereon.

(2) Except as hereinafter provided, the Commissioner shall not conduct an investigation under this Act in respect of any of the following matters, that is to say –

(a) any action in respect of which the person aggrieved has or had a right of appeal, reference or review to or before a tribunal constituted by or under any enactment or by virtue of Her Majesty's prerogative;
(b) any action in respect of which the person aggrieved has or had a remedy by way of proceedings in any court of law:

Provided that the Commissioner may conduct an investigation notwithstanding that the person aggrieved has or had such a right or remedy if satisfied that in the particular circumstances it is not reasonable to expect him to resort or have resorted to it.

(3) Without prejudice to subsection (2) of this section, the Commissioner shall not conduct an investigation under this Act in respect of any such action or matter as is described in Schedule 3 to this Act.

(4) Her Majesty may by Order in Council amend the said Schedule 3 so as to exclude from the provisions of that Schedule such actions or matters as may be

described in the Order; and any statutory instrument made by virtue of this subsection shall be subject to annulment in pursuance of a resolution of either House of Parliament.

(5) In determining whether to initiate, continue or discontinue an investigation under this Act, the Commissioner shall, subject to the foregoing provisions of this section, act in accordance with his own discretion; and any question whether a complaint is duly made under this Act shall be determined by the Commissioner.

(6) For the purposes of this section, administrative functions exercisable by any person appointed by the Lord Chancellor as a member of the administrative staff of any court or tribunal shall be taken to be administrative functions of the Lord Chancellor's Department or, in Northern Ireland, of the Northern Ireland Court Service.

(7) For the purposes of this section, administrative functions exercisable by any person appointed as a member of the administistative staff of a relevant tribunal –

(a) by a government department or authority to which this Act applies; or
(b) with the consent (whether as to remuneration and other terms and conditions of service or otherwise) of such a department or authority,

shall be taken to be administrative functions of that department or authority.

(8) In subsection (7) of this section, 'relevant tribunal' means a tribunal listed in Schedule 4 to this Act.

(9) Her Majesty may by Order in Council amend the said Schedule 4 by the alteration or removal of any entry or the insertion of any additional entry; and any statutory instrument made by virtue of this subsection shall be subject to annulment in pursuance of a resolution of either House of Parliament.

6 Provisions relating to complaints   [281]

(1) A complaint under this Act may be made by any individual, or by any body of persons whether incorporated or not, not being –

(a) a local authority or other authority or body constituted for purposes of the public service or of local government or for the purposes of carrying on under national ownership any industry or undertaking or part of an industry or undertaking;
(b) any other authority or body whose members are appointed by Her Majesty or any Minister of the Crown or government department, or whose revenues consist wholly or mainly of moneys provided by Parliament.

(2) Where the person by whom a complaint might have been made under the foregoing provisions of this Act has died or is for any reason unable to act for himself, the complaint may be made by his personal representative or by a member of his family or other individual suitable to represent him; but except as aforesaid a complaint shall not be entertained under this Act unless made by the person aggrieved himself.

(3) A complaint shall not be entertained under this Act unless it is made to a member of the House of Commons not later than twelve months from the day on which the person aggrieved first had notice of the matters alleged in the complaint; but the Commissioner may conduct an investigation pursuant to a complaint not made within that period if he considers that there are special circumstances which make it proper to do so.

(4) Except as provided in subsection (5) below a complaint shall not be entertained under this Act unless the person aggrieved is resident in the United Kingdom (or, if he is dead, was so resident at the time of his death) or the complaint relates to action taken in relation to him while he was present in the

United Kingdom or on an installation in a designated area within the meaning of the Continental Shelf Act 1964 or on a ship registered in the United Kingdom or an aircraft so registered, or in relation to rights or obligations which accrued or arose in the United Kingdom or on such an installation, ship or aircraft.

(5) A complaint may be entertained under this Act in circumstances not falling within subsection (4) above where –

(a) the complaint relates to action taken in any country or territory outside the United Kingdom by an officer (not being an honorary consular officer) in the exercise of a consular function on behalf of the Government of the United Kingdom; and

(b) the person aggrieved is a citizen of the United Kingdom and Colonies who, under section 2 of the Immigration Act 1971, has the right of abode in the United Kingdom.

7 Procedure in respect of investigations [282]

(1) Where the Commissioner proposes to conduct an investigation pursuant to a complaint under this Act, he shall afford to the principal officer of the department or authority concerned, and to any person who is alleged in the complaint to have taken or authorised the action complained of, an opportunity to comment on any allegations contained in the complaint.

(2) Every such investigation shall be conducted in private, but except as aforesaid the procedure for conducting an investigation shall be such as the Commissioner considers appropriate in the circumstances of the case; and without prejudice to the generality of the foregoing provision the Commissioner may obtain information from such persons and in such manner, and make such inquiries, as he thinks fit, and may determine whether any person may be represented, by counsel or solicitor or otherwise, in the investigation.

(3) The Commissioner may, if he thinks fit, pay to the person by whom the complaint was made and to any other person who attends or furnishes information for the purposes of an investigation under this Act –

(a) sums in respect of expenses properly incurred by them;

(b) allowances by way of compensation for the loss of their time,

in accordance with such scales and subject to such conditions as may be determined by the Treasury.

(4) The conduct of an investigation under this Act shall not affect any action taken by the department or authority concerned, or any power or duty of that department or authority to take further action with respect to any matters subject to the investigation ...

8 Evidence [283]

(1) For the purposes of an investigation under this Act the Commissioner may require any Minister, officer or member of the department or authority concerned or any other person who in his opinion is able to furnish information or produce documents relevant to the investigation to furnish any such information or produce any such document.

(2) For the purposes of any such investigation the Commissioner shall have the same powers as the Court in respect of the attendance and examination of witnesses (including the administration of oaths or affirmations and the examination of witnesses abroad) and in respect of the production of documents.

(3) No obligation to maintain secrecy or other restriction upon the disclosure of information obtained by or furnished to persons in Her Majesty's service, whether

imposed by any enactment or by any rule of law, shall apply to the disclosure of information for the purposes of an investigation under this Act; and the Crown shall not be entitled in relation to any such investigation to any such privilege in respect of the production of documents or the giving of evidence as is allowed by law in legal proceedings.

(4) No person shall be required or authorised by virtue of this Act to furnish any information or answer any question relating to proceedings of the Cabinet or of any committee of the Cabinet or to produce so much of any document as relates to such proceedings; and for the purposes of this subsection a certificate issued by the Secretary of the Cabinet with the approval of the Prime Minister and certifying that any information, question, document or part of a document so relates shall be conclusive.

(5) Subject to subsection (3) of this section, no person shall be compelled for the purposes of an investigation under this Act to give any evidence or produce any document which he could not be compelled to give or produce in civil proceedings before the Court.

9 Obstruction and contempt [284]

(1) If any person without lawful excuse obstructs the Commissioner or any officer of the Commissioner in the performance of his functions under this Act, or is guilty of any act or omission in relation to any investigation under this Act which, if that investigation were a proceeding in the Court, would constitute contempt of court, the Commissioner may certify the offence to the Court.

(2) Where an offence is certified under this section, the Court may inquire into the matter and, after hearing any witnesses who may be produced against or on behalf of the person charged with the offence, and after hearing any statement that may be offered in defence, deal with him in any manner in which the Court could deal with him if he had committed the like offence in relation to the Court.

(3) Nothing in this section shall be construed as applying to the taking of any such action as is mentioned in subsection (4) of section 7 of this Act.

10 Reports by Commissioner [285]

(1) In any case where the Commissioner conducts an investigation under this Act or decides not to conduct such an investigation, he shall sent to the member of the House of Commons by whom the request for investigation was made (or if he is no longer a member of that House, to such member of that House as the Commissioner thinks appropriate) a report of the results of the investigation or, as the case may be, a statement of his reasons for not conducting an investigation.

(2) In any case where the Commissioner conducts an investigation under this Act, he shall also send a report of the results of the investigation to the principal officer of the department or authority concerned and to any other person who is alleged in the relevant complaint to have taken or authorised the action complained of.

(3) If, after conducting an investigation under this Act, it appears to the Commissioner that injustice has been caused to the person aggrieved in consequence of maladministration and that the injustice has not been, or will not be, remedied, he may, if he thinks fit, lay before each House of Parliament a special report upon the case.

(4) The Commissioner shall annually lay before each House of Parliament a general report on the performance of his functions under this Act and may from time to time lay before each House of Parliament such other reports with respect to those functions as he thinks fit.

(5) For the purposes of the law of defamation, any such publication as is hereinafter mentioned shall be absolutely privileged, that is to say –

(a) the publication of any matter by the Commissioner in making a report to either House of Parliament for the purposes of this Act;

(b) the publication of any matter by a member of the House of Commons in communicating with the Commissioner or his officers for those purposes or by the Commissioner or his officers in communicating with such a member for those purposes;

(c) the publication by such a member to the person by whom a complaint was made under this Act of a report or statement sent to the member in respect of the complaint in pursuance of subsection (1) of this section;

(d) the publication by the Commissioner to such a person as is mentioned in subsection (2) of this section of a report to that person in pursuance of that subsection.

11 Provision for secrecy of information [286]

(2) Information obtained by the Commissioner or his officers in the course of or for the purposes of an investigation under this Act shall not be disclosed except –

(a) for the purposes of the investigation and of any report to be made thereon under this Act;

(b) for the purposes of any proceedings for an offence under the Official Secrets Acts 1911 to 1989 alleged to have been committed in respect of information obtained by the Commissioner or any of his officers by virtue of this Act or for an offence of perjury alleged to have been committed in the course of an investigation under this Act or for the purposes of an inquiry with a view to the taking of such proceedings; or

(c) for the purposes of any proceedings under section 9 of this Act;

and the Commissioner and his officers shall not be called upon to give evidence in any proceedings (other than such proceedings as aforesaid) of matters coming to his or their knowledge in the course of an investigation under this Act.

(2A) Where the Commissioner also holds office as a Health Service Commissioner and a person initiates a complaint to him in his capacity as such a Commissioner which relates partly to a matter with respect to which that person has previously initiated a complaint under this Act, or subsequently initiates such a complaint, information obtained by the Commissioner or his officers in the course of or for the purposes of investigating the complaint under this Act may be disclosed for the purposes of his carrying out his functions in relation to the other complaint.

(3) A Minister of the Crown may give notice in writing to the Commissioner, with respect to any document or information specified in the notice, or any class of documents or information so specified, that in the opinion of the Minister the disclosure of that document or information, or of documents or information of that class, would be prejudicial to the safety of the State or otherwise contrary to the public interest; and where such a notice is given nothing in this Act shall be construed as authorising or requiring the Commissioner or any officer of the Commissioner to communicate to any person or for any purpose any document or information specified in the notice, or any document or information of a class so specified.

(4) The references in this section to a Minister of the Crown include references to the Commissioners of Customs and Excise and the Commissioners of Inland Revenue.

11A Consultations between Parliamentary Commissioner and Health Service Commissioners [287]

(1) Where, at any stage in the course of conducting an investigation under this Act, the Commissioner forms the opinion that the complaint relates partly to a matter within the jurisdiction of the Health Service Commissioner for England, Wales or Scotland, he shall –

(a) unless he also holds office as that Commissioner, consult about the complaint with him; and

(b) if he considers it necessary, inform the person initiating the complaint under this Act of the steps necessary to initiate a complaint under the Health Services Commissioners Act 1993 (Health Service Commissioner for England and for Wales) or, as the case may be, Part VI of the National Health Service (Scotland) Act 1978 (Health Service Commissioner for Scotland).

(2) Where by virtue of subsection (1) above the Commissioner consults with the Health Service Commissioner in relation to a complaint under this Act, he may consult him about any matter relating to the complaint, including –

(a) the conduct of any investigation into the complaint; and

(b) the form, content and publication of any report of the results of such an investigation.

(3) Nothing in section 11(2) of this Act shall apply in relation to the disclosure of information by the Commissioner or any of his officers in the course of consultations held in accordance with this section.

12 Interpretation [288]

(1) In this Act the following expressions have the meanings hereby respectively assigned to them, that is to say –

'action' includes failure to act, and other expressions connoting action shall be construed accordingly;

'the Commissioner' means the Parliamentary Commissioner for Administration;

'the Court' means, in relation to England and Wales the High Court, in relation to Scotland the Court of Session, and in relation to Northern Ireland the High Court of Northern Ireland;

'enactment' includes an enactment of the Parliament of Northern Ireland and any instrument made by virtue of an enactment;

'officer' includes employee;

'person aggrieved' means the person who claims or is alleged to have sustained such injustice as is mentioned in section 5(1)(a) of this Act;

'tribunal' includes the person constituting a tribunal consisting of one person.

(2) References in this Act to any enactment are references to that enactment as amended or extended by or under any other enactment.

(3) It is hereby declared that nothing in this Act authorises or requires the Commissioner to question the merits of a decision taken without maladministration by a government department or other authority in the exercise of a discretion vested in that department or authority.

SCHEDULE 2

DEPARTMENTS, ETC SUBJECT TO INVESTIGATION

Advisory, Conciliation and Arbitration Service
Agricultural wages committee
Ministry of Agriculture, Fisheries and Food
Arts Council of Great Britain
British Council
British Library Board
Building Societies Commission
Bwrdd yr Iaith Gymraeg (Welsh Language Board)
Certification Officer
Charity Commission
Civil Service Commission
Co-operative Development Agency
Countryside Commission
Crafts Council
Crofters Commission
Crown Estate Office
Customs and Excise
Data Protection Registrar
Ministry of Defence
Development Commission
United Kingdom Ecolabelling Board
Department for Education
Education Assets Board
Central Bureau for Educational Visits and Exchanges
Office of the Director General of Electricity Supply
Department of Employment
Department of the Environment
Equal Opportunities Commission
Export Credits Guarantee Department
Office of the Director General of Fair Trading
British Film Institute
Foreign and Commonwealth Office
Forestry Commission
Registry of Friendly Societies
Friendly Societies Commission
Office of the Director General of Gas Supply
Health and Safety Commission
Health and Safety Executive
Department of Health
Highlands and Islands Development Board
Historic Buildings and Monuments Commission for England
Home Office
Horserace Betting Levy Board
Housing Corporation
Human Fertilisation and Embryology Authority
Office of the Commissioner for Protection Against Unlawful Industrial Action
Central Office of Information
Inland Revenue
Intervention Board for Agricultural Produce
Land Registry
Legal Aid Board

The following general lighthouse authorities –

(a) Corporation of the Trinity House of Deptford Strond;

(b) Commissioners of Northern Lighthouses

Local Government Commission for England
Traffic Director for London
Lord Chancellor's Department
Lord President of the Council's Office
Medical Practices Committee
Scottish Medical Practices Committee
Museums and Galleries Commission
National Debt Office
Department of National Heritage
Trustees of the National Heritage Memorial Fund
Office of the Director General of the National Lottery
Department for National Savings
Nature Conservancy Council for England
Commission for the New Towns
Development corporations for new towns
Northern Ireland Court Service
Northern Ireland Office
Ordnance Survey
Office of Population Censuses and Surveys
Office of the Commissioner or Protection Against Unlawful
    Industrial Action
Registrar of Public Lending Right
Public Record Office
Office of Public Service and Science
Scottish Record Office
Commission for Racial Equality
Red Deer Commission
Department of the Registers of Scotland
General Register Officer, Scotland
Agricultural and Food Research Council
Economic and Social Research Council
Medical Research Council
Natural Environment Research Council
Science and Engineering Research Council
International Rail Regulator
Residuary Bodies
National Rivers Authority
Royal Mint
Office of Her Majesty's Chief Inspector of Schools in England
Office of Her Majesty's Chief Inspector of Schools in Wales
Scottish Courts Administration
Scottish National Heritage
Scottish Homes
Scottish Legal Aid Board
Scottish Office
Council for Small Industries in Rural Areas
Department of Social Security
Central Council for Education and Training in Social Work
Sports Council
Scottish Sports Council
Sports Council for Wales

Stationery Office
Central Statistics Office of the Chancellor of the Exchequer
Office of the Director General of Telecommunications
English Tourist Board
Scottish Tourist Board
Wales Tourist Board
Board of Trade
Department of Trade and Industry
Office of the Commissioner for the Rights of Trade Union Members
Agricultural Training Board
Clothing and Allied Products Industry Training Board
Construction Industry Training Board
Engineering Industry Training Board
Hotel and Catering Industry Training Board
Plastics Processing Industry Training Board
Road Transport Industry Training Board
Department of Transport
Treasury
Treasury Solicitor
Urban development corporations
Urban Regeneration Agency
Countryside Council for Wales
Development Board for Rural Wales
Housing for Wales
Welsh Office
Office of the Director General of Water Services

SCHEDULE 3   [290]

MATTERS NOT SUBJECT TO INVESTIGATION

1 Action taken in matters certified by a Secretary of State or other Minister of the Crown to affect relations or dealings between the Government of the United Kingdom and any other Government or any international organisation of States or Governments.

2 Action taken, in any country or territory outside the United Kingdom, by or on behalf of any officer representing or acting under the authority of Her Majesty in respect of the United Kingdom, or any other officer of the Government of the United Kingdom other than action which is taken by an officer (not being an honorary consular officer) in the exercise of a consular function on behalf of the Government of the United Kingdom.

3 Action taken in connection with the administration of the government of any country or territory outside the United Kingdom which forms part of Her Majesty's dominions or in which Her Majesty has jurisdiction.

4 Action taken by the Secretary of State under the Extradition Act 1870, the Fugitive Offenders Act 1967 or the Extradition Act 1989.

5 Action taken by or with the authority of the Secretary of State for the purposes of investigating crime or of protecting the security of the State, including action so taken with respect to passports.

6 The commencement or conduct of civil or criminal proceedings before any court of law in the United Kingdom, of proceedings at any place under the Naval Discipline Act 1957, the Army Act 1955 or the Air Force Act 1955, or of proceedings before any international court or tribunal.

6A Action taken by any person appointed by the Lord Chancellor as a member of the administrative staff of any court or tribunal, so far as that action is taken at the direction, or on the authority (whether express or implied), of any person acting in a judicial capacity or in his capacity as a member of the tribunal.

6B – (1) Action taken by any member of the administrative staff of a relevant tribunal, so far as that action is taken at the direction, or on the authority (whether express or implied), of any person acting in his capacity as a member of the tribunal.

(2) In this paragraph, 'relevant tribunal' has the meaning given by section 5(8) of this Act.

7 Any exercise of the prerogative of mercy or of the power of a Secretary of State to make a reference in respect of any person to the Court of Appeal, the High Court of Justiciary or the Courts-Martial Appeal Court.

8 Action taken on behalf of the Minister of Health or the Secretary of State by a Regional Health Authority, an Area Health Authority, a District Health Authority, a special health authority, except the Rampton Review Board, the Rampton Hospital Board, the Broadmoor Hospital Board or the Moss Side and Park Law Hospital Board, a Family Practitioner Committee, a Health Board or the Common Services Agency for the Scottish Health Service, by the Dental Practice Board or the Scottish Dental Practice Board or by the Public Health Laboratory Service Board.

9 Action taken in matters relating to contractual or other commercial transactions, whether within the United Kingdom or elsewhere, being transactions of a government department or authority to which this Act applies or of any such authority or body as is mentioned in paragraph (a) or (b) of subsection (1) of section 6 of this Act and not being transactions for or relating to –

(a) the acquisition of land compulsorily or in circumstances in which it could be acquired compulsorily;
(b) the disposal as surplus of land acquired compulsorily or in such circumstances as aforesaid.

10 Action taken in respect of appointments or removals, pay, discipline, superannuation or other personnel matters, in relation to –

(a) service in any of the armed forces of the Crown, including reserve and auxiliary and cadet forces;
(b) service in any office or employment under the Crown or under any authority to which this Act applies; or
(c) service in any office or employment, or under any contract for services, in respect of which power to take action, or to determine or approve the action to be taken, in such matters is vested in Her Majesty, any Minister of the Crown or any such authority as aforesaid.

(2) Sub-paragraph (1)(c) above shall not apply to any action (not otherwise excluded from investigation by this Schedule) which is taken by the Secretary of State in connection with –

(a) the provision of information relating to the terms and conditions of any employment covered by an agreement entered into by him under section 12(1) of the Overseas Development and Cooperation Act 1980 or
(b) the provision of any allowance, grant or supplement or any benefit (other than those relating to superannuation) arising from the designation of any person in accordance with such an agreement.

11 The grant of honours, awards or privileges within the gift of the Crown, including the grant of Royal Charters.

SCHEDULE 4   [291]

RELEVANT TRIBUNALS FOR PURPOSES OF SECTION 5(7)

Tribunals constituted in Great Britain under regulations made under section 4 of the Vaccine Damage Payments Act 1979.

Child support appeal tribunals constituted under section 21 of the Child Support Act 1991.

Social security appeal tribunals constituted under section 41 of the Social Security Administration Act 1992.

Disability appeal tribunals constituted under section 43 of that Act.

Medical appeal tribunals constituted under section 50 of that Act.

[As amended by the Civil Evidence Act 1968, s17(1)(b); Parliamentary Commissioner (Consular Complaints) Act 1981, s1; Parliamentary and Health Service Commissioners Act 1987, ss1(1), (2), (3)(c), 2(1), 3, 4(1), (2), 6(1); Official Secrets Act 1989, s16(4), Schedules 1, para 1(a), 2; Courts and Legal Services Act 1990, ss10(2), 110(1); Trade Union Reform and Employment Rights Act 1993, s49(2), Schedule 8, para 2; Health Service Commissioners Act 1993, s20(1), Schedule 2, paras 1, 2; Welsh Language Act 1993, s4(2), Schedule 1, para 5; Trade Union Reform and Employment Rights Act 1993, s49(2), Schedule 8, para 2; National Lottery Act 1993, s3(2), Schedule 2, para 7; Parliamentary Commissioner Act 1994 s1. Detailed amendments were made to Schedules 2 and 3, above, by relevant Acts and orders.]

CRIMINAL LAW ACT 1967
(1967 c 58)

3 Use of force in making arrest, etc   [292]

(1) A person may use such force as is reasonable in the circumstances in the prevention of crime, or in effecting or assisting in the lawful arrest of offenders or suspected offenders or of persons unlawfully at large.

(2) Subsection (1) above shall replace the rules of the common law on the question when force used for a purpose mentioned in the subsection is justified by that purpose.

IMMIGRATION ACT 1971
(1971 c 77)

1 General principles   [293]

(1) All those who are in this Act expressed to have the right of abode in the United Kingdom shall be free to live in, and to come and go into and from, the United Kingdom without let or hindrance except such as may be required under and in accordance with this Act to enable their right to be established or as may be otherwise lawfully imposed on any person.

(2) Those not having the right may live, work and settle in the United Kingdom by permission and subject to such regulation and control of their entry into, stay in and departure from the United Kingdom as is imposed by this Act; and indefinite leave to enter or remain in the United Kingdom shall by virtue of this provision, be treated as having been given under this Act to those in the United

Kingdom at its coming into force, if they are then settled there (and not exempt under this Act from the provisions relating to leave to enter or remain) ...

2 Statement of right of abode in the United Kingdom [294]

(1) A person is under this Act to have the right of abode in the United Kingdom if –

(a) he is a British citizen; or

(b) he is a Commonwealth citizen who –

(i) immediately before the commencement of the British Nationality Act 1981 was a Commonwealth citizen having the right of abode in the United Kingdom by virtue of section 2(1)(d) or section 2(2) of this Act as then in force; and

(ii) has not ceased to be a Commonwealth citizen in the meanwhile.

(2) In relation to Commonwealth citizens who have the right of abode in the United Kingdom by virtue of subsection (1)(b) above, this Act, except this section and section 5(2), shall apply as if they were British citizens; and in this Act (except as aforesaid) 'British citizen' shall be construed accordingly.

3 General provisions for regulation and control [295]

(1) Except as otherwise provided by or under this Act, where a person is not a British citizen –

(a) he shall not enter the United Kingdom unless given leave to do so in accordance with this Act;

(b) he may be given leave to enter the United Kingdom (or, when already there, leave to remain in the United Kingdom) either for a limited or for an indefinite period;

(c) if he is given a limited leave to enter or remain in the United Kingdom, it may be given subject to conditions restricting his employment or occupation in the United Kingdom, or requiring him to register with the police, or both ...

(3) In the case of a limited leave to enter or remain in the United Kingdom –

(a) a person's leave may be varied, whether by restricting, enlarging or removing the limit on its duration, or by adding, varying or revoking conditions, but if the limit on its duration is removed, any conditions attached to the leave shall cease to apply; and

(b) the limitation on and any conditions attached to a person's leave whether imposed originally or on a variation shall, if not superseded, apply also to any subsequent leave he may obtain after an absence from the United Kingdom within the period limited for the duration of earlier leave ...

(5) A person who is not a British citizen shall be liable to deportation from the United Kingdom –

(a) if, having only a limited leave to enter or remain, he does not observe a condition attached to the leave or remains beyond the time limited by the leave; or

(b) if the Secretary of State deems his deportation to be conducive to the public good; or

(c) if another person to whose family he belongs is or has been ordered to be deported.

(6) Without prejudice to the operation of subsection (5) above, a person who is not a British citizen shall also be liable to deportation from the United Kingdom if, after he has attained the age of seventeen, he is convicted of an offence for which

he is punishable with imprisonment and on his conviction is recommended for deportation by a court empowered by this Act to do so ...

(8) Where any question arises under this Act whether or not a person is a British citizen, or is entitled to any exemption under this Act, it shall lie on the person asserting it to prove that he is ...

(9) A person seeking to enter the United Kingdom and claiming to have the right of abode there shall prove that he has that right by means of either –

(a) a United Kingdom passport describing him as a British citizen or as a citizen of the United Kingdom and Colonies having the right of abode in the United Kingdom; or
(b) a certificate of entitlement issued by or on behalf of the Government of the United Kingdom certifying that he has such a right of abode.

4 Administration of control   [296]

(1) The power under this Act to give or refuse leave to enter the United Kingdom shall be exercised by immigration officers, and the power to give leave to remain in the United Kingdom, or to vary any leave under section 3(3)(a) (whether as regards duration or conditions), shall be exercised by the Secretary of State; and, unless otherwise allowed by this Act, those powers shall be exercised by notice in writing given to the person affected ...

5 Procedure for, and further provision as to, deportation   [297]

(1) Where a person is under section 3(5) or (6) above liable to deportation, then subject to the following provisions of this Act the Secretary of State may make a deportation order against him, that is to say an order requiring him to leave and prohibiting him from entering the United Kingdom; and a deportation order against a person shall invalidate any leave to enter or remain in the United Kingdom given him before the order is made or while it is in force.

(2) A deportation order against a person may at any time be revoked by a further order of the Secretary of State, and shall cease to have effect if he becomes a British citizen.

(3) A deportation order shall not be made against a person as belonging to a family of another person if more than eight weeks have elapsed since the other person left the United Kingdom after the making of the deportation order against him; and a deportation order made against a person on that ground shall cease to have effect if he ceases to belong to the family of the other person, or if the deportation order made against the other person ceases to have effect.

(4) For purposes of deportation the following shall be those who are regarded as belonging to another person's family –

(a) where that other person is a man, his wife and his or her children under the age of eighteen; and
(b) where that other person is a woman, her children under the age of eighteen;

and for purposes of this subsection an adopted child, whether legally adopted or not, may be treated as the child of the adopter and, if legally adopted, shall be regarded as the child only of the adopter; an illegitimate child (subject to the foregoing rule as to adoptions) shall be regarded as the child of the mother; and 'wife' includes each of two or more wives ...

(6) Where a person is liable to deportation under section 3(5) or (6) above but, without a deportation order being made against him, leaves the United Kingdom

to live permanently abroad, the Secretary of State may make payments of such amounts as he may determine to meet the person's expenses in so leaving the United Kingdom, including travelling expenses for members of his family or household.

6 Recommendation by court for deportation [298]

(1) Where under section 3(6) above a person convicted of an offence is liable to deportation on the recommendation of a court, he may be recommended for deportation by any court having power to sentence him for the offence unless the court commits him to be sentenced or further dealt with for that offence by another court ...

(2) A court shall not recommend a person for deportation unless he has been given not less than seven days' notice in writing stating that a person is not liable to deportation if he is a British citizen, describing the persons who are British citizens and stating (so far as material) the effect of section 3(8) above and section 7 below ...

(5) Where a court recommends or purports to recommend a person for deportation, the validity of the recommendation shall not be called in question except on an appeal against the recommendation or against the conviction on which it is made; but –

(a) ... the recommendation shall be treated as a sentence for the purpose of any enactment providing an appeal against sentence ...

(6) A deportation order shall not be made on the recommendation of a court so long as an appeal or further appeal is pending against the recommendation or against the conviction on which it was made; and for this purpose an appeal or further appeal shall be treated as pending (where one is competent but has not been brought) until the expiration of the time for bringing that appeal ...

7 Exemption from deportation for certain existing residents [299]

(1) Notwithstanding anything in section 3(5) or (6) above but subject to the provisions of this section, a Commonwealth citizen or citizen of the Republic of Ireland who was such a citizen at the coming into force of this Act and was then ordinarily resident in the United Kingdom –

(a) shall not be liable to deportation under section 3(5)(b) if at the time of the Secretary of State's decision he had at all times since the coming into force of this Act been ordinarily resident in the United Kingdom and Islands; and
(b) shall not be liable to deportation under section 3(5)(a), (b) or (c) if at the time of the Secretary of State's decision he had for the last five years been ordinarily resident in the United Kingdom and Islands; and
(c) shall not on conviction of an offence be recommended for deportation under section 3(6) if at the time of the conviction he had for the last five years been ordinarily resident in the United Kingdom and Islands.

(2) A person who has at any time become ordinarily resident in the United Kingdom or in any of the Islands shall not be treated for the purposes of this section as having ceased to be so by reason only of his having remained there in breach of the immigration laws.

(3) The 'last five years' before the material time under subsection (1)(b) or (c) above is to be taken as a period amounting in total to five years exclusive of any time during which the person claiming exemption under this section was undergoing imprisonment or detention by virtue of a sentence passed for an

offence on a conviction in the United Kingdom and Islands, and the period for which he was imprisoned or detained by virtue of the sentence amounted to six months or more ...

13 Appeal against exclusion from the United Kingdom   [300]

(1) Subject to the provisions of this Part of this Act, a person who is refused leave to enter the United Kingdom under this Act may appeal to an adjudicator against the decision that he requires leave or against the refusal.

(2) Subject to the provisions of this Part of this Act, a person who, on an application duly made, is refused a certificate of entitlement or an entry clearance may appeal to an adjudicator against the refusal.

(3) A person shall not be entitled to appeal, on the ground that he has a right of abode in the United Kingdom, against a decision that he requires leave to enter the United Kingdom unless he holds such a passport or certificate as is mentioned in section 3(9) above; and a person shall not be entitled to appeal against a refusal of leave to enter so long as he is in the United Kingdom, unless he was refused leave at a port of entry and at a time when he held a current entry clearance or was a person named in a current work permit.

(3A) A person who seeks to enter the United Kingdom –

(a) as a visitor, or

(b) in order to follow a course of study of not more than six months' duration for which he has been accepted, or

(c) with the intention of studying but without having been accepted for any course of study, or

(d) as a dependent of a person within paragraph (a), (b) or (c) above,

shall not be entitled to appeal against a refusal of an entry clearance and shall not be entitled to appeal against a refusal of leave to enter unless he held a current entry clearance at the time of the refusal.

(3AA) The Secretary of State shall appoint a person, not being an officer of his, to monitor, in such manner as the Secretary of State may determine, refusals of entry clearance in cases where there is, by virtue of subsection (3A) above, no right of appeal; and the person so appointed shall make an annual report on the discharge of his functions to the Secretary of State who shall lay a copy of it before each House of Parliament.

(3AB) The Secretary of State may pay to a person appointed under subsection (3AA) above such fees and allowances as he may with the approval of the Treasury determine.

(3B) A person shall not be entitled to appeal against a refusal of an entry clearance if the refusal is on the ground that –

(a) he or any person whose dependant he is does not hold a relevant document which is required by the immigration rules; or

(b) he or any person whose dependant he is does not satisfy a requirement of the immigration rules as to age or nationality or citizenship; or

(c) he or any person whose dependant he is seeks entry for a period exceeding that permitted by the immigration rules;

and a person shall not be entitled to appeal against a refusal of leave to enter if the refusal is on any of those grounds.

(3C) For the purposes of subsection (3B)(a) above, the following are 'relevant documents' –

(a) entry clearances;

(b) passports or other identity documents; and
(c) work permits.

(4) An appeal against a refusal of leave to enter shall be dismissed by the adjudicator if he is satisfied that the appellant was at the time of the refusal an illegal entrant, and an appeal against a refusal of an entry clearance shall be dismissed by the adjudicator if he is satisfied that a deportation order was at the time of the refusal in force in respect of the appellant.

(5) A person shall not be entitled to appeal against a refusal of leave to enter, or against a refusal of an entry clearance, if the Secretary of State certifies that directions have been given by the Secretary of State (and not by a person acting under his authority) for the appellant not to be given entry to the United Kingdom on the ground that his exclusion is conducive to the public good, or if the leave to enter or entry clearance was refused in obedience to any such directions.

14 Appeals against conditions [301]

(1) Subject to the provisions of this Part of this Act, a person who has a limited leave under this Act to enter or remain in the United Kingdom may appeal to an adjudicator against any variation of the leave (whether as regards duration or conditions), or against any refusal to vary it; and a variation shall not take effect so long as an appeal is pending under this subsection against the variation, nor shall any appellant be required to leave the United Kingdom by reason of the expiration of his leave so long as his appeal is pending under this subsection against a refusal to enlarge or remove the limit on the duration of the leave ...

(3) A person shall not be entitled to appeal under subsection (1) above against any variation of his leave which reduces its duration, or against any refusal to enlarge or remove the limits of its duration, if the Secretary of State certifies that the appellant's departure from the United Kingdom would be conducive to the public good, as being in the interests of national security or of the relations between the United Kingdom and any other country or for any other reasons of a political nature, or the decision questioned by the appeal was taken on that ground by the Secretary of State (and not by a person acting under his authority) ...

(5) Where a deportation order is made against a person any pending appeal by that person under subsection (1) shall lapse.

15 Appeals in respect of deportation orders [302]

(1) Subject to the provisions of this Part of this Act, a person may appeal to an adjudicator against –

(a) a decision of the Secretary of State to make a deportation order against him by virtue of section 3(5) above; or
(b) a refusal by the Secretary of State to revoke a deportation order made against him.

(2) A deportation order shall not be made against a person by virtue of section 3(5) above so long as an appeal may be brought against the decision to make it nor, if such an appeal is duly brought, so long as the appeal is pending; but, in calculating the period of eight weeks limited by section 5(3) above for making a deportation order against a person as belonging to the family of another person, there shall be disregarded any period during which there is pending an appeal against the decision to make it.

(3) A person shall not be entitled to appeal against a decision to make a deportation order against him if the ground of the decision was that his

deportation is conducive to the public good as being in the interests of national security or of the relations between the United Kingdom and any other country or for other reasons of a political nature.

(4) A person shall not be entitled to appeal under this section against a refusal to revoke a deportation order, if the Secretary of State certifies that the appellant's exclusion from the United Kingdom is conducive to the public good or if revocation was refused on that ground by the Secretary of State (and not by a person acting under his authority).

(5) A person shall not be entitled to appeal under this section against a refusal to revoke a deportation order so long as he is in the United Kingdom, whether because he has not complied with the requirement to leave or because he has contravened the prohibition on entering.

(6) On an appeal against a decision to make a deportation order against a person as belonging to the family of another person, or an appeal against a refusal to revoke a deportation order so made, the appellant shall not be allowed, for the purpose of showing that he does not or did not belong to another person's family, to dispute any statement made with a view to obtaining leave for the appellant to enter or remain in the United Kingdom (including any statement made to obtain an entry clearance) unless the appellant shows that the statement was not so made by him or by any person acting with his authority and that, when he took the benefit of the leave, he did not know that any such statement had been made to obtain it or, if he did know, was under the age of eighteen.

(7) An appeal under this section shall be the Appeal Tribunal in the first instance, instead of to an adjudicator, if –

(a) it is an appeal against a decision to make a deportation order and the ground of the decision was that the deportation of the appellant is conducive to the public good; or

(b) it is an appeal against a decision to make a deportation order against a person as belonging to the family of another person, or an appeal against a refusal to revoke a deportation order so made; or

(c) there is pending a related appeal to which paragraph (b) above applies.

(8) Where an appeal to an adjudicator is pending under this section, and before the adjudicator has begun to hear it a related appeal is brought, the appeal to the adjudicator shall be dealt with instead by the Appeal Tribunal and be treated as an appeal duly made to the Tribunal in the first instance.

(9) In relation to an appeal under this section in respect of a deportation order against any person (whether an appeal against a decision to make or against a refusal to revoke the order), any other appeal under this section is a 'related appeal' if it is an appeal in respect of a deportation order against another person as belonging to the family of the first-mentioned person.

19 Determination of appeals by adjudicators [303]

(1) Subject to sections 13(4) and 16(4) above [illegal entrants], and to any restriction on the grounds of appeal, an adjudicator on an appeal to him under this Part of this Act –

(a) shall allow the appeal if he considers –

(i) that the decision or action against which the appeal is brought was not in accordance with the law or with any immigration rules applicable to the case; or

(ii) where the decision or action involved the exercise of discretion by the Secretary or State or an officer, that the discretion should have been exercised differently; and

(b) in any other case, shall dismiss the appeal.

(2) For the purposes of subsection (1)(a) above, the adjudicator may review any determination of a question of fact on which the decision or action was based; and for the purposes of subsection (1)(a)(ii) no decision or action which is in accordance with the immigration rules shall be treated as having involved the exercise of a discretion by the Secretary of State by reason only of the fact that he has been requested by or on behalf of the appellant to depart, or to authorise an officer to depart, from the rules and has refused to do so.

(3) Where an appeal is allowed, the adjudicator shall give such directions for giving effect to the determination as the adjudicator thinks requisite, and may also make recommendations with respect to any other action which the adjudicator considers should be taken in that case under this Act; and ... it shall be the duty of the Secretary of State and any officer to whom directions are given under this subsection to comply with them.

(4) Where in accordance with section 15 above a person appeals to the Appeal Tribunal in the first instance, this section shall apply with the substitution of references to the Tribunal for references to an adjudicator.

20 Appeal to tribunal from determination of adjudicators [304]

(1) Subject to any requirement of rules of procedure as to leave to appeal, any party to an appeal to an adjudicator may, if dissatisfied with his determination thereon, appeal to the Appeal Tribunal, and the Tribunal may affirm the determination or make any other determination which could have been made by the adjudicator ...

[As amended by the British Nationality Act 1981, s39(2), (3), (6), Schedule 4, paras 2, 3(1), 4; Criminal Justice Act 1982, ss77, 78, Schedule 15, para 16, Schedule 16; Immigration Act 1988, ss3(1), (2), (3), 10, Schedule, paras 1, 2, 3; Asylum and Immigration Appeals Act 1993, ss10, 11(1).]

EUROPEAN COMMUNITIES ACT 1972
(1972 c 68)

1 Short title and interpretation [305]

(1) This Act may be cited as the European Communities Act 1972.

(2) In this Act –

'the Communities' means the European Economic Community, the European Coal and Steel Community and the European Atomic Energy Community;

'the Treaties' or 'the Community Treaties' means, subject to subsection (3) below, the pre-accession treaties, that is to say, those described in Part I of Schedule 1 to this Act, taken with –

(a) the treaty relating to the accession of the United Kingdom to the European Economic Community and to the European Atomic Energy Community, signed at Brussels on the 22nd January 1972; and

(b) the decision, of the same date, of the Council of the European Communities relating to the accession of the United Kingdom to the European Coal and Steel Community; and

(c) the treaty relating to the accession of the Hellenic Republic to the European Economic Community and to the European Atomic Energy Community, signed at Athens on 28th May 1979; and

(d) the decision, of 24th May 1979, of the Council relating to the accession of

the Hellenic Republic to the European Coal and Steel Community; and
(e) the decisions, of 7th May 1985 and of 24th June 1988, of the Council on the Communities' system of own resources; and
(f) the undertaking by the Representatives of the Governments of the Member States, as confirmed at their meeting within the Council on 24th June 1988 in Luxembourg, to make payments to finance the Communities' general budget for the financial year 1988; and
(g) the treaty relating to the accession of the Kingdom of Spain and the Portuguese Republic to the European Economic Community and to the European Atomic Energy Community, signed at Lisbon and Madrid on 12th June 1985; and
(h) the decision, of 11th June 1985, of the Council relating to the accession of the Kingdom of Spain and the Portuguese Republic to the European Coal and Steel Community; and
(j) the following provisions of the Single European Act signed at Luxembourg and The Hague on 17th and 28th February 1986, namely Title II (amendment of the treaties establishing the Communities) and, so far as they relate to any of the Communities or any Community institution, the preamble and Titles I (common provisions) and IV (general and final provisions); and
(k) Titles II, III and IV of the Treaty on European Union signed at Maastricht on 7th February 1992, together with the other provisions of the Treaty so far as they relate to those Titles, and the Protocols adopted at Maastricht on that date and annexed to the Treaty establishing the European Community with the exception of the Protocol on Social Policy on page 117 of Cm 1934; and
(l) the decision, of 1st February 1993, of the Council amending the Act concerning the election of the representatives of the European Parliament by direct universal suffrage annexed to Council Decision 76/787/ECSC, EEC, Euratom of 20th September 1976; and
(m) the Agreement on the European Economic Area signed at Oporto on 2nd May 1992 together with the Protocol adjusting that Agreement signed at Brussels on 17th March 1993; and any other treaty entered into by any of the Communities, with or without any of the Member States, or entered into, as a treaty ancillary to any of the Treaties, by the United Kingdom;

and any expression defined in Schedule 1 to this Act has the meaning there given to it.

(3) If Her Majesty by Order in Council declares that a treaty specified in the Order is to be regarded as one of the Community Treaties as herein defined, the Order shall be conclusive that it is to be so regarded; but a treaty entered into by the United Kingdom after the 22nd January 1972, other than a pre-accession treaty to which the United Kingdom accedes on terms settled on or before that date, shall not be so regarded unless it is so specified, nor be so specified unless a draft of the Order in Council has been approved by resolution of each House of Parliament.

(4) For purposes of subsection (2) and (3) above, 'treaty' includes any international agreement, and any protocol or annex to a treaty or international agreement.

2 General implementation of treaties [306]

(1) All such rights, powers, liabilities, obligations and restrictions from time to time created or arising by or under the Treaties, and all such remedies and procedures from time to time provided for by or under the Treaties, as in accordance with the Treaties are without further enactment to be given legal effect or used in the United Kingdom, shall be recognised and available in law, and be

enforced, allowed or followed accordingly; and the expression 'enforceable Community right' and similar expressions shall be read as referring to one to which this subsection applies.

(2) Subject to Schedule 2 to this Act, at any time after its passing Her Majesty may by Order in Council, and any designated Minister or department may by regulations, make provision –

(a) for the purpose of implementing any Community obligation of the United Kingdom, or enabling any rights enjoyed or to be enjoyed by the United Kingdom under or by virtue of the Treaties to be exercised; or

(b) for the purpose of dealing with matters arising out of or related to any such obligation or rights or the coming into force, or the operation from time to time, of subsection (1) above; and in the exercise of any statutory power or duty, including any power to give directions or to legislate by means of orders, rules, regulations or other subordinate instrument, the person entrusted with the power or duty may have regard to the objects of the Communities and to any such obligations or rights as aforesaid ...

(4) The provision that may be made under subsection (2) above includes, subject to Schedule 2 to this Act, any such provision (of any such extent) as might be made by Act of Parliament, and any enactment passed or to be passed, other than one contained in this part of this Act, shall be construed and have effect subject to the foregoing provisions of this section; but, except as may be provided by any Act passed after this Act, Schedule 2 shall have effect in connection with the powers conferred by this and the following sections of this Act to make Orders in Council and regulations ...

3 Decisions on and proof of Treaties and Community Instruments [307]

(1) For the purpose of all legal proceedings any question as to the meaning or effect of any of the Treaties, or as to the validity, meaning or effect of any Community instrument, shall be treated as a question of law (and, if not referred to the European Court, be for determination as such in accordance with the principles laid down by and any relevant decision of the European Court or any court attached thereto).

(2) Judicial notice shall be taken of the Treaties, of the Official Journal of the Communities and of any decision of, or expression of opinion by, the European Court or any court attached thereto on any such question as aforesaid; and the Official Journal shall be admissible as evidence of any instrument or other act thereby communicated of any of the Communities or of any Community institution.

(3) Evidence of any instrument issued by a Community institution, including any judgment or order of the European Court or any court attached thereto, or of any document in the custody of a Community institution, or any entry in or extract from such a document, may be given by an official of that institution; and any document purporting to be such a copy shall be received in evidence without proof of the official position or handwriting of the person signing the certificate.

(4) Evidence of any Community instrument may also be given in any legal proceedings –

(a) by production of a copy purporting to be printed by the Queen's Printer;

(b) where the instrument is in the custody of a government department ... by production of a copy certified on behalf of the department to be a true copy by an officer of the department generally or specially authorised so to do;

and any document purporting to be such a copy as is mentioned in paragraph (b) above of an instrument in the custody of a department shall be received in evidence without proof of the official position or handwriting of the person signing the certificate, or of his authority to do so, or of the document being in the custody of the department ...

[As amended by the Interpretation Act 1978, s25(1), Schedule 3; European Communities (Greek Accession) Act 1979, s1; European Communities (Spanish and Portuguese) Accession Act 1985, s1; European Communities (Amendment) Act 1986, ss1, 2; European Communities (Finance) Act 1988, s1; European Communities (Amendment) Act 1993, s1(1); European Parliamentary Elections Act 1993, s3(2); European Economic Area Act 1993, s1.]

HOUSE OF COMMONS DISQUALIFICATION ACT 1975
(1975 c 24)

1 Disqualification of holders of certain offices and places   [308]

(1) Subject to the provisions of this Act, a person is disqualified for membership of the House of Commons who for the time being –

(a) holds any of the judicial offices specified in Part I of Schedule 1 to this Act;
(b) is employed in the civil service of the Crown, whether in an established capacity or not, and whether for the whole or part of his time;
(c) is a member of any of the regular armed forces of the Crown or the Ulster Defence Regiment.
(d) is a member of any police force maintained by a police authority;
(e) is a member of the legislature of any country or territory outside the Commonwealth; or
(f) holds any office described in Part II or Part III of Schedule 1.

(2) A person who for the time being holds any office described in Part IV of Schedule 1 is disqualified for membership of the House of Commons for any constituency specified in relation to that office in the second column of Part IV ...

(4) Except as provided by this Act, a person shall not be disqualified for membership of the House of Commons by reason of his holding an office or place of profit under the Crown or any other office or place; and a person shall not be disqualified for appointment to or for holding any office or place by reason of his being a member of that House.

2 Ministerial offices   [309]

(1) No more than ninety-five persons being the holders of office specified in Schedule 2 to this Act (in this section referred to as Ministerial offices) shall be entitled to sit and vote in the House of Commons at any one time.

(2) If at any time the number of members of the House of Commons who are holders of Ministerial offices exceeds the number entitled to sit and vote in that House under subsection (1) above, none except any who were both members of that House and holders of Ministerial offices before the excess occurred shall sit or vote therein until the number has been reduced, by death, resignation or otherwise, to the number entitled to sit and vote as aforesaid.

(3) A person holding a Ministerial office is not disqualified by this Act by reason of any office held by him ex officio as the holder of that Ministerial office.

4 Stewardship of the Chiltern Hundreds, etc [310]

For the purposes of the provisions of this Act relating to the vacation of the seat of a member of the House of Commons who becomes disqualified by this Act for membership of that House, the office of steward or bailiff of Her Majesty's three Chiltern Hundreds of Stoke, Desborough and Burnham, or of the Manor of Northstead, shall be treated as included among the office described in Part III of Schedule 1 to this Act.

6 Effect of disqualification and provisions for relief [311]

(1) Subject to any order made by the House of Commons under this section –

(a) if any person disqualified by this Act for membership of that House, or for membership for a particular constituency, is elected as a member or that House, or as a member for that constituency, as the case may be, his election shall be void; and

(b) if any person being a member of that House becomes disqualified by this Act for membership, or for membership for the constituency for which he is sitting, his seat shall be vacated.

(2) If, in a case falling or alleged to fall within subsection (1) above, it appears to the House of Commons that the grounds of disqualification or alleged disqualification under this Act which subsisted or arose at the material time have been removed, and that it is otherwise proper so to do, that House may by order direct that any such disqualification incurred on those grounds at that time shall be disregarded for the purposes of this section ...

SCHEDULE 1 [312]

OFFICES DISQUALIFYING FOR MEMBERSHIP

PART I

JUDICIAL OFFICES

Judge of the High Court of Justice or Court of Appeal

Judge of the Court of Session

Judge of the High Court of Justice or Court of Appeal in Northern Ireland

Judge of the Courts-Martial Appeal Court

Chairman of the Scottish Land Court

Circuit Judge

Sheriff Principal or Sheriff (other than Honorary Sheriff) appointed under the Sheriff Courts (Scotland) Act 1907, or Temporary Sheriff Principal or Temporary Sheriff appointed under the Sheriff Courts (Scotland) Act 1971

County Court Judge or deputy County Court Judge in Northern Ireland

Stipendiary Magistrate within the meaning of the Justices of the Peace Act 1979

Stipendiary Magistrate in Scotland

Resident Magistrate or Deputy Resident Magistrate appointed under the Magistrates' Courts Act (Northern Ireland) 1964

Chief of other Social Security Commissioner (not including a deputy Commissioner)

Chief or other Social Security Commissioner for Northern Ireland (not including a deputy Commissioner)

Commissioner for the special purposes of the Income Tax Acts appointed under section 4 of the Taxes Management Act 1970

Chief or other Child Support Commissioner (excluding a person appointed under paragraph 4 of Schedule 4 to the Child Support Act 1991)

Chief or other Child Support Commissioner for Northern Ireland (excluding a person appointed under paragraph 4 of Schedule 4 to the Child Support Act 1991).

PART II

[Lists bodies of which all members are disqualified, eg Broadcasting Standards Council, Friendly Societies Commission, Local Government Commission for England and National Rivers Authority.]

PART III

[Lists other disqualifying offices, eg Chairman of the Board of Governors of the Commonwealth Institute, district judge, Pensions Ombudsman and Secretary of the Medical Research Council.]

PART IV

[Lists offices disqualifying for particular constituencies, eg Governor of the Isle of Wight (Isle of Wight) and the High Sheriff of a county in England and Wales (any constituency comprising the whole or part of the area for which he is appointed).]

SCHEDULE 2 [313]

MINISTERIAL OFFICES

Prime Minister and First Lord of the Treasury
Lord President of the Council
Lord Privy Seal
Chancellor of the Duchy of Lancaster
Paymaster General
President of the Board of Trade
Secretary of State
Chancellor of the Exchequer
Minister of Agriculture, Fisheries and Food
Minister of State
Chief Secretary to the Treasury
Minister in charge of a public department of Her Majesty's Government in the United Kingdom (if not within the other provisions of this Schedule)
Attorney General

Lord Advocate

Solicitor General

Solicitor General for Scotland

Parliamentary Secretary to the Treasury

Financial Secretary to the Treasury

Parliamentary Secretary in a Government department other than the Treasury, or not in a department

Junior Lord of the Treasury

Treasurer of Her Majesty's Household

Comptroller of Her Majesty's Household

Vice-Chamberlain of Her Majesty's Household

Assistant Government Whip

[As amended by the Child Support Act 1991, s58(13), Schedule 5, para 3(1), (2); Social Security (Consequential Provisions) Act 1992, s4, Schedule 2, para 16. Detailed amendments were made to Schedule 1, Parts II, III and IV, above, by relevant Acts and orders.]

MINISTERS OF THE CROWN ACT 1975
(1975 c 26)

1 Power by Order in Council to transfer functions [314]
of Ministers

(1) Her Majesty may by Order in Council –

(a) provide for the transfer to any Minister of the Crown of any functions previously exercisable by another Minister of the Crown;

(b) provide for the dissolution of the government department in the charge of any Minister of the Crown and the transfer to or distribution among such other Minister or Ministers of the Crown as may be specified in the Order of any functions previously exercisable by the Minister in charge of that department;

(c) direct that functions of any Minister of the Crown shall be exercisable concurrently with another Minister of the Crown, or shall cease to be so exercisable.

(2) An Order in Council under this section may contain such incidental, consequential and supplemental provisions as may be necessary or expedient for the purpose of giving full effect to the Order, including provisions –

(a) for the transfer of any property, rights and liabilities held, enjoyed or incurred by any Minister of the Crown in connection with any functions transferred or distributed;

(b) for the carrying on and completion by or under the authority of the Minister to whom any functions are transferred of anything commenced by or under the authority of a minister of the Crown before the date when the Order takes effect;

(c) for such adaptations of the enactments relating to any functions transferred as may be necessary to enable them to be exercised by the Minister to whom they are transferred and his officers;

(d) for making in the enactments regulating the number of offices in respect of which salaries may be paid or in section 2 of, and Schedule 2 to, the House of Commons Disqualification Act 1975 (which regulate the number of office holders who may be elected, and sit and vote, as members of the House of

Commons), such modifications as may be expedient by reason of any transfer of functions or dissolutions of a Department effected by the Order;

(e) for the substitution of the Minister to whom functions are transferred for any other Minister of the Crown in any instrument, contract, or legal proceedings made or commenced before the date when the Order takes effect.

(3) No modifications shall be made by virtue of paragraph (d) of subsection (2) above, in any of the enactments mentioned in that paragraph, so as to increase the amount of any salary which may be paid, or the aggregate number of persons to whom salaries may be paid, under those enactments or the aggregate number of persons capable thereunder of sitting and voting as Members of the House of Commons.

(4) Where by any Order made under this section provision is made for the transfer of functions in respect of which any Minister may sue or be sued by virtue of any enactment, the Order shall make any provisions which may be required for enabling the Minister to whom those functions are transferred to sue or be sued in like manner.

(5) A certificate issued by a Minister of the Crown that any property vested in any other Minister immediately before an Order under this section takes effect has been transferred by virtue of the Order to the Minister issuing the certificate shall be conclusive evidence of the transfer.

2 Changes in departments of office of Secretary of State, [315] or in their functions

(1) Her Majesty may in connection with any change in the departments of the office of Secretary of State, or any change in the functions of a Secretary of State, by Order in Council make such incidental, consequential and supplemental provisions as may be necessary or expedient in connection with the change, including provisions –

(a) for making a Secretary of State a corporation sole,
(b) for the transfer of any property, rights or liabilities to or from a Secretary of State,
(c) for any adaptations of enactments relating to a Secretary of State, or to the department of a Secretary of State,
(d) for the substitution of one Secretary of State, or department of a Secretary of State, for another in any instrument, contract or legal proceedings made or commenced before the date when the Order takes effect.

(2) A certificate issued by a Minister of the Crown that any property vested in any other Minister immediately before an Order under this section takes effect has been transferred by virtue of the Order to the Minister issuing the certificate shall be conclusive evidence of the transfer.

(3) This section applies only to changes after 27th June 1974, and to the creation (in that year) of the Departments of Energy, Industry, Trade, and Prices and Consumer Protection.

3 Transfer of property etc by or to Secretary of State [316]

(1) This section applies where any enactment (including an order under this Act) provides that a named Secretary of State and his successors shall be a corporation sole, and applies whether or not the office of corporation sole is for the time being vacant.

(2) Anything done by or in relation to any other Secretary of State for the named Secretary of State as a corporation sole shall have effect as if done by or in relation to the named Secretary of State.

(3) Without prejudice to the preceding provisions of this section, any deed, contract or other instrument to be executed by or on behalf of the named Secretary of State as a corporation sole shall be valid if under the corporate seal of that Secretary of State authenticated by the signature of any other Secretary of State, or of a Secretary to any department of a Secretary of State, or of a person authorised by any Secretary of State to act in that behalf.

4 Change of title of Ministers [317]

If Her Majesty is pleased by Order in Council to direct that any change shall be made in the style and title of a Minister of the Crown, the Order may contain provisions substituting the new style and title –

(a) in the enactments (including those mentioned in section 1(2)(d) above) relating to the Minister;

(b) in any instrument, contract, or legal proceedings made or commenced before the date when the Order takes effect.

REPRESENTATION OF THE PEOPLE ACT 1981
(1981 c 34)

1 Disqualification of certain offenders for membership of [318] the House of Commons

A person found guilty of one or more offences (whether before or after the passing of this Act and whether in the United Kingdom or elsewhere), and sentenced or ordered to be imprisoned or detained indefinitely or for more than one year, shall be disqualified for membership of the House of Commons while detained anywhere in the British Islands or the Republic of Ireland in pursuance of the sentence or order or while unlawfully at large at a time when he would otherwise be so detained.

2 Effects of disqualification [319]

(1) If a person disqualified by this Act for membership of the House of Commons is elected to that House his election shall be void; and if such a person is nominated for election as a member of that House his nomination shall be void.

(2) If a member of the House of Commons becomes disqualified by this Act for membership of that House his seat shall be vacated.

CONTEMPT OF COURT ACT 1981
(1981 c 49)

1 The strict liability rule [320]

In this Act 'the strict liability rule' means the rule of law whereby conduct may be treated as a contempt of court as tending to interfere with the course of justice in particular legal proceedings regardless of intent to do so.

2 Limitation of scope of strict liability [321]

(1) The strict liability rule applies only in relation to publications, and for this purpose 'publication' includes any speech, writing, programme included in a service or other communication in whatever form, which is addressed to the public at large or any section of the public.

(2) The strict liability rule applies only to a publication which creates a substantial risk that the course of justice in the proceedings in question will be seriously impeded or prejudiced.

(3) The strict liability rule applies to a publication only if the proceedings in question are active within the meaning of this section at the time of the publication.

(4) Schedule 1 applies for determining the times at which proceedings are to be treated as active within the meaning of this section.

(5) In this section 'programme service' has the same meaning as in the Broadcasting Act 1990.

3 Defence of innocent publication or distribution [322]

(1) A person is not guilty of contempt of court under the strict liability rule as the publisher of any matter to which that rule applies if at the time of publication (having taken all reasonable care) he does not know and has no reason to suspect that relevant proceedings are active.

(2) A person is not guilty of contempt of court under the strict liability rule as the distributor of a publication containing any such matter if at the time of distribution (having taken all reasonable care) he does not know that it contains such matter and has no reason to suspect that it is likely to do so.

(3) The burden of proof of any fact tending to establish a defence afforded by this section to any person lies upon that person ...

4 Contemporary reports of proceedings [323]

(1) Subject to this section a person is not guilty of contempt of court under the strict liability rule in respect of a fair and accurate report of legal proceedings held in public, published contemporaneously and in good faith.

(2) In any such proceedings the court may, where it appears to be necessary for avoiding a substantial risk of prejudice to the administration of justice in those proceedings, or in any other proceedings pending or imminent, order that the publication of any report of the proceedings, or any part of the proceedings, be postponed for such period as the court thinks necessary for that purpose.

(3) For the purposes of subsection (1) of this section and of section 3 of the Law of Libel Amendment Act 1888 (privilege) a report of proceedings shall be treated as published contemporaneously –

(a) in the case of a report of which publication is postponed pursuant to an order under subsection (2) of this section, if published as soon as practicable after that order expires;

(b) in the case of a report of an application for dismissal under section 6 of the Magistrates' Courts Act 1980 of which publication is permitted by virtue only of subsection (5) or (7) of section 8A of that Act, if published as soon as practicable after publication is so permitted ...

5 Discussion of public affairs [324]

A publication made as or as part of a discussion in good faith of public affairs or other matters of general public interest is not to be treated as a contempt of court under the strict liability rule if the risk of impediment or prejudice to particular legal proceedings is merely incidental to the discussion.

6 Savings [325]

Nothing in the foregoing provisions of this Act –

(a) prejudices any defence available at common law to a charge of contempt of court under the strict liability rule;
(b) implies that any publication is punishable as contempt of court under that rule which would not be so punishable apart from those provisions;
(c) restricts liability for contempt of court in respect of conduct intended to impede or prejudice the administration of justice.

7 Consent required for institution of proceedings [326]

Proceedings for a contempt of court under the strict liability rule (other than Scottish proceedings) shall not be instituted except by or with the consent of the Attorney-General or on the motion of a court having jurisdiction to deal with it.

8 Confidentiality of jury's deliberations [327]

(1) Subject to subsection (2) below, it is a contempt of court to obtain, disclose or solicit any particulars of statements made, opinions expressed, arguments advanced or votes cast by members of a jury in the course of their deliberations in any legal proceedings.

(2) This section does not apply to any disclosure of any particulars –

(a) in the proceedings in question for the purpose of enabling the jury to arrive at their verdict, or in connection with the delivery of that verdict, or
(b) in evidence in any subsequent proceedings for an offence alleged to have been committed in relation to the jury in the first mentioned proceedings,

or to the publication of any particulars so disclosed.

(3) Proceedings for a contempt of court under this section (other than Scottish proceedings) shall not be instituted except by or with the consent of the Attorney-General or on the motion of a court having jurisdiction to deal with it.

10 Sources of information [328]

No court may require a person to disclose, nor is any person guilty of contempt of court for refusing to disclose, the source of information contained in a publication for which he is responsible, unless it be established to the satisfaction of the court that disclosure is necessary in the interests of justice or national security or for the prevention of disorder or crime.

11 Publication of matters exempted from disclosure in court [329]

In any case where a court (having power to do so) allows a name or other matter to be withheld from the public in proceedings before the court, the court may give such directions prohibiting the publication of that name or matter in connection with the proceedings as appear to the court to be necessary for the purpose for which it was so withheld.

19 Interpretation [330]

In this Act –

'court' includes any tribunal or body exercising the judicial power of the State, and 'legal proceedings' shall be construed accordingly ...

SCHEDULE 1

TIMES WHEN PROCEEDINGS ARE ACTIVE FOR PURPOSES OF SECTION 2

Preliminary [331]

1 In this Schedule 'criminal proceedings' means proceedings against a person in respect of an offence, not being appellate proceedings or proceedings commenced by motion for committal or attachment in England and Wales or Northern Ireland; and 'appellate proceedings' means proceedings on appeal from or for the review of the decision of a court in any proceedings.

2 Criminal, appellate and other proceedings are active within the meaning of section 2 at the times respectively prescribed by the following paragraphs of this Schedule; and in relation to proceedings in which more than one of the steps described in any of those paragraphs is taken, the reference in that paragraph is a reference to the first of those steps.

Criminal proceedings [332]

3 Subject to the following provisions of this Schedule, criminal proceedings are active from the relevant initial step specified in paragraph 4 until concluded as described in paragraph 5.

4 The initial steps of criminal proceedings are:

(a) arrest without warrant;
(b) the issue, or in Scotland the grant, of a warrant for arrest;
(c) the issue of a summons to appear, or in Scotland the grant of a warrant to cite;
(d) the service of an indictment or other document specifying the charge;
(e) except in Scotland, oral charge.

5 Criminal proceedings are concluded –

(a) by acquittal or, as the case may be, by sentence;
(b) by any other verdict, finding, order or decision which puts an end to the proceedings;
(c) by discontinuance or by operation of law.

6 The reference in paragraph 5(a) to sentence includes any order or decision consequent on conviction or finding of guilt which disposes of the case, either absolutely or subject to future events, and a deferment of sentence under section 1 of the Powers of Criminal Courts Act 1973, section 219 or 432 of the Criminal Procedure (Scotland) Act 1975 or Article 14 of the Treatment of Offenders (Northern Ireland) Order 1976.

7 Proceedings are discontinued within the meaning of paragraph 5(c) –

(a) in England and Wales or Northern Ireland, if the charge or summons is withdrawn or a nolle prosequi entered;
(aa) in England and Wales, if they are discontinued by virtue of section 23 of the Prosecution of Offences Act 1985 ...
(c) in the case of proceedings in England and Wales or Northern Ireland commenced by arrest without warrant, if the person arrested is released, otherwise than on bail, without having been charged.

8 Criminal proceedings before a court-martial or standing civilian court are not concluded until the completion of any review of finding or sentence.

9 Criminal proceedings in England and Wales or Northern Ireland cease to be

active if an order is made for the charge to lie on the file, but become active again if leave is later given for the proceedings to continue.

9A Where proceedings in England and Wales have been discontinued by virtue of section 23 of the Prosecution of Offences Act 1985, but notice is given by the accused under subsection (7) of that section to the effect that he wants the proceedings to continue, they become active again with the giving of that notice.

10 Without prejudice to paragraph 5(b) above, criminal proceedings against a person cease to be active –

(a) if the accused is found to be under a disability such as to render him unfit to be tried or unfit to plead ...; or

(b) if a hospital order is made in his case ...

but become active again if they are later resumed.

11 Criminal proceedings against a person which become active on the issue or the grant of a warrant for his arrest cease to be active at the end of the period of twelve months beginning with the date of the warrant unless he has been arrested within that period, but become active again if he is subsequently arrested.

Other proceedings at first instance [333]

12 Proceedings other than criminal proceedings and appellate proceedings are active from the time when arrangements for the hearing are made or, if no such arrangements are previously made, from the time the hearing begins, until the proceedings are disposed of or discontinued or withdrawn; and for the purposes of this paragraph any motion or application made in or for the purposes of any proceedings, and any pre-trial review in the county curt, is to be treated as a distinct proceeding.

13 In England and Wales or Northern Ireland arrangements for the hearing of proceedings to which paragraph 12 applies are made within the meaning of that paragraph –

(a) in the case of proceedings in the High Court for which provision is made by rules of court for setting down for trial, when the case is set down;

(b) in the case of any proceedings, when a date for the trial or hearing is fixed
...

Appellate proceedings [334]

15 Appellate proceedings are active from the time when they are commenced –

(a) by application for leave to appeal or apply for review, or by notice of such an application;

(b) by notice of appeal or of application for review;

(c) by other originating process,

until disposed of or abandoned, discontinued or withdrawn.

16 Where, in appellate proceedings relating to criminal proceedings, the court –

(a) remits the case to the court below; or

(b) orders a new trial or a venire de novo ...

any further or new proceedings which result shall be treated as active from the conclusion of the appellate proceedings.

[As amended by the Prosecution of Offences Act 1985, s31(5), Schedule 1, Part I, paras 4, 5; Broadcasting Act 1990, s203(1), Schedule 20, para 31(1); Criminal Justice and Public Order Act 1994, Schedule 4, para 50.]

SUPREME COURT ACT 1981
(1981 c 54)

30 Injunctions to restrain persons from acting in offices [335]
in which they are not entitled to act

(1) Where a person not entitled to do so acts in an office to which this section applies, the High Court may –

    (a) grant an injunction restraining him from so acting; and
    (b) if the case so requires, declare the office to be vacant.

(2) This section applies to any substantive office of a public nature and permanent character which is held under the Crown or which has been created by any statutory provision or royal charter.

31 Application for judicial review [336]

(1) An application to the High Court for one or more of the following forms of relief, namely –

    (a) an order of mandamus, prohibition or certiorari;
    (b) a declaration or injunction under subsection (2); or
    (c) an injunction under section 30 restraining a person not entitled to do so from acting in an office to which that section applies,

shall be made in accordance with rules of court by a procedure to be known as an application for judicial review.

(2) A declaration may be made or an injunction granted under this subsection in any case where an application for judicial review, seeking that relief, has been made and the High Court considers that, having regard to –

    (a) the nature of the matters in respect of which relief may be granted by orders of mandamus, prohibition or certiorari;
    (b) the nature of the persons and bodies against whom relief may be granted by such orders; and
    (c) all the circumstances of the case,

it would be just and convenient for the declaration to be made or the injunction to be granted, as the case may be.

(3) No application for judicial review shall be made unless the leave of the High Court has been obtained in accordance with rules of court; and the court shall not grant leave to make such an application unless it considers that the applicant has a sufficient interest in the matter to which the application relates.

(4) On an application for judicial review the High Court may award damages to the applicant if –

    (a) he has joined with his application a claim for damages arising from any matter to which the application relates; and
    (b) the court is satisfied that, if the claim has been made in an action begun by the applicant at the time of making his application, he would have been awarded damages.

(5) If, on an application for judicial review seeking an order of certiorari, the High Court quashes the decision to which the application relates, the High Court may remit the matter to the court, tribunal or authority concerned, with a direction to reconsider it and reach a decision in accordance with the findings of the High Court.

(6) Where the High Court considers that there has been undue delay in making an application for judicial review, the court may refuse to grant –

(a) leave for the making of the application; or

(b) any relief sought on the application,

if it considers that the granting of the relief sought would be likely to cause substantial hardship to, or substantially prejudice the rights of, any person or would be detrimental to good administration.

(7) Subsection (6) is without prejudice to any enactment or rule of court which has the effect of limiting the time within which an application for judicial review may be made.

REPRESENTATION OF THE PEOPLE ACT 1983
(1983 c 2)

1 Parliamentary electors   [337]

(1) A person entitled to vote as an elector at a parliamentary election in any constituency is one who –

(a) is resident there on the qualifying date (subject to subsection (2) below in relation to Northern Ireland); and

(b) on that date and on the date of the poll –

(i) is not subject to any legal incapacity to vote (age apart); and

(ii) is either a Commonwealth citizen or a citizen of the Republic of Ireland; and

(c) is of voting age (that is, 18 years or over) on the date of the poll.

(2) A person is not entitled to vote as an elector at a parliamentary election in any constituency in Northern Ireland unless he was resident in Northern Ireland during the whole of the period of three months ending on the qualifying date for that election.

(3) A person is not entitled to vote as an elector in any constituency unless registered there in the register of parliamentary electors to be used at the election.

(4) A person is not entitled to vote as an elector –

(a) more than once in the same constituency at any parliamentary election;

(b) in more than one constituency at a general election.

3 Disfranchisement of offenders in prison etc   [338]

(1) A convicted person during the time that he is detained in a penal institution in pursuance of his sentence or unlawfully at large when he would otherwise be so detained is legally incapable of voting at any parliamentary or local government election ...

4 Qualifying date   [339]

(1) In England and Wales and Scotland, 10th October in any year is the qualifying date for a parliamentary or local government election at which the date fixed for the poll falls within the period of twelve months beginning with 16th February in the next following year ...

67 Appointment of election agent   [340]

(1) Not later than the latest time for the delivery of notices of withdrawals for an election, a person shall be named by or on behalf of each candidate as the

candidate's election agent, and the name and address of the candidate's election agent shall be declared in writing by the candidate or some other person on his behalf to the appropriate officer not later than that time.

(2) A candidate may name himself as election agent, and upon doing so shall, so far as circumstances admit, be subject to the provisions of this Act both as a candidate and as an election agent, and, except where the context otherwise requires, any reference in this Act to an election agent shall be construed to refer to the candidate acting in his capacity of election agent.

(3) One election agent only shall be appointed for each candidate, but the appointment, whether the election agent appointed be the candidate himself or not, may be revoked ...

73 Payment of expenses through election agent [341]

(1) Except as permitted by section 74 below [candidate's personal expenses, etc], or in pursuance of section 78 [time for sending in and paying claims] or section 79 [disputed claims] below, no payment and no advance or deposit shall be made –

(a) by a candidate, or
(b) by any agent on behalf of a candidate, or
(c) by any other person,

at any time in respect of election expenses otherwise than by or through the candidate's election agent.

(2) Every payment made by an election agent in respect of any election expenses shall, except where less than £20, be vouched for by a bill stating the particulars and by a receipt.

(3) The references in the foregoing provisions of this section to an election agent shall, in relation to a parliamentary election where sub-agents are allowed, be taken as references to the election agent acting by himself or a sub-agent.

(4) All money provided by any person other than the candidate for any election expenses, whether as gift, loan, advance or deposit, shall be paid to the candidate or his election agent and not otherwise.

(5) The foregoing provisions of this section shall not be deemed to apply to any sum disbursed by any person out of his own money for any small expense legally incurred by him if the sum is not repaid to him.

(6) A person who makes any payment, advance or deposit in contravention of subsection (1) above, or pays in contravention of subsection (4) above any money so provided as mentioned above, shall be guilty of an illegal practice.

75 Prohibition of expenses not authorised by [342]
election agent

(1) No expenses shall, with a view to promoting or procuring the election of a candidate at an election, be incurred by any person other than the candidate, his election agent and persons authorised in writing by the election agent on account –

(a) of holding public meetings or organising any public display; or
(b) of issuing advertisements, circulars or publications; or
(c) of otherwise presenting to the electors the candidate or his views or the extent or nature of his backing or disparaging another candidate,

but paragraph (c) of this subsection shall not –

(i) restrict the publication of any matter relating to the election in a newspaper or other periodical or in a broadcast made by the British Broadcasting Corporation or by Sianel Pedwar Cymru or in a programme included in any service licensed under Part I or III of the Broadcasting Act 1990;

(ii) apply to any expenses not exceeding in the aggregate the sum of £5 which may be incurred by an individual and are not incurred in pursuance of a plan suggested by or concerted with others, or to expenses incurred by any person in travelling or in living away from home or similar personal expenses.

[As amended by the Representation of the People Act 1985, ss14(1), (3), 24, Schedule 4, para 1; Broadcasting Act 1990, s203(1), (4), Schedule 20, para 35(1), (2), Schedule 21, para 5.]

POLICE AND CRIMINAL EVIDENCE ACT 1984
(1984 c 60)

PART I

POWERS TO STOP AND SEARCH

1 Power of constable to stop and search persons,   **[343]** vehicles, etc

(1) A constable may exercise any power conferred by this section –

(a) in any place to which at the time when he proposes to exercise the power the public or any section of the public has access, on payment or otherwise, as of right or by virtue of express or implied permission; or

(b) in any other place to which people have ready access at the time when he proposes to exercise the power but which is not a dwelling.

(2) Subject to subsections (3) to (5) below, a constable –

(a) may search –

(i) any person or vehicle;

(ii) anything which is in or on a vehicle,

for stolen or prohibited articles or any article to which subsection (8A) below applies; and

(b) may detain a person or vehicle for the purpose of such a search.

(3) This section does not give a constable power to search a person or vehicle or anything in or on a vehicle unless he has reasonable grounds for suspecting that he will find stolen or prohibited articles or any article to which subsection (8A) below applies.

(4) If a person is in a garden or yard occupied with and used for the purposes of a dwelling or on other land so occupied and used, a constable may not search him in the exercise of the power conferred by this section unless the constable has reasonable grounds for believing –

(a) that he does not reside in the dwelling; and

(b) that he is not in the place in question with the express or implied permission of a person who resides in the dwelling.

(5) If a vehicle is in a garden or yard occupied with and used for the purposes of a dwelling or on other land so occupied and used, a constable may not search the vehicle or anything in or on it in the exercise of the power conferred by this section unless he has reasonable grounds for believing –

(a) that the person in charge of the vehicle does not reside in the dwelling; and

(b) that the vehicle is not in the place in question with the express or implied permission of a person who resides in the dwelling.

(6) If in the course of such a search a constable discovers an article which he has reasonable grounds for suspecting to be a stolen or prohibited article or an article to which subsection (8A) below applies, he may seize it.

(7) An article is prohibited for the purposes of this Part of this Act if it is –

(a) an offensive weapon; or

(b) an article –

(i) made or adapted for use in the course of or in connection with an offence to which this sub-paragraph applies; or

(ii) intended by the person having it with him for such use by him or by some other person.

(8) The offences to which subsection (7)(b)(i) above applies are –

(a) burglary;

(b) theft;

(c) offences under section 12 of the Theft Act 1968 (taking motor vehicle or other conveyance without authority); and

(d) offences under section 15 of that Act (obtaining property by deception).

(8A) This subsection applies to any article in relation to which a person has committed, or is committing or is going to commit an offence under section 139 of the Criminal Justice Act 1988.

(9) In this Part of this Act 'offensive weapon' means any article –

(a) made or adapted for use for causing injury to persons; or

(b) intended by the person having it with him for such use by him or by some other person.

2 Provisions relating to search under section 1 and other powers [344]

(1) A constable who detains a person or vehicle in the exercise –

(a) of the power conferred by section 1 above; or

(b) of any other power –

(i) to search a person without first arresting him; or

(ii) to search a vehicle without making an arrest,

need not conduct a search if it appears to him subsequently –

(i) that no search is required; or

(ii) that a search is impracticable.

(2) If a constable contemplates a search, other than a search of an unattended vehicle, in the exercise –

(a) of the power conferred by section 1 above; or

(b) of any other power, except the power conferred by section 6 below and the power conferred by section 27(2) of the Aviation Security Act 1982 –

(i) to search a person without first arresting him; or

(ii) to search a vehicle without making an arrest,

it shall be his duty, subject to subsection (4) below, to take reasonable steps before he commences the search to bring to the attention of the appropriate person –

(i) if the constable is not in uniform, documentary evidence that he is a constable; and

(ii) whether he is in uniform or not, the matters specified in subsection (3) below;

and the constable shall not commence the search until he has performed that duty.

(3) The matters referred to in subsection (2)(ii) above are –

(a) the constable's name and the name of the police station to which he is attached;
(b) the object of the proposed search;
(c) the constable's grounds for proposing to make it; and
(d) the effect of section 3(7) or (8) below, as may be appropriate.

(4) A constable need not bring the effect of section 3(7) or (8) below to the attention of the appropriate person if it appears to the constable that it will not be practicable to make the record in section 3(1) below.

(5) In this section 'the appropriate person' means –

(a) if the constable proposes to search a person, that person; and
(b) if he proposes to search a vehicle, or anything in or on a vehicle, the person in charge of the vehicle.

(6) On completing a search of an unattended vehicle or anything in or on such a vehicle in the exercise of any such power as is mentioned in subsection (2) above a constable shall leave a notice –

(a) stating that he has searched it;
(b) giving the name of the police station to which he is attached;
(c) stating that an application for compensation for any damage caused by the search may be made to that police station; and
(d) stating the effect of section 3(8) below.

(7) The constable shall leave the notice inside the vehicle unless it is not reasonably practicable to do so without damaging the vehicle.

(8) The time for which a person or vehicle may be detained for the purposes of such a search is such time as is reasonably required to permit a search to be carried out either at the place where the person or vehicle was first detained or nearby.

(9) Neither the power conferred by section 1 above nor any other power to detain and search a person without first arresting him or to detain and search a vehicle without making an arrest is to be construed –

(a) as authorising a constable to require a person to remove any of his clothing in public other than an outer coat, jacket or gloves; or
(b) as authorising a constable not in uniform to stop a vehicle.

(10) This section and section 1 above apply to vessels, aircraft and hovercraft as they apply to vehicles.

3 Duty to make records concerning searches   [345]

(1) Where a constable has carried out a search in the exercise of any such power as is mentioned in section 2(1) above, other than a search –

(a) under section 6 below; or
(b) under section 27(2) of the Aviation Security Act 1982,

he shall make a record of it in writing unless it is not practicable to do so.

(2) If –

(a) a constable is required by subsection (1) above to make a record of a search; but

(b) it is not practicable to make the record on the spot,

he shall make it as soon as practicable after the completion of the search.

(3) The record of a search of a person shall include a note of his name, if the constable knows it, but a constable may not detain a person to find out his name.

(4) If a constable does not know the name of a person whom he has searched, the record of the search shall include a note otherwise describing that person.

(5) The record of a search of a vehicle shall include a note describing the vehicle.

(6) The record of a search of a person or a vehicle –

(a) shall state –

(i) the object of the search;
(ii) the grounds for making it;
(iii) the date and time when it was made;
(iv) the place where it was made;
(v) whether anything, and if so what, was found;
(vi) whether any, and if so what, injury to a person or damage to property appears to the constable to have resulted from the search; and

(b) shall identify the constable making it.

(7) If a constable who conducted a search of a person made a record of it, the person who was searched shall be entitled to a copy of the record if he asks for one before the end of the period specified in subsection (9) below.

(8) If –

(a) the owner of a vehicle which has been searched or the person who was in charge of the vehicle at the time when it was searched asks for a copy of the record of the search before the end of the period specified in sub-section (9) below; and

(b) the constable who conducted the search made a record of it,

the person who made the request shall be entitled to a copy.

(9) The period mentioned in subsections (7) and (8) above is the period of 12 months beginning with the date on which the search was made.

(10) The requirements imposed by this section with regard to records of searches of vehicles shall apply also to records of searches of vessels, aircraft and hovercraft.

4 Road checks   [346]

(1) This section shall have effect in relation to the conduct of road checks by police officers for the purpose of ascertaining whether a vehicle is carrying –

(a) a person who has committed an offence other than a road traffic offence or a vehicles excise offence;
(b) a person who is a witness to such an offence;
(c) a person intending to commit such an offence; or
(d) a person who is unlawfully at large.

(2) For the purposes of this section a road check consists of the exercise in a locality of the power conferred by section 163 of the Road Traffic Act 1988 in such a way as to stop during the period for which its exercise in that way in that locality continues all vehicles or vehicles selected by any criterion.

(3) Subject to subsection (5) below, there may only be such a road check if a police officer of the rank of superintendent or above authorises it in writing.

(4) An officer may only authorise a road check under subsection (3) above –

(a) for the purpose specified in subsection (1)(a) above, if he has reasonable grounds –

(i) for believing that the offence is a serious arrestable offence; and
(ii) for suspecting that the person is, or is about to be, in the locality in which vehicles would be stopped if the road check were authorised;

(b) for the purpose specified in subsection (1)(b) above, if he has reasonable grounds for believing that the offence is a serious arrestable offence;

(c) for the purpose specified in subsection (1)(c) above, if he has reasonable grounds –

(i) for believing that the offence would be a serious arrestable offence; and
(ii) for suspecting that the person is, or is about to be, in the locality in which vehicles would be stopped if the road check were authorised;

(d) for the purpose specified in subsection (1)(d) above, if he has reasonable grounds for suspecting that the person is, or is about to be, in that locality.

(5) An officer below the rank of superintendent may authorise such a road check if it appears to him that it is required as a matter of urgency for one of the purposes specified in subsection (1) above.

(6) If an authorisation is given under subsection (5) above, it shall be the duty of the officer who gives it –

(a) to make a written record of the time at which he gives it; and
(b) to cause an officer of the rank of superintendent or above to be informed that it has been given.

(7) The duties imposed by subsection (6) above shall be performed as soon as it is practicable to do so.

(8) An officer to whom a report is made under subsection (6) above may, in writing, authorise the road check to continue.

(9) If such an officer considers that the road check should not continue, he shall record in writing –

(a) the fact that it took place; and
(b) the purpose for which it took place.

(10) An officer giving an authorisation under this section shall specify the locality in which vehicles are to be stopped.

(11) An officer giving an authorisation under this section, other than an authorisation under subsection (5) above –

(a) shall specify a period, not exceeding seven days, during which the road check may continue; and
(b) may direct that the road check –

(i) shall be continuous; or
(ii) shall be conducted at specified times,

during that period.

(12) If it appears to an officer of the rank of superintendent or above that a road check ought to continue beyond the period for which it has been authorised he may, from time to time, in writing specify a further period, not exceeding seven days, during which it may continue.

(13) Every written authorisation shall specify –

(a) the name of the officer giving it;
(b) the purpose of the road check; and
(c) the locality in which vehicles are to be stopped.

(14) The duties to specify the purposes of a road check imposed by subsections (9) and (13) above include duties to specify any relevant serious arrestable offence.

(15) Where a vehicle is stopped in a road check, the person in charge of the vehicle at the time when it is stopped shall be entitled to obtain a written statement of the purpose of the road check if he applies for such a statement not later than the end of the period of 12 months from the day on which the vehicle was stopped.

(16) Nothing in this section affects the exercise by police officers of any power to stop vehicles for purposes other than those specified in subsection (1) above.

6 Statutory undertakers, etc   [347]

(1) A constable employed by statutory undertakers may stop, detain and search any vehicle before it leaves a goods area included in the premises of the statutory undertakers.

(2) In this section 'goods area' means any area used wholly or mainly for the storage or handling of goods.

(3) For the purposes of section 6 of the Public Stores Act 1875, any person appointed under the Special Constables Act 1923 to be a special constable within any premises which are in the possession or under the control of British Nuclear Fuels Limited shall be deemed to be a constable deputed by a public department and any goods and chattels belonging to or in the possession of British Nuclear Fuels Limited shall be deemed to be Her Majesty's Stores ...

7 Part I – supplementary   [348]

(3) In this Part of this Act 'statutory undertakers' means persons authorised by any enactment to carry on any railway, light railway, road transport, water transport, canal, inland navigation, dock or harbour undertaking.

PART II

POWERS OF ENTRY, SEARCH AND SEIZURE

8 Power of justice of the peace to authorise entry   [349]
and search of premises

(1) If on an application made by a constable a justice of the peace is satisfied that there are reasonable grounds for believing –

(a) that a serious arrestable offence has been committed; and
(b) that there is material on premises specified in the application which is likely to be of substantial value (whether by itself or together with other material) to the investigation of the offence; and
(c) that the material is likely to be relevant evidence; and
(d) that it does not consist of or include items subject to legal privilege, excluded material or special procedure material; and
(e) that any of the conditions specified in subsection (3) below applies,

he may issue a warrant authorising a constable to enter and search the premises.

(2) A constable may seize and retain anything for which a search has been authorised under subsection (1) above.

(3) The conditions mentioned in subsection (1)(e) above are –

(a) that it is not practicable to communicate with any person entitled to grant entry to the premises;

(b) that it is practicable to communicate with a person entitled to grant entry to the premises but it is not practicable to communicate with any person entitled to grant access to the evidence;

(c) that entry to the premises will not be granted unless a warrant is produced;

(d) that the purpose of a search may be frustrated or seriously prejudiced unless a constable arriving at the premises can secure immediate entry to them.

(4) In this Act 'relevant evidence', in relation to an offence, means anything that would be admissible in evidence at a trial for the offence.

(5) The power to issue a warrant conferred by this section is in addition to any such power otherwise conferred.

9 Special provisions as to access [350]

(1) A constable may obtain access to excluded material or special procedure material for the purposes of a criminal investigation by making an application under Schedule 1 below and in accordance with that Schedule.

(2) Any Act (including a local Act) passed before this Act under which a search of premises for the purposes of a criminal investigation could be authorised by the issue of a warrant to a constable shall cease to have effect so far as it relates to the authorisation of searches –

(a) for items subject to legal privilege; or

(b) for excluded material; or

(c) for special procedure material consisting of documents or records other than documents.

10 Meaning of 'items subject to legal privilege' [351]

(1) Subject to subsection (2) below, in this Act 'items subject to legal privilege' means –

(a) communications between a professional legal adviser and his client or any person representing his client made in connection with the giving of legal advice to the client;

(b) communications between a professional legal adviser and his client or any person representing his client or between such an adviser or his client or any such representative and any other person made in connection with or in contemplation of legal proceedings and for the purposes of such proceedings; and

(c) items enclosed with or referred to in such communications and made –

(i) in connection with the giving of legal advice; or

(ii) in connection with or in contemplation of legal proceedings and for the purposes of such proceedings,

when they are in the possession of a person who is entitled to possession of them.

(2) Items held with the intention of furthering a criminal purpose are not items subject to legal privilege.

11 Meaning of 'excluded material' [352]

(1) Subject to the following provisions of this section, in this Act 'excluded material' means –

157

(a) personal records which a person has acquired or created in the course of any trade, business, profession or other occupation or for the purposes of any paid or unpaid office and which he holds in confidence;

(b) human tissue or tissue fluid which has been taken for the purposes of diagnosis or medical treatment and which a person holds in confidence;

(c) journalistic material which a person holds in confidence and which consists –

    (i) of documents; or

    (ii) of records other than documents.

(2) A person holds material other than journalistic material in confidence for the purposes of this section if he holds it subject –

(a) to an express or implied undertaking to hold it in confidence; or

(b) to a restriction on disclosure or an obligation of secrecy contained in any enactment, including an enactment contained in an Act passed after this Act.

(3) A person holds journalistic material in confidence for the purposes of this section if –

(a) he holds it subject to such an undertaking, restriction or obligation; and

(b) it has been continuously held (by one or more persons) subject to such an undertaking, restriction or obligation since it was first acquired or created for the purposes of journalism.

12 Meaning of 'personal records'   [353]

In this Part of this Act 'personal records' means documentary and other records concerning an individual (whether living or dead) who can be identified from them and relating –

(a) to his physical or mental health;

(b) to spiritual counselling or assistance given or to be given to him; or

(c) to counselling or assistance given or to be given to him, for the purposes of his personal welfare, by any voluntary organisations or by any individual who –

    (i) by reason of his office or occupation has responsibilities for his personal welfare; or

    (ii) by reason of an order of a court has responsibilities for his supervision.

13 Meaning of 'journalistic material'   [354]

(1) Subject to subsection (2) below, in this Act 'journalistic material' means material acquired or created for the purposes of journalism.

(2) Material is only journalistic material for the purposes of this Act if it is in the possession of a person who acquired or created it for the purposes of journalism.

(3) A person who receives material from someone who intends that the recipient shall use it for the purposes of journalism is to be taken to have acquired it for those purposes.

14 Meaning of 'special procedure material'   [355]

(1) In this Act 'special procedure material' means –

(a) material to which subsection (2) below applies; and

(b) journalistic material, other than excluded material.

(2) Subject to the following provisions of this section, this subsection applies to material, other than items subject to legal privilege and excluded material, in the possession of a person who –

(a) acquired or created it in the course of any trade, business, profession or other occupation or for the purpose of any paid or unpaid office; and

(b) holds it subject –

(i) to an express or implied undertaking to hold it in confidence; or

(ii) to a restriction or obligation such as is mentioned in section 11(2)(b) above.

(3) Where material is acquired –

(a) by an employee from his employer and in the course of his employment; or

(b) by a company from an associated company,

it is only special procedure material if it was special procedure material immediately before the acquisition.

(4) Where material is created by an employee in the course of his employment, it is only special procedure material if it would have been special procedure material had his employer created it.

(5) Where material is created by a company on behalf of an associated company, it is only special procedure material if it would have been special procedure material had the associated company created it.

(6) A company is to be treated as another's associated company for the purposes of this section if it would be so treated under section 302 of the Income and Corporation Taxes Act 1970.

15 Search warrants – safeguards [356]

(1) This section and section 16 below have effect in relation to the issue to constables under any enactment, including an enactment contained in an Act passed after this Act, of warrants to enter and search premises; and an entry on or search of premises under a warrant is unlawful unless it complies with this section and section 16 below.

(2) Where a constable applies for any such warrant, it shall be his duty –

(a) to state –

(i) the ground on which he makes the application; and

(ii) the enactment under which the warrant would be issued;

(b) to specify the premises which it is desired to enter and search; and

(c) to identify, so far as is practicable, the articles or persons to be sought.

(3) An application for such a warrant shall be made ex parte and supported by an information in writing.

(4) The constable shall answer on oath any question that the justice of the peace or judge hearing the application asks him.

(5) A warrant shall authorise an entry on one occasion only.

(6) A warrant –

(a) shall specify –

(i) the name of the person who applies for it;

(ii) the date on which it is issued;

(iii) the enactment under which it is issued; and

(iv) the premises to be searched; and

(b) shall identify, so far as is practicable, the articles or persons to be sought.

(7) Two copies shall be made of a warrant.

(8) The copies shall be clearly certified as copies.

16 Execution of warrants   [357]

(1) A warrant to enter and search premises may be executed by any constable.

(2) Such a warrant may authorise persons to accompany any constable who is executing it.

(3) Entry and search under a warrant must be within one month from the date of its issue.

(4) Entry and search under a warrant must be at a reasonable hour unless it appears to the constable executing it that the purpose of a search may be frustrated on an entry at a reasonable hour.

(5) Where the occupier of premises which are to be entered and searched is present at the time when a constable seeks to execute a warrant to enter and search them, the constable –

(a) shall identify himself to the occupier and, if not in uniform, shall produce to him documentary evidence that he is a constable;
(b) shall produce the warrant to him; and
(c) shall supply him with a copy of it.

(6) Where –

(a) the occupier of such premises is not present at the time when a constable seeks to execute such a warrant; but
(b) some other person who appears to the constable to be in charge of the premises is present,

subsection (5) above shall have effect as if any reference to the occupier were a reference to that other person.

(7) If there is no person present who appears to the constable to be in charge of the premises, he shall leave a copy of the warrant in a prominent place on the premises.

(8) A search under a warrant may only be a search to the extent required for the purpose for which the warrant was issued.

(9) A constable executing a warrant shall make an endorsement on it stating –

(a) whether the articles or persons sought were found; and
(b) whether any articles were seized, other than articles which were sought.

(10) A warrant which –

(a) has been executed; or
(b) has not been executed within the time authorised for its execution,

shall be returned –

(i) if it was issued by a justice of the peace, to the clerk to the justices for the petty sessions area for which he acts; and
(ii) if it was issued by a judge, to the appropriate officer of the court from which he issued it.

(11) A warrant which is returned under subsection (10) above shall be retained for 12 months from its return –

(a) by the clerk to the justices, if it was returned under paragraph (i) of that subsection; and
(b) by the appropriate officer, if it was returned under paragraph (ii).

(12) If during the period for which a warrant is to be retained the occupier of the premises to which it relates asks to inspect it, he shall be allowed to do so.

17 Entry for purpose of arrest, etc   [358]

(1) Subject to the following provisions of this section, and without prejudice to any other enactment, a constable may enter and search any premises for the purpose –

(a) of executing –

(i) a warrant of arrest issued in connection with or arising out of criminal proceedings; or
(ii) a warrant of commitment issued under section 76 of the Magistrates' Courts Act 1980;

(b) of arresting a person for an arrestable offence;
(c) of arresting a person for an offence under –

(i) section 1 (prohibition of uniforms in connection with political objects) of the Public Order Act 1936;
(ii) any enactment contained in sections 6 to 8 or 10 of the Criminal Law Act 1977 (offences relating to entering and remaining on property);
(iii) section 4 of the Public Order Act 1986 (fear or provocation of violence);
(iv) section 76 of the Criminal Justice and Public Order Act 1994 (failure to comply with interim possession order);

(d) of recapturing a person who is unlawfully at large and whom he is pursuing; or
(e) of saving life or limb or preventing serious damage to property.

(2) Except for the purpose specified in paragraph (e) of subsection (1) above, the powers of entry and search conferred by this section –

(a) are only exercisable if the constable has reasonable grounds for believing that the person whom he is seeking is on the premises; and
(b) are limited, in relation to premises consisting of two or more separate dwellings, to powers to enter and search –

(i) any parts of the premises which the occupiers of any dwelling comprised in the premises use in common with the occupiers of any other such dwelling; and
(ii) any such dwelling in which the constable has reasonable grounds for believing that the person whom he is seeking may be.

(3) The powers of entry and search conferred by this section are only exercisable for the purposes specified in subsection (1)(c)(ii) or (iv) above by a constable in uniform.

(4) The power of search conferred by this section is only a power to search to the extent that is reasonably required for the purpose for which the power of entry is exercised.

(5) Subject to subsection (6) below, all the rules of common law under which a constable has power to enter premises without a warrant are hereby abolished.

(6) Nothing in subsection (5) above affects any power of entry to deal with or prevent a breach of the peace.

18 Entry and search after arrest   [359]

(1) Subject to the following provisions of this section, a constable may enter and search any premises occupied or controlled by a person who is under arrest for an arrestable offence, if he has reasonable grounds for suspecting that there is on the premises evidence, other than items subject to legal privilege, that relates –

(a) to that offence; or
(b) to some other arrestable offence which is connected with or similar to that offence.

(2) A constable may seize and retain anything for which he may search under subsection (1) above.

(3) The power to search conferred by subsection (1) above is only a power to search to the extent that is reasonably required for the purpose of discovering such evidence.

(4) Subject to subsection (5) below, the powers conferred by this section may not be exercised unless an officer of the rank of inspector or above has authorised them in writing.

(5) A constable may conduct a search under subsection (1) above –

(a) before taking the person to a police station; and

(b) without obtaining an authorisation under subsection (4) above,

if the presence of that person at a place other than a police station is necessary for the effective investigation of the offence.

(6) If a constable conducts a search by virtue of subsection (5) above, he shall inform an officer of the rank of inspector or above that he has made the search as soon as practicable after he has made it.

(7) An officer who –

(a) authorises a search; or

(b) is informed of a search under subsection (6) above, shall make a record in writing –

(i) of the grounds for the search; and

(ii) of the nature of the evidence that was sought.

(8) If the person who was in occupation or control of the premises at the time of the search is in police detention at the time the record is to be made, the officer shall make the record as part of his custody record.

19 General power of seizure, etc [360]

(1) The powers conferred by subsections (2), (3) and (4) below are exercisable by a constable who is lawfully on any premises.

(2) The constable may seize anything which is on the premises if he has reasonable grounds for believing –

(a) that it has been obtained in consequence of the commission of an offence; and

(b) that it is necessary to seize it in order to prevent it being concealed, lost, damaged, altered or destroyed.

(3) The constable may seize anything which is on the premises if he has reasonable grounds for believing –

(a) that it is evidence in relation to an offence which he is investigating or any other offence; and

(b) that it is necessary to seize it in order to prevent the evidence being concealed, lost, altered or destroyed.

(4) The constable may require any information which is contained in a computer and is accessible from the premises to be produced in a form in which it can be taken away and in which it is visible and legible if he has reasonable grounds for believing –

(a) that –

(i) it is evidence in relation to an offence which he is investigating or any other offence; or

(ii) it has been obtained in consequence of the commission of an offence; and

(b) that it is necessary to do so in order to prevent it being concealed, lost, tampered with or destroyed.

(5) The powers conferred by this section are in addition to any power otherwise conferred.

(6) No power of seizure conferred on a constable under any enactment (including an enactment contained in an Act passed after this Act) is to be taken to authorise the seizure of an item which the constable exercising the power has reasonable grounds for believing to be subject to legal privilege.

20 Extension of powers of seizure to computerised information [361]

(1) Every power of seizure which is conferred by an enactment to which this section applies on a constable who has entered premises in the exercise of a power conferred by an enactment shall be construed as including a power to require any information contained in a computer and accessible from the premises to be produced in a form in which it can be taken away and in which it is visible and legible.

(2) This section applies –

(a) to any enactment contained in an Act passed before this Act;
(b) to sections 8 and 18 above;
(c) to paragraph 13 of Schedule 1 to this Act; and
(d) to any enactment contained in an Act passed after this Act.

21 Access and copying [362]

(1) A constable who seizes anything in the exercise of a power conferred by any enactment, including an enactment contained in an Act passed after this Act, shall, if so requested by a person showing himself –

(a) to be the occupier of premises on which it was seized; or
(b) to have had custody or control of it immediately before the seizure,

provide that person with a record of what he seized.

(2) The officer shall provide the record within a reasonable time from the making of the request for it.

(3) Subject to subsection (8) below, if a request for permission to be granted access to anything which –

(a) has been seized by a constable; and
(b) is retained by the police for the purpose of investigating an offence,

is made to the officer in charge of the investigation by a person who had custody or control of the thing immediately before it was so seized or by someone acting on behalf of such a person, the officer shall allow the person who made the request access to it under the supervision of a constable.

(4) Subject to subsection (8) below, if a request for a photograph or copy of any such thing is made to the officer in charge of the investigation by a person who had custody or control of the thing immediately before it was so seized, or by someone acting on behalf of such a person, the officer shall –

(a) allow the person who made the request access to it under the supervision of a constable for the purpose of photographing or copying it; or
(b) photograph or copy it, or cause it to be photographed or copied.

(5) A constable may also photograph or copy, or have photographed or copied, anything which he has power to seize, without a request being made under subsection (4) above.

(6) Where anything is photographed or copied under subsection (4)(b) above, the photograph or copy shall be supplied to the person who made the request.

(7) The photograph or copy shall be so supplied within a reasonable time from the making of the request.

(8) There is no duty under this section to grant access to, or to supply a photograph or copy of, anything if the officer in charge of the investigation for the purposes of which it was seized has reasonable grounds for believing that to do so would prejudice –

(a) that investigation;
(b) the investigation of an offence other than the offence for the purposes of investigating which the thing was seized; or
(c) any criminal proceedings which may be brought as a result of –

(i) the investigation of which he is in charge; or
(ii) any such investigation as is mentioned in paragraph (b) above.

22 Retention   [363]

(1) Subject to subsection (4) below, anything which has been seized by a constable or taken away by a constable following a requirement made by virtue of section 19 or 20 above may be retained so long as is necessary in all the circumstances.

(2) Without prejudice to the generality of subsection (1) above –

(a) anything seized for the purposes of a criminal investigation may be retained, except as provided by subsection (4) below –

(i) for use as evidence at a trial for an offence; or
(ii) for forensic examination or for investigation in connection with an offence; and

(b) anything may be retained in order to establish its lawful owner, where there are reasonable grounds for believing that it has been obtained in consequence of the commission of an offence.

(3) Nothing seized on the ground that it may be used –

(a) to cause physical injury to any person;
(b) to damage property;
(c) to interfere with evidence; or
(d) to assist in escape from police detention or lawful custody,

may be retained when the person from whom it was seized is no longer in police detention or the custody of a court or is in the custody of a court but has been released on bail.

(4) Nothing may be retained for either of the purposes mentioned in subsection (2)(a) above if a photograph or copy would be sufficient for that purpose.

(5) Nothing in this section affects any power of a court to make an order under section 1 of the Police (Property) Act 1897.

23 Meaning of 'premises', etc   [364]

In this Act –

'premises' includes any place and, in particular, includes –

(a) any vehicle, vessel, aircraft or hovercraft;
(b) any offshore installation; and
(c) any tent or movable structure; and

'offshore installation' has the meaning given to it by section 1 of the Mineral Workings (Offshore Installations) Act 1971.

PART III

ARREST

24 Arrest without warrant for arrestable offences [365]

(1) The powers of summary arrest conferred by the following subsections shall apply –

(a) to offences for which the sentence is fixed by law;

(b) to offences for which a person of 21 years of age or over (not previously convicted) may be sentenced to imprisonment for a term of five years (or might be so sentenced but for the restrictions imposed by section 33 of the Magistrates' Courts Act 1980); and

(c) to the offences to which subsection (2) below applies,

and in this Act 'arrestable offence' means any such offence.

(2) The offences to which this subsection applies are –

(a) offences for which a person may be arrested under the customs and excise Acts, as defined in section 1(1) of the Customs and Excise Management Act 1979;

(b) offences under the Official Secrets Act 1920 that are not arrestable offences by virtue of the term of imprisonment for which a person may be sentenced in respect of them;

(bb) offences under any provision of the Official Secrets Act 1989 except section 8(1), (4) or (5);

(c) offences under section 22 (causing prostitution of women) or 23 (procuration of girl under 21) of the Sexual Offences Act 1956;

(d) offences under section 12(1) (taking motor vehicle or other conveyance without authority, etc) or 25(1) (going equipped for stealing, etc) of the Theft Act 1968; and

(e) any offence under the Football (Offences) Act 1991.

(f) an offence under section 2 of the Obscene Publications Act 1959 (publication of obscene matter);

(g) an offence under section 1 of the Protection of Children Act 1978 (indecent photographs and pseudo-photographs of children);

(h) an offence under section 166 of the Criminal Justice and Public Order Act 1994 (sale of tickets by unauthorised persons);

(i) an offence under section 19 of the Public Order Act 1986 (publishing, etc material intended or likely to stir up racial hatred);

(j) an offence under section 167 of the Criminal Justice and Public Order Act 1994 (touting for hire car services).

(3) Without prejudice to section 2 of the Criminal Attempts Act 1981, the powers of summary arrest conferred by the following subsections shall also apply to the offences of –

(a) conspiring to commit any of the offences mentioned in subsection (2) above;

(b) attempting to commit any such offence other than an offence under s12(1) of the Theft Act 1968;

(c) inciting, aiding, abetting, counselling or procuring the commission of any such offence;

and such offences are also arrestable offences for the purposes of this Act.

(4) Any person may arrest without a warrant –

(a) anyone who is in the act of committing an arrestable offence;

(b) anyone whom he has reasonable grounds for suspecting to be committing such an offence.

(5) Where an arrestable offence has been committed, any person may arrest without a warrant –

(a) anyone who is guilty of the offence;
(b) anyone whom he has reasonable grounds for suspecting to be guilty of it.

(6) Where a constable has reasonable grounds for suspecting that an arrestable offence has been committed, he may arrest without a warrant anyone whom he has reasonable grounds for suspecting to be guilty of the offence.

(7) A constable may arrest without a warrant –

(a) anyone who is about to commit an arrestable offence;
(b) anyone whom he has reasonable grounds for suspecting to be about to commit an arrestable offence.

25 General arrest conditions   [366]

(1) Where a constable has reasonable grounds for suspecting that any offence which is not an arrestable offence has been committed or attempted, or is being committed or attempted, he may arrest the relevant person if it appears to him that service of a summons is impracticable or inappropriate because any of the general arrest conditions is satisfied.

(2) In this section 'the relevant person' means any person whom the constable has reasonable grounds to suspect of having committed or having attempted to commit the offence or of being in the course of committing or attempting to commit it.

(3) The general arrest conditions are –

(a) that the name of the relevant person is unknown to, and cannot be readily ascertained by, the constable;
(b) that the constable has reasonable grounds for doubting whether a name furnished by the relevant person as his name is his real name;
(c) that –

(i) the relevant person has failed to furnish a satisfactory address for service; or
(ii) the constable has reasonable grounds for doubting whether an address furnished by the relevant person is a satisfactory address for service;

(d) that the constable has reasonable grounds for believing that arrest is necessary to prevent the relevant person –

(i) causing physical injury to himself or any other person;
(ii) suffering physical injury;
(iii) causing loss of or damage to property;
(iv) committing an offence against public decency; or
(v) causing an unlawful obstruction of the highway;

(e) that the constable has reasonable grounds for believing that arrest is necessary to protect a child or other vulnerable person from the relevant person.

(4) For the purposes of subsection (3) above an address is a satisfactory address for service if it appears to the constable –

(a) that the relevant person will be at it for a sufficiently long period for it to be possible to serve him with a summons; or
(b) that some other person specified by the relevant person will accept service of a summons for the relevant person at it.

(5) Nothing in subsection (3)(d) above authorises the arrest of a person under sub-paragraph (iv) of that paragraph except where members of the public going

about their normal business cannot reasonably be expected to avoid the person to be arrested.

(6) This section shall not prejudice any power of arrest conferred apart from this section.

26 Repeal of statutory powers of arrest without warrant or order [367]

(1) Subject to subsection (2) below, so much of any Act (including a local Act) passed before this Act as enables a constable –

(a) to arrest a person for an offence without a warrant; or
(b) to arrest a person otherwise than for an offence without a warrant or an order of a court,

shall cease to have effect.

(2) Nothing in subsection (1) above affects the enactments specified in Schedule 2 to this Act.

27 Fingerprinting of certain offenders [368]

(1) If a person –

(a) has been convicted of a recordable offence;
(b) has not at any time been in police detention for the offence; and
(c) has not had his fingerprints taken –

(i) in the course of the investigation of the offence by the police; or
(ii) since the conviction,

any constable may at any time not later than one month after the date of the conviction require him to attend a police station in order that his fingerprints may be taken.

(2) A requirement under subsection (1) above –

(a) shall give the person a period of at least seven days within which he must so attend; and
(b) may direct him to so attend at a specified time of day or between specified times of day.

(3) Any constable may arrest without warrant a person who has failed to comply with a requirement under subsection (1) above.

(4) The Secretary of State may by regulations make provision for recording in national police records convictions for such offences as are specified in the regulations.

(5) Regulations under this section shall be made by statutory instrument and shall be subject to annulment in pursuance of a resolution of either House of Parliament.

28 Information to be given on arrest [369]

(1) Subject to subsection (5) below, where a person is arrested, otherwise than by being informed that he is under arrest, the arrest is not lawful unless the person arrested is informed that he is under arrest as soon as is practicable after his arrest.

(2) Where a person is arrested by a constable, subsection (1) above applies regardless of whether the fact of the arrest is obvious.

(3) Subject to subsection (5) below, no arrest is lawful unless the person arrested

is informed of the ground for the arrest at the time of, or as soon as is practicable after, the arrest.

(4) Where a person is arrested by a constable, subsection (3) above applies regardless of whether the ground for the arrest is obvious.

(5) Nothing in this section is to be taken to require a person to be informed –

(a) that he is under arrest; or
(b) of the ground for the arrest,

if it was not reasonably practicable for him to be so informed by reason of his having escaped from arrest before the information could be given.

29 Voluntary attendance at police station, etc   [370]

Where for the purpose of assisting with an investigation a person attends voluntarily at a police station or at any other place where a constable is present or accompanies a constable to a police station or any such other place without having been arrested –

(a) he shall be entitled to leave at will unless he is placed under arrest;
(b) he shall be informed at once that he is under arrest if a decision is taken by a constable to prevent him from leaving at will.

30 Arrest elsewhere than at police station   [371]

(1) Subject to the following provisions of this section, where a person –

(a) is arrested by a constable for an offence; or
(b) is taken into custody by a constable after being arrested for an offence by a person other than a constable,

at any place other than a police station, he shall be taken to a police station by a constable as soon as practicable after the arrest.

(2) Subject to subsections (3) and (5) below, the police station to which an arrested person is taken under subsection (1) above shall be a designated police station.

(3) A constable to whom this subsection applies may take an arrested person to any police station unless it appears to the constable that it may be necessary to keep the arrested person in police detention for more than six hours.

(4) Subsection (3) above applies –

(a) to a constable who is working in a locality covered by a police station which is not a designated police station; and
(b) to a constable belonging to a body of constables maintained by an authority other than a police authority.

(5) Any constable may take an arrested person to any police station if –

(a) either of the following conditions is satisfied –

(i) the constable has arrested him without the assistance of any other constable and no other constable is available to assist him;
(ii) the constable has taken him into custody from a person other than a constable without the assistance of any other constable and no other constable is available to assist him; and

(b) it appears to the constable that he will be unable to take the arrested person to a designated police station without the arrested person injuring himself, the constable or some other person.

(6) If the first police station to which an arrested person is taken after his arrest is

not a designated police station, he shall be taken to a designated police station not more than six hours after his arrival at the first police station unless he is released previously.

(7) A person arrested by a constable at a place other than a police station shall be released if a constable is satisfied, before the person arrested reaches a police station, that there are no grounds for keeping him under arrest.

(8) A constable who releases a person under subsection (7) above shall record the fact that he has done so.

(9) The constable shall make the record as soon as is practicable after the release.

(10) Nothing in subsection (1) above shall prevent a constable delaying taking a person who has been arrested to a police station if the presence of that person elsewhere is necessary in order to carry out such investigations as it is reasonable to carry out immediately.

(11) Where there is delay in taking a person who has been arrested to a police station after his arrest, the reasons for the delay shall be recorded when he first arrives at a police station.

(12) Nothing in subsection (1) above shall be taken to affect –

(a) paragraphs 16(3) or 18(1) of Schedule 2 to the Immigration Act 1971;
(b) section 34(1) of the Criminal Justice Act 1972; or
(c) section 15(6) and (9) of the Prevention of Terrorism (Temporary Provisions) Act 1989 and paragraphs 7(4) and 8(4) and (5) of Schedule 2 and paragraphs 6(6) and 7(4) and (5) of Schedule 5 to that Act.

(13) Nothing in subsection (10) above shall be taken to affect paragraph 18(3) of Schedule 2 to the Immigration Act 1971.

31 Arrest for further offence [372]

Where –

(a) a person –

(i) has been arrested for an offence; and
(ii) is at a police station in consequence of that arrest; and

(b) it appears to a constable that, if he were released from that arrest, he would be liable to arrest for some other offence,

he shall be arrested for that other offence.

32 Search upon arrest [373]

(1) A constable may search an arrested person, in any case where the person to be searched has been arrested at a place other than a police station, if the constable has reasonable grounds for believing that the arrested person may present a danger to himself or others.

(2) Subject to subsections (3) to (5) below, a constable shall also have power in any such case –

(a) to search the arrested person for anything –

(i) which he might use to assist him to escape from lawful custody; or
(ii) which might be evidence relating to an offence; and

(b) to enter and search any premises in which he was when arrested or immediately before he was arrested for evidence relating to the offence for which he has been arrested.

(3) The power to search conferred by subsection (2) above is only a power to

search to the extent that is reasonably required for the purpose of discovering any such thing or any such evidence.

(4) The powers conferred by this section to search a person are not to be construed as authorising a constable to require a person to remove any of his clothing in public other than an outer coat, jacket or gloves but they do authorise a search of a person's mouth.

(5) A constable may not search a person in the exercise of the power conferred by subsection (2)(a) above unless he has reasonable grounds for believing that the person to be searched may have concealed on him anything for which a search is permitted under that paragraph.

(6) A constable may not search premises in the exercise of the power conferred by subsection (2)(b) above unless he has reasonable grounds for believing that there is evidence for which a search is permitted under that paragraph on the premises.

(7) In so far as the power of search conferred by subsection (2)(b) above relates to premises consisting of two or more separate dwellings, it is limited to a power to search –

(a) any dwelling in which the arrest took place or in which the person arrested was immediately before his arrest; and
(b) any parts of the premises which the occupier of any such dwelling uses in common with the occupiers of any other dwellings comprised in the premises.

(8) A constable searching a person in the exercise of the power conferred by subsection (1) above may seize and retain anything he finds, if he has reasonable grounds for believing that the person searched might use it to cause physical injury to himself or to any other person.

(9) A constable searching a person in the exercise of the power conferred by subsection (2)(a) above may seize and retain anything he finds, other than an item subject to legal privilege, if he has reasonable grounds for believing –

(a) that he might use it to assist him to escape from lawful custody; or
(b) that it is evidence of an offence or has been obtained in consequence of the commission of an offence.

(10) Nothing in this section shall be taken to affect the power conferred by section 15(3), (4) and (5) of the Prevention of Terrorism (Temporary Provisions) Act 1989.

PART IV

DETENTION

34 Limitations on police detention   [374]

(1) A person arrested for an offence shall not be kept in police detention except in accordance with the provisions of this Part of this Act.

(2) Subject to subsection (3) below, if at any time a custody officer –

(a) becomes aware, in relation to any person in police detention, that the grounds for the detention of that person have ceased to apply; and
(b) is not aware of any other grounds on which the continued detention of that person could be justified under the provisions of this Part of this Act,

it shall be the duty of the custody officer, subject to subsection (4) below, to order his immediate release from custody.

(3) No person in police detention shall be released except on the authority of a custody officer at the police station where his detention was authorised or, if it

was authorised at more than one station, a custody officer at the station where it was last authorised.

(4) A person who appears to the custody officer to have been unlawfully at large when he was arrested is not to be released under subsection (2) above.

(5) A person whose release is ordered under subsection (2) above shall be released without bail unless it appears to the custody officer –

(a) that there is need for further investigation of any matter in connection with which he was detained at any time during the period of his detention; or
(b) that proceedings may be taken against him in respect of any such matter,

and, if it so appears, he shall be released on bail.

(6) For the purposes of this Part of this Act a person arrested under section 6(5) of the Road Traffic Act 1988 is arrested for an offence.

(7) For the purposes of this Part of this Act a person who returns to a police station to answer bail or is arrested under section 46A below shall be treated as arrested for an offence and the offence in connection with which he was granted bail shall be deemed to be that offence.

35 Designated police stations [375]

(1) The chief officer of police for each police area shall designate the police stations in his area which, subject to section 30(3) and (5) above, are to be the stations in that area to be used for the purpose of detaining arrested persons.

(2) A chief officer's duty under subsection (1) above is to designate police stations appearing to him to provide enough accommodation for that purpose.

(3) Without prejudice to section 12 of the Interpretation Act 1978 (continuity of duties) a chief officer –

(a) may designate a station which was not previously designated; and
(b) may direct that a designation of a station previously made shall cease to operate.

(4) In this Act 'designated police station' means a police station for the time being designated under this section.

36 Custody officers at police stations [376]

(1) One or more custody officers shall be appointed for each designated police station.

(2) A custody officer for a designated police station shall be appointed –

(a) by the chief officer of police for the area in which the designated police station is situated; or
(b) by such other police officer as the chief officer of police for that area may direct.

(3) No officer may be appointed a custody officer unless he is of at least the rank of sergeant.

(4) An officer of any rank may perform the functions of a custody officer at a designated police station if a custody officer is not readily available to perform them.

(5) Subject to the following provisions of this section and to section 39(2) below, none of the functions of a custody officer in relation to a person shall be performed by an officer who at the time when the function falls to be performed is involved in the investigation of an offence for which that person is in police detention at that time.

(6) Nothing in subsection (5) above is to be taken to prevent a custody officer –

(a) performing any function assigned to custody officers –

(i) by this Act; or
(ii) by a code of practice issued under this Act;

(b) carrying out the duty imposed on custody officers by section 39 below;
(c) doing anything in connection with the identification of a suspect; or
(d) doing anything under sections 7 and 8 of the Road Traffic Act 1988.

(7) Where an arrested person is taken to a police station which is not a designated police station, the functions in relation to him which at a designated police station would be the functions of a custody officer shall be performed –

(a) by an officer who is not involved in the investigation of an offence for which he is in police detention, if such an officer is readily available; and
(b) if no such officer is readily available, by the officer who took him to the station or any other officer.

(8) References to a custody officer in the following provisions of this Act include references to an officer other than a custody officer who is performing the functions of a custody officer by virtue of subsection (4) or (7) above.

(9) Where by virtue of subsection (7) above an officer of a force maintained by a police authority who took an arrested person to a police station is to perform the functions of a custody officer in relation to him, the officer shall inform an officer who –

(a) is attached to a designated police station; and
(b) is of at least the rank of inspector,

that he is to do so.

(10) The duty imposed by subsection (9) above shall be performed as soon as it is practicable to perform it.

37 Duties of custody officer before charge   [377]

(1) Where –

(a) a person is arrested for an offence –

(i) without a warrant; or
(ii) under a warrant not endorsed for bail,

the custody officer at each police station where he is detained after his arrest shall determine whether he has before him sufficient evidence to charge that person with the offence for which he was arrested and may detain him at the police station for such period as is necessary to enable him to do so.

(2) If the custody officer determines that he does not have such evidence before him, the person arrested shall be released either on bail or without bail, unless the custody officer has reasonable grounds for believing that his detention without being charged is necessary to secure or preserve evidence relating to an offence for which he is under arrest or to obtain such evidence by questioning him.

(3) If the custody officer has reasonable grounds for so believing, he may authorise the person arrested to be kept in police detention.

(4) Where a custody officer authorises a person who has not been charged to be kept in police detention, he shall, as soon as is practicable, make a written record of the grounds for the detention.

(5) Subject to subsection (6) below, the written record shall be made in the presence of the person arrested who shall at that time be informed by the custody officer of the grounds for his detention.

(6) Subsection (5) above shall not apply where the person arrested is, at the time when the written record is made –

(a) incapable of understanding what is said to him;
(b) violent or likely to become violent; or
(c) in urgent need of medical attention.

(7) Subject to section 41(7) below, if the custody officer determines that he has before him sufficient evidence to charge the person arrested with the offence for which he was arrested, the person arrested –

(a) shall be charged; or
(b) shall be released without charge, either on bail or without bail.

(8) Where –

(a) a person is released under subsection (7)(b) above; and
(b) at the time of his release a decision whether he should be prosecuted for the offence for which he was arrested has not been taken,

it shall be the duty of the custody officer so to inform him.

(9) If the person arrested is not in a fit state to be dealt with under subsection (7) above, he may be kept in police detention until he is.

(10) The duty imposed on the custody officer under subsection (1) above shall be carried out by him as soon as practicable after the person arrested arrives at the police station or, in the case of a person arrested at the police station, as soon as practicable after the arrest.

(15) In this Part of this Act –

'arrested juvenile' means a person arrested with or without a warrant who appears to be under the age of 17;
'endorsed for bail' means endorsed with a direction for bail in accordance with section 117(2) of the Magistrates' Courts Act 1980.

38 Duties of custody officer after charge [378]

(1) Where a person arrested for an offence otherwise than under a warrant endorsed for bail is charged with an offence, the custody officer shall, subject to section 25 of the Criminal Justice and Public Order Act 1994, order his release from police detention, either on bail or without bail, unless –

(a) if the person arrested is not an arrested juvenile –

(i) his name or address cannot be ascertained or the custody officer has reasonable grounds for doubting whether a name or address furnished by him as his name or address is his real name or address;
(ii) the custody officer has reasonable grounds for believing that the person arrested will fail to appear in court to answer to bail;
(iii) in the case of a person arrested for an imprisonable offence, the custody officer has reasonable grounds for believing that the detention of the person arrested is necessary to prevent him from committing an offence;
(iv) in the case of a person arrested for an offence which is not an imprisonable offence, the custody officer has reasonable grounds for believing that the detention of the person arrested is necessary to prevent him from causing physical injury to any other person or from causing loss of or damage to property;
(v) the custody officer has reasonable grounds for believing that the detention of the person arrested is necessary to prevent him from interfering with the administration of justice or with the investigation of offences or of a particular offence; or

(vi) the custody officer has reasonable grounds for believing that the detention of the person arrested is necessary for his own protection;

(b) if he is an arrested juvenile –

(i) any of the requirements of paragraph (a) above is satisfied; or
(ii) the custody officer has reasonable grounds for believing that he ought to be detained in his own interests.

(2) If the release of a person arrested is not required by subsection (1) above, the custody officer may authorise him to be kept in police detention.

(2A) The custody officer, in taking the decisions required by subsection 1(a) and (b) above (except (a)(i) and (vi) and (b)(ii)), shall have regard to the same considerations as those which a court is required to have regard to in taking the corresponding decisions under paragraph 2 of Part I of Schedule 1 to the Bail Act 1976.

(3) Where a custody officer authorises a person who has been charged to be kept in police detention, he shall, as soon as practicable, make a written record of the grounds for the detention.

(4) Subject to subsection (5) below, the written record shall be made in the presence of the person charged who shall at that time be informed by the custody officer of the grounds for his detention.

(5) Subsection (4) above shall not apply where the person charged is, at the time when the written record is made –

(a) incapable of understanding what is said to him;
(b) violent or likely to become violent; or
(c) in urgent need of medical attention.

(6) Where a custody officer authorises an arrested juvenile to be kept in police detention under subsection (1) above, the custody officer shall, unless he certifies –

(a) that, by reason of such circumstances as are specified in the certificate, it is impracticable for him to do so; or
(b) in the case of an arrested juvenile who has attained the age of 12 years, that no secure accommodation is available and that keeping him in other local authority accommodation would not be adequate to protect the public from serious harm from him,

secure that the arrested juvenile is moved to local authority accommodation.

(6A) In this section –

'local authority accommodation' means accommodation provided by or on behalf of a local authority (within the meaning of the Children Act 1989);
'secure accommodation' means accommodation provided for the purposes of restricting liberty;
'sexual offence' and 'violent offence' have the same meanings as in Part I of the Criminal Justice Act 1991;

and any reference, in relation to an arrested juvenile charged with a violent or sexual offence, to protecting the public from serious harm from him shall be construed as a reference to protecting members of the public from death or serious personal injury, whether physical or psychological, occasioned by further such offences committed by him.

(6B) Where an arrested juvenile is moved to local authority accommodation under subsection (6) above, it shall be lawful for any person acting on behalf of the authority to detain him.

(7) A certificate made under subsection (6) above in respect of an arrested

juvenile shall be produced to the court before which he is first brought thereafter.

(7A) In this section 'imprisonable offence' has the same meaning as in Schedule 1 to the Bail Act 1976.

(8) In this Part of this Act 'local authority' has the same meaning as in the Children Act 1989.

39 Responsibilities in relation to persons detained [379]

(1) Subject to subsections (2) and (4) below, it shall be the duty of the custody officer at a police station to ensure –

(a) that all persons in police detention at that station are treated in accordance with this Act and any code of practice issued under it and relating to the treatment of persons in police detention; and

(b) that all matters relating to such persons which are required by this Act or by such codes of practice to be recorded are recorded in the custody records relating to such persons.

(2) If the custody officer, in accordance with any code of practice issued under this Act, transfers or permits the transfer of a person in police detention –

(a) to the custody of a police officer investigating an offence for which that person is in police detention; or

(b) to the custody of an officer who has charge of that person outside the police station,

the custody officer shall cease in relation to that person to be subject to the duty imposed on him by subsection (1)(a) above; and it shall be the duty of the officer to whom the transfer is made to ensure that he is treated in accordance with the provisions of this Act and of any such codes of practice as are mentioned in subsection (1) above.

(3) If the person detained in subsequently returned to the custody of the custody officer, it shall be the duty of the officer investigating the offence to report to the custody officer as to the manner in which this section and the codes of practice have been complied with while that person was in his custody.

(4) If an arrested juvenile is moved to local authority accommodation in pursuance of arrangements made under section 38(6) above, the custody officer shall cease in relation to that person to be subject to the duty imposed on him by subsection (1) above.

40 Review of police detention [380]

(1) Reviews of the detention of each person in police detention in connection with the investigation of an offence shall be carried out periodically in accordance with the following provisions of this section –

(a) in the case of a person who has been arrested and charged, by the custody officer; and

(b) in the case of a person who has been arrested but not charged, by an officer of at least the rank of inspector who has not been directly involved in the investigation.

(2) The officer to whom it falls to carry out a review is referred to in this section as a 'review officer'.

(3) Subject to subsection (4) below –

(a) the first review shall be not later than six hours after the detention was first authorised;

(b) the second review shall be not later than nine hours after the first;

(c) subsequent reviews shall be at intervals of not more than nine hours.

(4) A review may be postponed –

(a) if, having regard to all the circumstances prevailing at the latest time for it specified in subsection (3) above, it is not practicable to carry out the review at that time;

(b) without prejudice to the generality of paragraph (a) above –

(i) if at that time the person in detention is being questioned by a police officer and the review officer is satisfied that an interruption of the questioning for the purpose of carrying out the review would prejudice the investigation in connection with which he is being questioned; or

(ii) if at that time no review officer is readily available.

(5) If a review is postponed under subsection (4) above it shall be carried out as soon as practicable after the latest time specified for it in subsection (3) above.

(6) If a review is carried out after postponement under subsection (4) above, the fact that it was so carried out shall not affect any requirements of this section as to the time at which any subsequent review is to be carried out.

(7) The review officer shall record the reasons for any postponement of a review in the custody record.

(8) Subject to subsection (9) below, where the person whose detention is under review has not been charged before the time of the review, section 37(1) to (6) above shall have effect in relation to him, but with the substitution –

(a) of references to the person whose detention is under review for references to the person arrested; and

(b) of references to the review officer for references to the custody officer.

(9) Where a person has been kept in police detention by virtue of section 37(9) above, section 37(1) to (6) shall not have effect in relation to him but it shall be the duty of the review officer to determine whether he is yet in a fit state.

(10) Where the person whose detention is under review has been charged before the time of the review, section 38(1) to (6) above shall have effect in relation to him, but with the substitution of references to the person whose detention is under review for references to the person arrested.

(11) Where –

(a) an officer of higher rank than the review officer gives directions relating to a person in police detention; and

(b) the directions are at variance –

(i) with any decision made or action taken by the review officer in the performance of a duty imposed on him under this Part of this Act; or

(ii) with any decision or action which would but for the directions have been made or taken by him in the performance of such a duty,

the review officer shall refer the matter at once to an officer of the rank of superintendent or above who is responsible for the police station for which the review officer is acting as review officer in connection with the detention.

(12) Before determining whether to authorise a person's continued detention the review officer shall give –

(a) that person (unless he is asleep); or

(b) any solicitor representing him who is available at the time of the review,

an opportunity to make representations to him about the detention.

(13) Subject to subsection (14) below, the person whose detention is under review or his solicitor may make representations under subsection (12) above either orally or in writing.

(14) The review officer may refuse to hear oral representations from the person whose detention is under review if he considers that he is unfit to make such representations by reason of his condition or behaviour.

41 Limits on period of detention without charge [381]

(1) Subject to the following provisions of this section and to sections 42 and 43 below, a person shall not be kept in police detention for more than 24 hours without being charged.

(2) The time from which the period of detention of a person is to be calculated (in this Act referred to as 'the relevant time') –

(a) in the case of a person to whom this paragraph applies, shall be –

(i) the time at which that person arrives at the relevant police station; or
(ii) the time 24 hours after the time of that person's arrest,

whichever is the earlier;
(b) in the case of a person arrested outside England and Wales, shall be –

(i) the time at which that person arrives at the first police station to which he is taken in the police area in England or Wales in which the offence for which he was arrested is being investigated; or
(ii) the time 24 hours after the time of that person's entry into England and Wales,

whichever is the earlier;
(c) in the case of a person who –

(i) attends voluntarily at a police station; or
(ii) accompanies a constable to a police station without having been arrested,

and is arrested at the police station, the time of his arrest;
(d) in any other case, except where subsection (5) below applies, shall be the time at which the person arrested arrives at the first police station to which he is taken after his arrest.

(3) Subsection (2)(a) above applies to a person if –

(a) his arrest is sought in one police area in England and Wales;
(b) he is arrested in another police area; and
(c) he is not questioned in the area in which he is arrested in order to obtain evidence in relation to an offence for which he is arrested;

and in sub-paragraph (i) of that paragraph 'the relevant police station' means the first police station to which he is taken in the police area in which his arrest was sought.

(4) Subsection (2) above shall have effect in relation to a person arrested under section 31 above as if every reference in it to his arrest or his being arrested were a reference to his arrest or his being arrested for the offence for which he was originally arrested.

(5) If –

(a) a person is in police detention in a police area in England and Wales ('the first area'); and
(b) his arrest for an offence is sought in some other police area in England and Wales ('the second area'); and
(c) he is taken to the second area for the purposes of investigating that offence, without being questioned in the first area in order to obtain evidence in relation to it,

the relevant time shall be –

(i) the time 24 hours after he leaves the place where he is detained in the first area; or

(ii) the time at which he arrives at the first police station to which he is taken in the second area,

whichever is the earlier.

(6) When a person who is in police detention is removed to hospital because he is in need of medical treatment, any time during which he is being questioned in hospital or on the way there or back by a police officer for the purpose of obtaining evidence relating to an offence shall be included in any period which falls to be calculated for the purposes of this Part of this Act, but any other time while he is in hospital or on his way there or back shall not be so included.

(7) Subject to subsection (8) below, a person who at the expiry of 24 hours after the relevant time is in police detention and has not been charged shall be released at that time either on bail or without bail.

(8) Subsection (7) above does not apply to a person whose detention for more than 24 hours after the relevant time has been authorised or is otherwise permitted in accordance with section 42 or 43 below.

(9) A person released under subsection (7) above shall not be re-arrested without a warrant for the offence for which he was previously arrested unless new evidence justifying a further arrest has come to light since his release, but this subsection does not prevent an arrest under section 46A below.

42 Authorisation of continued detention   [382]

(1) Where a police officer of the rank of superintendent or above who is responsible for the police station at which a person is detained has reasonable grounds for believing that –

(a) the detention of that person without charge is necessary to secure or preserve evidence relating to an offence for which he is under arrest or to obtain such evidence by questioning him;

(b) an offence for which he is under arrest is a serious arrestable offence; and

(c) the investigation is being conducted diligently and expeditiously,

he may authorise the keeping of that person in police detention for a period expiring at or before 36 hours after the relevant time.

(2) Where an officer such as is mentioned in subsection (1) above has authorised the keeping of a person in police detention for a period expiring less than 36 hours after the relevant time, such an officer may authorise the keeping of that person in police detention for a further period expiring not more than 36 hours after that time if the conditions specified in subsection (1) above are still satisfied when he gives the authorisation.

(3) If it is proposed to transfer a person in police detention to another police area, the officer determining whether or not to authorise keeping him in detention under subsection (1) above shall have regard to the distance and the time the journey would take.

(4) No authorisation under subsection (1) above shall be given in respect of any person –

(a) more than 24 hours after the relevant time; or

(b) before the second review of his detention under section 40 above has been carried out.

(5) Where an officer authorises the keeping of a person in police detention under subsection (1) above, it shall be his duty –

(a) to inform that person of the grounds for his continued detention; and

(b) to record the grounds in that person's custody record.

(6) Before determining whether to authorise the keeping of a person in detention under subsection (1) or (2) above, an officer shall give –

(a) that person; or

(b) any solicitor representing him who is available at the time when it falls to the officer to determine whether to give the authorisation,

an opportunity to make representations to him about the detention.

(7) Subject to subsection (8) below, the person in detention or his solicitor may make representations under subsection (6) above either orally or in writing.

(8) The officer to whom it falls to determine whether to give the authorisation may refuse to hear oral representations from the person in detention if he considers that he is unfit to make such representations by reason of his condition or behaviour.

(9) Where –

(a) an officer authorises the keeping of a person in detention under subsection (1) above; and

(b) at the time of the authorisation he has not yet exercised a right conferred on him by section 56 or 58 below,

the officer –

(i) shall inform him of that right;

(ii) shall decide whether he should be permitted to exercise it;

(iii) shall record the decision in his custody record; and

(iv) if the decision is to refuse to permit the exercise of the right, shall also record the grounds for the decision in that record.

(10) Where an officer has authorised the keeping of a person who has not been charged in detention under subsection (1) or (2) above, he shall be released from detention, either on bail or without bail, not later than 36 hours after the relevant time, unless –

(a) he has been charged with an offence; or

(b) his continued detention is authorised or otherwise permitted in accordance with section 43 below.

(11) A person released under subsection (10) above shall not be re-arrested without a warrant for the offence for which he was previously arrested unless new evidence justifying a further arrest has come to light since his release, but this subsection does not prevent an arrest under section 46A below.

43 Warrants of further detention [383]

(1) Where, on an application on oath made by a constable and supported by an information, a magistrates' court is satisfied that there are reasonable grounds for believing that the further detention of the person to whom the application relates is justified, it may issue a warrant of further detention authorising the keeping of that person in police detention.

(2) A court may not hear an application for a warrant of further detention unless the person to whom the application relates –

(a) has been furnished with a copy of the information; and

(b) has been brought before the court for the hearing.

(3) The person to whom the application relates shall be entitled to be legally represented at the hearing and, if he is not so represented but wishes to be so represented –

(a) the court shall adjourn the hearing to enable him to obtain representation; and

(b) he may be kept in police detention during the adjournment.

(4) A person's further detention is only justified for the purposes of this section or section 44 below if –

(a) his detention without charge is necessary to secure or preserve evidence relating to an offence for which he is under arrest or to obtain such evidence by questioning him;

(b) an offence for which he is under arrest is a serious arrestable offence; and

(c) the investigation is being conducted diligently and expeditiously.

(5) Subject to subsection (7) below, an application for a warrant of further detention may be made –

(a) at any time before the expiry of 36 hours after the relevant time; or

(b) in a case where –

(i) it is not practicable for the magistrates' court to which the application will be made to sit at the expiry of 36 hours after the relevant time; but

(ii) the court will sit during the six hours following the end of that period,

at any time before the expiry of the said six hours.

(6) In a case to which subsection (5)(b) above applies –

(a) the person to whom the application relates may be kept in police detention until the application is heard; and

(b) the custody officer shall make a note in that person's custody record –

(i) of the fact that he was kept in police detention for more than 36 hours after the relevant time; and

(ii) of the reason why he was so kept.

(7) If –

(a) an application for a warrant of further detention is made after the expiry of 36 hours after the relevant time; and

(b) it appears to the magistrates' court that it would have been reasonable for the police to make it before the expiry of that period,

the court shall dismiss the application.

(8) Where on an application such as is mentioned in subsection (1) above a magistrates' court is not satisfied that there are reasonable grounds for believing that the further detention of the person to whom the application relates is justified, it shall be its duty –

(a) to refuse the application; or

(b) to adjourn the hearing of it until a time not later than 36 hours after the relevant time.

(9) The person to whom the application relates may be kept in police detention during the adjournment.

(10) A warrant of further detention shall –

(a) state the time at which it is issued;

(b) authorise the keeping in police detention of the person to whom it relates for the period stated in it.

(11) Subject to subsection (12) below, the period stated in a warrant of further detention shall be such period as the magistrates' court thinks fit, having regard to the evidence before it.

(12) The period shall not be longer than 36 hours.

(13) If it is proposed to transfer a person in police detention to a police area other

than that in which he is detained when the application for a warrant of further detention is made, the court hearing the application shall have regard to the distance and the time the journey would take.

(14) Any information submitted in support of an application under this section shall state –

(a) the nature of the offence for which the person to whom the application relates has been arrested;

(b) the general nature of the evidence on which that person was arrested;

(c) what inquiries relating to the offence have been made by the police and what further inquiries are proposed by them;

(d) the reasons for believing the continued detention of that person to be necessary for the purposes of such further inquiries.

(15) Where an application under this section is refused, the person to whom the application relates shall forthwith be charged or, subject to subsection (16) below, released, either on bail or without bail.

(16) A person need not be released under subsection (15) above –

(a) before the expiry of 24 hours after the relevant time; or

(b) before the expiry of any longer period for which his continued detention is or has been authorised under section 42 above.

(17) Where an application under this section is refused, no further application shall be made under this section in respect of the person to whom the refusal relates, unless supported by evidence which has come to light since the refusal.

(18) Where a warrant of further detention is issued, the person to whom it relates shall be released from police detention, either on bail or without bail, upon or before the expiry of the warrant unless he is charged.

(19) A person released under subsection (18) above shall not be re-arrested without a warrant for the offence for which he was previously arrested unless new evidence justifying a further arrest has come to light since his release, but this subsection does not prevent an arrest under section 46A below.

44 Extension of warrants of further detention [384]

(1) On an application on oath made by a constable and supported by an information a magistrates' court may extend a warrant of further detention issued under section 43 above if it is satisfied that there are reasonable grounds for believing that the further detention of the person to whom the application relates is justified.

(2) Subject to subsection (3) below, the period for which a warrant of further detention may be extended shall be such period as the court thinks fit, having regard to the evidence before it.

(3) The period shall not –

(a) be longer than 36 hours; or

(b) end later than 96 hours after the relevant time.

(4) Where a warrant of further detention has been extended under subsection (1) above, or further extended under this subsection, for a period ending before 96 hours after the relevant time, on an application such as is mentioned in that subsection a magistrates' court may further extend the warrant if it is satisfied as there mentioned; and subsections (2) and (3) above apply to such further extensions as they apply to extensions under subsection (1) above.

(5) A warrant of further detention shall, if extended or further extended under this section, be endorsed with a note of the period of the extension.

(6) Subsections (2), (3) and (14) of section 43 above shall apply to an application made under this section as they apply to an application made under that section.

(7) Where an application under this section is refused, the person to whom the application relates shall forthwith be charged or, subject to subsection (8) below, released, either on bail or without bail.

(8) A person need not be released under subsection (7) above before the expiry of any period for which a warrant of further detention issued in relation to him has been extended or further extended on an earlier application made under this section.

45 Detention before charge – supplementary [385]

(1) In sections 43 and 44 of this Act 'magistrates' court' means a court consisting of two or more justices of the peace sitting otherwise than in open court.

(2) Any reference in this Part of this Act to a period of time or a time of day is to be treated as approximate only.

46 Detention after charge [386]

(1) Where a person –

(a) is charged with an offence; and
(b) after being charged –

(i) is kept in police detention; or
(ii) is detained by a local authority in pursuance of arrangements made under section 38(6) above,

he shall be brought before a magistrates' court in accordance with the provisions of this section.

(2) If he is to be brought before a magistrates' court for the petty sessions area in which the police station at which he was charged is situated, he shall be brought before such a court as soon as is practicable and in any event not later than the first sitting after he is charged with the offence.

(3) If no magistrates' court for that area is due to sit either on the day on which he is charged or on the next day, the custody officer for the police station at which he was charged shall inform the clerk to the justices for the area that there is a person in the area to whom subsection (2) above applies.

(4) If the person charged is to be brought before a magistrates' court for a petty sessions area other than that in which the police station at which he was charged is situated, he shall be removed to that area as soon as is practicable and brought before such a court as soon as is practicable after his arrival in the area and in any event not later than the first sitting of a magistrates' court for that area after his arrival in the area.

(5) If no magistrates' court for that area is due to sit either on the day on which he arrives in the area or on the next day –

(a) he shall be taken to a police station in the area; and
(b) the custody officer at that station shall inform the clerk to the justices for the area that there is a person in the area to whom subsection (4) applies.

(6) Subject to subsection (8) below, where a clerk to the justices for a petty sessions area has been informed –

(a) under subsection (3) above that there is a person in the area to whom subsection (2) above applies; or
(b) under subsection (5) above that there is a person in the area to whom subsection (4) above applies,

the clerk shall arrange for a magistrates' court to sit not later than the day next following the relevant day.

(7) In this section 'the relevant day' –

(a) in relation to a person who is to be brought before a magistrates' court for the petty sessions area in which the police station at which he was charged is situated, means the day on which he was charged; and
(b) in relation to a person who is to be brought before a magistrates' court for any other petty sessions area, means the day on which he arrives in the area.

(8) Where the day next following the relevant day is Christmas Day, Good Friday or a Sunday, the duty of the clerk under subsection (6) above is a duty to arrange for a magistrates' court to sit not later than the first day after the relevant day which is not one of those days.

(9) Nothing in this section requires a person who is in hospital to be brought before a court if he is not well enough.

46A Power of arrest for failure to answer to police bail   [387]

(1) A constable may arrest without a warrant any person who, having been released on bail under this Part of this Act subject to a duty to attend at a police station, fails to attend at that police station at the time appointed for him to do so.

(2) A person who is arrested under this section shall be taken to the police station appointed as the place at which he is to surrender to custody as soon as practicable after the arrest.

(3) For the purposes of –

(a) section 30 above (subject to the obligation in subsection (2) above), and
(b) section 32 above,

an arrest under this section shall be treated as an arrest for an offence.

47 Bail after arrest   [388]

(1) Subject to subsection (2) below, a release on bail of a person under this Part of this Act shall be a release on bail granted in accordance with sections 3, 3A, 5 and 5A of the Bail Act 1976 as they apply to bail granted by a constable.

(1A) The normal powers to impose conditions of bail shall be available to him where a custody officer releases a person on bail under section 38(1) above (including that subsection as applied by section 40(10) above) but not in any other cases.

In this subsection, 'the normal powers to impose conditions of bail' has the meaning given in section 3(6) of the Bail Act 1976.

(2) Nothing in the Bail Act 1976 shall prevent the re-arrest without warrant of a person released on bail subject to a duty to attend at a police station if new evidence justifying a further arrest has come to light since his release.

(3) Subject to subsection (4) below, in this Part of this Act references to 'bail' are references to bail subject to a duty –

(a) to appear before a magistrates' court at such time and such place; or
(b) to attend at such police station at such time,

as the custody officer may appoint.

(4) Where a custody officer has granted bail to a person subject to a duty to appear at a police station, the custody officer may give notice in writing to that person that his attendance at the police station is not required.

(6) Where a person who has been granted bail and either has attended at the police station in accordance with the grant of bail or has been arrested under section 46A above is detained at a police station, any time during which he was in police detention prior to being granted bail shall be included as part of any period which falls to be calculated under this Part of this Act.

(7) Where a person who was released on bail subject to a duty to attend at a police station is re-arrested, the provisions of this Part of this Act shall apply to him as they apply to a person arrested for the first time, but this subsection does not apply to a person who is arrested under section 46A above or has attended a police station in accordance with the grant of bail (and who accordingly is deemed by section 34(7) above to have been arrested for an offence).

51 Savings [389]

Nothing in this Part of this Act shall affect –

(a) the powers conferred on immigration officers by section 4 of and Schedule 2 to the Immigration Act 1971 (administrative provisions as to control on entry, etc);
(b) the powers conferred by or by virtue of section 14 of the Prevention of Terrorism (Temporary Provisions) Act 1989 or Schedule 2 or 5 to that Act (powers of arrest and detention and control of entry and procedure for removal);
(c) any duty of a police officer under –

(i) sections 129, 190 or 202 of the Army Act 1955 (duties of governors of prisons and others to receive prisoners, deserters, absentees and persons under escort);
(ii) sections 129, 190 or 202 of the Air Force Act 1955 (duties of governors of prisons and others to receive prisoners, deserters, absentees and persons under escort);
(iii) section 107 of the Naval Discipline Act 1957 (duties of governors of civil prisons, etc); or
(iv) paragraph 5 of Schedule 5 to the Reserve Forces Act 1980 (duties of governors of civil prisons); or

(d) any right of a person in police detention to apply for a writ of habeas corpus or other prerogative remedy.

PART V

QUESTIONING AND TREATMENT OF PERSONS BY POLICE

53 Abolition of certain powers of constables [390]
to search persons

(1) Subject to subsection (2) below, there shall cease to have effect any Act (including a local Act) passed before this Act in so far as it authorises –

(a) any search by a constable of a person in police detention at a police station; or
(b) an intimate search of a person by a constable;

and any rule of common law which authorises a search such as is mentioned in paragraph (a) or (b) above is abolished.

54 Searches of detained persons [391]

(1) The custody officer at a police station shall ascertain and record or cause to be recorded everything which a person has with him when he is –

(a) brought to the station after being arrested elsewhere or after being committed to custody by an order or sentence of a court; or
(b) arrested at the station or detained there as a person falling within section 34(7) under section 37 above.

(2) In the case of an arrested person the record shall be made as part of his custody record.

(3) Subject to subsection (4) below, a custody officer may seize and retain any such thing or cause any such thing to be seized and retained.

(4) Clothes and personal effects may only be seized if the custody officer –

(a) believes that the person from whom they are seized may use them –

(i) to cause physical injury to himself or any other person;
(ii) to damage property;
(iii) to interfere with evidence; or
(iv) to assist him to escape; or

(b) has reasonable grounds for believing that they may be evidence relating to an offence.

(5) Where anything is seized, the person from whom it is seized shall be told the reason for the seizure unless he is –

(a) violent or likely to become violent; or
(b) incapable of understanding what is said to him.

(6) Subject to subsection (7) below, a person may be searched if the custody officer considers it necessary to enable him to carry out his duty under subsection (1) above and to the extent that the custody officer considers necessary for that purpose.

(6A) A person who is in custody at a police station or is in police detention otherwise than at a police station may at any time be searched in order to ascertain whether he has with him anything which he could use for the purposes specified in subsection (4)(a) above.

(6B) Subject to subsection (6C) below, a constable may seize and retain, or cause to be seized and retained, anything found on such a search.

(6C) A constable may only seize clothes and personal effects in the circumstances specified in subsection (4) above.

(7) An intimate search may not be conducted under this section.

(8) A search under this section shall be carried out by a constable.

(9) The constable carrying out a search shall be of the same sex as the person searched.

55 Intimate searches [392]

(1) Subject to the following provisions of this section, if an officer of at least the rank of superintendent has reasonable grounds for believing –

(a) that a person who has been arrested and is in police detention may have concealed on him anything which –

(i) he could use to cause physical injury to himself or others; and
(ii) he might so use while he is in police detention or in the custody of a court; or

(b) that such a person –

(i) may have a Class A drug concealed on him; and
(ii) was in possession of it with the appropriate criminal intent before his arrest,

he may authorise an intimate search of that person.

(2) An officer may not authorise an intimate search of a person for anything unless he has reasonable grounds for believing that it cannot be found without his being intimately searched.

(3) An officer may give an authorisation under subsection (1) above orally or in writing but, if he gives it orally, he shall confirm it in writing as soon as is practicable.

(4) An intimate search which is only a drug offence search shall be by way of examination by a suitably qualified person.

(5) Except as provided by subsection (4) above, an intimate search shall be by way of examination by a suitably qualified person unless an officer of at least the rank of superintendent considers that this is not practicable.

(6) An intimate search which is not carried out as mentioned in subsection (5) above shall be carried out by a constable.

(7) A constable may not carry out an intimate search of a person of the opposite sex.

(8) No intimate search may be carried out except –

(a) at a police station;
(b) at a hospital;
(c) at a registered medical practitioner's surgery; or
(d) at some other place used for medical purposes.

(9) An intimate search which is only a drug offence search may not be carried out at a police station.

(10) If an intimate search of a person is carried out, the custody record relating to him shall state –

(a) which parts of his body were searched; and
(b) why they were searched.

(11) The information required to be recorded by subsection (10) above shall be recorded as soon as practicable after the completion of the search.

(12) The custody officer at a police station may seize and retain anything which is found on an intimate search of a person, or cause any such thing to be seized and retained –

(a) if he believes that the person from whom it is seized may use it –

(i) to cause physical injury to himself or any other person;
(ii) to damage property;
(iii) to interfere with evidence; or
(iv) to assist him to escape; or

(b) if he has reasonable grounds for believing that it may be evidence relating to an offence.

(13) Where anything is seized under this section, the person from whom it is seized shall be told the reason for the seizure unless he is –

(a) violent or likely to become violent; or
(b) incapable of understanding what is said to him ...

(17) In this section –

'the appropriate criminal intent' means an intent to commit an offence under –

(a) section 5(3) of the Misuse of Drugs Act 1971 (possession of controlled drug with intent to supply to another); or

(b) section 68(2) of the Customs and Excise Management Act 1979 (exportation etc with intent to evade a prohibition of restriction);

'Class A drug' has the meaning assigned to it by section 2(1)(b) of the Misuse of Drugs Act 1971;

'drug offence search' means an intimate search for a Class A drug which an officer has authorised by virtue of subsection (1)(b) above; and

'suitably qualified person' means –

(a) a registered medical practitioner; or

(b) a registered nurse.

56 Right to have someone informed when arrested [393]

(1) Where a person has been arrested and is being held in custody in a police station or other premises, he shall be entitled, if he so requests, to have one friend or relative or other person who is known to him or who is likely to take an interest in his welfare told, as soon as is practicable except to the extent that delay is permitted by this section, that he has been arrested and is being detained there.

(2) Delay is only permitted –

(a) in the case of a person who is in police detention for a serious arrestable offence; and

(b) if an officer of at least the rank of superintendent authorises it.

(3) In any case the person in custody must be permitted to exercise the right conferred by subsection (1) above within 36 hours from the relevant time, as defined in section 41(2) above.

(4) An officer may give an authorisation under subsection (2) above orally or in writing but, if he gives it orally, he shall confirm it in writing as soon as is practicable.

(5) Subject to subsection (5A) below, an officer may only authorise delay where he has reasonable grounds for believing that telling the named person of the arrest –

(a) will lead to interference with or harm to evidence connected with a serious arrestable offence or interference with or physical injury to other persons; or

(b) will lead to the alerting of other persons suspected of having committed such an offence but not yet arrested for it; or

(c) will hinder the recovery of any property obtained as a result of such an offence.

(5A) An officer may also authorise delay where the serious arrestable offence is a drug trafficking offence or an offence to which Part VI of the Criminal Justice Act 1988 applies (offences in respect of which confiscation orders under that Part may be made) and the officer has reasonable grounds for believing –

(a) where the offence is a drug trafficking offence, that the detained person has benefited from drug trafficking and that the recovery of the value of that person's proceeds of drug trafficking will be hindered by telling the named person of the arrest; and

(b) where the offence is one to which Part VI of the Criminal Justice Act 1988 applies, that the detained person has benefited from the offence and that the recovery of the value of the property obtained by that person from or in connection with the offence or of the pecuniary advantage derived by him from or in connection with it will be hindered by telling the named person of the arrest.

(6) If a delay is authorised –

    (a) the detained person shall be told the reason for it; and

    (b) the reason shall be noted on his custody record.

(7) The duties imposed by subsection (6) above shall be performed as soon as is practicable.

(8) The rights conferred by this section on a person detained at a police station or other premises are exercisable whenever he is transferred from one place to another; and this section applies to each subsequent occasion on which they are exercisable as it applies to the first such occasion.

(9) There may be no further delay in permitting the exercise of the right conferred by subsection (1) above once the reason for authorising delay ceases to subsist.

(10) In the foregoing provisions of this section references to a person who has been arrested include references to a person who has been detained under the terrorism provisions and 'arrest' includes detention under those provisions.

(11) In its application to a person who has been arrested or detained under the terrorism provisions –

    (a) subsection (2)(a) above shall have effect as if for the words 'for a serious arrestable offence' there were substituted the words 'under the terrorism provisions';

    (b) subsection (3) above shall have effect as if for the words from 'within' onwards there were substituted the words 'before the end of the period beyond which he may no longer be detained without the authority of the Secretary of State'; and

    (c) subsection (5) above shall have effect as if at the end there were added 'or

    (d) will lead to interference with the gathering of information about the commission, preparation or instigation of acts of terrorism; or

    (e) by alerting any person, will make it more difficult –

        (i) to prevent an act of terrorism; or

        (ii) to secure the apprehension, prosecution or conviction of any person in connection with the commission, preparation or instigation of an act of terrorism.'.

58 Access to legal advice [394]

(1) A person arrested and held in custody in a police station or other premises shall be entitled, if he so requests, to consult a solicitor privately at any time.

(2) Subject to subsection (3) below, a request under subsection (1) above and the time at which it was made shall be recorded in the custody record.

(3) Such a request need not be recorded in the custody record of a person who makes it at a time while he is at a court after being charged with an offence.

(4) If a person makes such a request, he must be permitted to consult a solicitor as soon as is practicable except to the extent that delay is permitted by this section.

(5) In any case he must be permitted to consult a solicitor within 36 hours from the relevant time, as defined in section 41(2) above.

(6) Delay in compliance with a request is only permitted –

    (a) in the case of a person who is in police detention for a serious arrestable offence; and

    (b) if an officer of at least the rank of superintendent authorises it.

(7) An officer may give an authorisation under subsection (6) above orally or in writing but, if he gives it orally, he shall confirm it in writing as soon as is practicable.

(8) Subject to subsection (8A) below, an officer may only authorise delay where he has reasonable grounds for believing that the exercise of the right conferred by subsection (1) above at the time when the person detained desires to exercise it –

(a) will lead to interference with or harm to evidence connected with a serious arrestable offence or interference with or physical injury to other persons; or
(b) will lead to the alerting of other persons suspected of having committed such an offence but not yet arrested for it; or
(c) will hinder the recovery of any property obtained as a result of such an offence.

(8A) An officer may also authorise delay where the serious arrestable offence is a drug trafficking offence or an offence to which Part VI of the Criminal Justice Act 1988 applies and the officer has reasonable grounds for believing –

(a) where the offence is a drug trafficking offence, that the detained person has benefited from drug trafficking and that the recovery of the value of that person's proceeds of drug trafficking will be hindered by the exercise of the right conferred by subsection (1) above; and
(b) where the offence is one to which Part VI of the Criminal Justice Act 1988 applies, that the detained person has benefited from the offence and that the recovery of the value of the property obtained by that person from or in connection with the offence or of the pecuniary advantage derived by him from or in connection with it will be hindered by the exercise of the right conferred by subsection (1) above.

(9) If delay is authorised –

(a) the detained person shall be told the reason for it; and
(b) the reason shall be noted on his custody record.

(10) The duties imposed by subsection (9) above shall be performed as soon as is practicable.

(11) There may be no further delay in permitting the exercise of the right conferred by subsection (1) above once the reason for authorising delay ceases to subsist.

(12) The reference in subsection (1) above to a person arrested includes a reference to a person who has been detained under the terrorism provisions.

(13) In the application of this section to a person who has been arrested or detained under the terrorism provisions –

(a) subsection (5) above shall have effect as if for the words from 'within' onwards there were substituted the words 'before the end of the period beyond which he may no longer be detained without the authority of the Secretary of State';
(b) subsection (6)(a) above shall have effect as if for the words 'for a serious arrestable offence' there were substituted the words 'under the terrorism provisions'; and
(c) subsection (8) above shall have effect as if at the end there were added 'or
(d) will lead to interference with the gathering of information about the commission, preparation or instigation of acts of terrorism; or
(e) by alerting any person, will make it more difficult –

(i) to prevent an act of terrorism; or
(ii) to secure the apprehension, prosecution or conviction of any person in connection with the commission, preparation or instigation of an act of terrorism.'.

(14) If an officer of appropriate rank has reasonable grounds for believing that, unless he gives a direction under subsection (15) below, the exercise by a person

arrested or detained under the terrorism provisions of the right conferred by subsection (1) above will have any of the consequences specified in subsection (8) above (as it has effect by virtue of subsection (13) above), he may give a direction under that subsection.

(15) A direction under this subsection is a direction that a person desiring to exercise the right conferred by subsection (1) above may only consult a solicitor in the sight and hearing of a qualified officer of the uniformed branch of the force of which the officer giving the direction is a member.

(16) An officer is qualified for the purpose of subsection (15) above if –

(a) he is of at least the rank of inspector; and
(b) in the opinion of the officer giving the direction he has no connection with the case.

(17) An officer is of appropriate rank to give a direction under subsection (15) above if he is of at least the rank of Commander or Assistant Chief Constable.

(18) A direction under subsection (15) above shall cease to have effect once the reason for giving it ceases to subsist.

61 Fingerprinting   [395]

(1) Except as provided by this section no person's fingerprints may be taken without the appropriate consent.

(2) Consent to the taking of a person's fingerprints must be in writing if it is given at a time when he is at a police station.

(3) The fingerprints of a person detained at a police station may be taken without the appropriate consent –

(a) if an officer of at least the rank of superintendent authorises them to be taken; or
(b) if –

(i) he has been charged with a recordable offence or informed that he will be reported for such an offence; and
(ii) he has not had his fingerprints taken in the course of the investigation of the offence by the police.

(4) An officer may only give an authorisation under subsection (3)(a) above if he has reasonable grounds –

(a) for suspecting the involvement of the person whose fingerprints are to be taken in a criminal offence; and
(b) for believing that his fingerprints will tend to confirm or disprove his involvement.

(5) An officer may give an authorisation under subsection (3)(a) above orally or in writing but, if he gives it orally, he shall confirm it in writing as soon as is practicable.

(6) Any person's fingerprints may be taken without the appropriate consent if he has been convicted of a recordable offence.

(7) In a case where by virtue of subsection (3) or (6) above a person's fingerprints are taken without the appropriate consent –

(a) he shall be told the reason before his fingerprints are taken; and
(b) the reason shall be recorded as soon as is practicable after the fingerprints are taken.

(7A) If a person's fingerprints are taken at a police station, whether with or without the appropriate consent –

(a) before the fingerprints are taken, an officer shall inform him that they may be the subject of a speculative search; and

(b) the fact that the person has been informed of this possibility shall be recorded as soon as is practicable after the fingerprints have been taken.

(8) If he is detained at a police station when the fingerprints are taken, the reason for taking them and, in the case falling within subsection (7A) above, the fact referred to in paragraph (b) of that subsection shall be recorded on his custody record.

(9) Nothing in this section –

(a) affects any power conferred by paragraph 18(2) of Schedule 2 to the Immigration Act 1971; or

(b) except as provided in section 15(10) of, and paragraph 7(6) of Schedule 5 to, the Prevention of Terrorism (Temporary Provisions) Act 1989, applies to a person arrested or detained under the terrorism provisions.

62 Intimate samples [396]

(1) An intimate sample may be taken from a person in police detention only –

(a) if a police officer of at least the rank of superintendent authorises it to be taken; and

(b) if the appropriate consent is given.

(1A) An intimate sample may be taken from a person who is not in police detention but from whom, in the course of the investigation of an offence, two or more non-intimate samples suitable for the means of analysis have been taken which have proved insufficient –

(a) if a police officer of at least the rank of superintendent authorises it to be taken; and

(b) if the appropriate consent is given.

(2) An officer may only give an authorisation under subsection (1) or (1A) above if he has reasonable grounds –

(a) for suspecting the involvement of the person from whom the sample is to be taken in a recordable offence; and

(b) for believing that the sample will tend to confirm or disprove his involvement.

(3) An officer may give an authorisation under subsection (1) or (1A) above orally or in writing but, if he gives it orally, he shall confirm it in writing as soon as is practicable.

(4) The appropriate consent must be given in writing.

(5) Where –

(a) an authorisation has been given; and

(b) it is proposed that an intimate sample shall be taken in pursuance of the authorisation,

an officer shall inform the person from whom the sample is to be taken –

(i) of the giving of the authorisation; and

(ii) of the grounds for giving it.

(6) The duty imposed by subsection (5)(ii) above includes a duty to state the nature of the offence in which it is suspected that the person from whom the sample is to be taken has been involved.

(7) If an intimate sample is taken from a person –

(a) the authorisation by virtue of which it was taken;

(b) the grounds for giving the authorisation; and

(c) the fact that the appropriate consent was given,

shall be recorded as soon as is practicable after the sample is taken.

(7A) If an intimate sample is taken from a person at a police station –

(a) before the sample is taken, an officer shall inform him that it may be the subject of a speculative search; and

(b) the fact that the person has been informed of this possibility shall be recorded as soon as practicable after the sample has been taken.

(8) If an intimate sample is taken from a person detained at a police station, the matters required to be recorded by subsection (7) or (7A) above shall be recorded in his custody record.

(9) An intimate sample, other than a sample of urine or a dental impression, may only be taken from a person by a registered medical practitioner, and a dental impression may only be taken by a registered dentist.

(10) Where the appropriate consent to the taking of an intimate sample from a person was refused without good cause, in any proceedings against that person for an offence –

(a) the court, in determining –

(i) whether to grant an application for dismissal made by that person under section 6 of the Magistrates' Courts Act 1980 (application for dismissal of charge in course of proceedings with a view to transfer for trial); or

(ii) whether there is a case to answer; and

(aa) a judge, in deciding whether to grant an application made by the accused under –

(i) section 6 of the Criminal Justice Act 1987 (application for dismissal of charge of serious fraud in respect of which notice of transfer has been given under section 4 of that Act);

or

(ii) paragraph 5 of Schedule 6 to the Criminal Justice Act 1991 (application for dismissal of charge of violent or sexual offence involving child in respect of which notice of transfer has been given under section 53 of that Act); and

(b) the court or jury, in determining whether that person is guilty of the offence charged,

may draw such inferences from the refusal as appear proper.

(11) Nothing in this section affects sections 4 to 11 of the Road Traffic Act 1988.

(12) Nothing in this section, except as provided in section 15(11) and (12) of, and paragraph 7(6A) and (6B) of Schedule 5 to, the Prevention of Terrorism (Temporary Provisions) Act 1989, applies to a person arrested or detained under the terrorism provisions.

63 Other samples [397]

(1) Except as provided by this section, a non-intimate sample may not be taken from a person without the appropriate consent.

(2) Consent to the taking of a non-intimate sample must be given in writing.

(3) A non-intimate sample may be taken from a person without the appropriate consent if –

(a) he is in police detention or is being held in custody by the police on the authority of a court; and

(b) an officer of at least the rank of superintendent authorises it to be taken without the appropriate consent.

(3A) A non-intimate sample may be taken from a person (whether or not he falls within subsection (3)(a) above) without the appropriate consent if –

(a) he has been charged with a recordable offence or informed that he will be reported for such an offence; and
(b) either he has not had a non-intimate sample taken from him in the course of the investigation of the offence by the police or he has had a non-intimate sample taken from him but either it was not suitable for the same means of analysis or, though so suitable, the sample proved insufficient.

(3B) A non-intimate sample may be taken from a person without the appropriate consent if he has been convicted of a recordable offence.

(4) An officer may only give an authorisation under subsection (3) above if he has reasonable grounds –

(a) for suspecting the involvement of the person from whom the sample is to be taken in a recordable offence; and
(b) for believing that the sample will tend to confirm or disprove his involvement.

(5) An officer may give an authorisation under subsection (3) above orally or in writing but, if he gives it orally, he shall confirm it in writing as soon as is practicable.

(6) Where –

(a) an authorisation has been given; and
(b) it is proposed that a non-intimate sample shall be taken in pursuance of the authorisation,

an officer shall inform the person from whom the sample is to be taken –

(i) of the giving of the authorisation; and
(ii) of the grounds for giving it.

(7) The duty imposed by subsection (6)(ii) above includes a duty to state the nature of the offence in which it is suspected that the person from whom the sample is to be taken has been involved.

(8) If a non-intimate sample is taken from a person by virtue of subsection (3) above –

(a) the authorisation by virtue of which it was taken; and
(b) the grounds for giving the authorisation,

shall be recorded as soon as is practicable after the sample is taken.

(8A) In a case where by virtue of subsection (3A) or (3B) a sample is taken from a person without the appropriate consent –

(a) he shall be told the reason before the sample is taken; and
(b) the reason shall be recorded as soon as practicable after the sample is taken.

(8B) If a non-intimate sample is taken from a person at a police station, whether with or without the appropriate consent –

(a) before the sample is taken, an officer shall inform him that it may be the subject of a speculative search; and
(b) the fact that the person has been informed of this possibility shall be recorded as soon as practicable after the sample has been taken.

(9) If a non-intimate sample is taken from a person detained at a police station, the matters required to be recorded by subsection (8) or (8A) or (8B) above shall be recorded in his custody record.

(10) Subsection (3B) above shall not apply to persons convicted before the date on which that subsection comes into force.

(10) Nothing in this section, except as provided in section 15(13) and (14) of, and paragraph 7(6C) and (6D) of Schedule 5 to, the Prevention of Terrorism (Temporary Provision) Act 1989, applies to a person arrested or detained under the terrorism provisions.*

63A Fingerprints and samples: supplementary provisions   [398]

(1) Fingerprints or samples or the information derived from samples taken under any power conferred by this Part of this Act from a person who has been arrested on suspicion of being involved in a recordable offence may be checked against other fingerprints or samples or the information derived from other samples contained in records held by or on behalf of the police or held in connection with or as a result of an investigation of an offence.

(2) Where a sample of hair other than pubic hair is to be taken the sample may be taken either by cutting hairs or by plucking hairs with their roots so long as no more are plucked than the person taking the sample reasonably considers to be necessary for a sufficient sample.

(3) Where any power to take a sample is exercisable in relation to a person the sample may be taken in a prison or other institution to which the Prison Act 1952 applies.

(4) Any constable may, within the allowed period, require a person who is neither in police detention nor held in custody by the police on the authority of a court to attend a police station in order to have a sample taken where –

(a) the person has been charged with a recordable offence or informed that he will be reported for such an offence and either he has not had a sample taken from him in the course of the investigation of the offence by the police or he has had a sample so taken from him but either it was not suitable for the same means of analysis or, though so suitable, the sample proved insufficient; or
(b) the person has been convicted of a recordable offence and either he has not had a sample taken from him since the conviction or he has had a sample taken from him (before or after his conviction) but either it was not suitable for the same means of analysis or, though so suitable, the sample proved insufficient.

(5) The period allowed for requiring a person to attend a police station for the purpose specified in subsection (4) above is –

(a) in the case of a person falling within paragraph (a), one month beginning with the date of the charge or one month beginning with the date on which the appropriate officer is informed of the fact that the sample is not suitable for the same means of analysis or has proved insufficient, as the case may be;
(b) in the case of a person falling within paragraph (b), one month beginning with the date of the conviction or one month beginning with the date on which the appropriate officer is informed of the fact that the sample is not suitable for the same means of analysis or has proved insufficient, as the case may be.

(6) A requirement under subsection (4) above –

(a) shall give the person at least 7 days within which he must so attend; and
(b) may direct him to attend at a specified time of day or between specified times of day.

(7) Any constable may arrest without a warrant a person who has failed to comply with a requirement under subsection (4) above.

(8) In this section 'the appropriate officer' is –

(a) in the case of a person falling within subsection (4)(a), the officer investigating the offence with which that person has been charged or as to which he was informed that he would be reported;
(b) in the case of a person falling within subsection (4)(b), the officer in charge of the police station from which the investigation of the offence of which he was convicted was conducted.

64 Destruction of fingerprints and samples [399]

(1) If –

(a) fingerprints or samples are taken from a person in connection with the investigation of an offence; and
(b) he is cleared of that offence,

they must except as provided in subsection (3A) below be destroyed as soon as is practicable after the conclusion of the proceedings.

(2) If –

(a) fingerprints or samples are taken from a person in connection with such an investigation; and
(b) it is decided that he shall not be prosecuted for the offence and he has not admitted it and been dealt with by way of being cautioned by a constable,

they must except as provided in subsection (3A) below be destroyed as soon as is practicable after that decision is taken.

(3) If –

(a) fingerprints or samples are taken from a person in connection with the investigation of an offence; and
(b) that person is not suspected of having committed the offence,

they must except as provided in subsection (3A) below be destroyed as soon as they have fulfilled the purpose for which they were taken.

(3A) Samples which are required to be destroyed under subsection (1), (2) or (3) above need not be destroyed if they were taken for the purpose of the same investigation of an offence of which a person from whom one was taken has been convicted, but the information derived from the sample of any person entitled (apart from this subsection) to its destruction under subsection (1), (2) or (3) above shall not be used –

(a) in evidence against the person so entitled; or
(b) for the purposes of any investigation of an offence.

(3B) Where samples are required to be destroyed under subsections (1), (2) or (3) above, and subsection (3A) above does not apply, information derived from the sample of any person entitled to its destruction under subsection (1), (2) or (3) above shall not be used –

(a) in evidence against the person so entitled; or
(b) for the purposes of any investigation of an offence.

(4) Proceedings which are discontinued are to be treated as concluded for the purposes of this section.

(5) If fingerprints are destroyed –

(a) any copies of the fingerprints shall also be destroyed; and
(b) any chief officer of police controlling access to computer data relating to the fingerprints shall make access to the data impossible, as soon as it is practicable to do so.

(6) A person who asks to be allowed to witness the destruction of his fingerprints or copies of them shall have a right to witness it.

(6A) If –

(a) subsection (5)(b) above falls to be complied with; and
(b) the person to whose fingerprints the data relate asks for a certificate that it has been complied with,

such a certificate shall be issued to him, not later than the end of the period of three months beginning with the day on which he asks for it, by the responsible chief officer of police or a person authorised by him or on his behalf for the purposes of this section.

(6B) In this section –

'chief officer of police' means the chief officer of police for an area mentioned in Schedule 8 to the Police Act 1964; and
'the responsible chief officer of police' means the chief officer of police in whose area the computer data were put on to the computer.

(7) Nothing in this section –

(a) affects any power conferred by paragraph 18(2) of Schedule 2 to the Immigration Act 1971; or
(b) applies to a person arrested or detained under the terrorism provisions.

65 Part V – supplementary   [400]

In this Part of this Act –

'appropriate consent' means –

(a) in relation to a person who has attained the age of 17 years, the consent of that person;
(b) in relation to a person who has not attained that age but has attained the age of 14 years, the consent of that person and his parent or guardian; and
(c) in relation to a person who has not attained the age of 14 years, the consent of his parent or guardian;

'drug trafficking' and 'drug trafficking offence' have the same meaning as in the Drug Trafficking Offences Act 1986;
'fingerprints' includes palm prints;
'intimate sample means

(a) a sample of blood, semen or any other tissue fluid, urine or pubic hair;
(b) a dental impression;
(c) a swab taken from a person's body orifice other than the mouth;

'intimate search' means a search which consists of the physical examination of a person's body orifices other than the mouth;
'non-intimate sample' means –

(a) a sample of hair other than pubic hair;
(b) a sample taken from a nail or from under a bail;
(c) a swab taken from any part of a person's body including the mouth but not any other body orifice;
(d) saliva;
(e) a footprint or a similar impression of any part of a person's body other than a part of his hand;

'registered dentist' has the same meaning as in the Dentists Act 1984;
'speculative search', in relation to a person's fingerprints or samples, means

such a check against other fingerprints or samples or against information derived from other samples as is referred to in section 63A(1) above;

'sufficient' and 'insufficient', in relation to a sample, means sufficient or insufficient (in point of quantity or quality) for the purpose of enabling information to be produced by the means of analysis used or to be used in relation to the sample.

'the terrorism provisions' means section 14(1) of the Prevention of Terrorism (Temporary Provisions) Act 1989 and any provision of Schedule 2 or 5 to that Act conferring a power of arrest or detention; and

'terrorism' has the meaning assigned to it by section 20(1) of that Act.

References in this Part to any person's proceeds of drug trafficking are to be construed in accordance with the Drug Trafficking Offences Act 1986.

PART VI

CODES OF PRACTICE – GENERAL

66 Codes of practice [401]

The Secretary of State shall issue codes of practice in connection with –

(a) the exercise by police officers of statutory powers –

(i) to search a person without first arresting him; or
(ii) to search a vehicle without making an arrest;

(b) the detention, treatment, questioning and identification of persons by police officers;

(c) searches of premises by police officers; and

(d) the seizure of property found by police officers on persons or premises.

67 Codes of practice – supplementary [402]

(1) When the Secretary of State proposes to issue a code of practice to which this section applies, he shall prepare and publish a draft of that code, shall consider any representations made to him about the draft and may modify the draft accordingly.

(2) This section applies to a code of practice under section 60 or 66 above.

(3) The Secretary of State shall lay before both Houses of Parliament a draft of any code of practice prepared by him under this section.

(4) When the Secretary of State has laid the draft of a code before Parliament, he may bring the code into operation by order made by statutory instrument.

(5) No order under subsection (4) above shall have effect until approved by a resolution of each House of Parliament.

(6) An order bringing a code of practice into operation may contain such transitional provisions or savings as appear to the Secretary of State to be necessary or expedient in connection with the code of practice thereby brought into operation.

(7) The Secretary of State may from time to time revise the whole or any part of a code of practice to which this section applies and issue that revised code; and the foregoing provisions of this section shall apply (with appropriate modifications) to such a revised code as they apply to the first issue of a code.

(9) Persons other than police officers who are charged with the duty of investigating offences or charging offenders shall in the discharge of that duty have regard to any relevant provision of such a code.

(10) A failure on the part –

(a) of a police officer to comply with any provision of such a code; or

(b) of any person other than a police officer who is charged with the duty of investigating offences or charging offenders to have regard to any relevant provision of such a code in the discharge of that duty,

shall not of itself render him liable to any criminal or civil proceedings.

(11) In all criminal and civil proceedings any such code shall be admissible in evidence; and if any provision of such a code appears to the court or tribunal conducting the proceedings to be relevant to any question arising in the proceedings it shall be taken into account in determining that question.

(12) In this section 'criminal proceedings' includes –

(a) proceedings in the United Kingdom or elsewhere before a court-martial constituted under the Army Act 1955, the Air Force Act 1955 or the Naval Discipline Act 1957 or a disciplinary court constituted under section 50 of the said Act of 1957;

(b) proceedings before the Courts-Martial Appeal Court; and

(c) proceedings before a Standing Civilian Court.

PART VIII

EVIDENCE IN CRIMINAL PROCEEDINGS – GENERAL

76 Confessions   [403]

(1) In any proceedings a confession made by an accused person may be given in evidence against him in so far as it is relevant to any matter in issue in the proceedings and is not excluded by the court in pursuance of this section.

(2) If, in any proceedings where the prosecution proposes to give in evidence a confession made by an accused person, it is represented to the court that the confession was or may have been obtained –

(a) by oppression of the person who made it; or

(b) in consequence of anything said or done which was likely, in the circumstances existing at the time, to render unreliable any confession which might be made by him in consequence thereof,

the court shall not allow the confession to be given in evidence against him except in so far as the prosecution proves to the court beyond reasonable doubt that the confession (notwithstanding that it may be true) was not obtained as aforesaid.

(3) In any proceedings where the prosecution proposes to give in evidence a confession made by an accused person, the court may of its own motion require the prosecution, as a condition of allowing it to do so, to prove that the confession was not obtained as mentioned in subsection (2) above.

(4) The fact that a confession is wholly or partly excluded in pursuance of this section shall not affect the admissibility in evidence –

(a) of any facts discovered as a result of the confession; or

(b) where the confession is relevant as showing that the accused speaks, writes or expresses himself in a particular way, of so much of the confession as is necessary to show that he does so.

(5) Evidence that a fact to which this subsection applies was discovered as a result of a statement made by an accused person shall not be admissible unless evidence of how it was discovered is given by him or on his behalf.

(6) Subsection (5) above applies –

(a) to any fact discovered as a result of a confession which is wholly excluded in pursuance of this section; and

(b) to any fact discovered as a result of a confession which is partly so excluded, if the fact is discovered as a result of the excluded part of the confession.

(7) Nothing in Part VII of this Act shall prejudice the admissibility of a confession made by an accused person.

(8) In this section 'oppression' includes torture, inhuman or degrading treatment, and the use or threat of violence (whether or not amounting to torture).

77 Confessions by mentally handicapped persons [404]

(1) Without prejudice to the general duty of the court at a trial on indictment to direct the jury on any matter on which it appears to the court appropriate to do so, where at such a trial –

(a) the case against the accused depends wholly or substantially on a confession by him; and

(b) the court is satisfied –

(i) that he is mentally handicapped; and

(ii) that the confession was not made in the presence of an independent person,

the court shall warn the jury that there is special need for caution before convicting the accused in reliance on the confession, and shall explain that the need arises because of the circumstances mentioned in paragraphs (a) and (b) above.

(2) In any case where at the summary trial of a person for an offence it appears to the court that a warning under subsection (1) above would be required if the trial were on indictment, the court shall treat the case as one in which there is a special need for caution before convicting the accused on his confession.

(3) In this section –

'independent person' does not include a police officer or a person employed for, or engaged on, police purposes;

'mentally handicapped', in relation to a person, means that he is in a state of arrested or incomplete development of mind which includes significant impairment of intelligence and social functioning; and

'police purposes' has the meaning assigned to it by section 64 of the Police Act 1964.

78 Exclusion of unfair evidence [405]

(1) In any proceedings the court may refuse to allow evidence on which the prosecution proposes to rely to be given if it appears to the court that, having regard to all the circumstances, including the circumstances in which the evidence was obtained, the admission of the evidence would have such an adverse effect on the fairness of the proceedings that the court ought not to admit it.

(2) Nothing in this section shall prejudice any rule of law requiring a court to exclude evidence.

82 Part VIII – interpretation [406]

(1) In this Part of this Act –

'confession' includes any statement wholly or partly adverse to the person who made it, whether made to a person in authority or not and whether made in words or otherwise;

'court-martial' means a court-martial constituted under the Army Act 1955, the Air Force Act 1955 or the Naval Discipline Act 1957 or a disciplinary court constituted under section 50 of the said Act of 1957;

'proceedings' means criminal proceedings, including –

(a) proceedings in the United Kingdom or elsewhere before a court-martial constituted under the Army Act 1955 or the Air Force Act 1955;

(b) proceedings in the United Kingdom or elsewhere before the Courts-Martial Appeal Court –

(i) on an appeal from a court-martial so constituted or from a court-martial constituted under the Naval Discipline Act 1957; or

(ii) on a reference under section 34 of the Courts-Martial (Appeals) Act 1968; and

(b) proceedings before a Standing Civilian Court; and

'Service court' means a court-martial or a Standing Civilian Court.

(2) In this Part of this Act references to conviction before a Service court are references –

(a) as regards a court-martial constituted under the Army Act 1955 or the Air Force Act 1955, to a finding of guilty which is, or falls to be treated as, a finding of the court duly confirmed;

(b) as regards –

(i) a court-martial; or

(ii) a disciplinary court,

constituted under the Naval Discipline Act 1957, to a finding of guilty which is, or falls to be treated as, the finding of the court;

and 'convicted' shall be construed accordingly.

(3) Nothing in this Part of this Act shall prejudice any power of a court to exclude evidence (whether by preventing questions from being put or otherwise) at its discretion.

PART IX

POLICE COMPLAINTS AND DISCIPLINE

83 Establishment of Police Complaints Authority   [407]

(1) There shall be an authority to be known as 'the Police Complaints Authority' and in this Part of this Act referred to as 'the Authority'.

(2) Schedule 4 to this Act shall have effect in relation to the Authority.

(3) The Police Complaints Board is hereby abolished.

84 Preliminary   [408]

(1) Where a complaint is submitted to the chief officer of police for a police area, it shall be his duty to take any steps that appear to him to be desirable for the purpose of obtaining or preserving evidence relating to the conduct complained of.

(2) After performing the duties imposed on him by subsection (1) above, the chief officer shall determine whether he is the appropriate authority in relation to the officer against whom the complaint was made.

(3) If he determines that he is not the appropriate authority, it shall be his duty –

(a) to send the complaint or, if it was made orally, particulars of it, to the appropriate authority; and

(b) to give notice that he has done so to the person by or on whose behalf the complaint was made.

(4) In this Part of this Act –

'complaint' means any complaint about the conduct of a police officer which is submitted –

(a) by a member of the public; or

(b) on behalf of a member of the public and with his written consent;

'the appropriate authority' means –

(a) in relation to an officer of the metropolitan police, the Commissioner of Police of the Metropolis; and

(b) in relation to an officer of any other police force –

(i) if he is a senior officer, the police authority for the force's area; and

(ii) if he is not a senior officer, the chief officer of the force;

'senior officer' means an officer holding a rank above the rank of superintendent;

'disciplinary proceedings' means proceedings identified as such by regulations under section 33 of the Police Act 1964.

(5) Nothing in this Part of this Act has effect in relation to a complaint in so far as it relates to the direction or control of the police force by the chief officer or the person performing the functions of the chief officer.

(6) If any conduct to which a complaint wholly or partly relates is or has been the subject of criminal or disciplinary proceedings, none of the provisions of this Part of this Act which relate to the recording and investigation of complaints have effect in relation to the complaint in so far as it relates to that conduct.

85 Investigation of complaints: standard procedure [409]

(1) If a chief officer determines that he is the appropriate authority in relation to an officer about whose conduct a complaint has been made and who is not a senior officer, he shall record it.

(2) After doing so he shall consider whether the complaint is suitable for informal resolution and may appoint an officer from his force to assist him.

(3) If it appears to the chief officer that the complaint is not suitable for informal resolution, he shall appoint an officer from his force or some other force to investigate it formally.

(4) If it appears to him that it is suitable for informal resolution, he shall seek to resolve it informally and may appoint an officer from his force to do so on his behalf.

(5) If it appears to the chief officer, after attempts have been made to resolve a complaint informally –

(a) that informal resolution of the complaint is impossible; or

(b) that the complaint is for any other reason not suitable for informal resolution,

he shall appoint an officer from his force or some other force to investigate it formally.

(6) An officer may not be appointed to investigate a complaint formally if he has previously been appointed to act in relation to it under subsection (4) above.

(7) If a chief officer requests the chief officer of some other force to provide an officer of his force for appointment under subsection (3) or (5) above, that chief officer shall provide an officer to be so appointed.

(9) Unless the investigation is supervised by the Authority under section 89 below, the investigating officer shall submit his report on the investigation to the chief officer.

(10) A complaint is not suitable for informal resolution unless –

(a) the member of the public concerned gives his consent; and
(b) the chief officer is satisfied that the conduct complained of, even if proved, would not justify criminal or disciplinary proceedings.

86 Investigation of complaints against senior officers   [410]

(1) Where a complaint about the conduct of a senior officer –

(a) is submitted to the appropriate authority; or
(b) is sent to the appropriate authority under section 84(3) above,

it shall be the appropriate authority's duty to record it and, subject to subsection (2) below, to investigate it.

(2) The appropriate authority may deal with the complaint according to the appropriate authority's discretion, if satisfied that the conduct complained of, even if proved, would not justify criminal or disciplinary proceedings.

(3) In any other case the appropriate authority shall appoint an officer from the appropriate authority's force or from some other force to investigate the complaint.

(4) A chief officer shall provide an officer to be appointed, if a request is made to him for one to be appointed under subsection (3) above.

(5) No officer may be appointed unless he is of at least the rank of the officer against whom the complaint is made.

(6) Unless an investigation under this section is supervised by the Authority under section 89 below, the investigating officer shall submit his report on it to the appropriate authority.

87 References of complaints to Authority   [411]

(1) The appropriate authority –

(a) shall refer to the Authority –

(i) any complaint alleging that the conduct complained of resulted in the death of or serious injury to some other person; and
(ii) any complaint of a description specified for the purposes of this section in regulations made by the Secretary of State; and

(b) may refer to the Authority any complaint which is not required to be referred to them.

(2) The Authority may require the submission to them for consideration of any complaint not referred to them by the appropriate authority; and it shall be the appropriate authority's duty to comply with any such requirement not later than the end of a period specified in regulations made by the Secretary of State.

(3) Where a complaint falls to be referred to the Authority under subsection (1)(a) above, it shall be the appropriate authority's duty to refer it to them not later than the end of a period specified in such regulations.

(4) In this Part of this Act 'serious injury' means a fracture, damage to an internal organ, impairment of bodily function, a deep cut or a deep laceration.

PART XI

MISCELLANEOUS AND SUPPLEMENTARY

116 Meaning of 'serious arrestable offence' [412]

(1) This section has effect for determining whether an offence is a serious arrestable offence for the purposes of this Act.

(2) The following arrestable offences are always serious –

(a) an offence (whether at common law or under any enactment) specified in Part I of Schedule 5 to this Act; and

(aa) any of the offences mentioned in paragraphs (a) to (d) of the definition of 'drug trafficking offence' in section 38(1) of the Drug Trafficking Offences Act 1986; and

(b) an offence under an enactment specified in Part II of that Schedule.

(3) Subject to subsections (4) and (5) below, any other arrestable offence is serious only if its commission –

(a) has led to any of the consequences specified in subsection (6) below; or

(b) is intended or is likely to lead to any of those consequences.

(4) An arrestable offence which consists of making a threat is serious if carrying out the threat would be likely to lead to any of the consequences specified in subsection (6) below.

(5) An offence under section 2, 8, 9, 10 or 11 of the Prevention of Terrorism (Temporary Provisions) Act 1989 is always a serious arrestable offence for the purposes of section 56 or 58 above, and an attempt or conspiracy to commit any such offence is also always a serious arrestable offence for those purposes.

(6) The consequences mentioned in subsections (3) and (4) above are –

(a) serious harm to the security of the State or to public order;

(b) serious interference with the administration of justice or with the investigation of offences or of a particular offence;

(c) the death of any person;

(d) serious injury to any person;

(e) substantial financial gain to any person; and

(f) serious financial loss to any person.

(7) Loss is serious for the purposes of this section if, having regard to all the circumstances, it is serious for the person who suffers it.

(8) In this section 'injury' includes any disease and any impairment of a person's physical or mental condition.

117 Power of constable to use reasonable force [413]

Where any provision of this Act –

(a) confers a power on a constable; and

(b) does not provide that the power may only be exercised with the consent of some person, other than a police officer,

the officer may use reasonable force, if necessary, in the exercise of the power.

118 General interpretation   [414]

(1) In this Act –

'arrestable offence' has the meaning assigned to it by section 24 above;
'designated police station' has the meaning assigned to it by section 35 above;
'document' has the same meaning as in Part I of the Civil Evidence Act 1968;
'item subject to legal privilege' has the meaning assigned to it by section 10 above;
'parent or guardian' means –

(a) in the case of a child or young person in the care of a local authority, that authority;

'premises' has the meaning assigned to it by section 23 above;
'recordable offence' means any offence to which regulations under section 27 above apply;
'vessel' includes any ship, boat, raft or other apparatus constructed or adapted for floating on water.

(2) A person is in police detention for the purposes of this Act if –

(a) he has been taken to a police station after being arrested for an offence or after being arrested under section 14 of the Prevention of Terrorism (Temporary Provisions) Act 1989 or under paragraph 6 of Schedule 5 to that Act by an examining officer who is a constable; or
(b) he is arrested at a police station after attending voluntarily at the station or accompanying a constable to it,

and is detained there or is detained elsewhere in the charge of a constable, except that a person who is at a court after being charged is not in police detention for those purposes.

SCHEDULE 1   [415]

SPECIAL PROCEDURE

1. If on an application made by a constable a circuit judge is satisfied that one or other of the sets of access conditions is fulfilled, he may make an order under paragraph 4 below.

2. The first set of access conditions is fulfilled if –

(a) there are reasonable grounds for believing –

(i) that a serious arrestable offence has been committed;
(ii) that there is material which consists of special procedure material or includes special procedure material and does not also include excluded material on premises specified in the application;
(iii) that the material is likely to be of substantial value (whether by itself or together with other material) to the investigation in connection with which the application is made; and
(iv) that the material is likely to be relevant evidence;

(b) other methods of obtaining the material –

(i) have been tried without success; or
(ii) have not been tried because it appeared that they were bound to fail; and

(c) it is in the public interest, having regard –

(i) to the benefit likely to accrue to the investigation if the material is obtained; and

(ii) to the circumstances under which the person in possession of the material holds it,

that the material should be produced or that access to it should be given.

3. The second set of access conditions is fulfilled if –

(a) there are reasonable grounds for believing that there is material which consists of or includes excluded material or special procedure material on premises specified in the application;

(b) but for section 9(2) above a search of the premises for that material could have been authorised by the issue of a warrant to a constable under an enactment other than this Schedule; and

(c) the issue of such a warrant would have been appropriate.

4. An order under this paragraph is an order that the person who appears to the circuit judge to be in possession of the material to which the application relates shall –

(a) produce it to a constable for him to take away; or

(b) give a constable access to it,

not later than the end of the period of seven days from the date of the order or the end of such longer period as the order may specify.

5. Where the material consists of information contained in a computer –

(a) an order under paragraph 4(a) above shall have effect as an order to produce the material in a form in which it can be taken away and in which it is visible and legible; and

(b) an order under paragraph 4(b) above shall have effect as an order to give a constable access to the material in a form in which it is visible and legible.

6. For the purposes of sections 21 and 22 above material produced in pursuance of an order under paragraph 4(a) above shall be treated as if it were material seized by a constable ...

11. Where notice of an application for an order under paragraph 4 above has been served on a person, he shall not conceal, destroy, alter or dispose of the material to which the application relates except –

(a) with the leave of a judge; or

(b) with the written permission of a constable,

until –

(i) the application is dismissed or abandoned; or

(ii) he has complied with an order under paragraph 4 above made on the application.

12. If on an application made by a constable a circuit judge –

(a) is satisfied –

(i) that either set of access conditions is fulfilled; and

(ii) that any of the further conditions set out in paragraph 14 below is also fulfilled; or

(b) is satisfied –

(i) that the second set of access conditions is fulfilled; and

(ii) that an order under paragraph 4 above relating to the material has not been complied with,

he may issue a warrant authorising a constable to enter and search the premises.

13. A constable may seize and retain anything for which a search has been authorised under paragraph 12 above.

14. The further conditions mentioned in paragraph 12(a)(ii) above are –

(a) that it is not practicable to communicate with any person entitled to grant entry to the premises to which the application relates;

(b) that it is practicable to communicate with a person entitled to grant entry to the premises but it is not practicable to communicate with any person entitled to grant access to the material;

(c) that the material contains information which –

(i) is subject to a restriction or obligation such as is mentioned in section 11(2)(b) above; and

(ii) is likely to be disclosed in breach of it if a warrant is not issued;

(d) that service of notice of an application for an order under paragraph 4 above may seriously prejudice the investigation.

15. (1) If a person fails to comply with an order under paragraph 4 above, a circuit judge may deal with him as if he had committed a contempt of the Crown Court.

(2) Any enactment relating to contempt of the Crown Court shall have effect in relation to such a failure as if it were such a contempt.

16. The costs of any application under this Schedule and of anything done or to be done in pursuance of an order made under it shall be in the discretion of the judge.

SCHEDULE 2   **[416]**

PRESERVED POWERS OF ARREST

Section 17(2) of the Military Lands Act 1892.

Section 12(1) of the Protection of Animals Act 1911.

Section 2 of the Emergency Powers Act 1920.

Section 7(3) of the Public Order Act 1936.

Section 49 of the Prison Act 1952.

Section 13 of the Visiting Forces Act 1952.

Sections 186 and 190B of the Army Act 1955.

Section 186 and 190B of the Air Force Act 1955.

Sections 104 and 105 of the Naval Discipline Act 1957.

Section 1(3) of the Street Offences Act 1959.

Section 32 of the Children and Young Persons Act 1969.

Section 24(2) of the Immigration Act 1971 and paragraphs 17, 24 and 33 of Schedule 2 and paragraph 7 of Schedule 3 to that Act.

Section 7 of the Bail Act 1976.

Sections 6(6), 7(11), 8(4), 9(7) and 10(5) of the Criminal Law Act 1977.

Schedule 5 to the Reserve Forces Act 1980.

Sections 60(5) and 61(1) of the Animal Health Act 1981.

Rule 36 in Schedule 1 to the Representation of the People Act 1983.

Sections 18, 35(10), 36(8), 38(7), 136(1) and 138 of the Mental Health Act 1983.

Section 5(5) of the Repatriation of Prisoners Act 1984.

SCHEDULE 5 **[417]**

SERIOUS ARRESTABLE OFFENCES

PART I

OFFENCES MENTIONED IN SECTION 116(2)(a)

1. Treason.
2. Murder.
3. Manslaughter.
4. Rape.
5. Kidnapping.
6. Incest with a girl under the age of 13.
7. Buggery with a person under the age of 16.
8. Indecent assault which constitutes an act of gross indecency.

PART II

OFFENCES MENTIONED IN SECTION 116(2)(b)

Explosive Substances Act 1883 (c 3)

Section 2 (causing explosion likely to endanger life or property).

Sexual Offences Act 1956 (c 69)

Section 5 (intercourse with a girl under the age of 13).

Firearms Act 1968 (c 27)

Section 16 (possession of firearms with intent to injure).
Section 17(1) (use of firearms and imitation firearms to resist arrest).
Section 18 (carrying firearms with criminal intent).

Taking of Hostages Act 1982 (c 28)

Section 1 (hostage-taking).

Aviation Security Act 1982 (c 36)

Section 1 (hi-jacking).

Road Traffic Act 1988 (c 52)

Section 1 (causing death by dangerous driving).

Section 3A (causing death by careless driving when under the influence of drink or drugs).

Criminal Justice Act 1988 (c 33)

Section 134 (torture).

Protection of Children Act 1978 (c37)

Section 1 (indecent photographs and pseudo-photographs of children).

Obscene Publications Act 1959 (c66)

Section 2 (publication of obscene matter).

[As amended by the Sexual Offences Act 1985, s5(3), Schedule; Representation of the People Act 1985, s25(1); Public Order Act 1986, s40(2), (3), Schedule 2, para 7, Schedule 3; Drug Trafficking Offences Act 1986, ss32(1), (3), 36; Criminal Justice Act 1988, ss99(1), (2), 140(1), 147, 148, 170, Schedule 15, paras 97, 98, 99, 100, 102, Schedule 16; Road Traffic (Consequential Provisions) Act 1988, ss3, 4, Schedules 1, 3, para 27(1), (3), (4), (5); Children Act 1989, s108(5), (7), Schedule 13, paras 53, 54, 55, Schedule 15; Official Secrets Act 1989, s11(1); Prevention of Terrorism (Temporary Provisions) Act 1989, s25(1), Schedule 8, para 6(1), (2), (3), (4), (5), (6), (7), (8); Football (Offences) Act 1991, s5(1); Criminal Justice Act 1991, s59; Road Traffic Act 1991, s48, Schedule 4, para 39; Police and Magistrates' Courts Act 1994, s37(a), Schedule 5, paras 24–26; Criminal Justice and Public Order Act 1994, ss24, 27(1), 28(2), (3), (4)(c)–(e), 29(2), (3), (4)(a) and (b), 54(2)–(5), 55(2), (3), (5), (6), 56, 57(2), (3), 58(2)–(4), 59(1)–(2), 85(1)–(3), 155, 166(4), 167(7), Schedule 4, para 58, Schedule 9, para 24, Schedule 10, paras 4(a), 53–59, 62(4)(a) and (b).]

Note (* on page 194): An apparent legislative oversight has resulted in s55(6) and Schedule 10, para 62(4)(b) of the Criminal Justice and Public Order Act 1994 *both* adding a new subsection (10) to s63 of the Police and Criminal Evidence Act 1984. This error will presumably be rectified in subsequent legislation.

INTERCEPTION OF COMMUNICATIONS ACT 1985
(1985 c 56)

1 Prohibition on interception   [418]

(1) Subject to the following provisions of this section, a person who intentionally intercepts a communication in the course of its transmission by post or by means of a public telecommunication system shall be guilty of an offence and liable –

    (a) on summary conviction, to a fine not exceeding the statutory maximum;

    (b) on conviction on indictment, to imprisonment for a term not exceeding two years or to a fine or to both.

(2) A person shall not be guilty of an offence under this section if –

    (a) the communication is intercepted in obedience to a warrant issued by the Secretary of State under section 2 below; or

(b) that person has reasonable grounds for believing that the person to whom, or the person by whom, the communication is sent has consented to the interception.

(3) A person shall not be guilty of an offence under this section if –

(a) the communication is intercepted for purposes connected with the provision of postal or public telecommunication services or with the enforcement of any enactment relating to the user of those services; or
(b) the communication is being transmitted by wireless telegraphy and is intercepted, with the authority of the Secretary of State, for purposes connected with the issue of licences under the Wireless Telegraphy Act 1949 or the prevention or detection of interference with wireless telegraphy.

(4) No proceedings in respect of an offence under this section shall be instituted –

(a) in England and Wales, except by or with the consent of the Director of Public Prosecutions;
(b) In Northern Ireland, except by or with the consent of the Director of Public Prosecutions for Northern Ireland.

2 Warrants for interception [419]

(1) Subject to the provisions of this section and section 3 below, the Secretary of State may issue a warrant requiring the person to whom it is addressed to intercept, in the course of their transmission by post or by means of a public telecommunication system, such communications as are described in the warrant; and such a warrant may also require the person to whom it is addressed to disclose the intercepted material to such persons and in such manner as are described in the warrant.

(2) The Secretary of State shall not issue a warrant under this section unless he considers that the warrant is necessary –

(a) in the interests of national security;
(b) for the purpose of preventing or detecting serious crime; or
(c) for the purpose of safeguarding the economic well-being of the United Kingdom.

(3) The matters to be taken into account in considering whether a warrant is necessary as mentioned in subsection (2) above shall include whether the information which it is considered necessary to acquire could reasonably be acquired by other means.

(4) A warrant shall not be considered necessary as mentioned in subsection (2)(c) above unless the information which it is considered necessary to acquire is information relating to the acts or intentions of persons outside the British Islands
...

3 Scope of warrants [420]

(1) Subject to subsection (2) below, the interception required by a warrant shall be the interception of –

(a) such communications as are sent to or from one or more addresses specified in the warrant, being an address or addresses likely to be used for the transmission of communications to or from –

(i) one particular person specified or described in the warrant; or
(ii) one particular set of premises so specified or described; and

(b) such other communications (if any) as it is necessary to intercept in order to intercept communications falling within paragraph (a) above.

(2) Subsection (1) above shall not apply to a warrant if –

(a) the interception required by the warrant is the interception, in the course of their transmission by means of a public telecommunication system, of –

(i) such external communications as are described in the warrant; and
(ii) such other communications (if any) as it is necessary to intercept in order to intercept such external communications as are so described; and

(b) at the time when the warrant is issued, the Secretary of State issues a certificate certifying the descriptions of intercepted material the examination of which he considers necessary as mentioned in section 2(2) above.

(3) A certificate such as is mentioned in subsection (2) above shall not specify an address in the British Islands for the purpose of including communications sent to or from that address in the certified material unless –

(a) the Secretary of State considers that the examination of communications sent to or from that address is necessary for the purpose of preventing or detecting acts of terrorism; and
(b) communications sent to or from that address are included in the certified material only in so far as they are sent within such a period, not exceeding three months, as is specified in the certificate.

(4) A certificate such as is mentioned in subsection (2) above shall not be issued except under the hand of the Secretary of State.

(5) References in the following provisions of this Act to a certificate are references to a certificate such as is mentioned in subsection (2) above.

4 Issue and duration of warrants   [421]

(1) A warrant shall not be issued except –

(a) under the hand of the Secretary of State; or
(b) in an urgent case where the Secretary of State has expressly authorised its issue and a statement of that fact is endorsed thereon, under the hand of an official of his department of or above the rank of Assistant Under Secretary of State.

(2) A warrant shall, unless renewed under subsection (3) below, cease to have effect at the end of the relevant period.

(3) The Secretary of State may, at any time before the end of the relevant period, renew a warrant if he considers that the warrant continues to be necessary as mentioned in section 2(2) above.

(4) If, at any time before the end of the relevant period, the Secretary of State considers that a warrant is no longer necessary as mentioned in section 2(2) above, he shall cancel the warrant.

(5) A warrant shall not be renewed except by an instrument under the hand of the Secretary of State.

(6) In this section 'the relevant period' –

(a) in relation to a warrant which has not been renewed, means –

(i) if the warrant was issued under subsection (1)(a) above, the period of two months beginning with the day on which it was issued; and
(ii) if the warrant was issued under subsection (1)(b) above, the period ending with the second working day following that day;

(b) in relation to a warrant which was last renewed within the period mentioned in paragraph (a)(ii) above, means the period of two months beginning with the day on which it was so renewed; and

(c) in relation to a warrant which was last renewed at any other time, means –

(i) if the instrument by which it was so renewed is endorsed with a statement that the renewal is considered necessary as mentioned in section 2(2)(a) or (c) above, the period of six months beginning with the day on which it was so renewed; and
(ii) if that instrument is not so endorsed, the period of one month beginning with that day.

5 Modification of warrants, etc [422]

(1) The Secretary of State may at any time –

(a) modify a warrant by the insertion of any address which he considers likely to be used as mentioned in section 3(1)(a) above; or
(b) modify a certificate so as to include in the certified material any material the examination of which he considers necessary as mentioned in section 2(2) above.

(2) If at any time the Secretary of State considers that any address specified in a warrant is no longer likely to be used as mentioned in section 3(1)(a) above, he shall modify the warrant by the deletion of that address.

(3) If at any time the Secretary of State considers that the material certified by a certificate includes any material the examination of which is no longer necessary as mentioned in section 2(2) above, he shall modify the certificate so as to exclude that material from the certified material.

(4) A warrant or certificate shall not be modified under subsection (1) above except by an instrument under the hand of the Secretary of State or, in an urgent case –

(a) under the hand of a person holding office under the Crown who is expressly authorised by the warrant or certificate to modify it on the Secretary of State's behalf; or
(b) where the Secretary of State has expressly authorised the modification and a statement of that fact is endorsed on the instrument, under the hand of such an officer as is mentioned in section 4(1)(b) above.

(5) An instrument made under subsection (4)(a) or (b) above shall cease to have effect at the end of the fifth working day following the day on which it was issued.

6 Safeguards [423]

(1) Where the Secretary of State issues a warrant he shall, unless such arrangements have already been made, make such arrangements as he considers necessary for the purpose of securing –

(a) that the requirements of subsections (2) and (3) below are satisfied in relation to the intercepted material; and
(b) where a certificate is issued in relation to the warrant, that so much of the intercepted material as is not certified by the certificate is not read, looked at or listened to by any person.

(2) The requirements of this subsection are satisfied in relation to any intercepted material if each of the following, namely –

(a) the extent to which the material is disclosed;
(b) the number of persons to whom any of the material is disclosed;
(c) the extent to which the material is copied; and
(d) the number of copies made of any of the material,

is limited to the minimum that is necessary as mentioned in section 2(2) above.

(3) The requirements of this subsection are satisfied in relation to any intercepted material if each copy made of any of that material is destroyed as soon as its retention is no longer necessary as mentioned in section 2(2) above.

7 The Tribunal [424]

(1) There shall be a tribunal (in this Act referred to as 'the Tribunal') in relation to which the provisions of Schedule 1 to this Act shall apply.

(2) Any person who believes that communications sent to or by him have been intercepted in the course of their transmission by post or by means of a public telecommunication system may apply to the Tribunal for an investigation under this section.

(3) On such an application (other than one appearing to the Tribunal to be frivolous or vexatious), the Tribunal shall investigate –

(a) whether there is or has been a relevant warrant or a relevant certificate; and

(b) where there is or has been such a warrant or certificate, whether there has been any contravention of sections 2 to 5 above in relation to that warrant or certificate.

(4) If, on an investigation, the Tribunal, applying the principles applicable by a court on an application for judicial review, conclude that there has been a contravention of sections 2 to 5 above in relation to a relevant warrant or a relevant certificate, they shall –

(a) give notice to the applicant stating that conclusion;

(b) make a report of their findings to the Prime Minister; and

(c) if they think fit, make an order under subsection (5) below.

(5) An order under this subsection may do one or more of the following, namely –

(a) quash the relevant warrant or the relevant certificate;

(b) direct the destruction of copies of the intercepted material or, as the case may be, so much of it as is certified by the relevant certificate;

(c) direct the Secretary of State to pay to the applicant such sum by way of compensation as may be specified in the order.

(6) A notice given or report made under subsection (4) above shall state the effect of any order under subsection (5) above made in the case in question.

(7) If, on an investigation, the Tribunal come to any conclusion other than that mentioned in subsection (4) above, they shall give notice to the applicant stating that there has been no contravention of sections 2 to 5 above in relation to a relevant warrant or a relevant certificate.

(8) The decisions of the Tribunal (including any decisions as to their jurisdiction) shall not be subject to appeal or liable to be questioned in any court.

(9) For the purposes of this section –

(a) a warrant is a relevant warrant in relation to an applicant if –

(i) the applicant is specified or described in the warrant; or

(ii) an address used for the transmission of communications to or from a set of premises in the British Islands where the applicant resides or works is so specified;

(b) a certificate is a relevant certificate in relation to an applicant if and to the extent that an address used as mentioned in paragraph (a)(ii) above is specified in the certificate for the purpose of including communications sent to or from that address in the certified material.

PARLIAMENTARY CONSTITUENCIES ACT 1986
(1986 c 56)

1 Parliamentary constituencies　　　　**[425]**

(1) There shall for the purpose of parliamentary elections be the county and borough constituencies (or in Scotland the county and burgh constituencies), each returning a single member, which are described in Orders in Council made under this Act.

(2) In this Act and, except where the context otherwise requires, in any Act passed after the Representation of the People Act 1948, 'constituency' means an area having separate representation in the House of Commons.

2 The Boundary Commissions　　　　**[426]**

(1) For the purpose of the continuous review of the distribution of seats at parliamentary elections, there shall continue to be four permanent Boundary Commissions, namely a Boundary Commission for England, a Boundary Commission for Scotland, a Boundary Commission for Wales and a Boundary Commission for Northern Ireland.

(2) Schedule 1 to this Act shall have effect with respect to the constitution of, and other matters relating to, the Boundary Commissions.

3 Reports of the Commissions　　　　**[427]**

(1) Each Boundary Commission shall keep under review the representation in the House of Commons of the part of the United Kingdom with which they are concerned and shall, in accordance with subsection (2) below, submit to the Secretary of State reports with respect to the whole of that part of the United Kingdom, either –

　(a) showing the constituencies into which they recommend that it should be divided in order to give effect to the rules set out in paragraphs 1 to 6 of Schedule 2 to this Act (read with paragraph 7 of that Schedule), or
　(b) stating that, in the opinion of the Commission, no alteration is required to be made in respect of that part of the United Kingdom in order to give effect to the said rules (read with paragraph 7).

(2) Reports under subsection (1) above shall be submitted by a Boundary Commission not less than eight or more than twelve years from the date of the submission of their last report under that subsection.

(2A) A failure by a Boundary Commission to submit a report within the time limit which is appropriate to that report shall not be regarded as invalidating the report for the purposes of any enactment.

(3) Any Boundary Commission may also from time to time submit to the Secretary of State reports with respect to the area comprised in any particular constituency or constituencies in the part of the United Kingdom with which they are concerned, showing the constituencies into which they recommend that that area should be divided in order to give effect to the rules set out in paragraphs 1 to 6 of Schedule 2 to this Act (read with paragraph 7 of that Schedule).

(4) A report of a Boundary Commission under this Act showing the constituencies into which they recommend that any area should be divided shall state, as respects each constituency, the name by which they recommend that it should be known, and whether they recommend that it should be a county constituency or a borough constituency (or in Scotland a county constituency or a burgh constituency).

(5) As soon as may be after a Boundary Commission have submitted a report to the Secretary of State under this Act, he shall lay the report before Parliament together, except in a case where the report states that no alteration is required to be made in respect of the part of the United Kingdom with which the Commission are concerned, with the draft of an Order in Council for giving effect, whether with or without modifications, to the recommendations contained in the report.

(6) Schedule 2 to this Act which contains the rules referred to above and related provisions shall have effect.

4 Orders in Council [428]

(1) The draft of any Order in Council laid before Parliament by the Secretary of State under this Act for giving effect, whether with or without modifications, to the recommendations contained in the report of a Boundary Commission may make provisions for any matters which appear to him to be incidental to, or consequential on, the recommendations.

(2) Where any such draft gives effect to any such recommendations with modifications, the Secretary of State shall lay before Parliament together with the draft a statement of the reasons for the modifications.

(3) If any such draft is approved by resolution of each House of Parliament, the Secretary of State shall submit it to Her Majesty in Council.

(4) If a motion for the approval of any such draft is rejected by either House of Parliament or withdrawn by leave of the House, the Secretary of State may amend the draft and lay the amended draft before Parliament, and if the draft as so amended is approved by resolution of each House of Parliament, the Secretary of State shall submit it to Her Majesty in Council.

(5) Where the draft of an Order in Council is submitted to Her Majesty in Council under this Act, Her Majesty in Council may make an Order in terms of the draft which (subject to subsection (6) below) shall come into force on such date as may be specified in the Order and shall have effect notwithstanding anything in any enactment.

(6) The coming into force of any such Order shall not affect any parliamentary election until a proclamation is issued by Her Majesty summoning a new Parliament, or affect the constitution of the House of Commons until the dissolution of the Parliament then in being.

(7) The validity of any Order in Council purporting to be made under this Act and reciting that a draft of the Order has been approved by resolution of each House of Parliament shall not be called in question in any legal proceedings whatsoever.

SCHEDULE 1 [429]

THE BOUNDARY COMMISSIONS

1 The Speaker of the House of Commons shall be the chairman of each of the Commissions.

2 Each of the four Commissions shall consist of the chairman, a deputy chairman and other members appointed by the Secretary of State ...

NB. In relation to reports under s3(1) above, the first such report due to be made after the passing of the Boundary Commissions Act 1992 had to be submitted not later than 31 December 1994: ibid, s2(2).

[As amended by the Boundary Commissions Act 1992, s2(1), (3), (4).]

PUBLIC ORDER ACT 1986
(1986 c 64)

1 Riot [430]

(1) Where 12 or more persons who are present together use or threaten unlawful violence for a common purpose and the conduct of them (taken together) is such as would cause a person of reasonable firmness present at the scene to fear for his personal safety, each of the persons using unlawful violence for the common purpose is guilty of riot.

(2) It is immaterial whether or not the 12 or more use or threaten unlawful violence simultaneously.

(3) The common purpose may be inferred from conduct.

(4) No person of reasonable firmness need actually be, or be likely to be, present at the scene.

(5) Riot may be committed in private as well as in public places.

(6) A person guilty of riot is liable on conviction on indictment to imprisonment for a term not exceeding ten years or a fine or both.

2 Violent disorder [431]

(1) Where three or more persons who are present together use or threaten unlawful violence and the conduct of them (taken together) is such as would cause a person of reasonable firmness present at the scene to fear for his personal safety, each of the persons using or threatening unlawful violence is guilty of violent disorder.

(2) It is immaterial whether or not the three or more use or threaten unlawful violence simultaneously.

(3) No person of reasonable firmness need actually be, or be likely to be, present at the scene.

(4) Violent disorder may be committed in private as well as in public places.

(5) A person guilty of violent disorder is liable on conviction on indictment to imprisonment for a term not exceeding five years or a fine or both, or on summary conviction to imprisonment for a term not exceeding six months or a fine not exceeding the statutory maximum or both.

3 Affray [432]

(1) A person is guilty of affray if he uses or threatens unlawful violence towards another and his conduct is such as would cause a person of reasonable firmness present at the scene to fear for his personal safety.

(2) Where two or more persons use or threaten the unlawful violence, it is the conduct of them taken together that must be considered for the purposes of subsection (1).

(3) For the purposes of this section a threat cannot be made by the use of words alone.

(4) No person of reasonable firmness need actually be, or be likely to be, present at the scene.

(5) Affray may be committed in private as well as in public places.

(6) A constable may arrest without warrant anyone he reasonably suspects is committing affray.

(7) A person guilty of affray is liable on conviction on indictment to imprisonment for a term not exceeding three years or a fine or both, or on summary conviction to imprisonment for a term not exceeding six months or a fine not exceeding the statutory maximum or both.

4 Fear or provocation of violence   [433]

(1) A person is guilty of an offence if he –

(a) uses towards another person threatening, abusive or insulting words or behaviour, or

(b) distributes or displays to another person any writing, sign or other visible representation which is threatening, abusive or insulting,

with intent to cause that person to believe that immediate unlawful violence will be used against him or another by any person, or to provoke the immediate use of unlawful violence by that person or another, or whereby that person is likely to believe that such violence will be used or it is likely that such violence will be provoked.

(2) An offence under this section may be committed in a public or a private place, except that no offence is committed where the words or behaviour are used, or the writing, sign or other visible representation is distributed or displayed, by a person inside a dwelling and the other person is also inside that or another dwelling.

(3) A constable may arrest without warrant anyone he reasonably suspects is committing an offence under this section.

(4) A person guilty of an offence under this section is liable on summary conviction to imprisonment for a term not exceeding six months or a fine not exceeding level 5 on the standard scale or both.

4A Intentional harassment, alarm or distress   [434]

(1) A person is guilty of an offence if, with intent to cause a person harassment, alarm or distress, he –

(a) uses threatening, abusive or insulting words or behaviour, or disorderly behaviour, or

(b) displays any writing, sign or other visible representation which is threatening, abusive or insulting,

thereby causing that or another person harassment, alarm or distress.

(2) An offence under this section may be committed in a public or a private place, except that no offence is committed where the words or behaviour are used, or the writing, sign or other visible representation is displayed, by a person inside a dwelling and the person who is harassed, alarmed or distressed is also inside that or another dwelling.

(3) It is a defence for the accused to prove –

(a) that he was inside a dwelling and had no reason to believe that the words or behaviour used, or the writing, sign or other visible representation displayed, would be heard or seen by a person outside that or any other dwelling, or

(b) that his conduct was reasonable.

(4) A constable may arrest without warrant anyone he reasonably suspects is committing an offence under this section.

(5) A person guilty of an offence under this section is liable on summary

conviction to imprisonment for a term not exceeding 6 months or a fine not exceeding level 5 on the standard scale or both.

5 Harassment, alarm or distress [435]

(1) A person is guilty of an offence if he –

(a) uses threatening, abusive or insulting words or behaviour, or disorderly behaviour, or

(b) displays any writing, sign or other visible representation which is threatening, abusive or insulting,

within the hearing or sight of a person likely to be caused harassment, alarm or distress thereby.

(2) An offence under this section may be committed in a public or a private place, except that no offence is committed where the words or behaviour are used, or the writing, sign or other visible representation is displayed, by a person inside a dwelling and the other person is also inside that or another dwelling.

(3) It is a defence for the accused to prove –

(a) that he had no reason to believe that there was any person within hearing or sight who was likely to be caused harassment, alarm or distress, or

(b) that he was inside a dwelling and had no reason to believe that the words or behaviour used, or the writing, sign or other visible representation displayed, would be heard or seen by a person outside that or any other dwelling, or

(c) that his conduct was reasonable.

(4) A constable may arrest a person without warrant if –

(a) he engages in offensive conduct which the constable warns him to stop, and

(b) he engages in further offensive conduct immediately or shortly after the warning.

(5) In subsection (4) 'offensive conduct' means conduct the constable reasonably suspects to constitute an offence under this section, and the conduct mentioned in paragraph (a) and the further conduct need not be of the same nature.

(6) A person guilty of an offence under this section is liable on summary conviction to a fine not exceeding level 3 on the standard scale.

6 Mental element: miscellaneous [436]

(1) A person is guilty of riot only if he intends to use violence or is aware that his conduct may be violent.

(2) A person is guilty of violent disorder or affray only if he intends to use or threaten violence or is aware that his conduct may be violent or threaten violence.

(3) A person is guilty of an offence under section 4 only if he intends his words or behaviour, or the writing, sign or other visible representation, to be threatening, abusive or insulting, or is aware that it may be threatening, abusive or insulting.

(4) A person is guilty of an offence under section 5 only if he intends his words or behaviour, or the writing, sign or other visible representation, to be threatening, abusive or insulting, or is aware that it may be threatening, abusive or insulting or (as the case may be) he intends his behaviour to be or is aware that it may be disorderly.

(5) For the purposes of this section a person whose awareness is impaired by intoxication shall be taken to be aware of that of which he would be aware if not

intoxicated, unless he shows either that his intoxication was not self-induced or that it was caused solely by the taking or administration of a substance in the course of medical treatment.

(6) In subsection (5) 'intoxication' means any intoxication, whether caused by drink, drugs or other means, or by a combination of means.

(7) Subsections (1) and (2) do not affect the determination for the purposes of riot or violent disorder of the number of persons who use or threaten violence.

7 Procedure: miscellaneous   [437]

(1) No prosecution for an offence of riot or incitement to riot may be instituted except by or with the consent of the Director of Public Prosecutions.

(2) For the purposes of the rules against charging more than one offence in the same count or information, each of sections 1 to 5 creates one offence.

(3) If on the trial on indictment of a person charged with violent disorder or affray the jury find him not guilty of the offence charged, they may (without prejudice to section 6(3) of the Criminal Law Act 1967) find him guilty of an offence under section 4.

(4) The Crown Court has the same powers and duties in relation to a person who is by virtue of subsection (3) convicted before it of an offence under section 4 as a magistrates' court would have on convicting him of the offence.

8 Interpretation   [438]

In this Part –

'dwelling' means any structure or part of a structure occupied as a person's home or as other living accommodation (whether the occupation is separate or shared with others) but does not include any part not so occupied, and for this purpose 'structure' includes a tent, caravan, vehicle, vessel or other temporary or movable structure;

'violence' means any violent conduct, so that –

(a) except in the context of affray, it includes violent conduct towards property as well as violent conduct towards persons, and
(b) it is not restricted to conduct causing or intended to cause injury or damage but includes any other violent conduct (for example, throwing at or towards a person a missile of a kind capable of causing injury which does not hit or falls short).

9 Offences abolished   [439]

(1) The common law offences of riot, rout, unlawful assembly and affray are abolished ...

11 Advance notice of public processions   [440]

(1) Written notice shall be given in accordance with this section of any proposal to hold a public procession intended –

(a) to demonstrate support for or opposition to the views or actions of any person or body of persons,
(b) to publicise a cause or campaign, or
(c) to mark or commemorate an event,

unless it is not reasonably practicable to give any advance notice of the procession.

(2) Subsection (1) does not apply where the procession is one commonly or customarily held in the police area (or areas) in which it is proposed to be held or is a funeral procession organised by a funeral director acting in the normal course of his business.

(3) The notice must specify the date when it is intended to hold the procession, the time when it is intended to start it, its proposed route, and the name and address of the person (or of one of the persons) proposing to organise it.

(4) Notice must be delivered to a police station –

(a) in the police area in which it is proposed the procession will start, or
(b) where it is proposed the procession will start in Scotland and cross into England, in the first police area in England on the proposed route.

(5) If delivered not less than six clear days before the date when the procession is intended to be held, the notice may be delivered by post under the recorded delivery service; but section 7 of the Interpretation Act 1978 (under which a document sent by post is deemed to have been served when posted and to have been delivered in the ordinary course of post) does not apply.

(6) If not delivered in accordance with subsection (5), the notice must be delivered by hand not less than six clear days before the date when the procession is intended to be held or, if that is not reasonably practicable, as soon as delivery is reasonably practicable.

(7) Where a public procession is held, each of the persons organising it is guilty of an offence if –

(a) the requirements of this section as to notice have not been satisfied, or
(b) the date when it is held, the time when it starts, or its route, differs from the date, time or route specified in the notice.

(8) It is a defence for the accused to prove that he did not know of, and neither suspected nor had reason to suspect, the failure to satisfy the requirements or (as the case may be) the difference of date, time or route.

(9) To the extent that an alleged offence turns on a difference of date, time or route, it is a defence for the accused to prove that the difference arose from circumstances beyond his control or from something done with the agreement of a police officer or by his direction.

(10) A person guilty of an offence under subsection (7) is liable on summary conviction to a fine not exceeding level 3 on the standard scale.

12 Imposing conditions on public processions   [441]

(1) If the senior police officer, having regard to the time or place at which and the circumstances in which any public procession is being held or is intended to be held and to its route or proposed route, reasonably believes that –

(a) it may result in serious public disorder, serious damage to property or serious disruption to the life of the community, or
(b) the purpose of the persons organising it is the intimidation of others with a view to compelling them not to do an act they have a right to do, or to do an act they have a right not to do,

he may give directions imposing on the persons organising or taking part in the procession such conditions as appear to him necessary to prevent such disorder, damage, disruption or intimidation, including conditions as to the route of the procession or prohibiting it from entering any public place specified in the directions.

(2) In subsection (1) 'the senior police officer' means –

(a) in relation to a procession being held, or to a procession intended to be held in a case where persons are assembling with a view to taking part in it, the most senior in rank of the police officers present at the scene, and
(b) in relation to a procession intended to be held in a case where paragraph (a) does not apply, the chief officer of police.

(3) A direction given by a chief officer of police by virtue of subsection (2)(b) shall be given in writing.

(4) A person who organises a public procession and knowingly fails to comply with a condition imposed under this section is guilty of an offence, but it is a defence for him to prove that the failure arose from circumstances beyond his control.

(5) A person who takes part in a public procession and knowingly fails to comply with a condition imposed under this section is guilty of an offence, but it is a defence for him to prove that the failure arose from circumstances beyond his control.

(6) A person who incites another to commit an offence under subsection (5) is guilty of an offence.

(7) A constable in uniform may arrest without warrant anyone he reasonably suspects is committing an offence under subsection (4), (5) or (6).

(8) A person guilty of an offence under subsection (4) is liable on summary conviction to imprisonment for a term not exceeding three months or a fine not exceeding level 4 on the standard scale or both.

(9) A person guilty of an offence under subsection (5) is liable on summary conviction to a fine not exceeding level 3 on the standard scale.

(10) A person guilty of an offence under subsection (6) is liable on summary conviction to imprisonment for a term not exceeding three months or a fine not exceeding level 4 on the standard scale or both, notwithstanding section 45(3) of the Magistrates' Courts Act 1980 (inciter liable to same penalty as incited) ...

13 Prohibiting public processions [442]

(1) If at any time the chief officer of police reasonably believes that, because of particular circumstances existing in any district or part of a district, the powers under section 12 will not be sufficient to prevent the holding of public processions in that district or part from resulting in serious public disorder, he shall apply to the council of the district for an order prohibiting for such period not exceeding three months as may be specified in the application the holding of all public processions (or of any class of public procession so specified) in the district or part concerned.

(2) On receiving such an application, a council may with the consent of the Secretary of State make an order either in the terms of the application or with such modifications as may be approved by the Secretary of State.

(3) Subsection (1) does not apply in the City of London or the metropolitan police district.

(4) If at any time the Commissioner of Police for the City of London or the Commissioner of Police of the Metropolis reasonably believes that, because of particular circumstances existing in his police area or part of it, the powers under section 12 will not be sufficient to prevent the holding of public processions in that area or part from resulting in serious public disorder, he may with the consent of the Secretary of State make an order prohibiting for such period not exceeding three months as may be specified in the order the holding of all public processions (or of any class of public procession so specified) in the area or part concerned.

(5) An order made under this section may be revoked or varied by a subsequent order made in the same way, that is, in accordance with subsections (1) and (2) or subsection (4), as the case may be.

(6) Any order under this section shall, if not made in writing, be recorded in writing as soon as practicable after being made.

(7) A person who organises a public procession the holding of which he knows is prohibited by virtue of an order under this section is guilty of an offence.

(8) A person who takes part in a public procession the holding of which he knows is prohibited by virtue of an order under this section is guilty of an offence.

(9) A person who incites another to commit an offence under subsection (8) is guilty of an offence.

(10) A constable in uniform may arrest without warrant anyone he reasonably suspects is committing an offence under subsection (7), (8) or (9).

(11) A person guilty of an offence under subsection (7) is liable on summary conviction to imprisonment for a term not exceeding three months or a fine not exceeding level 4 on the standard scale or both.

(12) A person guilty of an offence under subsection (8) is liable on summary conviction to a fine not exceeding level 3 on the standard scale.

(13) A person guilty of an offence under subsection (9) is liable on summary conviction to imprisonment for a term not exceeding three months or a fine not exceeding level 4 on the standard scale or both, notwithstanding section 45(3) of the Magistrates' Courts Act 1980.

14 Imposing conditions on public assemblies   [443]

(1) If the senior police officer, having regard to the time or place at which and the circumstances in which any public assembly is being held or is intended to be held, reasonably believes that –

(a) it may result in serious public disorder, serious damage to property or serious disruption to the life of the community, or

(b) the purpose of the persons organising it is the intimidation of others with a view to compelling them not to do an act they have a right to do, or to do an act they have a right not to do,

he may give directions imposing on the persons organising or taking part in the assembly such conditions as to the place at which the assembly may be (or continue to be) held, its maximum duration, or the maximum number of persons who may constitute it, as appear to him necessary to prevent such disorder, damage, disruption or intimidation.

(2) In subsection (1) 'the senior police officer' means –

(a) in relation to an assembly being held, the most senior in rank of the police officers present at the scene, and

(b) in relation to an assembly intended to be held, the chief officer of police.

(3) A direction given by a chief officer of police by virtue of subsection (2)(b) shall be given in writing.

(4) A person who organises a public assembly and knowingly fails to comply with a condition imposed under this section is guilty of an offence, but it is a defence for him to prove that the failure arose from circumstances beyond his control.

(5) A person who takes part in a public assembly and knowingly fails to comply with a condition imposed under this section is guilty of an offence, but it is a

defence for him to prove that the failure arose from circumstances beyond his control.

(6) A person who incites another to commit an offence under subsection (5) is guilty of an offence.

(7) A constable in uniform may arrest without warrant anyone he reasonably suspects is committing an offence under subsection (4), (5) or (6).

(8) A person guilty of an offence under subsection (4) is liable on summary conviction to imprisonment for a term not exceeding three months or a fine not exceeding level 4 on the standard scale or both.

(9) A person guilty of an offence under subsection (5) is liable on summary conviction to a fine not exceeding level 3 on the standard scale.

(10) A person guilty of an offence under subsection (6) is liable on summary conviction to imprisonment for a term not exceeding three months or a fine not exceeding level 4 on the standard scale or both, notwithstanding section 45(3) of the Magistrates' Courts Act 1980.

14A Prohibiting trespassory assemblies   [444]

(1) If at any time the chief officer of police reasonably believes that an assembly is intended to be held in any district at a place on land to which the public has no right of access or only a limited right of access and that the assembly –

   (a) is likely to be held without the permission of the occupier of the land or to conduct itself in such a way as to exceed the limits of any permission of his or the limits of the public's right of access, and
   (b) may result –

      (i) in serious disruption to the life of the community, or
      (ii) where the land, or a building or monument on it, is of historical, architectural, archaeological or scientific importance, in significant damage to the land, building or monument,

he may apply to the council of the district for an order prohibiting for a specified period the holding of all trespassory assemblies in the district or a part of it, as specified.

(2) On receiving such an application, a council may –

   (a) in England and Wales, with the consent of the Secretary of State make an order either in the terms of the application or with such modifications as may be approved by the Secretary of State; or
   (b) in Scotland, make an order in the terms of the application.

(3) Subsection (1) does not apply in the City of London or the metropolitan police district.

(4) If at any time the Commissioner of Police for the City of London or the Commissioner of Police of the Metropolis reasonably believes that an assembly is intended to be held at a place on land to which the public has no right of access or only a limited right of access in his police area and that the assembly –

   (a) is likely to be held without the permission of the occupier of the land or to conduct itself in such a way as to exceed the limits of any permission of his or the limits of the public's right of access, and
   (b) may result –

      (i) in serious disruption to the life of the community, or
      (ii) where the land, or a building or monument on it, is of historical, architectural, archaeological or scientific importance, in significant damage to the land, building or monument,

he may with the consent of the Secretary of State make an order prohibiting for a specified period the holding of all trespassory assemblies in the area or a part of it, as specified.

(5) An order prohibiting the holding of trespassory assemblies operates to prohibit any assembly which –

(a) is held on land to which the public has no right of access or only a limited right of access, and

(b) takes place in the prohibited circumstances, that is to say, without the permission of the occupier of the land or so as to exceed the limits of any permission of his or the limits of the public's right of access.

(6) No order under this section shall prohibit the holding of assemblies for a period exceeding 4 days or in an area exceeding an area represented by a circle with a radius of 5 miles from a specified centre.

(7) An order made under this section may be revoked or varied by a subsequent order made in the same way, that is, in accordance with subsection (1) and (2) or subsection (4), as the case may be.

(8) Any order under this section shall, if not made in writing, be recorded in writing as soon as practicable after being made.

(9) In this section and sections 14B and 14C –

'assembly' means an assembly of 20 or more persons;

'land' means land in the open air;

'limited', in relation to a right of access by the public to land, means that their use of it is restricted to use for a particular purpose (as in the case of a highway or road) or is subject to other restrictions;

'occupier' means –

(a) in England and Wales, the person entitled to possession of the land by virtue of an estate or interest held by him; or

(b) in Scotland, the person lawfully entitled to natural possession of the land,

and in subsections (1) and (4) includes the person reasonably believed by the authority applying for or making the order to be the occupier;

'public' includes a section of the public; and

'specified' means specified in an order under this section.

(10) In relation to Scotland, the references in subsection (1) above to a district and to the council of the district shall be construed –

(a) as respects applications before 1st April 1996, as references to the area of a regional or islands authority and to the authority in question; and

(b) as respects applications on and after that date, as references to a local government area and to the council for that area.

(11) In relation to Wales, the references in subsection (1) above to a district and to the council of the district shall be construed, as respects applications on and after 1st April 1996, as references to a county or county borough and to the council for that county or county borough.

14B Offices in connection with trespassory assemblies and arrest therefor　　　　　　　　　　　　　　　　　　　　　**[445]**

(1) A person who organises an assembly the holding of which he knows is prohibited by an order under section 14A is guilty of an offence.

(2) A person who takes part in an assembly which he knows is prohibited by an order under section 14A is guilty of an offence.

(3) In England and Wales, a person who incites another to commit an offence under subsection (2) is guilty of an offence.

(4) A constable in uniform may arrest without a warrant anyone he reasonably suspects to be committing an offence under this section.

(5) A person guilty of an offence under subsection (1) is liable on summary conviction to imprisonment for a term not exceeding 3 months or a fine not exceeding level 4 on the standard scale or both.

(6) A person guilty of an offence under subsection (2) is liable of summary conviction to a fine not exceeding level 3 on the standard scale.

(7) A person guilty of an offence under subsection (3) is liable on summary conviction to imprisonment for a term not exceeding 3 months or a fine not exceeding level 4 on the standard scale or both, notwithstanding section 45(3) of the Magistrates' Courts Act 1980.

(8) Subsection (3) above is without prejudice to the application of any principle of Scots Law as respects art and part guilt to such incitement as is mentioned in that subsection.

14C Stopping persons from proceeding to   [446]
trespassory assemblies

(1) If a constable in uniform reasonably believes that a person is on his way to an assembly within the area to which an order under section 14A applies which the constable reasonably believes is likely to be an assembly which is prohibited by that order, he may, subject to subsection (2) below –

(a) stop that person, and
(b) direct him not to proceed in the direction of the assembly.

(2) The power conferred by subsection (1) may only be exercised within the area to which the order applies.

(3) A person who fails to comply with a direction under subsection (1) which he knows has been given to him is guilty of an offence.

(4) A constable in uniform may arrest without a warrant anyone he reasonably suspects to be committing an offence under this section.

(5) A person guilty of an offence under subsection (3) is liable on summary conviction to a fine not exceeding level 3 on the standard scale.

16 Interpretation   [447]

In this Part –

'the City of London' means the City as defined for the purposes of the Acts relating to the City of London police;

'the metropolitan police district' means that district as defined in section 76 of the London Government Act 1963;

'public assembly' means an assembly of 20 or more persons in a public place which is wholly or partly open to the air;

'public place' means –

(a) any highway, or in Scotland any road within the meaning of the Roads (Scotland) Act 1984, and
(b) any place to which at the material time the public or any section of the public has access, on payment or otherwise, as of rights or by virtue of express or implied permission;

'public procession' means a procession in a public place.

[As amended by the Criminal Justice and Public Order Act 1994, ss70–71, 154.]

CROWN PROCEEDINGS (ARMED FORCES) ACT 1987
(1987 c 25)

1 Repeal of section 10 of the Crown Proceedings Act 1947   [448]

Subject to section 2 below, section 10 of the Crown Proceedings Act 1947 (exclusions from liability in tort cases involving the armed forces) shall cease to have effect except in relation to anything suffered by a person in consequence of an act or omission committed before the date on which this Act is passed.

2 Revival of section 10   [449]

(1) Subject to the following provisions of this section, the Secretary of State may, at any time after the coming into force of section 1 above, by order –

(a) revive the effect of section 10 of the Crown Proceedings Act 1947 either for all purposes or for such purposes as may be described in the order; or
(b) where that section has effect for the time being in pursuance of an order made by virtue of paragraph (a) above, provide for that section to cease to have effect either for all of the purposes for which it so has effect or for such of them as may be described.

(2) The Secretary of State shall not make an order reviving the effect of the said section 10 for any purposes unless it appears to him necessary or expedient to do so –

(a) by reason of any imminent national danger or of any great emergency that has arisen; or
(b) for the purposes of any warlike operations in any part of the world outside the United Kingdom or of any other operations which are or are to be carried out in connection with the warlike activity of any persons in any such part of the world.

(3) Subject to subsection (4) below, an order under this section describing purposes for which the effect of the said section 10 is to be revived, or for which that section is to cease to have effect, may describe those purposes by reference to any matter whatever and may make different provisions for different cases, circumstances or persons.

(4) Nothing in any order under this section shall revive the effect of the said section 10, or provide for that section to cease to have effect, in relation to anything suffered by a person in consequence of an act or omission committed before the date on which the order comes into force.

(5) The power to make an order under this section shall be exercisable by statutory instrument subject to annulment in pursuance of a resolution of either House of Parliament.

NB. This Act came into effect on 15 May 1987.

IMMIGRATION ACT 1988
(1988 c 14)

2 Restriction on exercise of right of abode in cases of polygamy   [450]

(1) This section applies to any woman who –

(a) has the right of abode in the United Kingdom under section 2(1)(b) of the principal Act [ie the Immigration Act 1971] as, or as having been, the wife of a man ('the husband') –

(i) to whom she is or was polygamously married; and
(ii) who is or was such a citizen of the United Kingdom and Colonies, Commonwealth citizen or British subject as is mentioned in section 2(2)(a) or (b) of that Act as in force immediately before the commencement of the British Nationality Act 1981; and

(b) has not before the coming into force of this section and since her marriage to the husband been in the United Kingdom.

(2) A woman to whom this section applies shall not be entitled to enter the United Kingdom in the exercise of the right of abode mentioned in subsection (1)(a) above or to be granted a certificate of entitlement in respect of that right if there is another woman living (whether or not one to whom this section applies) who is the wife or widow of the husband and who –

(a) is, or at any time since her marriage to the husband has been, in the United Kingdom; or

(b) has been granted a certificate of entitlement in respect of the right of abode mentioned in subsection (1)(a) above or an entry clearance to enter the United Kingdom as the wife of the husband.

(3) So long as a woman is precluded by subsection (2) above from entering the United Kingdom in the exercise of her right of abode or being granted a certificate of entitlement in respect of that right the principal Act shall apply to her as it applies to a person not having a right of abode.

(4) Subsection (2) above shall not preclude a woman from re-entering the United Kingdom if since her marriage to the husband she has at any time previously been in the United Kingdom and there was at that time no such other woman living as is mentioned in that subsection.

(5) Where a woman claims that this section does not apply to her because she has been in the United Kingdom before the coming into force of this section and since her marriage to the husband it shall be for her to prove that fact.

(6) For the purposes of this section a marriage may be polygamous although at its inception neither party has any spouse additional to the other.

(7) For the purposes of subsections (1)(b), (2)(a), (4) and (5) above there shall be disregarded presence in the United Kingdom as a visitor or an illegal entrant and presence in circumstances in which a person is deemed by section 11(1) of the principal Act not to have entered the United Kingdom.

(8) In subsection (2)(b) above the reference to a certificate of entitlement includes a reference to a certificate treated as such a certificate by virtue of section 39(8) of the British Nationality Act 1981.

(9) No application by a woman for a certificate of entitlement in respect of such a right of abode as is mentioned in subsection (1)(a) above or for an entry clearance shall be granted if another application for such a certificate or clearance

is pending and that application is made by a woman as the wife or widow of the same husband.

(10) For the purposes of subsection (9) above an application shall be regarded as pending so long as it and any appeal proceedings relating to it have not been finally determined.

5 Restricted right of appeal against deportation   [451]
in cases of breach of limited leave

(1) A person to whom this subsection applies shall not be entitled to appeal under section 15 of the principal Act against a decision to make a deportation order against him –

    (a) by virtue of section 3(5)(a) of that Act (breach of limited leave); or
    (b) by virtue of section 3(5)(c) of that Act as belonging to the family of a person who is or has been ordered to be deported by virtue of section 3(5)(a),

except on the ground that on the facts of his case there is in law no power to make the deportation order for the reasons stated in the notice of the decision.

(2) Subsection (1) above applies to any person who was last given leave to enter the United Kingdom less than seven years before the date of the decision in question but the Secretary of State may by order exempt any such persons from that subsection in such circumstances and to such extent as may be specified in the order.

(3) The power to make an order under subsection (2) above shall be exercisable by statutory instrument subject to annulment in pursuance of a resolution of either House of Parliament.

(4) It shall be presumed for the purposes of this section that a person was last given leave as mentioned in subsection (2) above unless he proves the contrary.

(5) Subsection (1) above shall not affect the grounds on which a person may appeal where written notice of the decision in question was given to him before the coming into force of this section.

7 Persons exercising Community rights and nationals   [452]
of Member States

(1) A person shall not under the principal Act require leave to enter or remain in the United Kingdom in any case in which he is entitled to do so by virtue of an enforceable Community right or of any provision made under section 2(2) of the European Communities Act 1972.

(2) The Secretary of State may by order made by statutory instrument give leave to enter the United Kingdom for a limited period to any class of persons who are nationals of Member States but who are not entitled to enter the United Kingdom as mentioned in subsection (1) above; and any such order may give leave subject to such conditions as may be imposed by the order.

(3) References in the principal Act to limited leave shall include references to leave given by an order under subsection (2) above and a person having leave by virtue of such an order shall be treated as having been given that leave by a notice given to him by an immigration officer within the period specified in paragraph 6(1) of Schedule 2 to that Act.

PREVENTION OF TERRORISM (TEMPORARY PROVISIONS) ACT 1989
(1989 c 4)

1 Proscribed organisations [453]

(1) Any organisation for the time being specified in Schedule 1 to this Act is a proscribed organisation for the purposes of this Act; and any organisation which passes under a name mentioned in that Schedule shall be treated as proscribed whatever relationship (if any) it has to any other organisation of the same name.

(2) The Secretary of State may by order made by statutory instrument –

(a) add to Schedule 1 to this Act any organisation that appears to him to be concerned in, or in promoting or encouraging, terrorism occurring in the United Kingdom and connected with the affairs of Northern Ireland;
(b) remove an organisation from that Schedule.

(3) No order shall be made under this section unless –

(a) a draft of the order has been laid before and approved by a resolution of each House of Parliament; or
(b) it is declared in the order that it appears to the Secretary of State that by reason of urgency it is necessary to make the order without a draft having been so approved.

(4) An order under this section of which a draft has not been approved under subsection (3) above –

(a) shall be laid before Parliament; and
(b) shall cease to have effect at the end of the period of forty days beginning with the day on which it was made unless, before the end of that period, the order has been approved by a resolution of each House of Parliament, but without prejudice to anything previously done or to the making of a new order.

(5) In reckoning for the purposes of subsection (4) above any period of forty days, no account shall be taken of any period during which Parliament is dissolved or prorogued or during which both Houses are adjourned for more than four days.

(6) In this section 'organisation' includes any association or combination of persons.

2 Membership, support and meetings [454]

(1) Subject to subsection (3) below, a person is guilty of an offence if he –

(a) belongs or professes to belong to a proscribed organisation;
(b) solicits or invites support for a proscribed organisation other than support with money or other property; or
(c) arranges or assists in the arrangement or management of, or addresses, any meeting of three or more persons (whether or not it is a meeting to which the public are admitted) knowing that the meeting is –

(i) to support a proscribed organisation;
(ii) to further the activities of such an organisation; or
(iii) to be addressed by a person belonging or professing to belong to such an organisation.

(2) A person guilty of an offence under subsection (1) above is liable –

(a) on conviction on indictment, to imprisonment for a term not exceeding ten years or a fine or both;

(b) on summary conviction, to imprisonment for a term not exceeding six months or a fine not exceeding the statutory maximum or both.

(3) A person belonging to a proscribed organisation is not guilty of an offence under this section by reason of belonging to the organisation if he shows –

(a) that he became a member when it was not a proscribed organisation under the current legislation; and
(b) that he has not since he became a member taken part in any of its activities at any time while it was a proscribed organisation under that legislation.

(4) In subsection (3) above 'the current legislation', in relation to any time, means whichever of the following was in force at that time –

(a) the Prevention of Terrorism (Temporary Provisions) Act 1974;
(b) the Prevention of Terrorism (Temporary Provisions) Act 1976;
(c) the Prevention of Terrorism (Temporary Provisions) Act 1984; or
(d) this Act.

(5) The reference in subsection (3) above to a person becoming a member of an organisation is a reference to the only or last occasion on which he became a member.

3 Display of support in public [455]

(1) Any person who in a public place –

(a) wears any item of dress; or
(b) wears, carries or displays any article,

in such a way or in such circumstances as to arouse reasonable apprehension that he is a member or supporter of a proscribed organisation, is guilty of an offence and liable on summary conviction to imprisonment for a term not exceeding six months or a fine not exceeding level 5 on the standard scale or both ...

(3) In this section 'public place' includes any highway or, in Scotland, any road within the meaning of the Roads (Scotland) Act 1984 and any premises to which at the material time the public have, or are permitted to have, access, whether on payment or otherwise.

4 Exclusion orders: general [456]

(1) The Secretary of State may exercise the powers conferred on him by this Part of this Act in such a way as appears to him expedient to prevent acts of terrorism to which this Part of this Act applies.

(2) The acts of terrorism to which this Part of this Act applies are acts of terrorism connected with the affairs of Northern Ireland.

(3) An order under section 5, 6 or 7 below is referred to in this Act as an 'exclusion order'.

(4) Schedule 2 to this Act shall have effect with respect to the duration of exclusion orders, the giving of notices, the right to make representations, powers of removal and detention and other supplementary matters for this Part of this Act.

(5) The exercise of the detention powers conferred by that Schedule shall be subject to supervision in accordance with Schedule 3 to this Act.

5 Orders excluding persons from Great Britain [457]

(1) If the Secretary of State is satisfied that any person –

(a) is or has been concerned in the commission, preparation or instigation of acts of terrorism to which this Part of this Act applies; or

(b) is attempting or may attempt to enter Great Britain with a view to being concerned in the commission, preparation or instigation of such acts of terrorism,

the Secretary of State may make an exclusion order against him.

(2) An exclusion order under this section is an order prohibiting a person from being in, or entering, Great Britain.

(3) In deciding whether to make an exclusion order under this section against a person who is ordinarily resident in Great Britain, the Secretary of State shall have regard to the question whether that person's connection with any country or territory outside Great Britain is such as to make it appropriate that such an order should be made.

(4) An exclusion order shall not be made under this section against a person who is a British citizen and who –

(a) is at the time ordinarily resident in Great Britain and has then been ordinarily resident in Great Britain throughout the last three years; or

(b) is at the time subject to an order under section 6 below.

6 Orders excluding persons from Northern Ireland [458]

(1) If the Secretary of State is satisfied that any person –

(a) is or has been concerned in the commission, preparation or instigation of acts of terrorism to which this Part of this Act applies; or

(b) is attempting or may attempt to enter Northern Ireland with a view to being concerned in the commission, preparation or instigation of such acts of terrorism,

the Secretary of State may make an exclusion order against him.

(2) An exclusion order under this section is an order prohibiting a person from being in, or entering, Northern Ireland.

(3) In deciding whether to make an exclusion order under this section against a person who is ordinarily resident in Northern Ireland, the Secretary of State shall have regard to the question whether that person's connection with any country or territory outside Northern Ireland is such as to make it appropriate that such an order should be made.

(4) An exclusion order shall not be made under this section against a person who is a British citizen and who –

(a) is at the time ordinarily resident in Northern Ireland and has then been ordinarily resident in Northern Ireland throughout the last three years; or

(b) is at the time subject to an order under section 5 above.

7 Orders excluding persons from the United Kingdom [459]

(1) If the Secretary of State is satisfied that any person –

(a) is or has been concerned in the commission, preparation or instigation of acts of terrorism to which this Part of this Act applies; or

(b) is attempting or may attempt to enter Great Britain or Northern Ireland with a view to being concerned in the commission, preparation or instigation of such acts of terrorism,

the Secretary of State may make an exclusion order against him.

(2) An exclusion order under this section is an order prohibiting a person from being in, or entering, the United Kingdom.

(3) In deciding whether to make an exclusion order under this section against a person who is ordinarily resident in the United Kingdom, the Secretary of State shall have regard to the question whether that person's connection with any country or territory outside the United Kingdom is such as to make it appropriate that such an order should be made.

(4) An exclusion order shall not be made under this section against a person who is a British citizen.

8 Offences in respect of exclusion orders　　　　　　　　[460]

(1) A person who is subject to an exclusion order is guilty of an offence if he fails to comply with the order at a time after he has been, or has become liable to be, removed under Schedule 2 to this Act.

(2) A person is guilty of an offence –

(a) if he is knowingly concerned in arrangements for securing or facilitating the entry into Great Britain, Northern Ireland or the United Kingdom of a person who he knows, or has reasonable grounds for believing, to be an excluded person; or
(b) if he knowingly harbours such a person in Great Britain, Northern Ireland or the United Kingdom.

(3) In subsection (2) above 'excluded person' means –

(a) in relation to Great Britain, a person subject to an exclusion order made under section 5 above who has been, or has become liable to be, removed from Great Britain under Schedule 2 to this Act.
(b) in relation to Northern Ireland, a person subject to an exclusion order made under section 6 above who has been, or has become liable to be, removed from Northern Ireland under that Schedule; and
(c) in relation to the United Kingdom, a person subject to an exclusion order made under section 7 above who has been, or has become liable to be, removed from the United Kingdom under that Schedule.

(4) A person guilty of an offence under this section is liable –

(a) on conviction on indictment, to imprisonment for a term not exceeding five years or a fine or both;
(b) on summary conviction, to imprisonment for a term not exceeding six months or a fine not exceeding the statutory maximum or both.

9 Contributions towards acts of terrorism　　　　　　　　[461]

(1) A person is guilty of an offence if he –

(a) solicits or invites any other person to give, lend or otherwise make available, whether for consideration or not, any money or other property; or
(b) receives or accepts from any other person, whether for consideration or not, any money or other property, or
(c) uses or has possession of, whether for consideration or not, any money or other property,

intending that it shall be applied or used for the commission of, or in furtherance of or in connection with, acts of terrorism to which this section applies or having reasonable cause to suspect that it may be so used or applied.

(2) A person is guilty of an offence if he –

(a) gives, lends or otherwise makes available to any other person, whether for consideration or not, any money or other property; or

(b) enters into or is otherwise concerned in an arrangement whereby money or other property is or is to be made available to another person,

knowing or having reasonable cause to suspect that it will or may be applied or used as mentioned in subsection (1) above.

(3) The acts of terrorism to which this section applies are –

(a) acts of terrorism connected with the affairs of Northern Ireland; and

(b) subject to subsection (4) below, acts of terrorism of any other description except acts connected solely with the affairs of the United Kingdom or any part of the United Kingdom other than Northern Ireland.

(4) Subsection (3)(b) above does not apply to an act done or to be done outside the United Kingdom unless it constitutes or would constitute an offence triable in the United Kingdom.

(5) In proceedings against a person for an offence under this section in relation to an act within subsection (3)(b) above done or to be done outside the United Kingdom –

(a) the prosecution need not prove that that person knew or had reasonable cause to suspect that the act constituted or would constitute such an offence as is mentioned in subsection (4) above; but

(b) it shall be a defence to prove that he did not know and had no reasonable cause to suspect that the facts were such that the act constituted or would constitute such an offence.

10 Contributions to resources of proscribed organisations   [462]

(1) A person is guilty of an offence if he –

(a) solicits or invites any other person to give, lend or otherwise make available, whether for consideration or not, any money or other property for the benefit of a proscribed organisation;

(b) gives, lends or otherwise makes available or receives or accepts, or uses or has possession of whether for consideration or not, any money or other property for the benefit of such an organisation; or

(c) enters into or is otherwise concerned in an arrangement whereby money or other property is or is to be made available for the benefit of such an organisation.

(2) In proceedings against a person for an offence under subsection (1)(b) above it is a defence to prove that he did not know and had no reasonable cause to suspect that the money or property was for the benefit of a proscribed organisation; and in proceedings against a person for an offence under subsection (1)(c) above it is a defence to prove that he did not know and had no reasonable cause to suspect that the arrangement related to a proscribed organisation.

(3) In this section and sections 11 and 13 below 'proscribed organisation' includes a proscribed organisation for the purposes of section 28 of the Northern Ireland (Emergency Provisions) Act 1991.

11 Assisting in retention or control of terrorist funds   [463]

(1) A person is guilty of an offence if he enters into or is otherwise concerned in an arrangement whereby the retention or control by or on behalf of another person of terrorist funds is facilitated, whether by concealment, removal from the jurisdiction, transfer to nominees or otherwise.

(2) In proceedings against a person for an offence under this section it is a defence to prove that he did not know and had no reasonable cause to suspect that the arrangement related to terrorist funds.

(3) In this section and section 12 below 'terrorist funds' means –

(a) funds which may be applied or used for the commission of, or in furtherance of or in connection with, acts of terrorism to which section 9 above applies;
(b) the proceeds of the commission of such acts of terrorism or of activities engaged in furtherance of or in connection with such acts; and
(c) the resources of a proscribed organisation.

(4) Paragraph (b) of subsection (3) includes any property which in whole or in part directly or indirectly represents such proceeds as are mentioned in that paragraph; and paragraph (c) of that subsection includes any money or other property which is or is to be applied or made available for the benefit of a proscribed organisation.

12 Disclosure of information about terrorist funds   [464]

(1) A person may notwithstanding any restriction on the disclosure of information imposed by statute or otherwise disclose to a constable a suspicion or belief that any money or other property is or is derived from terrorist funds or any matter on which such a suspicion or belief is based.

(2) A person who enters into or is otherwise concerned in any such transaction or arrangement as is mentioned in section 9, 10 or 11 above does not commit an offence under that section if he is acting with the express consent of a constable or if –

(a) he discloses to a constable his suspicion or belief that the money or other property concerned is or is derived from terrorist funds or any matter on which such a suspicion or belief is based; and
(b) the disclosure is made after he enters into or otherwise becomes concerned in the transaction or arrangement in question but is made on his own initiative and as soon as it is reasonable for him to make it,

but paragraphs (a) and (b) above do not apply in a case where, having disclosed any such suspicion, belief or matter to a constable and having been forbidden by a constable to enter into or otherwise be concerned in the transaction or arrangement in question, he nevertheless does so.

(2A) For the purposes of subsection (2) above a person who uses or has possession of money or other property shall be taken to be concerned in a transaction or arrangement.

(3) In proceedings against a person for an offence under section 9(1)(b) or (c) or (2), 10(1)(b) or (c) or 11 above it is a defence to prove –

(a) that he intended to disclose to a constable such a suspicion, belief or matter as is mentioned in paragraph (a) of subsection (2) above; and
(b) that there is a reasonable excuse for his failure to make the disclosure as mentioned in paragraph (b) of that subsection.

(4) In the case of a person who was in employment at the relevant time,

subsections (1) to (3) above shall have effect in relation to disclosures, and intended disclosures, to the appropriate person in accordance with the procedure established by his employer for the making of such disclosures as they have effect in relation to disclosures, and intended disclosures, to a constable.

(5) No constable or other person shall be guilty of an offence under section 9(1)(b) or (c) or (2) or 10(1)(b) or (c) above in respect of anything done by him in the course of acting in connection with the enforcement, or intended enforcement, of any provision of this Act or of any other enactment relating to terrorism or the proceeds or resources of terrorism.

(6) For the purposes of subsection (5) above, having possession of any property shall be taken to be doing an act in relation to it.

13 Penalties and forfeiture [465]

(1) A person guilty of an offence under section 9, 10 or 11 above is liable –

(a) on conviction on indictment, to imprisonment for a term not exceeding fourteen years or a fine or both;

(b) on summary conviction, to imprisonment for a term not exceeding six months or a fine not exceeding the statutory maximum or both.

(2) Subject to the provisions of this section, the court by or before which a person is convicted of an offence under section 9(1) or (2)(a) above may order the forfeiture of any money or other property –

(a) which, at the time of the offence, he had in his possession or under his control; and

(b) which, at that time –

(i) in the case of an offence under subsection (1) of section 9, he intended should be applied or used, or had reasonable cause to suspect might be applied or used, as mentioned in that subsection;

(ii) in the case of an offence under subsection (2)(a) of that section, he knew or had reasonable cause to suspect would or might be applied or used as mentioned in subsection (1) of that section.

(3) Subject to the provisions of this section, the court by or before which a person is convicted of an offence under section 9(2)(b), 10(1)(c) or 11 above may order the forfeiture of the money or other property to which the arrangement in question related and which, in the case of an offence under section 9(2)(b), he knew or had reasonable cause to suspect would or might be applied or used as mentioned in section 9(1) above.

(4) Subject to the provisions of this section, the court by or before which a person is convicted of an offence under section 10(1)(a) or (b) above may order the forfeiture of any money or other property which, at the time of the offence, he had in his possession or under his control for the use or benefit of a proscribed organisation.

(5) The court shall not under this section make an order forfeiting any money or other property unless the court considers that the money or property may, unless forfeited, be applied or used as mentioned in section 9(1) above but the court may, in the absence of evidence to the contrary, assume that any money or property may be applied or used as there mentioned.

(6) Where a person other than the convicted person claims to be the owner of or otherwise interested in anything which can be forfeited by an order under this section, the court shall, before making such an order in respect of it, give him an opportunity to be heard ...

13A Powers to stop and search vehicles, etc and persons   [466]

(1) Where it appears to –

(a) any officer of police of or above the rank of commander of the metropolitan police, as respects the metropolitan police area;

(b) any officer of police of or above the rank of commander of the City of London police, as respects the City of London; or

(c) any officer of police of or above the rank of assistant chief constable for any other police area,

that it is expedient to do so in order to prevent acts of terrorism to which this section applies he may give an authorisation that the powers to stop and search vehicles and persons conferred by this section shall be exercisable at any place within his area or a specified locality in his area for a specified period not exceeding twenty eight days.

(2) The acts of terrorism to which this section applies are –

(a) acts of terrorism connected with the affairs of Northern Ireland; and

(b) acts of terrorism of any other description except acts connected solely with the affairs of the United Kingdom or any part of the United Kingdom other than Northern Ireland.

(3) This section confers on any constable in uniform power –

(a) to stop any vehicle;

(b) to search any vehicle, its driver or any passenger for articles of a kind which could be used for a purpose connected with the commission, preparation or instigation of acts of terrorism to which this section applies;

(c) to stop any pedestrian and search any thing carried by him for articles of a kind which could be used for a purpose connected with the commission, preparation or instigation of acts of terrorism to which this section applies.

(4) A constable may, in the exercise of those powers, stop any vehicle or person and make any search he thinks fit whether or not he has any grounds for suspecting that the vehicle or person is carrying articles of that kind.

(5) This section applies (with the necessary modifications) to ships and aircraft as it applies to vehicles.

(6) A person is guilty of an offence if he –

(a) fails to stop or (as the case may be) to stop the vehicle when required to do so by a constable in the exercise of his powers under this section; or

(b) wilfully obstructs a constable in the exercise of those powers.

(7) A person guilty of an offence under subsection (6) above shall be liable on summary conviction to imprisonment for a term not exceeding six months or a fine not exceeding level 5 on the standard scale or both.

(8) If it appears to a police officer of the rank specified in subsection (1)(a), (b) or (c) (as the case may be) that the exercise of the powers conferred by this section ought to continue beyond the period for which their exercise has been authorised under this section he may, from time to time, authorise the exercise of those powers for a further period, not exceeding twenty eight days.

(9) Where a vehicle is stopped by a constable under this section, the driver shall be entitled to obtain a written statement that the vehicle was stopped under the powers conferred by this section if he applies for such a statement not later than the end of the period of twelve months from the day on which the vehicle was stopped; and similarly as respects a pedestrian who is stopped under this section for a search of anything carried by him.

(10) In this section –

'authorise' and 'authorisation' mean authorise or an authorisation in writing signed by the officer giving it; and
'specified' means specified in an authorisation under this section.

(11) Nothing in this section affects the exercise by constables of any power to stop vehicles for purposes other than those specified in subsection (1) above.

14   Arrest and detention of suspected persons   [467]

(1) Subject to subsection (2) below, a constable may arrest without warrant a person whom he has reasonable grounds for suspecting to be –

(a) a person guilty of an offence under section 2, 8, 9, 10 or 11 above;
(b) a person who is or has been concerned in the commission, preparation or instigation of acts of terrorism to which this section applies; or
(c) a person subject to an exclusion order.

(2) The acts of terrorism to which this section applies are –

(a) acts of terrorism connected with the affairs of Northern Ireland; and
(b) acts of terrorism of any other description except acts connected solely with the affairs of the United Kingdom or any part of the United Kingdom other than Northern Ireland.

(3) The power of arrest conferred by subsection (1)(c) above is exercisable only –

(a) in Great Britain if the exclusion order was made under section 5 above; and
(b) in Northern Ireland if it was made under section 6 above.

(4) Subject to subsection (5) below, a person arrested under this section shall not be detained in right of the arrest for more than forty-eight hours after his arrest.

(5) The Secretary of State may, in any particular case, extend the period of forty-eight hours mentioned in subsection (4) above by a period or periods specified by him, but any such further period or periods shall not exceed five days in all and if an application for such an extension is made the person detained shall as soon as practicable be given written notice of that fact and of the time when the application was made.

(6) The exercise of the detention powers conferred by this section shall be subject to supervision in accordance with Schedule 3 to this Act.

(7) The provisions of this section are without prejudice to any power of arrest exercisable apart from this section.

15 Provisions supplementary to section 14   [468]

(1) If a justice of the peace is satisfied that there are reasonable grounds for suspecting that a person whom a constable believes to be liable to arrest under section 14(1)(b) above is to be found on any premises he may grant a search warrant authorising any constable to enter those premises for the purpose of searching for and arresting that person ...

(3) In any circumstances in which a constable has power under section 14 above to arrest a person, he may also, for the purpose of ascertaining whether he has in his possession any document or other article which may constitute evidence that he is a person liable to arrest, stop that person and search him.

(4) Where a constable has arrested a person under that section for any reason other than the commission of a criminal offence, he, or any other constable, may search him for the purpose of ascertaining whether he has in his possession any

document or other article which may constitute evidence that he is a person liable to arrest.

(5) A search of a person under subsection (3) or (4) above may only be carried out by a person of the same sex.

(6) A person detained under section 14 above shall be deemed to be in legal custody at any time when he is so detained and may be detained in such a place as the Secretary of State may from time to time direct ...

(9) Where a person is detained under section 14 above, any constable or prison officer, or any other person authorised by the Secretary of State, may take all such steps as may be reasonably necessary for photographing, measuring or otherwise identifying him.

(10) Section 61(1) to (8) of the Police and Criminal Evidence Act 1984 (fingerprinting) shall apply to the taking of a person's fingerprints by a constable under subsection (9) above as if for subsection (4) there were substituted –

'(4) An officer may only give an authorisation under subsection (3)(a) above for the taking of a person's fingerprints if he is satisfied that it is necessary to do so in order to assist in determining –

(a) whether that person is or has been concerned in the commission, preparation or instigation of acts of terrorism to which section 14 of the Prevention of Terrorism (Temporary Provisions) Act 1989 applies; or
(b) whether he is subject to an exclusion order under that Act;
or if the officer has reasonable grounds for suspecting that person's involvement in an offence under any of the provisions mentioned in subsection (1)(a) of that section and for believing that his fingerprints will tend to confirm or disprove his involvement.'.

(11) Section 62(1) to (11) of the Police and Criminal Evidence Act 1984 (regulation of taking of intimate samples) shall apply to the taking of an intimate sample from a person under subsection (9) above as if –

(a) for subsection (2) there were substituted –

'(2) An officer may only give an authorisation under subsection (1) or (1A) above for the taking of an intimate sample if he is satisfied that it is necessary to do so in order to assist in determining –

(a) whether that person is or has been concerned in the commission, preparation or instigation of acts of terrorism to which section 14 of the Prevention of Terrorism (Temporary Provisions) Act 1989 applies; or
(b) whether he is subject to an exclusion order under that Act;

or if the officer has reasonable grounds for suspecting that person's involvement in an offence under any of the provisions mentioned in subsection (1)(a) of that section and for believing that an intimate sample will tend to confirm or disprove his involvement'; and

(b) in subsection (6), after the word 'includes', there were inserted the words 'where relevant'.

(12) In this section, 'intimate sample' has the same meaning as in section 65 of the Police and Criminal Evidence Act 1984.

(13) Section 63(1) to (9) of the Police and Criminal Evidence Act 1984 (regulation of taking of non-intimate samples) shall apply to the taking of a non-intimate sample from a person by a constable under subsection (9) above as if –

(a) for subsection (4) there we re substituted –

'(4) An officer may only give an authorisation under subsection (3) above for the taking of a non-intimate sample if he is satisfied that it is necessary to do so in order to assist in determining –

(a) whether that person is or has been concerned in the commission, preparation or instigation of acts of terrorism to which section 14 of the Prevention of Terrorism (Temporary Provisions) Act 1989 applies; or

(b) whether he is subject to an exclusion order under that Act;

or if the officer has reasonable grounds for suspecting that person's involvement in an offence under any of the provisions mentioned in subsection (1)(a) of that section and for believing that a non-intimate sample will tend to confirm or disprove his involvement'; and

(b) in subsection (7), after the word 'includes' there were inserted the words 'where relevant'.

(14) In this section, 'non-intimate sample' has the same meaning as in section 65 of the Police and Criminal Evidence Act 1984.

16 Port and border controls   [469]

(1) Schedule 5 to this Act shall have effect for conferring powers to examine persons arriving in or leaving Great Britain or Northern Ireland and for connected purposes.

(2) The exercise of the examination and detention powers conferred by paragraphs 2 and 6 of that Schedule shall be subject to supervision in accordance with Schedule 3 to this Act.

(3) The designated ports for the purposes of paragraph 8 of Schedule 5 to this Act shall be those specified in Schedule 6 to this Act but the Secretary of State may by order add any port to, or remove any port from, that Schedule.

(4) Without prejudice to the provisions of Schedule 5 to this Act with respect to persons who enter or leave Northern Ireland by land or who seek to do so, the Secretary of State may by order make such further provision with respect to those persons as appears to him to be expedient.

(5) The power to make orders under this section shall be exercisable by statutory instrument.

(6) An order under subsection (4) above may contain transitional provisions and savings and shall be subject to annulment in pursuance of a resolution of either House of Parliament.

16A Possession of articles for suspected terrorist purposes   [470]

(1) A person is guilty of an offence if he has any article in his possession in circumstances giving rise to a reasonable suspicion that the article is in his possession for a purpose connected with the commission, preparation or instigation of acts of terrorism to which this section applies.

(2) The acts of terrorism to which this section applies are –

(a) acts of terrorism connected with the affairs of Northern Ireland; and

(b) acts of terrorism of any other description except acts connected solely with the affairs of the United Kingdom or any part of the United Kingdom other than Northern Ireland.

(3) It is a defence for a person charged with an offence under this section to prove that at the time of the alleged offence the article in question was not in his possession for such a purpose as is mentioned in subsection (1) above.

(4) Where a person is charged with an offence under this section and it is proved that at the time of the alleged offence –

(a) he and that article were both present in any premises; or

(b) the article was in premises of which he was the occupier or which he habitually used otherwise than as a member of the public,

the court may accept the fact proved as sufficient evidence of his possessing that article at that time unless it is further proved that he did not at that time know of its presence in the premises in question, or, if he did know, that he had no control over it.

(5) A person guilty of an offence under this section is liable –

(a) on conviction on indictment, to imprisonment for a term not exceeding ten years or a fine or both;

(b) on summary conviction, to imprisonment for a term not exceeding six months or a fine not exceeding the statutory maximum or both.

(6) This section applies to vessels, aircraft and vehicles as it applies to premises.

16B   Unlawful collection, etc of information   [471]

(1) No person shall, without lawful authority or reasonable excuse (the proof of which lies on him) –

(a) collect or record any information which is of such a nature as is likely to be useful to terrorists in planning or carrying out any act of terrorism to which this section applies; or

(b) have in his possession any record or document containing any such information as is mentioned in paragraph (a) above.

(2) The acts of terrorism to which this section applies are –

(a) acts of terrorism connected with the affairs of Northern Ireland; and

(b) acts of terrorism of any other description except acts connected solely with the affairs of the United Kingdom or any part of the United Kingdom other than Northern Ireland.

(3) In subsection (1) above the reference to recording information includes a reference to recording it by means of photography or by any other means.

(4) Any person who contravenes this section is guilty of an offence and liable –

(a) on conviction on indictment, to imprisonment for a term not exceeding ten years or a fine or both;

(b) on summary conviction, to imprisonment for a term not exceeding six months or a fine not exceeding the statutory maximum or both.

(5) The court by or before which a person is convicted of an offence under this section may order the forfeiture of any record or document mentioned in subsection (1) above which is found in his possession.

17   Investigation of terrorist activities   [472]

(1) Schedule 7 to this Act shall have effect for conferring powers to obtain information for the purposes of terrorist investigations, that is to say –

(a) investigations into –

(i) the commission, preparation or instigation of acts of terrorism to which section 14 above applies; or

(ii) any other act which appears to have been done in furtherance of or in connection with such acts of terrorism, including any act which appears to constitute an offence under section 2, 9, 10, 11, 18 or 18(A) of this Act or section 27, 28, 53, 54, 54(A) of the Northern Ireland (Emergency Provisions) Act 1991; or

(iii) without prejudice to sub-paragraph (ii) above, the resources of a proscribed organisation within the meaning of this Act or a proscribed organisation for the purposes of section 21 of the said Act of 1978; and

(b) investigations into whether there are grounds justifying the making of an order under section 1(2)(a) above or section 28(3) of that Act.

(2) A person is guilty of an offence if, knowing or having reasonable cause to suspect that a constable is acting, or is proposing to act, in connection with a terrorist investigation which is being, or is about to be, conducted, he –

(a) discloses to any other person information or any other matter which is likely to prejudice the investigation or proposed investigation, or

(b) falsifies, conceals or destroys or otherwise disposes of, or causes or permits the falsification, concealment, destruction or disposal of, material which is or is likely to be relevant to the investigation, or proposed investigation.

(2A) A person is guilty of an offence if, knowing or having reasonable cause to suspect that a disclosure ('the disclosure') has been made to a constable under section 12, 18 or 18A of this Act or section 53, 54 or 54A of the Northern Ireland (Emergency Provisions) Act 1991, he –

(a) discloses to any other person information or any other matter which is likely to prejudice any investigation which might be conducted following the disclosure; or

(b) falsifies, conceals or destroys or otherwise disposes of, or causes or permits the falsification, concealment, destruction or disposal of, material which is or is likely to be relevant to any such investigation.

(2B) A person is guilty of an offence if, knowing or having reasonable cause to suspect that a disclosure ('the disclosure') of a kind mentioned in section 12(4) or 18A(5) of this Act or section 53(4A), 54(5D) or 54A(5) of the Act of 1991 has been made, he –

(a) discloses to any person information or any other matter which is likely to prejudice any investigation which might be conducted following the disclosure; or

(b) falsifies, conceals or destroys or otherwise disposes of, or causes or permits the falsification, concealment, destruction or disposal of, material which is or is likely to be relevant to any such investigation.

(2C) Nothing in subsections (2) to (2B) above makes it an offence for a professional legal adviser to disclose any information or other matter –

(a) to, or to a representative of, a client of his in connection with the giving by the adviser of legal advice to the client; or

(b) to any person –

(i) in contemplation of, or in connection with, legal proceedings; and

(ii) for the purpose of those proceedings.

(2D) Subsection (2C) above does not apply in relation to any information or other matter which is disclosed with a view to furthering any criminal purpose.

(2E) No constable or other person shall be guilty of an offence under this section in respect of anything done by him in the course of acting in connection with the enforcement, or intended enforcement, of any provision of this Act or of any other enactment relating to terrorism or the proceeds or resources of terrorism.

(3) In proceedings against a person for an offence under subsection (2)(a) above it is a defence to prove –

(a) that he did not know and had no reasonable cause to suspect that the disclosure was likely to prejudice the investigation or proposed investigation; or

(b) that he had lawful authority or reasonable excuse for making the disclosure.

(3A) In proceedings against a person for an offence under subsection (2A)(a) or (2B)(a) above it is a defence to prove –

(a) that he did not know and had no reasonable cause to suspect that his disclosure was likely to prejudice the investigation in question; or
(b) that he had lawful authority or reasonable excuse for making his disclosure.

(4) In proceedings against a person for an offence under subsection (2)(b) above it is a defence to prove that he had no intention of concealing any information contained in the material in question from any person conducting, or likely to be conducting, the investigation or proposed investigation.

(4A) In proceedings against a person for an offence under subsection (2A)(b) or (2B)(b) above, it is a defence to prove that he had no intention of concealing any information contained in the material in question from any person who might carry out the investigation in question ...

(6) For the purposes of subsection (1) above, as it applies to any offence under section 18 or 18A below or sections 54A of the Act of 1991, 'act' includes 'omission'.

18 Information about acts of terrorism [473]

(1) A person is guilty of an offence if he has information which he knows or believes might be of material assistance –

(a) in preventing the commission by any other person of an act of terrorism connected with the affairs of Northern Ireland; or
(b) in securing the apprehension, prosecution or conviction of any other person for an offence involving the commission, preparation or instigation of such an act,

and fails without reasonable excuse to disclose that information as soon as reasonably practicable –

(i) in England and Wales, to a constable; or ...
(iii) in Northern Ireland, to a constable or a member of Her Majesty's Forces.

(2) A person guilty of an offence under this section is liable –

(a) on conviction on indictment, to imprisonment for a term not exceeding five years or a fine or both;
(b) on summary conviction, to imprisonment for a term not exceeding six months or a fine not exceeding the statutory maximum or both.

(3) Proceedings for an offence under this section may be taken, and the offence may for the purposes of those proceedings be treated as having been committed, in any place where the person to be charged is or has at any time been since he first knew or believed that the information might be of material assistance as mentioned in subsection (1) above.

18A Failure to disclose knowledge or suspicion [474]
of offences under sections 9 to 11

(1) A person is guilty of an offence if –

(a) he knows, or suspects, that another person is providing financial assistance for terrorism;

(b) the information, or other matter, on which that knowledge or suspicion is based came to his attention in the course of his trade, profession, business or employment; and

(c) he does not disclose the information or other matter to a constable as soon as is reasonably practicable after it comes to his attention.

(2) Subsection (1) above does not make it an offence for a professional legal adviser to fail to disclose any information or other matter which has come to him in privileged circumstances.

(3) It is a defence to a charge of committing an offence under this section that the person charged had a reasonable excuse for not disclosing the information or other matter in question …

(7) In this section 'providing financial assistance for terrorism' means doing any act which constitutes an offence under section 9, 10 or 11 above or, in the case of an act done otherwise than in the United Kingdom, which would constitute such an offence if done in the United Kingdom.

(8) For the purposes of subsection (7) above, having possession of any property shall be taken to be doing an act in relation to it.

(9) For the purposes of this section, any information or other matter comes to a professional legal adviser in privileged circumstances if it is communicated, or given, to him –

(a) by, or by a representative of, a client of his in connection with the giving by the adviser of legal advice to the client;

(b) by, or by a representative of, a person seeking legal advice from the adviser; or

(c) by any person –

(i) in contemplation of, or in connection with, legal proceedings; and

(ii) for the purpose of those proceedings.

(10) No information or other matter shall be treated as coming to a professional legal adviser in privileged circumstances if it is communicated or given with a view to furthering any criminal purpose.

(11) A person guilty of an offence under this section shall be liable –

(a) on summary conviction, to imprisonment for a term not exceeding six months or a fine not exceeding the statutory maximum or to both; or

(b) on conviction on indictment, to imprisonment for a term not exceeding five years or a fine or to both.

20 Interpretation [475]

(1) In this Act –

'aircraft' includes hovercraft;

'captain' means master of a ship or commander of an aircraft;

'Concessionaires' has the same meaning as in the Channel Tunnel Act 1987;

'examining officer' has the meaning given in paragraph 1 of Schedule 5 to this Act;

'exclusion order' has the meaning given by section 4(3) above but subject to section 25(3) below;

'the Islands' means the Channel Islands or the Isle of Man;

'port' includes airport and hoverport;

'premises' includes any place and in particular includes –

(a) any vehicle, vessel or aircraft;

(b) any offshore installation as defined in section 1 of the Mineral Workings (Offshore Installations) Act 1971; and

(c) any tent or moveable structure;

'property' includes property wherever situated and whether real or personal, heritable or moveable and things in action and other intangible or incorporeal property;

'ship' includes every description of vessel used in navigation;

'terrorism' means the use of violence for political ends, and includes any use of violence for the purpose of putting the public or any section of the public in fear;

'tunnel system' has the same meaning as in the Channel Tunnel Act 1987;

'vehicle' includes a train and carriages forming part of a train.

(2) A constable or examining officer may, if necessary, use reasonable force for the purpose of exercising any powers conferred on him under or by virtue of any provision of this Act other than paragraph 2 of Schedule 5; but this subsection is without prejudice to any provision of this Act, or of any instrument made under it, which implies that a person may use reasonable force in connection with that provision.

(3) The powers conferred by Part II [sections 4–8] and section 16 of, and Schedules 2 and 5 to, this Act shall be exercisable notwithstanding the rights conferred by section 1 of the Immigration Act 1971 (general principles regulating entry into and staying in the United Kingdom).

(4) Any reference in a provision of this Act to a person having been concerned in the commission, preparation or instigation of acts of terrorism shall be taken to be a reference to his having been so concerned at any time, whether before or after the passing of this Act.

[As amended by the Channel Tunnel (Fire Services, Immigration and Prevention of Terrorism) Order 1990; Northern Ireland (Emergency Provisions) Act 1991, s70(3), Schedule 7, para 5(1), (2); Criminal Justice Act 1993, ss49(1), (2), (3), (4), (5), (6), 50(2)(a), (b), (3), (4), (5), (6), (7), 51; Criminal Justice and Public Order Act 1994, ss81–82, 168(2), Schedule 10, paras 62(1)–(2) and 63(2).]

OFFICIAL SECRETS ACT 1989
(1989 c 6)

1 Security and intelligence [476]

(1) A person who is or has been –

(a) a member of the security and intelligence services; or

(b) a person notified that he is subject to the provisions of this subsection,

is guilty of an offence if without lawful authority he discloses any information, document or other article relating to security or intelligence which is or has been in his possession by virtue of his position as a member of any of those services or in the course of his work while the notification is or was in force.

(2) The reference in subsection (1) above to disclosing information relating to security or intelligence includes a reference to making any statement which purports to be a disclosure of such information or is intended to be taken by those to whom it is addressed as being such a disclosure.

(3) A person who is or has been a Crown servant or government contractor is guilty of an offence if without lawful authority he makes a damaging disclosure of

any information, document or other article relating to security or intelligence which is or has been in his possession by virtue of his position as such but otherwise than as mentioned in subsection (1) above.

(4) For the purposes of subsection (3) above a disclosure is damaging if –

(a) it causes damage to the work of, or of any part of, the security and intelligence services; or

(b) it is of information or a document or other article which is such that its unauthorised disclosure would be likely to cause such damage or which falls within a class or description of information or articles the unauthorised disclosure of which would be likely to have that effect.

(5) It is a defence for a person charged with an offence under this section to prove that at the time of the alleged offence he did not know, and has no reasonable cause to believe, that the information, document or article in question related to security or intelligence or, in the case of an offence under subsection (3), that the disclosure would be damaging within the meaning of that subsection.

(6) Notification that a person is subject to subsection (1) above shall be effected by a notice in writing served on him by a Minister of the Crown; and such a notice may be served if, in the Minister's opinion, the work undertaken by the person in question is or includes work connected with the security and intelligence services and its nature is such that the interests of national security require that he should be subject to the provisions of that subsection.

(7) Subject to subsection (8) below, a notification for the purposes of subsection (1) above shall be in force for the period of five years beginning with the day on which it is served but may be renewed by further notices under subsection (6) above for periods of five years at a time.

(8) A notification for the purposes of subsection (1) above may at any time be revoked by a further notice in writing served by the Minister on the person concerned; and the Minister shall serve such a further notice as soon as, in his opinion, the work undertaken by that person ceases to be such as is mentioned in subsection (6) above.

(9) In this section 'security or intelligence' means the work of, or in support of, the security and intelligence services or any part of them, and references to information relating to security or intelligence include references to information held or transmitted by those services or by persons in support of, or of any part of, them.

2 Defence [477]

(1) A person who is or has been a Crown servant or government contractor is guilty of an offence if without lawful authority he makes a damaging disclosure of any information, document or other article relating to defence which is or has been in his possession by virtue of his position as such.

(2) For the purposes of subsection (1) above a disclosure is damaging if –

(a) it damages the capability of, or of any part of, the armed forces of the Crown to carry out their tasks or leads to loss of life or injury to members of those forces or serious damage to the equipment or installation of those forces; or

(b) otherwise than as mentioned in paragraph (a) above, it endangers the interests of the United Kingdom abroad, seriously obstructs the promotion or protection by the United Kingdom of those interests or endangers the safety of British citizens abroad; or

(c) it is of information or of a document or article which is such that its unauthorised disclosure would be likely to have any of those effects.

(3) It is a defence for a person charged with an offence under this section to prove that at the time of the alleged offence he did not know, and had no reasonable cause to believe, that the information, document or article in question related to defence or that its disclosure would be damaging within the meaning of subsection (1) above.

(4) In this section 'defence' means –

(a) the size, shape, organisation, logistics, order of battle, deployment, operations, state of readiness and training of the armed forces of the Crown;

(b) the weapons, stores or other equipment of those forces and the invention, development, production and operation of such equipment and research relating to it;

(c) defence policy and strategy and military planning and intelligence;

(d) plans and measures for the maintenance of essential supplies and services that are or would be needed in time of war.

3 International relations [478]

(1) A person who is or has been a Crown servant or government contractor is guilty of an offence if without lawful authority he makes a damaging disclosure of –

(a) any information, document or other article relating to international relations; or

(b) any confidential information, document or other article which was obtained from a State other than the United Kingdom or an international organisation,

being information or a document or article which is or has been in his possession by virtue of his position as a Crown servant or government contractor.

(2) For the purposes of subsection (1) above a disclosure is damaging if –

(a) it endangers the interests of the United Kingdom abroad, seriously obstructs the promotion or protection by the United Kingdom of those interests or endangers the safety of British citizens abroad; or

(b) it is of information or of a document or article which is such that its unauthorised disclosure would be likely to have any of those effects.

(3) In the case of information or a document or article within subsection (1)(b) above –

(a) the fact that it is confidential, or

(b) its nature or contents,

may be sufficient to establish for the purposes of subsection (2)(b) above that the information, document or article is such that its unauthorised disclosure would be likely to have any of the effects there mentioned.

(4) It is a defence for a person charged with an offence under this section to prove that at the time of the alleged offence he did not know, and had no reasonable cause to believe, that the information, document or article in question was such as is mentioned in subsection (1) above or that its disclosure would be damaging within the meaning of that subsection.

(5) In this section 'international relations' means the relations between States, between international organisations or between one or more States and one or more such organisations and includes any matter relating to a State other than the United Kingdom or to an international organisation which is capable of affecting the relations of the United Kingdom with another State or with an international organisation.

(6) For the purposes of this section any information, document or article obtained from a State or organisation is confidential at any time while the terms on which it was obtained require it to be held in confidence or while the circumstances in which it was obtained make it reasonable for the State or organisation to expect that it would be so held.

4 Crime and special investigation powers   [479]

(1) A person who is or has been a Crown servant or government contractor is guilty of an offence if without lawful authority he discloses any information, document or other article to which this section applies and which is or has been in his possession by virtue of his position as such.

(2) This section applies to any information, document or other article –

(a) the disclosure of which –

(i) results in the commission of an offence; or
(ii) facilitates an escape from legal custody or the doing of any other act prejudicial to the safekeeping of persons in legal custody; or
(iii) impedes the prevention or detection of offences or the apprehension or prosecution of suspected offenders; or

(b) which is such that its unauthorised disclosure would be likely to have any of those effects.

(3) This section also applies to –

(a) any information obtained by reason of the interception of any communication in obedience to a warrant issued under section 2 of the Interception of Communications Act 1985, any information relating to the obtaining of information by reason of any such interception and any document or other article which is or has been used or held for use in, or has been obtained by reason of, any such interception; and

(b) any information obtained by reason of action authorised by a warrant issued under section 3 of the Security Service Act 1989, any information relating to the obtaining of information by reason of any such action and any document or other article which is or has been used or held for use in, or has been obtained by reason of, any such action.

(4) It is a defence for a person charged with an offence under this section in respect of a disclosure falling within subsection (2)(a) above to prove that at the time of the alleged offence he did not know, and had no reasonable cause to believe, that the disclosure would have any of the effects there mentioned.

(5) It is a defence for a person charged with an offence under this section in respect of any other disclosure to prove that at the time of the alleged offence he did not know, and had no reasonable cause to believe, that the information, document or article in question was information or a document or article to which this section applies.

(6) In this section 'legal custody' includes detention in pursuance of any enactment or any instrument made under an enactment.

5 Information resulting from unauthorised disclosures   [480]
or entrusted in confidence

(1) Subsection (2) below applies where –

(a) any information, document or other article protected against disclosure by the foregoing provisions of this Act has come into a person's possession as a result of having been –

(i) disclosed (whether to him or another) by a Crown servant or government contractor without lawful authority; or

(ii) entrusted to him by a Crown servant or government contractor on terms requiring it to be held in confidence or in circumstances in which the Crown servant or government contractor could reasonably expect that it would be so held; or

(iii) disclosed (whether to him or another) without lawful authority by a person to whom it was entrusted as mentioned in sub-paragraph (ii) above; and

(b) the disclosure without lawful authority of the information, document or article by the person into whose possession it has come is not an offence under any of those provisions.

(2) Subject to subsections (3) and (4) below, the person into whose possession the information, document or article has come is guilty of an offence if he discloses it without lawful authority knowing, or having reasonable cause to believe, that it is protected against disclosure by the foregoing provisions of this Act and that it has come into his possession as mentioned in subsection (1) above.

(3) In the case of information or a document or article protected against disclosure by sections 1 to 3 above, a person does not commit an offence under subsection (2) above unless –

(a) the disclosure by him is damaging; or

(b) he makes it knowing, or having reasonable cause to believe, that it would be damaging;

and the question whether a disclosure is damaging shall be determined for the purposes of this subsection as it would be in relation to a disclosure of that information, document or article by a Crown servant in contravention of section 1(3), 2(1) or 3(1) above.

(4) A person does not commit an offence under subsection (2) above in respect of information or a document or other article which has come into his possession as a result of having been disclosed –

(a) as mentioned in subsection (1)(a)(i) above by a government contractor; or

(b) as mentioned in subsection (1)(a)(iii) above,

unless that disclosure was by a British citizen or took place in the United Kingdom, in any of the Channel Islands or in the Isle of Man or a colony.

(5) For the purposes of this section information or a document or article is protected against disclosure by the foregoing provisions of this Act if –

(a) it relates to security or intelligence, defence or international relations within the meaning of section 1, 2 or 3 above or is such as is mentioned in section 3(1)(b) above; or

(b) it is information or a document or article to which section 4 above applies;

and information or a document or article is protected against disclosure by sections 1 to 3 above if it falls within paragraph (a) above.

(6) A person is guilty of an offence if without lawful authority he discloses any information, document or other article which he knows, or has reasonable cause to believe, to have come into his possession as a result of a contravention of section 1 of the Official Secrets Act 1911.

6 Information entrusted in confidence to other States [481]
or international organisations

(1) This section applies where –

  (a) any information, document or other article which –

    (i) relates to security or intelligence, defence or international relations; and
    (ii) has been communicated in confidence by or on behalf of the United Kingdom to another State or to an international organisation,

has come into a person's possession as a result of having been disclosed (whether to him or another) without the authority of that State or organisation or, in the case of an organisation, of a member of it; and

  (b) the disclosure without lawful authority of the information, document or article by the person into whose possession it has come is not an offence under any of the foregoing provisions of this Act.

(2) Subject to subsection (3) below, the person into whose possession the information, document or article has come is guilty of an offence if he makes a damaging disclosure of it knowing, or having reasonable cause to believe, that it is such as is mentioned in subsection (1) above, that it has come into his possession as there mentioned and that its disclosure would be damaging.

(3) A person does not commit an offence under subsection (2) above if the information, document or article is disclosed by him with lawful authority or has previously been made available to the public with the authority of the State or organisation concerned or, in the case of an organisation, of a member of it.

(4) For the purposes of this section 'security or intelligence', 'defence' and 'international relations' have the same meaning as in sections 1, 2 and 3 above and the question whether a disclosure is damaging shall be determined as it would be in relation to a disclosure of the information, document or article in question by a Crown servant in contravention of section 1(3), 2(1) and 3(1) above.

(5) For the purposes of this section information or a document or article is communicated in confidence if it is communicated on terms requiring it to be held in confidence or in circumstances in which the person communicating it could reasonably expect that it would be so held.

7 Authorised disclosures [482]

(1) For the purposes of this Act a disclosure by –

  (a) a Crown servant; or
  (b) a person, not being a Crown servant or government contractor, in whose case a notification for the purposes of section 1(1) above is in force,

is made with lawful authority if, and only if, it is made in accordance with his official duty.

(2) For the purposes of this Act a disclosure by a government contractor is made with lawful authority if, and only if, it is made –

  (a) in accordance with an official authorisation; or
  (b) for the purposes of the functions by virtue of which he is a government contractor and without contravening an official restriction.

(3) For the purposes of this Act a disclosure made by any other person is made with lawful authority if, and only if, it is made –

  (a) to a Crown servant for the purposes of his functions as such; or
  (b) in accordance with an official authorisation.

(4) It is a defence for a person charged with an offence under any of the

foregoing provisions of this Act to prove that at the time of the alleged offence he believed that he had lawful authority to make the disclosure in question and had no reasonable cause to believe otherwise.

(5) In this section 'official authorisation' and 'official restriction' mean, subject to subsection (6) below, an authorisation or restriction duly given or imposed by a Crown servant or government contractor or by or on behalf of a prescribed body or a body of a prescribed class.

(6) In relation to subsection 5 above 'official authorisation' includes an authorisation duly given by or on behalf of the State or organisation concerned or, in the case of an organisation, a member of it.

8 Safeguarding of information [483]

(1) Where a Crown servant or government contractor, by virtue of his position as such, has in his possession or under his control any document or other article which it would be an offence under any of the foregoing provisions of this Act for him to disclose without lawful authority he is guilty of an offence if –

(a) being a Crown servant, he retains the document or article contrary to his official duty; or
(b) being a government contractor, he fails to comply with an official direction for the return or disposal of the document or article,

or if he fails to take such care to prevent the unauthorised disclosure of the document or article as a person in his position may reasonably be expected to take.

(2) It is a defence for a Crown servant charged with an offence under subsection (1)(a) above to prove that at the time of the alleged offence he believed that he was acting in accordance with his official duty and had no reasonable cause to believe otherwise.

(3) In subsections (1) and (2) above references to a Crown servant include any person, not being a Crown servant or government contractor, in whose case a notification for the purposes of section 1(1) above is in force.

(4) Where a person has in his possession or under his control any document or other article which it would be an offence under section 5 above for him to disclose without lawful authority, he is guilty of an offence if –

(a) he fails to comply with an official direction for its return or disposal; or
(b) where he obtained it from a Crown servant or government contractor on terms requiring it to be held in confidence or in circumstances in which that servant or contractor could reasonably expect that it would be so held, he fails to take such care to prevent its unauthorised disclosure as a person in his position may reasonably be expected to take.

(5) Where a person has in his possession or under his control any document or other article which it would be an offence under section 6 above for him to disclose without lawful authority, he is guilty of an offence if he fails to comply with an official direction for its return or disposal.

(6) A person is guilty of an offence if he discloses any official information, document or other article which can be used for the purpose of obtaining access to any information, document or other article protected against disclosure by the foregoing provisions of this Act and the circumstances in which it is disclosed are such that it would be reasonable to expect that it might be used for that purpose without authority.

(7) For the purposes of subsection (6) above a person discloses information or a document or article which is official if –

(a) he had or has had it in his possession by virtue of his position as a Crown servant or government contractor; or

(b) he knows or has reasonable cause to believe that a Crown servant or government contractor has or has had it in his possession by virtue of his position as such.

(8) Subsection (5) of section 5 above applies for the purposes of subsection (6) above as it applies for the purposes of that section.

(9) In this section 'official direction' means a direction duly given by a Crown servant or government contractor or by or on behalf of a prescribed body or a body of a prescribed class.

9 Prosecutions   [484]

(1) Subject to subsection (2) below, no prosecution for an offence under this Act shall be instituted in England and Wales or in Northern Ireland except by or with the consent of the Attorney General or, as the case may be, the Attorney General for Northern Ireland.

(2) Subsection (1) above does not apply to an offence in respect of any such information, document or article as is mentioned in section 4(2) above but no prosecution for such an offence shall be instituted in England and Wales or in Northern Ireland except by or with the consent of the Director of Public Prosecutions or, as the case may be, the Director or Public Prosecutions for Northern Ireland

12 'Crown servant' and 'government contractor'   [485]

(1) In this Act 'Crown servant' means –

(a) a Minister of the Crown;

(b) a person appointed under section 8 of the Northern Ireland Constitution Act 1973 (the Northern Ireland Executive etc);

(c) any person employed in the civil service of the Crown, including Her Majesty's Diplomatic Service, Her Majesty's Overseas Civil Service, the civil service of Northern Ireland and the Northern Ireland Court Service;

(d) any member of the naval, military or air forces of the Crown including any person employed by an association established for the purposes of the Reserve Forces Act 1980;

(e) any constable and any other person employed or appointed in or for the purposes of any police force (including a police force within the meaning of the Police Act (Northern Ireland) 1970);

(f) any person who is a member or employee of a prescribed body or a body of a prescribed class and either is prescribed for the purposes of this paragraph or belongs to a prescribed class of members or employees of any such body;

(g) any person who is the holder of a prescribed office or who is an employee of such a holder and either is prescribed for the purposes of this paragraph or belongs to a prescribed class of such employees.

(2) In this Act 'government contractor' means, subject to subsection (3) below, any person who is not a Crown servant but who provides, or is employed in the provision of, goods or services –

(a) for the purposes of any Minister or person mentioned in paragraph (a) or

(b) of subsection (1) above, of any of the services, forces or bodies mentioned in that subsection or of the holder of any office prescribed under that subsection; or

(b) under an agreement or arrangement certified by the Secretary of State as being one to which the government of a State other than the United Kingdom or an international organisation is a party or which is subordinate to, or made for the purposes of implementing, any such agreement or arrangement.

(3) Where an employee or class of employees of any body, or of any holder of an office, is prescribed by an order made for the purposes of subsection (1) above –

(a) any employee of that body, or of the holder of that office, who is not prescribed or is not within the prescribed class; and
(b) any person who does not provide, or is not employed in the provision of, goods or services for the purposes of the performance of those functions of the body or the holder of the office in connection with which the employee or prescribed class of employees is engaged,

shall not be a government contractor for the purposes of this Act.

13 Other interpretation provisions [486]

(1) In this Act –

'disclose' and 'disclosure', in relation to a document or other article, include parting with possession of it;

'international organisation' means, subject to subsections (2) and (3) below, an organisation of which only States are members and includes a reference to any organ of such an organisation;

'prescribed' means prescribed by an order made by the Secretary of State;

'State' includes the government of a State and any organ of its government and references to a State other than the United Kingdom include references to any territory outside the United Kingdom.

(2) In section 12(2)(b) above the reference to an international organisation includes a reference to any such organisation whether or not one of which only States are members and includes a commercial organisation.

(3) In determining for the purposes of subsection (1) above whether only States are members of an organisation, any member which is itself an organisation of which only States are members, or which is an organ of such an organisation, shall be treated as a State.

15 Acts done abroad and extent [487]

(1) Any Act –

(a) done by a British citizen or Crown servant; or
(b) done by any person in any of the Channel Islands or the Isle of Man or any colony,

shall, if it would be an offence by that person under any provision of this Act other than section 8(1), (4) or (5) when done by him in the United Kingdom, be an offence under that provision.

(2) This Act extends to Northern Ireland.

(3) Her Majesty may by Order in Council provide that any provision of this Act shall extend, with such exceptions, adaptations and modifications as may be specified in the Order, to any of the Channel Islands or the Isle of Man or any colony.

TRIBUNALS AND INQUIRIES ACT 1992
(1992 c 53)

1 The Council on Tribunals   [488]

(1) There shall continue to be a council entitled the Council on Tribunals (in this Act referred to as 'the Council') –

(a) to keep under review the constitution and working of the tribunals specified in Schedule 1 (being the tribunals constituted under or for the purposes of the statutory provisions specified in that Schedule) and, from time to time, to report on their constitution and working;

(b) to consider and report on such particular matters as may be referred to the Council under this Act with respect to tribunals other than the ordinary courts of law, whether or not specified in Schedule 1, or any such tribunal; and

(c) to consider and report on such matters as may be referred to the Council under this Act, or as the Council may determine to be of special importance, with respect to administrative procedures involving, or which may involve, the holding by or on behalf of a Minister of a statutory inquiry, or any such procedure.

(2) Nothing in this section authorises or requires the Council to deal with any matter with respect to which the Parliament of Northern Ireland had power to make laws.

2 Composition of the Council and the Scottish Committee   [489]

(1) Subject to subsection (3), the Council shall consist of not more than fifteen nor less than ten members appointed by the Lord Chancellor and the Lord Advocate, and one of the members shall be so appointed to be chairman of the Council.

(2) There shall be a Scottish Committee of the Council (in this Act referred to as 'the Scottish Committee') which, subject to subsection (3), shall consist of –

(a) either two or three members of the council designated by the Lord Advocate, and

(b) either three or four persons, not being members of the Council, appointed by the Lord Advocate;

and the Lord Advocate shall appoint one of the members of the Scottish Committee (being a member of the Council) to be chairman of the Scottish Committee.

(3) In addition to the persons appointed or designated under subsection (1) or (2), the Parliamentary Commissioner for Administration shall, by virtue of his office, be a member of the Council and of the Scottish Committee.

(4) In appointing members of the Council regard shall be had to the need for representation of the interests of persons in Wales.

4 Reports of, and references to, Council and   [490]
Scottish Committee

(1) Subject to the provisions of this section, any report by, or reference to, the Council shall be made to or, as the case may be, by, the Lord Chancellor and the Lord Advocate ...

(7) The Council shall make an annual report to the Lord Chancellor and the Lord Advocate on their proceedings and those of the Scottish Committee, and those Ministers shall lay the report before Parliament with such comments (if any) as they think fit.

5 Recommendations of Council as to appointment of members of tribunals [491]

(1) Subject to section 6 but without prejudice to the generality of section 1(1)(a), the Council may make to the appropriate Minister general recommendations as to the making of appointments to membership of any tribunals mentioned in Schedule 1 or of panels constituted for the purposes of any such tribunals; and (without prejudice to any statutory provisions having effect with respect to such appointments) the appropriate Minister shall have regard to recommendations under this section.

(2) In this section 'the appropriate Minister', in relation to appointments of any description, means the Minister making the appointments or, if they are not made by a Minister, the Minister in charge of the government department concerned with the tribunals in question ...

6 Appointment of chairmen of certain tribunals [492]

(1) The chairman, or any person appointed to act as chairman, of any of the tribunals to which this subsection applies shall (without prejudice to any statutory provisions as to qualifications) be selected by the appropriate authority from a panel of persons appointed by the Lord Chancellor.

(2) Members of panels constituted under this section shall hold and vacate office under the terms of the instruments under which they are appointed, but may resign office by notice in writing to the Lord Chancellor; and any such member who ceases to hold office shall be eligible for re-appointment.

(3) Subsection (1) applies to any tribunal specified in paragraph 7, 38(a), 41(a), (b), (c) or (e) or 43 of Schedule 1.

(4) In relation to the tribunals specified in paragraph 41(a), (b) and (c) of Schedule 1, this section has effect subject to sections 41 (social security appeals tribunals), 43 (disability appeal tribunals) and 50 (medical appeal tribunals) of the Social Security Administration Act 1992.

(5) The person or persons constituting any tribunal specified in paragraph 31 of Schedule 1 shall be appointed by the Lord Chancellor, and where such a tribunal consists of more than one person the Lord Chancellor shall designate which of them is to be the chairman.

(6) In this section, 'the appropriate authority' means the Minister who apart from this Act would be empowered to appoint or select the chairman, person to act as chairman, members or members of the tribunal in question.

(7) A panel may be constituted under this section for the purposes either of a single tribunal or of two or more tribunals, whether or not of the same description ...

(9) In relation to any of the tribunals referred to in this section which sits in Northern Ireland, this section shall have effect with the substitution for any reference to the Lord Chancellor of a reference to the Lord Chief Justice of Northern Ireland.

7 Concurrence required for removal of members of certain tribunals [493]

(1) Subject to subsection (2), the power of a Minister, other than the Lord Chancellor, to terminate a person's membership of any tribunal specified in Schedule 1, or of a panel constituted for the purposes of any such tribunal, shall be exercisable only with the consent of –

(a) the Lord Chancellor, the Lord President of the Court of Session and the Lord Chief Justice of Northern Ireland, if the tribunal sits in all parts of the United Kingdom;

(b) the Lord Chancellor and the Lord President of the Court of Session, if the tribunal sits in all parts of Great Britain;

(c) the Lord Chancellor and the Lord Chief Justice of Northern Ireland if the tribunal sits both in England and Wales and in Northern Ireland;

(d) the Lord Chancellor, if the tribunal does not sit outside England and Wales;

...

(f) the Lord Chief Justice of Northern Ireland, if the tribunal sits only in Northern Ireland.

(2) This section does not apply to any tribunal specified in paragraph 3, 4, 12, 14, 17, 18, 21A, 26, 33(a), 33A, 34, 35(d) or (e), 36(a), 36A, 39(b), 40, 43, 48, 56(a) or 56A of Schedule 1.

(3) For the purposes of this section in its application to any tribunal specified in paragraph 22(a) of Schedule 1, an adjudicator who has sat only in England and Wales, who has sat only in Scotland or who has sat only in Northern Ireland shall be deemed to constitute a tribunal which does not sit outside England and Wales, which sits only in Scotland or which sits only in Northern Ireland, as the case may be.

8 Procedural rules for tribunals   [494]

(1) The power of a Minister, the Lord President of the Court of Session, the Commissioners of Inland Revenue or the Foreign Compensation Commission to make, approve, confirm or concur in procedural rules for any tribunal specified in Schedule 1 shall be exercisable only after consultation with the Council.

(2) The power of the Treasury to make –

(a) regulations under section 48(3) of the Building Societies Act 1986 (regulations with respect to appeals to the tribunal established under section 47 of that Act), or

(b) regulations under section 30 of the Banking Act 1987 (regulations with respect to appeals under Part I of that Act),

shall be exercisable only after consultation with the Council.

(3) The Council shall consult the Scottish Committee in relation to the exercise of their functions under this section –

(a) with respect to any tribunal specified in Part II of Schedule 1, or

(b) with respect to any regulations under section 30 of the Banking Act 1987 which (by virtue of subsection (4) of that section) are made by the Lord Advocate.

(4) In this section 'procedural rules' includes any statutory provision relating to the procedure of the tribunal in question.

9 Procedure in connection with statutory inquiries   [495]

(1) The Lord Chancellor, after consultation with the Council, may make rules regulating the procedure to be followed in connection with statutory inquiries held by or on behalf of Ministers; and different provision may be made by any such rules in relation to different classes of such inquiries.

(2) Any rules made by the Lord Chancellor under this section shall have effect, in relation to any statutory inquiry, subject to the provisions of the enactment under which the inquiry is held, and of any rules or regulations made under that enactment.

(3) Subject to subsection (2), rules made under this section may regulate procedure in connection with matters preparatory to such statutory inquiries as are mentioned in subsection (1), and in connection with matters subsequent to such inquiries, as well as in connection with the conduct of proceedings at such inquiries ...

10 Reasons to be given for decisions of tribunals and Ministers [496]

(1) Subject to the provisions of this section and of section 14, where –

(a) any tribunal specified in Schedule 1 gives any decision, or
(b) any Minister notifies any decision taken by him –

(i) after a statutory inquiry has been held by him or on his behalf, or
(ii) in a case in which a person concerned could (whether by objecting or otherwise) have required a statutory inquiry to be so held,

it shall be the duty of the tribunal or Minister to furnish a statement, either written or oral, of the reasons for the decision if requested, on or before the giving or notification of the decision, to state the reasons.

(2) The statement referred to in subsection (1) may be refused, or the specification of the reasons restricted, on grounds of national security.

(3) A tribunal or Minister may refuse to furnish a statement under subsection (1) to a person not primarily concerned with the decision if of the opinion that to furnish it would be contrary to the interests of any person primarily concerned.

(4) Subsection (1) does not apply to any decision taken by a Minister after the holding by him or on his behalf of an inquiry or hearing which is a statutory inquiry by virtue only of an order made under section 16(2) unless the order contains a direction that this section is to apply in relation to any inquiry or hearing to which the order applies.

(5) Subsection (1) does not apply –

(a) to decisions in respect of which any statutory provision has effect, apart from this section, as to the giving of reasons,
(b) to decisions of a Minister in connection with the preparation, making, approval, confirmation, or concurrence in regulations, rules or bye-laws, or orders or schemes of a legislative and not executive character, or
(c) to decisions of the Occupational Pensions Board referred to in paragraph 35(d) of Schedule 1.

(6) Any statement of the reasons for a decision referred to in paragraph (a) or (b) of subsection (1), whether given in pursuance of that subsection or of any other statutory provision, shall be taken to form part of the decision and accordingly to be incorporated in the record.

(7) If, after consultation with the Council, it appears to the Lord Chancellor and the Lord Advocate that it is expedient that –

(a) decisions of any particular tribunal or any description of such decisions, or
(b) any description of decisions of a Minister,

should be excluded from the operation of subsection (1) on the ground that the subject-matter of such decisions, or the circumstances in which they are made, make the giving of reasons unnecessary or impracticable, the Lord Chancellor and the Lord Advocate may by order direct that subsection (1) shall not apply to such decisions.

(8) Where an order relating to any decisions has been made under subsection (7), the Lord Chancellor and the Lord Advocate may, by a subsequent order made

after consultation with the Council, revoke or vary the earlier order so that subsection (1) applies to any of those decisions.

11 Appeals from certain tribunals   [497]

(1) Subject to subsection (2), if any party to proceedings before any tribunal specified in paragraph 8, 15(a), (d) or (e), 16, 18, 24, 26, 31, 33(b), 37, 40A, 44 or 45 of Schedule 1 is dissatisfied in point of law with a decision of the tribunal he may, according as rules of court may provide, either appeal from the tribunal to the High Court or require the tribunal to state and sign a case for the opinion of the High Court.

(2) Subsection (1) shall not apply in relation to proceedings before industrial tribunals which arise under or by virtue of any of the enactments mentioned in section 136(1) of the Employment Protection (Consolidation) Act 1978.

(3) Rules of court made with respect to all or any of the tribunals referred to in subsection (1) may provide for authorising or requiring a tribunal, in the course of proceedings before it, to state, in the form of a special case for the decision of the High Court, any question of law arising in the proceedings; and a decision of the High Court on a case stated by virtue of this subsection shall be deemed to be a judgment of the Court within the meaning of section 16 of the Supreme Court Act 1981 (jurisdiction of Court of Appeal to hear and determine appeals from judgments of the High Court).

(4) In relation to proceedings in the High Court or the Court of Appeal brought by virtue of this section, the power to make rules of court shall include power to make rules prescribing the powers of the High Court or the Court of Appeal with respect to –

(a) the giving of any decision which might have been given by the tribunal;
(b) the remitting of the matter with the opinion or direction of the court for re-hearing and determination by the tribunal;
(c) the giving of directions to the tribunal;

and different provisions may be made for different tribunals.

(5) An appeal to the Court of Appeal shall not be brought by virtue of this section except with the leave of the High Court or the Court of Appeal.

(6) Subsection (1) shall apply to a decision of the Secretary of State on an appeal under section 41 of the Consumer Credit Act 1974 from a determination of the Director General of Fair Trading as it applies to a decision of any of the tribunals mentioned in that subsection, but with the substitution for the reference to a party to proceedings of a reference to any person who had a right to appeal to the Secretary of State (whether or not he has exercised that right); and accordingly references in subsections (1) and (4) to a tribunal shall be construed, in relation to such an appeal, as references to the Secretary of State ...

(10) In this section 'decision' includes any direction or order, and references to the giving of a decision shall be construed accordingly.

12 Supervisory functions of superior courts not   [498]
excluded by Acts passed before 1st August 1958

(1) As respects England and Wales –

(a) any provision in an Act passed before 1st August 1958 that any order or determination shall not be called into question in any court, or
(b) any provision in such an Act which by similar words excludes any of the powers of the High Court,

shall not have effect so as to prevent the removal of the proceedings into the High Court by order of certiorari or to prejudice the powers of the High Court to make orders of mandamus ...

(3) Nothing in this section shall apply –

(a) to any order or determination of a court of law, or

(b) where an Act makes special provision for application to the High Court or the Court of Session within a time limited by the Act.

16 Interpretation [499]

(1) In this Act, except where the context otherwise requires ...

'statutory inquiry' means –

(a) an inquiry or hearing held or to be held in pursuance of a duty imposed by any statutory provision, or

(b) an inquiry or hearing, or an inquiry or hearing of a class, designated for the purposes of this section by an order under subsection (2) ...

(2) The Lord Chancellor and the Lord Advocate may by order designate for the purposes of this section any inquiry or hearing held or to be held in pursuance of a power conferred by any statutory provision specified or described in the order, or any class of such inquiries or hearings ...

SCHEDULE 1 [500]

TRIBUNALS UNDER GENERAL SUPERVISION OF COUNCIL

PART I

Matters with which tribunal concerned	*Tribunal and statutory authority*
Agriculture	1 (a) The Agricultural Land Tribunals establishedunder section 73 of the Agriculture Act 1947 (c 48)
	(b) arbitrators appointed (otherwise than by agreement) under Schedule 11 to the Agricultural Holdings Act 1986 (c 5) ...
Building societies	6 The tribunal constituted in accordance with section 47 of the Building Societies Act 1986 (c 53)
Child support maintenance	7 (a) The child support appeal tribunals established under section 21 of the Child Support Act 1991 (c 48);
	(b) a Child Support Commissioner appointed under section 22 of that Act and any tribunal presided over by such a Commissioner ...
Conveyancing	10 A Conveyancing Appeals Tribunal constituted under section 39 of the Courts and Legal Services Act 1990 (c 41) ...

Criminal injuries compensation	12 The Criminal Injuries Compensation Board constituted under Part VII of the Criminal Justice Act 1988 (c 33) ...
Education	15 (a) Independent Schools Tribunals constituted under section 72 of, and Schedule 6 to the Education Act 1944 (c 31);
	(b) appeal committees constituted in accordance with Part I of Schedule 2 to the Education Act 1980 (c 20); ...
	(d) a tribunal constituted in accordance with Schedule 3 to the Education (Schools) Act 1992 (c 38).
Employment	16 The industrial tribunals for England and Wales established under section 128 of the Employment Protection (Consolidation) Act 1978 (c 44).
Fair trading	17 The Director General of Fair Trading in respect of his functions under the Consumer Credit Act 1974 (c 39) and the Estate Agents Act 1979 (c 38), and any member of the Director's staff authorised to exercise those functions under paragraph 7 of Schedule 1 to the Fair Trading Act 1973 (c 41).
Financial services	18 The Financial Services Tribunal established by section 96 of the Financial Services Act 1986 (c 60) ...
Immigration appeals	22 (a) The adjudicators established under section 12 of the Immigration Act 1971 (c 77);
	(b) the Immigration Appeal Tribunal established under that section ...
Land	27 The Lands Tribunal constituted under section 1(1)(b) of the Lands Tribunal Act 1949 (c 42) ...
Mental health	30 The Mental Health Review Tribunals constituted or having effect as if constituted under section 65 of the Mental Health Act 1983 (c 20) ...
National Health Service	33 (a) Family Health Services Authorities established in pursuance of section 10 of the National Health Service Act 1977 (c 49);
	(b) the tribunal constituted under section 46 of that Act;

National Health Service (*contd.*)	(c) service committees of Family Health Services Authorities, being committees constituted in accordance with regulations made under that Act …
Rents	37 Rent assessment committees constituted in accordance with Schedule 10 to the Rent Act 1977 (c 42) …
Revenue	39 (a) The Commissioners for the general purposes of the income tax acting under section 2 of the Taxes Management Act 1970 (c 9) for any division in England and Wales;
	(b) the Commissioners for the special purposes of the Income Tax Acts appointed under section 4 of that Act;
	(c) the tribunal constituted for the purposes of Chapter I of Part XVII of the Income and Corporation Taxes Act 1988 (c 1).
Road traffic	40 (a) The traffic commissioner for any area constituted for the purposes of the Public Passenger Vehicles Act 1981 (c 14);
	(b) a parking adjudicator appointed under section 73(3)(a) of the Road Traffic Act 1991 (c 40).
Sea fish (conservation)	40A The Sea Fish Licence Tribunal established under section 4AA of the Sea Fish (Conservation) Act 1967 (c 84).
Social security	41 (a) Social security appeal tribunals constituted under section 41 of the Social Security Administration Act 1992 (c 5);
	(b) disability appeal tribunals constituted under section 43 of that Act;
	(c) medical appeal tribunals constituted under section 50 of that Act;
	(d) a Commissioner appointed under section 52 of that Act and any tribunal presided over by a Commissioner so appointed;
	(e) a tribunal constituted under regulations made under section 58 of that Act.

Value added tax

44 Value added tax tribunals for England and Wales and for Northern Ireland, constituted under section 40 of, and Schedule 8 to,the Value Added Tax Act 1983 (c 55) ...

[As amended by the Sea Fish (Conservation) Act 1992, s9; Friendly Societies Act 1992, s120(1), Schedule 21, paras 12, 13; National Lottery, etc Act 1993, s3(2), Schedule 2, para 8(1); Education Act 1993, s181(2); Police and Magistrates' Courts Act 1994, Schedule 5, para 39(a), (b).]

ASYLUM AND IMMIGRATION APPEALS ACT 1993
(1993 c 23)

1 Interpretation [501]

In this Act –

'the 1971 Act' means the Immigration Act 1971;

'claim for asylum' means a claim made by a person (whether before or after the coming into force of this section) that it would be contrary to the United Kingdom's obligations under the Convention for him to be removed from, or required to leave, the United Kingdom; and

'the Convention' means the Convention relating to the Status of Refugees done at Geneva on 28th July 1951 and the Protocol to that Convention.

2 Primacy of Convention [502]

Nothing in the immigration rules (within the meaning of the 1971 Act) shall lay down any practice which would be contrary to the Convention.

7 Curtailment of leave to enter or remain [503]

(1) Where –

(a) a person who has limited leave under the 1971 Act to enter or remain in the United Kingdom claims that it would be contrary to the United Kingdom's obligations under the Convention for him to be required to leave the United Kingdom after the time limited by the leave, and

(b) the Secretary of State has considered the claim and given to the person notice in writing of his rejection of it,

the Secretary of State may by notice in writing, given to the person concurrently with the notice under paragraph (b) above, curtail the duration of the leave.

(2) No appeal may be brought under section 14 of the 1971 Act or section 8(2) below against the curtailment of leave under subsection (1) above.

(3) The power conferred by subsection (1) above is without prejudice to sections 3(3) and 4 of the 1971 Act and the immigration rules (within the meaning of that Act).

(4) Where –

(a) the duration of a person's leave under the 1971 Act to enter or remain in the United Kingdom has been curtailed under subsection (1) above, and

(b) the Secretary of State has decided to make a deportation order against him by virtue of section 3(5) of that Act,

he may be detained under the authority of the Secretary of State pending the making of the deportation order; and the references to sub-paragraph (2) of paragraph 2 of Schedule 3 to that Act in sub-paragraphs (3), (4) and (6) of that paragraph (provisions about detention under sub-paragraph (2)) shall include references to this subsection.

8 Appeals to special adjudicator   [504]

(1) A person who is refused leave to enter the United Kingdom under the 1971 Act may appeal against the refusal to a special adjudicator on the ground that his removal in consequence of the refusal would be contrary to the United Kingdom's obligations under the Convention.

(2) A person who has limited leave under the 1971 Act to enter or remain in the United Kingdom may appeal to a special adjudicator against any variation of, or refusal to vary, the leave on the ground that it would be contrary to the United Kingdom's obligations under the Convention for him to be required to leave the United Kingdom after the time limited by the leave.

(3) Where the Secretary of State –

(a) has decided to make a deportation order against a person by virtue of section 3(5) of the 1971 Act, or
(b) has refused to revoke a deportation order made against a person by virtue of section 3(5) or (6) of that Act,

the person may appeal to a special adjudicator against the decision or refusal on the ground that his removal in pursuance of the order would be contrary to the United Kingdom's obligations under the Convention; but a person may not bring an appeal under both paragraph (a) and paragraph (b) above.

(4) Where directions are given as mentioned in section 16(1)(a) or (b) of the 1971 Act for a person's removal from the United Kingdom, the person may appeal to a special adjudicator against the directions on the ground that his removal in pursuance of the directions would be contrary to the United Kingdom's obligations under the Convention.

(5) The Lord Chancellor shall designate such number of the adjudicators appointed for the purposes of Part II of the 1971 Act as he thinks necessary to act as special adjudicators for the purposes of this section and may from time to time vary that number and the persons who are so designated.

(6) Schedule 2 to this Act (which makes supplementary provision about appeals under this section) shall have effect; and the preceding provisions of this section shall have effect subject to that Schedule.

9 Appeals from Immigration Appeal Tribunal   [505]

(1) Where the Immigration Appeal Tribunal has made a final determination of an appeal brought under Part II of the 1971 Act (including that Part as it applies by virtue of Schedule 2 to this Act) any party to the appeal may bring a further appeal to the appropriate appeal court on any question of law material to that determination.

(2) An appeal under this section may be brought only with the leave of the Immigration Appeal Tribunal or, if such leave is refused, with the leave of the appropriate appeal court.

(3) In this section 'the appropriate appeal court' means –

(a) if the appeal is from the determination of an adjudicator or special adjudicator and that determination was made in Scotland, the Court of Session; and

(b) in any other case, the Court of Appeal.

(4) Rules of procedure under section 22 of the 1971 Act may include provision regulating, and prescribing the procedure to be followed on, applications to the Immigration Appeal Tribunal for leave to appeal under this section ...

SCHEDULE 2   **[506]**

APPEALS TO SPECIAL ADJUDICATOR: SUPPLEMENTARY

1 No appeal may be brought under Part II of the 1971 Act on any of the grounds mentioned in subsections (1) to (4) of section 8 of this Act.

2 A person may not bring an appeal on any of the grounds mentioned in subsections (1) to (4) of section 8 of this Act unless, before the time of the refusal, variation, decision or directions (as the case may be), he has made a claim for asylum.

3 Where an appeal is brought by a person on any of the grounds mentioned in subsections (1) to (4) of section 8 of this Act, the special adjudicator shall in the same proceedings deal with –

(a) any appeal against the refusal, variation, decision or directions (as the case may be) which the person is entitled to bring under Part II of the 1971 Act on any other ground on which he seeks to rely; and

(b) any appeal brought by the person under that Part of that Act against any other decision or action ...

5–(1) Subject to sub-paragraph (2) below, this paragraph applies to an appeal by a person under subsection (1), (3)(b) or (4) of section 8 of this Act if the Secretary of State has certified that, in his opinion, the person's claim on the ground that it would be contrary to the United Kingdom's obligations under the Convention for him to be removed from the United Kingdom is without foundation.

(2) This paragraph does not apply to an appeal on the ground mentioned in subsection (1) of section 8 of this Act if, by virtue of section 13(3) of the 1971 Act (right of appeal for person with current entry clearance or work permit), the appellant seeks to rely on another ground.

(3) For the purposes of this paragraph a claim is without foundation if (and only if) –

(a) it does not raise any issue as to the United Kingdom's obligations under the Convention; or

(b) it is otherwise frivolous or vexatious.

(4) Rules of procedure under 22 of the 1971 Act may make special provision in relation to appeals to which this paragraph applies.

(5) If on an appeal to which this paragraph applies the special adjudicator agrees that the claim is without foundation, section 20(1) of that Act shall not confer on the appellant any right to appeal to the Immigration Appeal Tribunal.

(6) If the special adjudicator does not agree that the claim is without foundation, he may (as an alternative to allowing or dismissing the appeal) refer the case to the Secretary of State for reconsideration; and the making of such a reference shall, accordingly, be regarded as disposing of the appeal.

6 Subsection (5) of section 13, subsection (3) of section 14 and subsections (3) and (4) of section 15 of the 1971 Act shall have effect in relation to the rights of appeal conferred by section 8(1), (2) and (3)(a) and (b) of this Act respectively as they have effect in relation to the rights of appeal conferred by subsection (1) of those sections of that Act but as if references to a person's exclusion, departure or

262

deportation being conducive to the public good were references to its being in the interests of national security.

7 The limitation on the taking effect of a variation and on a requirement to leave the United Kingdom contained in subsection (1) of section 14 of the 1971 Act shall have effect as if appeals under section 8(2) of this Act were appeals under that subsection.

8 In section 15(2) of the 1971 Act references to an appeal against a decision to make a deportation order shall include references to an appeal against such a decision under section 8(3)(a) of this Act.

9 Part II of Schedule 2, and paragraph 3 of Schedule 3, to the 1971 Act shall have effect as if the references to appeals under section 13(1), 15(1)(a) and 16 of that Act included (respectively) appeals under section 8(1), (3) and (4) of this Act and as if sub-paragraph (5) of paragraph 28 of Schedule 2 were omitted.

EUROPEAN COMMUNITIES (AMENDMENT) ACT 1993
(1993 c 32)

1 Treaty on European Union [507]

...

(2) For the purpose of section 6 of the European Parliamentary Elections Act 1978 (approval of treaties increasing the Parliament's powers) the Treaty on European Union signed at Maastricht on 7th February 1992 is approved.

2 Economic and monetary union [508]

No notification shall be given to the Council of the European Communities that the United Kingdom intends to move to the third stage of economic and monetary union (in accordance with the Protocol on certain provisions relating to the United Kingdom adopted at Maastricht on 7th February 1992) unless a draft of the notification has first been approved by Act of Parliament and unless Her Majesty's Government has reported to Parliament on its proposals for the co-ordination of economic policies, its role in the European Council of Finance Ministers (ECOFIN) in pursuit of the objectives of Article 2 of the Treaty establishing the European Community as provided for in Articles 103 and 102a, and the work of the European Monetary Institute in preparation for economic and monetary union.

3 Annual report by Bank of England [509]

In implementing Article 108 of the Treaty establishing the European Community, and ensuring compatibility of the statutes of the national central bank, Her Majesty's Government shall, by order, make provision for the Governor of the Bank of England to make an annual report to Parliament, which shall be subject to approval by a Resolution of each House of Parliament.

4 Information for Commission [510]

In implementing the provisions of Article 103(3) of the Treaty establishing the European Community, information shall be submitted to the Commission from the United Kingdom indicating performance on economic growth, industrial investment, employment and balance of trade, together with comparisons with those items of performance from other member States.

5 Convergence criteria: assessment of deficits   [511]

Before submitting the information required in implementing Article 103(3) of the Treaty establishing the European Community, Her Majesty's Government shall report to Parliament for its approval an assessment of the medium term economic and budgetary position in relation to public investment expenditure and to the social, economic and environmental goals set out in Article 2, which report shall form the basis of any submission to the Council and Commission in pursuit of their responsibilities under Articles 103 and 104c.

6 Committee of the Regions   [512]

A person may be proposed as a member or alternate member for the United Kingdom by the Committee of the Regions constituted under Article 198a of the Treaty establishing the European Community only if, at the time of the proposal, he is an elected member of a local authority.

7 Commencement (Protocol on Social Policy)   [513]

This Act shall come into force only when each House of Parliament has come to a Resolution on a motion tabled by a Minister of the Crown considering the question of adopting the Protocol on Social Policy.

CRIMINAL JUSTICE AND PUBLIC ORDER ACT 1994
(1994 c 23)

PART III

COURTS OF JUSTICE: EVIDENCE, PROCEDURE, ETC

34 Effect of accused's failure to mention facts   [514]
when questioned or charged

(1) Where, in any proceedings against a person for an offence, evidence is given that the accused –

(a) at any time before he was charged with the offence, on being questioned under caution by a constable trying to discover whether or by whom the offence had been committed, failed to mention any fact relied on in his defence in those proceedings; or

(b) on being charged with the offence or officially informed that he might be prosecuted for it, failed to mention any such fact,

being a fact which in the circumstances existing at the time the accused could reasonably have been expected to mention when so questioned, charged or informed, as the case may be, subsection (2) below applies.

(2) Where this subsection applies –

(a) a magistrates' court, in deciding whether to grant an application for dismissal made by the accused under section 6 of the Magistrates' Courts Act 1980 (application for dismissal of charge in course of proceedings with a view to transfer for trial);

(b) a judge, in deciding whether to grant an application made by the accused under –

(i) section 6 of the Criminal Justice Act 1987 (application for dismissal of charge of serious fraud in respect of which notice of transfer has been given under section 4 of that Act); or

(ii) paragraph 5 of Schedule 6 to the Criminal Justice Act 1991 (application for dismissal of charge of violent or sexual offence involving child in respect of which notice of transfer has been given under section 53 of that Act);

(c) the court, in determining whether there is a case to answer; and
(d) the court or jury, in determining whether the accused is guilty of the offence charged,

may draw such inferences from the failure as appear proper.

(3) Subject to any directions by the court, evidence tending to establish the failure may be given before or after evidence tending to establish the fact which the accused is alleged to have failed to mention.

(4) This section applies in relation to questioning by persons (other than constables) charged with the duty of investigating offences or charging offenders as it applies in relation to questioning by constables; and in subsection (1) above 'officially informed' means informed by a constable or any such person.

(5) This section does not –

(a) prejudice the admissibility in evidence of the silence or other reaction of the accused in the face of anything said in his presence relating to the conduct in respect of which he is charged, in so far as evidence thereof would be admissible apart from this section; or
(b) preclude the drawing of any inference from any such silence or other reaction of the accused which could properly be drawn apart from this section.

(6) This section does not apply in relation to a failure to mention a fact if the failure occurred before the commencement of this section.

(7) In relation to any time before the commencement of section 44 of this Act, this section shall have effect as if the reference in subsection (2)(a) to the grant of an application for dismissal was a reference to the committal of the accused for trial.

35 Effect of accused's silence at trial [515]

(1) At the trial of any person who has attained the age of fourteen years for an offence, subsections (2) and (3) below apply unless –

(a) the accused's guilt is not in issue; or
(b) it appears to the court that the physical or mental condition of the accused makes it undesirable for him to give evidence;

but subsection (2) below does not apply if, at the conclusion of the evidence for the prosecution, his legal representative informs the court that the accused will give evidence or, where he is unrepresented, the court ascertains from him that he will give evidence.

(2) Where this subsection applies, the court shall, at the conclusion of the evidence for the prosecution, satisfy itself (in the case of proceedings on indictment, in the presence of the jury) that the accused is aware that the stage has been reached at which evidence can be given for the defence and that he can, if he wishes, give evidence and that, if he chooses not to give evidence, or having been sworn, without good cause refuses to answer any question, it will be permissible for the court or jury to draw such inferences as appear proper from his failure to give evidence or his refusal, without good cause, to answer any question.

(3) Where this subsection applies, the court or jury, in determining whether the accused is guilty of the offence charged, may draw such inferences as appear proper from the failure of the accused to give evidence or his refusal, without good cause, to answer any question.

(4) This section does not render the accused compellable to give evidence on his own behalf, and he shall accordingly not be guilty of contempt of court by reason of a failure to do so.

(5) For the purposes of this section a person who, having been sworn, refuses to answer any question shall be taken to do so without good cause unless –

(a) he is entitled to refuse to answer the question by virtue of any enactment, whenever passed or made, or on the ground of privilege; or
(b) the court in the exercise of its general discretion excuses him from answering it.

(6) Where the age of any person is material for the purposes of subsection (1) above, his age shall for the purposes be taken to be that which appears to the court to be his age.

(7) This section applies –

(a) in relation to proceedings on indictment for an offence, only if the person charged with the offence is arraigned on or after the commencement of this section;
(b) in relation to proceedings in a magistrates' court, only if the time when the court begins to receive evidence in the proceedings falls after the commencement of this section.

36 Effect of accused's failure or refusal to account   **[516]**
for objects, substances or marks

(1) Where –

(a) a person is arrested by a constable, and there is –

(i) on his person; or
(ii) in or on his clothing or footwear; or
(iii) otherwise in his possession; or
(iv) in any place in which he is at the time of his arrest,

any object, substance or mark, or there is any mark on any such object; and
(b) that or another constable investigating the case reasonably believes that the presence of the object, substance or mark may be attributable to the participation of the person arrested in the commission of an offence specified by the constable; and
(c) the constable informs the person arrested that he so believes, and requests him to account for the presence of the object, substance or mark; and
(d) the person fails or refuses to do so,

then if, in any proceedings against the person for the offence so specified, evidence of those matters is given, subsection (2) below applies.

(2) Where this subsection applies –

(a) a magistrates' court, in deciding whether to grant an application for dismissal made by the accused under section 6 of the Magistrates' Courts Act 1980 (application for dismissal of charge in course of proceedings with a view to transfer for trial);
(b) a judge, in deciding whether to grant an application made by the accused under –

(i) section 6 of the Criminal Justice Act 1987 (application for dismissal of charge of serious fraud in respect of which notice of transfer has been given under section 4 of that Act); or
(ii) paragraph 5 of Schedule 6 to the Criminal Justice Act 1991 (application for dismissal of charge of violent or sexual offence involving child in

respect of which notice of transfer has been given under section 53 of that Act);

(c) the court, in determining whether there is a case to answer; and

(d) the court or jury, in determining whether the accused is guilty of the offence charged,

may draw such in inferences from the failure or refusal as appear proper.

(3) Subsections (1) and (2) above apply to the condition of clothing or footwear as they apply to a substance or mark thereon.

(4) Subsections (1) and (2) above do not apply unless the accused was told in ordinary language by the constable when making the request mentioned in subsection (1)(c) above what the effect of this section would be if he failed or refused to comply with the request.

(5) This section applies in relation to officers of customs and exercise as it applies in relation to constables.

(6) This section does not preclude the drawing of any inference from a failure or refusal of the accused to account for the presence of an object, substance or mark or from the condition of clothing or footwear which could properly be drawn apart from this section.

(7) This section does not apply in relation to a failure or refusal which occurred before the commencement of this section.

(8) In relation to any time before the commencement of section 44 of this Act, this section shall have effect as if the reference in subsection (2)(a) to the grant of an application for dismissal was a reference to the committal of the accused for trial.

37 Effect of accused's failure or refusal to account for presence at a particular place   [517]

(1) Where –

(a) a person arrested by a constable was found by him at a place at or about the time the offence for which he was arrested is alleged to have been committed; and

(b) that or another constable investigating the offence reasonably believes that the presence of the person at that place and at that time may be attributable to his participation in the commission of the offence; and

(c) the constable informs the person that he so believes, and requests him to account for that presence; and

(d) the person fails or refuses to do so,

then if, in any proceedings against the person for the offence, evidence of those matters is given, subsection (2) below applies.

(2) Where this subsection applies –

(a) a magistrates' court, in deciding whether to grant an application for dismissal made by the accused under section 6 of the Magistrates' Courts Act 1980 (application for dismissal of charge in course of proceedings with a view to transfer for trial);

(b) a judge, in deciding whether to grant an application made by the accused under –

(i) section 6 of the Criminal Justice Act 1987 (application for dismissal of charge of serious fraud in respect of which notice of transfer has been given under section 4 of that Act); or

(ii) paragraph 5 of Schedule 6 to the Criminal Justice Act 1991 (application for dismissal of charge of violent or sexual offence involving child in respect of which notice of transfer has been given under section 53 of that Act);

(c) the court, in determining whether there is a case to answer; and

(d) the court or jury, in determining whether the accused is guilty of the offence charged,

may draw such inferences from the failure or refusal as appear proper.

(3) Subsections (1) and (2) do not apply unless the accused was told in ordinary language by the constable when making the request mentioned in subsection (1)(c) above what the effect of this section would be if he failed or refused to comply with the request.

(4) This section applies in relation to officers of customs and excise as it applies in relation to constables.

(5) This section does not preclude the drawing of any inference from a failure or refusal of the accused to account for his presence at a place which could properly be drawn apart from this section.

(6) This section does not apply in relation to a failure or refusal which occurred before the commencement of this section.

(7) In relation to any time before the commencement of section 44 of this Act, this section shall have effect as if the reference in subsection (2)(a) to the grant of an application for dismissal was a reference to the committal of the accused for trial.

38 Interpretation and savings for sections 34, 35, 36 and 37   [518]

(1) In sections 34, 35, 36 and 37 of this Act –

'legal representative' means an authorised advocate or authorised litigator, as defined by section 119(1) of the Courts and Legal Services Act 1990; and

'place' includes any building or part of a building, any vehicle, vessel, aircraft or hovercraft and any other place whatsoever.

(2) In sections 34(2), 35(3), 36(2) and 37(2), references to an offence charged include references to any other offence of which the accused could lawfully be convicted on that charge.

(3) A person shall not have the proceedings against him transferred to the Crown Court for trial, have a case to answer or be convicted of an offence solely on an inference drawn from such a failure or refusal as is mentioned in section 34(2), 35(3), 36(2) or 37(2).

(4) A judge shall not refuse to grant such an application as is mentioned in section 34(2)(b), 36(2)(b) and 37(2)(b) solely on an inference drawn from such a failure as is mentioned in section 34(2), 36(2) or 37(2).

(5) Nothing in sections 34, 35, 36 or 37 prejudices the operation of a provision of any enactment which provides (in whatever words) that any answer or evidence given by a person in specified circumstances shall not be admissible in evidence against him or some other person in any proceedings or class of proceedings (however described, and whether civil or criminal).

In this subsection, the reference to giving evidence is a reference to giving evidence in any manner, whether by furnishing information, making discovery, producing documents or otherwise.

(6) Nothing in section 34, 35, 36 or 37 prejudices any power of a court, in any proceedings, to exclude evidence (whether by preventing questions being put or otherwise) at its discretion.

PART IV

POLICE POWERS

60 Powers to stop and search in anticipation of violence [519]

(1) Where a police officer of or above the rank of superintendent reasonably believes that –

(a) incidents involving serious violence may take place in any locality in his area, and

(b) it is expedient to do so to prevent their occurrence,

he may give an authorisation that the powers to stop and search person and vehicles conferred by this section shall be exercisable at any place within that locality for a period not exceeding twenty four hours.

(2) The power conferred by subsection (1) above may be exercised by a chief inspector or an inspector if he reasonably believes that incidents involving serious violence are imminent and no superintendent is available.

(3) If it appears to the officer who gave the authorisation or to a superintendent that it is expedient to do so, having regard to offences which have, or are reasonably suspected to have, been committed in connection with any incident falling within the authorisation, he may direct that the authorisation shall continue in being for a further six hours.

(4) This section confers on any constable in uniform power –

(a) to stop any pedestrian and search him or anything carried by him for offensive weapons or dangerous instruments;

(b) to stop any vehicle and search the vehicle, its driver and any passenger for offensive weapons or dangerous instruments.

(5) A constable may, in the exercise of those powers, stop any person or vehicle and make any search he thinks fit whether or not he has any grounds for suspecting that the person or vehicle is carrying weapons or articles of that kind.

(6) If in the course of a search under this section a constable discovers a dangerous instrument or an article which he has reasonable grounds for suspecting to be an offensive weapon, he may seize it.

(7) This section applies (with the necessary modifications) to ships, aircraft and hovercraft as it applies to vehicles.

(8) A person who fails to stop or (as the case may be) to stop the vehicle when required to do so by a constable in the exercise of his powers under this section shall be liable on summary conviction to imprisonment for a term not exceeding one month or to a fine not exceeding level 3 on the standard scale or both.

(9) Any authorisation under this section shall be in writing signed by the officer giving it and shall specify the locality in which and the period during which the powers conferred by this section are exercisable and a direction under subsection (3) above shall also be given in writing or, where that is not practicable, recorded in writing as soon as it is practicable to do so.

(10) Where a vehicle is stopped by a constable under this section, the driver shall be entitled to obtain a written statement that the vehicle was stopped under the powers conferred by this section if he applies for such a statement not later than the end of the period of twelve months from the day on which the vehicle was stopped and similarly as respects a pedestrian who is stopped and searched under this section.

(11) In this section –

'dangerous instruments' means instruments which have a blade or are sharply pointed;

'offensive weapon' has the meaning given by section 1(9) of the Police and Criminal Evidence Act 1984; and

'vehicle' includes a caravan as defined in section 29(1) of the Caravan Sites and Control of Development Act 1960.

(12) The powers conferred by this section are in addition to and not in derogation of, any power otherwise conferred.

PART V

PUBLIC ORDER: COLLECTIVE TRESPASS OR NUISANCE ON LAND

61 Power to remove trespassers on land   [520]

(1) If the senior police officer present at the scene reasonably believes that two or more persons are trespassing on land and are present there with the common purpose of residing there for any period, that reasonable steps have been taken by or on behalf of the occupier to ask them to leave and –

    (a) that any of those persons has caused damage to the land or to property on the land or used threatening, abusive or insulting words or behaviour towards the occupier, a member of his family or an employee or agent of his, or

    (b) that those persons have between them six or more vehicles on the land,

he may direct those persons, or any of them, to leave the land and to remove any vehicles or other property they have with them on the land.

(2) Where the persons in question are reasonably believed by the senior police officer to be persons who were not originally trespassers but have become trespassers on the land, the officer must reasonably believe that the other conditions specified in subsection (1) are satisfied after those persons became trespassers before he can exercise the power conferred by that subsection.

(3) A direction under subsection (1) above, if not communicated to the persons referred to in subsection (1) by the police officer giving the direction, may be communicated to them by any constable at the scene.

(4) If a person knowing that a direction under subsection (1) above has been given which applies to him –

    (a) fails to leave the land as soon as reasonably practicable, or

    (b) having left again enters the land as a trespasser within the period of three months beginning with the day on which the direction was given,

he commits an offence and is liable on summary conviction to imprisonment for a term not exceeding three months or a fine not exceeding level 4 on the standard scale, or both.

(5) A constable in uniform who reasonably suspects that a person is committing an offence under this section may arrest him without a warrant.

(6) In proceedings for an offence under this section it is a defence for the accused to show –

    (a) that he was not trespassing on the land, or

    (b) that he had a reasonable excuse for failing to leave the land as soon as reasonably practicable or, as the case may be, for again entering the land as a trespasser.

(7) In its application in England and Wales to common land this section has effect as if in the preceding subsections of it –

(a) references to trespassing or trespassers were references to acts and persons doing acts which constitute either a trespass as against the occupier or an infringement of the commoners' rights; and

(b) references to 'the occupier' included the commoners or any of them or, in the case of common land to which the public has access, the local authority as well as any commoner.

(8) Subsection (7) above does not –

(a) require action by more than one occupier; or

(b) constitute persons trespassers as against any commoner or the local authority if they are permitted to be there by the other occupier.

(9) In this section –

'common land' means common land as defined in section 22 of the Commons Registration Act 1965;

'commoner' means a person with rights of common as defined in section 22 of the Commons Registration Act 1965;

'land' does not include –

(a) buildings other than –

(i) agricultural buildings within the meaning of, in England and Wales, paragraphs 3 to 8 of Schedule 5 to the Local Government Finance Act 1988 or, in Scotland, section 7(2) of the Valuation and Rating (Scotland) Act 1956, or

(ii) scheduled monuments within the meaning of the Ancient Monuments and Archaeological Areas Act 1979;

(b) land forming part of –

(i) a highway unless it falls within the classifications in section 54 of the Wildlife and Countryside Act 1981 (footpath, bridleway or byway open to all traffic or road used as a public path) or is a cycle track under the Highways Act 1980 or the Cycle Tracks Act 1984; or

(ii) a road within the meaning of the Roads (Scotland) Act 1984 unless it falls within the definitions in section 151(2)(a)(ii) or (b) (footpaths and cycle tracks) of that Act or is a bridleway within the meaning of section 47 of the Countryside (Scotland) Act 1967;

'the local authority', in relation to common land, means any local authority which has powers in relation to the land under section 9 of the Commons Registration Act 1965;

'occupier' (and in subsection (8) 'the other occupier') means –

(a) in England and Wales, the person entitled to possession of the land by virtue of an estate or interest held by him; and

(b) in Scotland, the person lawfully entitled to natural possession of the land;

'property', in relation to damage to property on land, means –

(a) in England and Wales, property within the meaning of section 10(1) of the Criminal Damage Act 1971; and

(b) in Scotland, either –

(i) heritable property other than land; or

(ii) corporeal moveable property,

and 'damage' includes the deposit of any substance capable of polluting the land;

'trespass' means, in the application of this section –

(a) in England and Wales, subject to the extensions effected by subsection (7) above, trespass as against the occupier of the land;
(b) in Scotland, entering, or as the case may be remaining on, land without lawful authority and without the occupier's consent; and

'trespassing' and 'trespasser' shall be construed accordingly;

'vehicle' includes –

(a) any vehicle, whether or not it is in a fit state for use on roads, and includes any chassis or body, with or without wheels, appearing to have formed part of such a vehicle, and any load carried by, and anything attached to, such a vehicle; and
(b) a caravan as defined in section 29(1) of the Caravan Sites and Control of Development Act 1960;

and a person may be regarded for the purposes of this section as having a purpose of residing in a place notwithstanding that he has a home elsewhere.

62 Supplementary powers of seizure [521]

(1) If a direction has been given under section 61 and a constable reasonably suspects that any person to whom the direction applies has, without reasonable excuse –

(a) failed to remove any vehicle on the land which appears to the constable to belong to him or to be in his possession or under his control; or
(b) entered the land as a trespasser with a vehicle within the period of three months beginning with the day on which the direction was given,

the constable may seize and remove the vehicle.

(2) In this section, 'trespasser' and 'vehicle' have the same meaning as in section 61.

63 Powers to remove persons attending or preparing for a rave [522]

(1) This section applies to a gathering on land in the open air of 100 or more persons (whether or not trespassers) at which amplified music is played during the night (with or without intermissions) and is such as, by reason of its loudness and duration and the time at which it is played, is likely to cause serious distress to the inhabitants of the locality; and for this purpose –

(a) such a gathering continues during intermissions in the music and, where the gathering extends over several days, throughout the period during which amplified music is played at night (with or without intermissions); and
(b) 'music' includes sounds wholly or predominantly characterised by the emission of a succession of repetitive beats.

(2) If, as respects any land in the open air, a police officer of at least the rank of superintendent reasonably believes that –

(a) two or more persons are making preparations for the holding there of a gathering to which this section applies,
(b) ten or more persons are waiting for such a gathering to begin there, or
(c) ten or more persons are attending such a gathering which is in progress,

he may give a direction that those persons and any other persons who come to prepare or wait for or to attend the gathering are to leave the land and remove any vehicles or other property which they have with them on the land.

(3) A direction under subsection (2) above, if not communicated to the persons referred to in subsection (2) by the police officer giving the direction, may be communicated to them by any constable at the scene.

(4) Persons shall be treated as having had a direction under subsection (2) above communicated to them if reasonable steps have been taken to bring it to their attention.

(5) A direction under subsection (2) above does not apply to an exempt person.

(6) If a person knowing that a direction has been given which applies to him –

(a) fails to leave the land as soon as reasonably practicable, or
(b) having left again enters the land within the period of 7 days beginning with the day on which the direction was given,

he commits an offence and is liable on summary conviction to imprisonment for a term not exceeding three months or a fine not exceeding level 4 on the standard scale, or both.

(7) In proceedings for an offence under this section it is a defence for the accused to show that he had a reasonable excuse for failing to leave the land as soon as reasonably practicable or, as the case may be, for again entering the land.

(8) A constable in uniform who reasonably suspects that a person is committing an offence under this section may arrest him without a warrant.

(9) This section does not apply –

(a) in England and Wales, to a gathering licensed by an entertainment licence; or
(b) in Scotland, to a gathering in premises which, by virtue of section 41 of the Civic Government (Scotland) Act 1982, are licensed to be used as a place of public entertainment.

(10) In this section –

'entertainment licence' means a licence granted by a local authority under –

(a) Schedule 12 to the London Government Act 1963;
(b) section 3 of the Private Places of Entertainment (Licensing) Act 1967; or
(c) Schedule 1 to the Local Government (Miscellaneous Provisions) Act 1982;

'exempt person', in relation to land (or any gathering on land), means the occupier, any member of his family and any employee or agent of his and any person whose home is situated on the land;

'land in the open air' includes a place partly open to the air;

'local authority' means –

(a) in Greater London, a London borough council or the Common Council of the City of London;
(b) in England outside Greater London, a district council or the council of the Isles of Scilly;
(c) in Wales, a county council or county borough council; and

'occupier', 'trespasser' and 'vehicle' have the same meaning as in section 61.

64 Supplementary powers of entry and seizure [523]

(1) If a police officer of at least the rank of superintendent reasonably believes that circumstances exist in relation to any land which would justify the giving of a direction under section 63 in relation to a gathering to which that section applies he may authorise any constable to enter the land for any of the purposes specified in subsection (2) below.

(2) Those purposes are –

(a) to ascertain whether such circumstances exist; and

(b) to exercise any power conferred on a constable by section 63 or subsection (4) below.

(3) A constable who is so authorised to enter land for any purpose may enter the land without a warrant.

(4) If a direction has been given under section 63 and a constable reasonably suspects that any person to whom the direction applies has, without reasonable excuse –

(a) failed to remove any vehicle or sound equipment on the land which appears to the constable to belong to him or to be in his possession or under his control; or

(b) entered the land as a trespasser with a vehicle or sound equipment within the period of 7 days beginning with the day on which the direction was given,

the constable may seize and remove that vehicle or sound equipment.

(5) Subsection (4) above does not authorise the seizure of any vehicle or sound equipment of an exempt person.

(6) In this section –

'exempt person' has the same meaning as in section 63;

'sound equipment' means equipment designed or adapted for amplifying music and any equipment suitable for use in connection

with such equipment, and 'music' has the same meaning as in section 63; and

'vehicle' has the same meaning as in section 61.

65 Raves: power to stop persons from proceeding   [524]

(1) If a constable in uniform reasonably believes that a person is on his way to a gathering to which section 63 applies in relation to which a direction under section 63(2) is in force, he may, subject to subsections (2) and (3) below –

(a) stop that person, and

(b) direct him not to proceed in the direction of the gathering.

(2) The power conferred by subsection (1) above may only be exercised at a place within 5 miles of the boundary of the site of the gathering.

(3) No direction may be given under subsection (1) above to an exempt person.

(4) If a person knowing that a direction under subsection (1) above has been given to him fails to comply with that direction, he commits an offence and is liable on summary conviction to a fine not exceeding level 3 on the standard scale.

(5) A constable in uniform who reasonably suspects that a person is committing an offence under this section may arrest him without a warrant.

(6) In this section, 'exempt person' has the same meaning as in section 63.

66 Power of court to forfeit sound equipment   [525]

(1) Where a person is convicted of an offence under section 63 in relation to a gathering to which that section applies and the court is satisfied that any sound equipment which has been seized from him under section 64(4), or which was in his possession or under his control at the relevant time, has been used at the gathering the court may make an order for forfeiture under this subsection in respect of that property.

(2) The court may make an order under subsection (1) above whether or not it also deals with the offender in respect of the offence in any other way and without regard to any restrictions on forfeiture in any enactment.

(3) In considering whether to make an order under subsection (1) above in respect of any property a court shall have regard –

(a) to the value of the property; and
(b) to the likely financial and other effects on the offender of the making of the order (taken together with any other order that the court contemplates making).

(4) An order under subsection (1) above shall operate to deprive the offender of his rights, if any, in the property to which it relates, and the property shall (if not already in their possession) be taken into the possession of the police.

(5) Except in a case to which subsection (6) below applies, where any property has been forfeited under subsection (1) above, a magistrates' court may, on application by a claimant of the property, other than the offender from whom it was forfeited under subsection (1) above, make an order for delivery of the property to the applicant if it appears to the court that he is the owner of the property.

(6) In a case where forfeiture under subsection (1) above has been by order of a Scottish court, a claimant such as is mentioned in subsection (5) above may, in such manner as may be prescribed by act of adjournal, apply to that court for an order for the return of the property in question.

(7) No application shall be made under subsection (5), or by virtue of subsection (6), above by any claimant of the property after the expiration of 6 months from the date on which an order under subsection (1) above was made in respect of the property.

(8) No such application shall succeed unless the claimant satisfies the court either that he had not consented to the offender having possession of the property or that he did not know, and had no reason to suspect, that the property was likely to be used at a gathering to which section 63 applies.

(9) An order under subsection (5), or by virtue of subsection (6), above shall not affect the right of any person to take, within the period of 6 months from the date of an order under subsection (5), or as the case may be by virtue of subsection (6), above, proceedings for the recovery of the property from the person in possession of it in pursuance of the order, but on the expiration of that period the right shall cease.

(10) The Secretary of State may make regulations for the disposal of property, and for the application of the proceeds of sale of property, forfeited under subsection (1) above where no application by a claimant of the property under subsection (5), or by virtue of subsection (6), above has been made within the period specified in subsection (7) above or no such application has succeeded.

(11) The regulations may also provide for the investment of money and for the audit of accounts.

(12) The power to make regulations under subsection (10) above shall be exercisable by statutory instrument which shall be subject to annulment in pursuance of a resolution of either House of Parliament.

(13) In this section –

'relevant time', in relation to a person –

(a) convicted in England and Wales of an offence under section 63, means the time of his arrest for the offence or of the issue of a summons in respect of it;

(b) so convicted in Scotland, means the time of his arrest for, or of his being cited as an accused in respect of, the offence;

'sound equipment' has the same meaning as in section 64.

67 Retention and charges for seized property   [526]

(1) Any vehicles which have been seized and removed by a constable under section 62(1) or 64(4) may be retained in accordance with regulations made by the Secretary of State under subsection (3) below.

(2) Any sound equipment which has been seized and removed by a constable under section 64(4) may be retained until the conclusion of proceedings against the person from whom it was seized for an offence under section 63.

(3) The Secretary of State may make regulations –

(a) regulating the retention and safe keeping and the disposal and the destruction in prescribed circumstances of vehicles; and
(b) prescribing charges in respect of the removal, retention, disposal and destruction of vehicles.

(4) Any authority shall be entitled to recover from a person from whom a vehicle has been seized such charges as may be prescribed in respect of the removal, retention, disposal and destruction of the vehicle by the authority.

(5) Regulations under subsection (3) above may make different provisions for different classes of vehicles or for different circumstances.

(6) Any charges under subsection (4) above shall be recoverable as a simple contract debt.

(7) Any authority having custody of vehicles under regulations under subsection (3) above shall be entitled to retain custody until any charges under subsection (4) are paid.

(8) The power to make regulations under subsection (3) above shall be exercisable by statutory instrument which shall be subject to annulment in pursuance of a resolution of either House of Parliament.

(9) In this section –

'conclusion of proceedings' against a person means –

(a) his being sentenced or otherwise dealt with for the offence or his acquittal;
(b) the discontinuance of the proceedings; or
(c) the decision not to prosecute him,

whichever is the earlier;

'sound equipment' has the same meaning as in section 64; and

'vehicle' has the same meaning as in section 61.

68 Offence of aggravated trespass   [527]

(1) A person commits the offence of aggravated trespass if he trespasses on land in the open air and, in relation to any lawful activity which persons are engaging in or are about to engage in on that or adjoining land in the open air, does there anything which is intended by him to have the effect –

(a) of intimidating those persons or any of them so as to deter them or any of them from engaging in that activity,
(b) of obstructing that activity, or
(c) of disrupting that activity.

(2) Activity on any occasion on the part of a person or persons on land is 'lawful'

for the purposes of this section if he or they may engage in the activity on the land on that occasion without committing an offence or trespassing on the land.

(3) A person guilty of an offence under this section is liable on summary conviction to imprisonment for a term not exceeding three months or a fine not exceeding level 4 on the standard scale, or both.

(4) A constable in uniform who reasonably suspects that a person is committing an offence under this section may arrest him without a warrant.

(5) In this section 'land' does not include –

(a) the highways and roads excluded from the application of section 61 by paragraph (b) of the definition of 'land' in subsection (9) of that section; or
(b) a road within the meaning of the Roads (Northern Ireland) Order 1993.

69 Powers to remove persons committing or participating in aggravated trespass [528]

(1) If the senior police officer present at the scene reasonably believes –

(a) that a person is committing, has committed or intends to commit the offence of aggravated trespass on land in the open air; or
(b) that two or more persons are trespassing on land in the open air and are present there with the common purpose of intimidating persons so as to deter them from engaging in a lawful activity or of obstructing or disrupting a lawful activity,

he may direct that person or (as the case may be) those persons (or any of them) to leave the land.

(2) A direction under subsection (1) above, if not communicated to the persons referred to in subsection (1) by the police officer giving the direction, may be communicated to them by any constable at the scene.

(3) If a person knowing that a direction under subsection (1) above has been given which applies to him –

(a) fails to leave the land as soon as practicable, or
(b) having left again enters the land as a trespasser within the period of three months beginning with the day on which the direction was given,

he commits an offence and is liable on summary conviction to imprisonment for a term not exceeding three months or a fine not exceeding level 4 on the standard scale, or both.

(4) In proceedings for an offence under subsection (3) it is a defence for the accused to show –

(a) that he was not trespassing on the land, or
(b) that he had a reasonable excuse for failing to leave the land as soon as practicable or, as the case may be, for again entering the land as a trespasser.

(5) A constable in uniform who reasonably suspects that a person is committing an offence under this section may arrest him without a warrant.

(6) In this section 'lawful activity' and 'land' have the same meaning as in section 68.

PART XII

MISCELLANEOUS AND GENERAL

166 Sale of tickets by unauthorised persons   [529]

(1) It is an offence for an unauthorised person to sell, or offer or expose for sale, a ticket for a designated football match in any public place or place to which the public has access or, in the course of a trade or business, in any other place.

(2) For this purpose –

(a) a person is 'unauthorised' unless he is authorised in writing to sell tickets for the match by the home club or by the organisers of the match;
(b) a 'ticket' means anything which purports to be a ticket; and
(c) a 'designated football match' means a football match, or football match of a description, for the time being designated under section 1(1) of the Football (Offences) Act 1991.

(3) A person guilty of an offence under this section is liable on summary conviction to a fine not exceeding level 5 on the standard scale.

(5) Section 32 of the Police and Criminal Evidence Act 1984 (search of persons and premises (including vehicles) upon arrest) shall have effect, in its application in relation to an offence under this section, as if the power conferred on a constable to enter and search any vehicle extended to any vehicle which the constable has reasonable grounds for believing was being used for any purpose connected with the offence.

Treaties

EUROPEAN CONVENTION FOR THE PROTECTION OF HUMAN RIGHTS AND FUNDAMENTAL FREEDOMS 1950
(Cmd 8969)

Article 1 [530]

The High Contracting Parties shall secure to everyone within their jurisdiction the rights and freedoms in Section 1 of this Convention [Articles 2 to 18].

Article 2 [531]

1 Everyone's right to life shall be protected by law. No one shall be deprived of his life intentionally save in the execution of a sentence of a court following his conviction of a crime for which this penalty is provided by law.

2 Deprivation of life shall not be regarded as inflicted in contravention of this Article when it results from the use of force which is no more than absolutely necessary:

(a) in defence of any person from unlawful violence;
(b) in order to effect a lawful arrest or to prevent the escape of a person lawfully detained;
(c) in action lawfully taken for the purpose of quelling a riot or insurrection.

Article 3 [532]

No one shall be subjected to torture or to inhuman or degrading treatment or punishment.

Article 4 [533]

1 No one shall be held in slavery or servitude.

2 No one shall be required to perform forced or compulsory labour.

3 For the purpose of this Article the term 'forced or compulsory labour' shall not include:

(a) any work required to be done in the ordinary course of detention imposed according to the provisions of Article 5 of this Convention or during conditional release from such detention;

(b) any service of a military character or, in case of conscientious objectors in countries where they are recognised, service exacted instead of compulsory military service;

(c) any service exacted in case of an emergency or calamity threatening the life or well-being of the community;

(d) any work or service which forms part of normal civil obligations.

Article 5 [534]

1 Everyone has the right to liberty and security of person. No one shall be deprived of his liberty save in the following cases and in accordance with a procedure prescribed by law:

(a) the lawful detention of a person after conviction by a competent court;

(b) the lawful arrest or detention of a person for non-compliance with the lawful order of a court or in order to secure the fulfilment of any obligation prescribed by law;

(c) the lawful arrest or detention of a person effected for the purpose of bringing him before the competent legal authority on reasonable suspicion of having committed an offence or when it is reasonably considered necessary to prevent his committing an offence or fleeing after having done so;

(d) the detention of a minor by lawful order for the purpose of educational supervision or his lawful detention for the purpose of bringing him before the competent legal authority;

(e) the lawful detention of persons for the prevention of the spreading of infectious diseases, of persons of unsound mind, alcoholics or drug addicts or vagrants;

(f) the lawful arrest or detention of a person to prevent his effecting an unauthorised entry into the country or of a person against whom action is being taken with a view to deportation or extradition.

2 Everyone who is arrested shall be informed promptly, in a language which he understands, of the reasons for his arrest and of any charge against him.

3 Everyone arrested or detained in accordance with the provisions of paragraph 1(c) of this Article shall be brought promptly before a judge or other officer authorised by law to exercise judicial power and shall be entitled to trial within a reasonable time or to release pending trial. Release may be conditioned by guarantees to appear for trial.

4 Everyone who is deprived of his liberty by arrest or detention shall be entitled to take proceedings by which the lawfulness of his detention shall be decided speedily by a court and his release ordered if the detention is not lawful.

5 Everyone who has been the victim of arrest or detention in contravention of the provisions of this Article shall have an enforceable right to compensation.

Article 6 [535]

1 In the determination of his civil rights and obligations or of any criminal charge against him, everyone is entitled to a fair and public hearing within a reasonable time by an independent and impartial tribunal established by law. Judgment shall be pronounced publicly but the press and public may be excluded from all or part of the trial in the interest of morals, public order or national security in a democratic society, where the interests of juveniles or the protection of the private life of the parties so require, or to the extent strictly necessary in the opinion of

the court in special circumstances where publicity would prejudice the interests of justice.

2 Everyone charged with a criminal offence shall be presumed innocent until proved guilty according to law.

3 Everyone charged with a criminal offence has the following minimum rights:

(a) to be informed promptly, in a language which he understands and in detail, of the nature and cause of the accusation against him;

(b) to have adequate time and facilities for the preparation of his defence;

(c) to defend himself in person or through legal assistance of his own choosing or, if he has not sufficient means to pay for legal assistance, to be given it free when the interests of justice so require;

(d) to examine or have examined witnesses against him and to obtain the attendance and examination of witnesses on his behalf under the same conditions as witnesses against him;

(e) to have the free assistance of an interpreter if he cannot understand or speak the language used in court.

Article 7   [536]

1 No one shall be held guilty of any criminal offence on account of any act or omission which did not constitute a criminal offence under national or international law at the time when it was committed. Nor shall a heavier penalty be imposed than the one that was applicable at the time the criminal offence was committed.

2 This Article shall not prejudice the trial and punishment of any person for any act or omission which, at the time when it was committed, was criminal according to the general principles of law recognised by civilised nations.

Article 8   [537]

1 Everyone has the right to respect for his private and family life, his home and his correspondence.

2 There shall be no interference by a public authority with the exercise of this right except such as is in accordance with the law and is necessary in a democratic society in the interests of national security, public safety or the economic well-being of the country, for the prevention of disorder or crime, for the protection of health or morals, or for the protection of the rights and freedoms of others.

Article 9   [538]

1 Everyone has the right to freedom of thought, conscience and religion; this right includes freedom to change his religion or beliefs and freedom, either alone or in community with others and in public or private, to manifest his religion or belief, in worship, teaching, practice and observance.

2 Freedom to manifest one's religion or beliefs shall be subject only to such limitations as are prescribed by law and are necessary in a democratic society in the interests of public safety, for the protection of public order, health or morals, or for the protection of the rights and freedoms of others.

Article 10   [539]

1 Everyone has the right to freedom of expression. This right shall include freedom to hold opinions and to receive and impart information and ideas without interference by public authority and regardless of frontiers. This Article shall not prevent States from requiring the licensing of broadcasting, television or cinema enterprises.

2 The exercise of these freedoms, since it carries with it duties and responsibilities, may be subject to such formalities, conditions, restrictions or penalties as are prescribed by law and are necessary in a democratic society, in the interests of national security, territorial integrity or public safety, for the prevention of disorder or crime, for the protection of health or morals, for the protection of the reputation or rights of others, for preventing the disclosure of information received in confidence, or for maintaining the authority and impartiality of the judiciary.

Article 11   [540]

1 Everyone has the right to freedom of peaceful assembly and to freedom of association with others, including the right to form and to join trade unions for the protection of his interests.

2 No restrictions shall be placed on the exercise of these rights other than such as are prescribed by law and are necessary in a democratic society in the interests of national security or public safety, for the prevention of disorder or crime, for the protection of health or morals or for the protection of the rights and freedoms of others. This Article shall not prevent the imposition of lawful restrictions on the exercise of these rights by members of the armed forces, of the police or of the administration of the State.

Article 12   [541]

Men and women of marriageable age have the right to marry and to found a family, according to the national laws governing the exercise of this right.

Article 13   [542]

Everyone whose rights and freedoms as set forth in this Convention are violated shall have an effective remedy before a national authority notwithstanding that the violation has been committed by persons acting in an official capacity.

Article 14   [543]

The enjoyment of the rights and freedoms set forth in this Convention shall be secured without discrimination on any ground such as sex, race, colour, language, religion, political or other opinion, national or social origin, association with a national minority, property, birth or other status.

Article 15   **[544]**

1 In time of war or other public emergency threatening the life of the nation any High Contracting Party may take measures derogating from its obligations under this Convention to the extent strictly required by the exigencies of the situation, provided that such measures are not inconsistent with its other obligations under international law.

2 No derogation from Article 2, except in respect of deaths resulting from lawful acts of war, or from Articles 3, 4 (paragraph 1) and 7 shall be made under this provision.

3 Any High Contracting Party availing itself of this right of derogation shall keep the Secretary-General of the Council of Europe fully informed of the measures which it has taken and the reasons therefor. It shall also inform the Secretary-General of the Council of Europe when such measures have ceased to operate and the provisions of the Convention are again fully executed.

Article 16   **[545]**

Nothing in Articles 10, 11 and 14 shall be regarded as preventing the High Contracting Parties from imposing restrictions on the political activity of aliens.

Article 17   **[546]**

Nothing in this Convention may be interpreted as implying for any State, group or person any right to engage in any activity or perform any act aimed at the destruction of any of the rights and freedoms set forth herein or at their limitation to a greater extent than is provided for in the Convention.

Article 18   **[547]**

The restrictions permitted under this Convention to the said rights and freedoms shall not be applied for any purpose other than those for which they have been prescribed.

Glossary
of Latin and other words and phrases

Ab extra. From outside.

Ab inconvenienti. *See* ARGUMENTUM

Ab initio. From the beginning.

Accessio. Addition; appendage. The combination of two chattels belonging to different persons into a single article.

Acta exteriora indicant interiora secreta. A man's outward actions are evidence of his innermost thoughts and intentions.

Actio personalis moritur cum persona. A personal right of action dies on the death of the person by or against whom it could be enforced.

Actus non facit reum, nisi mens sit rea. The act itself does not make a man guilty, unless he does it with a guilty intention.

Ad colligenda bona. To collect the goods.

Ad hoc. Arranged for this purpose; special.

Ad idem. *See* CONSENSUS.

Ad infinitum. To infinity; without limit; for ever.

Ad litem. For the purpose of the law suit.

Ad opus. For the benefit of: on behalf of.

Ad valorem. Calculated in proportion to the value or price of the property.

Adversus extraneos vitiosa possessio prodesse solet. Possession, though supported only by a defective title, will prevail over the claims of strangers other than the true owner.

A fortiori (ratione). For a stronger reason; by even more convincing reasoning.

Aliter. Otherwise; the result would be different, if ...; (also, used of a judge who thinks differently from his fellow judges).

Aliud est celare; aliud est tacere; neque enim id est celare quicquid reticeas. Mere silence is one thing but active concealment is quite another thing; for it is not disguising something when you say nothing about it.

Aliunde. From elsewhere; from other sources.

A mensa et thoro. A separation from the 'table and bed' of one's spouse.

Amicus curiae. A friend of the court.

Animo contrahendi. With the intention of contracting.

Animo revocandi. With the intention of revoking.

Animus deserendi. The intention of deserting.

Animus donandi. The intention of giving.

Animus possidendi. The intention of possessing.

Animus revertendi. The intention of returning.

Animus testandi. The intention of making a will.

Ante. Before; (also used of a case referred to earlier on a page or in a book).

A posteriori. From effect to cause; inductively; from subsequent conclusions.

A priori. From cause to effect; deductively; from previous assumptions or reasoning.

Argumentum ab inconvenienti. An argument devised because of the existence of an awkward problem so as to provide an explanation for it.

Asportatio. The act of carrying away.

Assensus. *See* CONSENSUS.

Assensus ad idem. Agreement as to the same terms.

Assumpsit (super se). He undertook.

Ats. (ad sectam). At the suit of. (The opposite of VERSUS.)

Autrefois acquit. Formerly acquitted.

Autrefois convict. Formerly convicted.

Bis dat qui cito dat. He gives doubly who gives swiftly; a quick gift is worth two slow ones.

Bona fide. In good faith; sincere.

Bona vacantia. Goods without an owner.

Brutum fulmen. A silent thunderbolt; an empty threat.

Cadit quaestio. The matter admits of no further argument.

Caeterorum. Of the things which are left.

Capias ad satisfaciendum. A writ commanding the sheriff to take the body of the defendant in order that he may make satisfaction for the plaintiff's claim.

Causa causans. The immediate cause of something; the last link in the chain of causation.

Causa proxima non remota spectatur. Regard is paid to the immediate, not to the remote cause.

Causa sine qua non. A preceding link in the chain of causation without which the causa causans could not be operative.

Caveat emptor. The buyer must look out for himself.

Cessante ratione legis, cessat lex ipsa. When the reason for its existence ceases, the law itself ceases to exist.

Cestui(s) que trust. A person (or persons) for whose benefit property is held on trust; a beneficiary (beneficiaries).

Cestui que vie. Person for the duration of whose life an estate is granted to another person.

Chose in action. Intangible personal property or rights, which can be enjoyed or enforced only by legal action, and not by taking physical possession (eg debts).

Chose jugée. Thing it is idle to discuss.

Coitus interruptus. Interrupted sexual intercourse, i.e. withdrawal before emission.

Colore officii. Under the pretext of a person's official position.

Commorientes. Persons who die at the same time.

Confusio. A mixture; union. The mixture of things of the same nature, but belonging to different persons so that identification of the original things becomes impossible.

Consensu. By general consent; unanimously.

Consensus ad idem. Agreement as to the same thing.

Consortium. Conjugal relations with and companionship of a spouse.

Contra. To the contrary. (Used of a case in which the decision was contrary to the doctrine or cases previously cited; also of a judge who delivers a dissenting judgment.)

Contra bonos mores. Contrary to good morals.

Contra mundum. Against the world.

Contra proferentem. Against the party who puts forward a clause in a document.

Cor. (coram). In the presence of; before (a judge).

Coram non judice. Before one who is not a judge. Corpus. Body; capital.

Corpus. Body; capital.

Coverture. Marriage.

Cri de coeur. Heartfelt cry.

Cujus est solum, ejus est usque ad coelum et ad inferos. Whosoever owns the soil also owns everything above it as far as the heavens and everything below it as far as the lower regions of the earth.

Culpa. Wrongful default.

Cum onere. Together with the burden.

Cum testamento annexo. With the will annexed.

Cur. adv. vult. (curia advisari vult). The court wishes time to consider the matter.

Cy-pres. For a purpose resembling as nearly as possible the purpose originally proposed.

Damage feasant. *See* DISTRESS.

Damnosa hereditas. An insolvent inheritance.

Damnum. Loss; damage.

Damnum absque injuria. *See* DAMNUM SINE INJURIA.

Damnum emergens. A loss which arises.

Damnum fatale. Damage resulting from the workings of fate for which human negligence is not to blame.

Damnum sine (or absque) injuria. Damage which is not the result of a legally remediable wrong.

De bene esse. Evidence or action which a court allows to be given or done provisionally, subject to further consideration at a later stage.

Debitor non praesumitur donare. A debtor is presumed to give a legacy to a creditor to discharge his debt and not as a gift.

Debitum in praesenti. A debt which is due at the present time.

Debitum in futuro solvendum. A debt which will be due to be paid at a future time.

De bonis asportatis. Of goods carried away.

De bonis non administratis. Of the assets which have not been administered .

De die in diem. From day to day.

De facto. In fact.

De futuro. Regarding the future; in the future; about something which will exist in the future.

Dehors. Outside (the document or matter in question); irrelevant.

De integro. As regards the whole; entirely.

De jure. By right; rightful.

Del credere agent. An agent who for an extra commission guarantees the due performance of contracts by persons whom he introduces to his principal.

Delegatus non potest delegare. A person who is entrusted with a duty has no right to appoint another person to perform it in his place.

De minimis non curat lex. The law does not concern itself with trifles.

De novo. Anew; starting afresh.

Deodand. A chattel which caused the death of a human being and was forfeited to the Crown.

De praerogativa regis. Concerning the royal prerogative.

De son tort. Of his wrong.

Deus est procurator fatuorum. God is the protector of the simpleminded.

Devastavit. Where an executor 'has squandered' the estate.

Dictum. Saying. *See* OBITER DICTUM.

Dies non (jurisdicus). Day on which no legal business can be transacted.

Dissentiente. Delivering a dissenting judgment.

Distress damage feasant. The detention by a landowner of an animal or chattel while it is doing damage on his land.

Distringas. That you may distrain.

Doli incapax. Incapable of crime.

Dolus qui dat locum contractui. A deception which clears the way for the other party to enter into a contract.

Dominium. Ownership.

Dominus litis. The principal in a suit.

Dominus pro tempore. The master for the time being.

Donatio mortis causa. A gift made in contemplation of death and conditional thereon.

Dubitante. Doubting the correctness of the decision.

Durante absentia. During an executor's absence abroad.

Durante minore aetate. While an executor remains an infant.

Durante viduitate. During widowhood.

Ei incumbit probatio qui dicit, non qui negat. The onus of proving a fact rests upon the man who asserts its truth, not upon the man who denies it.

Ejusdem generis. General words following a list of specific things are construed as relating to things 'of the same kind' as those specifically listed.

Enceinte. Pregnant.

En ventre sa mère. Conceived but not yet born.

Eodem modo quo oritur, eodem modo dissolvitur. What has been created by a certain method may be extinguished by the same method.

Eo instanti. At that instant.

Escrow. A document delivered subject to a condition which must be fulfilled before it becomes a deed.

Estoppel. A rule of evidence which applies in certain circumstances and stops a person from denying the truth of a statement previously made by him.

Et cetera. (Etc.) And other things of that sort.

Et seq. (et sequentes). And subsequent pages.

Ex. From; by virtue of.

Ex abundanti cautela. From an abundance of caution.

Ex aequo et bono. According to what is just and equitable.

Ex cathedra. From his seat of office: an authoritative statement made by someone in his official capacity.

Ex concessis. In view of what has already been accepted.

Ex contractu. Arising out of contract.

Ex converso. Conversely.

Ex debito justitiae. That which is due as of right; which the court has no discretion to refuse.

Ex delicto. Arising out of a wrongful act or tort.

Ex dolo malo non oritur actio. No right of action arises out of a fraud.

Ex facie. On the face of it; ostensibly.

Ex gratia. Out of the kindness. Gratuitous; voluntary.

Ex hypothesi. In view of what has already been assumed.

Ex improviso. Unexpectedly, without forethought.

Ex officio. By virtue of one's official position.

Ex pacto illicito non oritur actio. No action can be brought on an unlawful contract.

Ex parte. Proceedings brought on behalf of one interested party without notice to, and in the absence of, the other.

Ex post facto. By reason of a subsequent act; acting retrospectively.

Ex relatione. An action instituted by the Attorney-General on behalf of the Crown on the information of a member of the public who is interested in the matter (the relator).

Expressio unius est exclusio alterius. When one thing is expressly specified, then it prevents anything else being implied.

Expressum facit cessare tacitum. Where terms are expressed, no other terms can be implied.

Ex turpi causa non oritur actio. No action can be brought where the parties are guilty of illegal or immoral conduct.

Faciendum. Something which is to be done.

Factum. Deed; that which has been done; statement of facts or points in issue.

Fait accompli. An accomplished fact.

Falsa demonstratio non nocet cum de corpore constat. Where the substance of the property in question is clearly identified, the addition of an incorrect description of the property does no harm.

Falsus in ono, falsus in omnibus. False in one, false in all.

Fecundatio ab extra. Conception from outside, i.e. where there has been no penetration.

Feme covert. A married woman.

Feme sole. An unmarried woman.

Ferae naturae. Animals which are by nature dangerous to man.

Fieri facias. A writ addressed to the sheriff: 'that you cause to be made' from the defendant's goods the sum due to the plaintiff under the judgment.

Force majeure. Irresistible compulsion.

Fructus industriales. Cultivated crops.

Fructus naturales. Vegetation which grows naturally without cultivation.

Functus officio. Having discharged his duty; having exhausted its powers.

Genus numquam perit. Particular goods which have been identified may be destroyed, but 'a category or type of article can never perish'.

Habeas corpus (ad subjiciendum). A writ addressed to one who detains another in custody, requiring him 'that you produce the prisoner's body to answer' to the court.

Habitue. A frequent visitor to a place.

Ibid. (ibidem). In the same place, book, or source.

Id certum est quod certum reddi potest. That which is capable of being reduced to a certainty is already a certainty.

Idem. The same thing, or person.

Ideo consideratum est per. Therefore it is considered by the court.

Ignorantia juris haud (neminem) (non) excusat, ignorantia facti excusat. A man may be excused for mistaking facts, but not for mistaking the law.

Ignorantia juris non excusat. Ignorance of the law is no excuse.

Imperitia culpae adnumeratur. Lack of skill is accounted a fault.

In aequali jure melior est conditio possidentis. Where the legal rights of the parties are equal, the party with possession is in the stronger position.

In articulo mortis. On the point of death.

In bonis. In the goods (or estate) of a deceased person.

In capite. In chief; holding as tenant directly under the Crown.

In consimili casu. In a similar case.

In custodia legis. In the keeping of the law.

Indebitatus assumpsit. A form of action in which the plaintiff alleges the defendant 'being already indebted to the plaintiff undertook' to do something.

In delicto. At fault.

Indicia. Signs; marks.

Indicium. Indication; sign; mark.

In esse. In existence.

In expeditione. On actual military service.

In extenso. At full length.

In fieri. In the course of being performed or established.

In flagrante delicto. In the act of committing the offence.

In forma pauperis. In the character of a poor person.

Infra. Below; lower down on a page; later in a book. In futuro. In the future.

In futuro. In the future.

In hac re. In this matter; in this particular aspect.

In jure non remota causa sed proxima spectatur. In law it is the immediate and not the remote cause which is considered.

Injuria. A wrongful act for which the law provides a remedy.

Injuria sine damno. A wrongful act unaccompanied by any damage yet actionable at law.

In lieu of. In place of.

In limine. On the threshold; at the outset.

In loco parentis. In the place of a parent.

In minore delicto. A person who is 'less at fault'.

In omnibus. In every respect.

Inops consilii. Lacking facilities for legal advice.

In pari delicto, potior est conditio defendentis (or possidentis). Where both parties are equally at fault, the defendant (or the party in possession) is in the stronger position.

In pari materia. In an analogous case or position.

In personam. *See* JUS IN PERSONAM.

In pleno. In full.

In praesenti. At the present time.

In propria persona. In his own capacity. In re. In the matter of. In rem. *See* JUS IN REM.

In re. In the matter of.

In rem. *See* JUS IN REM.

In situ. In its place.

In specie. In its own form; not converted into anything else.

In statu quo ante. In the condition in which it, or a person, was before.

Inter alia. Amongst other things.

Inter alios. Amongst other persons.

Interest reipublicae ut sit finis litium. It is in the interests of the community that every law suit should reach a final conclusion (and not be reopened later).

Interim. In the meanwhile; temporary.

Inter partes. Between (the) parties.

In terrorem. As a warning; as a deterrent.

Inter se. Between themselves.

Inter vivos. Between persons who are alive.

In toto. In its entirety; completely.

In transitu. In passage from one place to another.

Intra vires. Within the powers recognised by law as belonging to the person or body in question.

In utero. In the womb.

In vacuo. In the abstract; without considering the circumstances.

In vitro. In glass; in a test tube.

Ipsissima verba. 'The very words' of a speaker.

Ipso facto. By that very fact.

Jura. Rights.

Jura mariti. By virtue of the right of a husband to the goods of his wife.

Jus. A right which is recognised in law.

Jus accrescendi. The right of survivorship; the right of joint tenants to have their interests in the joint property increased by inheriting the interests of the deceased joint tenants until the last survivor inherits the entire property.

Jus in personam. A right which can be enforced against a particular person only.

Jus in rem. A right which can be enforced over the property in question against all other persons.

Jus naturale. Natural justice.

Jus neque in re neque ad rem. A right which is enforceable neither over the property in question against all the world nor against specific persons only.

Jus quaesitum tertio. A right vested in a third party (who is not a party to the contract).

Jus tertii. *See* JUS QUAESITUM TERTIO

Laches. Slackness or delay in pursuing a legal remedy which disentitles a person from action at a later date.

Laesio fidei. Breach of faith.

Laissez faire. 'Let him do what he likes'; permissive.

Lapsus linguae. Slip of the tongue.

Lex domicilii. The law of domicile.

Lex fori. The law of the court in which the case is being heard.

Lex loci celebrationis. The law of the place where the marriage was celebrated.

Lex loci contractus. The law of the place where the contract was made.

Lex loci delicti. The law of the place where the wrong was committed.

Lex loci situs. *See* LEX SITUS.

Lex loci solutionis. The law of the place where the contract is to be performed.

Lex situs. The law of the place where the thing in question is situated.

Lien. The rights to retain possession of goods, deeds or other property belonging to another as security for payment of money.

Lis pendens. Pending action.

Loc. cit. (loco citato). In the passage previously mentioned.

Locus classicus. Authoritative passage in a book or judgment; the principal authority or source for the subject.

Locus in quo. Scene of the event.

Locus poenitentiae. Scope or opportunity for repentance.

Locus standi. Recognised position or standing; the right to appear in court.

Lucrum cessans. A benefit which is terminated.

Magnum opus. A great work of literature.

Mala fide(s). (In) bad faith.

Malitia supplet aetatem. Malice supplements the age of an infant wrongdoer who would (in the absence of malice) be too young to be responsible for his acts.

Malum in se. An act which in itself is morally wrong, e.g. murder.

Malum prohibitum. An act which is wrong because it is prohibited by human law but is not morally wrong.

Malus animus. Evil intent.

Mansuetae naturae. Animals which are normally of a domesticated disposition.

Mesne. Intermediate; middle; dividing.

Mesne profits. Profits of land lost by the plaintiff while the defendant remained wrongfully in possession.

Mobilia sequuntur personam. The domicile of movable property follows the owner's personal domicile.

Molliter manus imposuit. Gently laid his hand upon the other party.

Mutatis mutandis. With the necessary changes of detail being made.

Natura negotii. The nature of the transaction.

Negotiorum gestio. Handling of other people's affairs.

Nemo dat quod non habet. No one has power to transfer the ownership of that which he does not own.

Nemo debet bis vexari, si constat curiae quod sit pro una et eadem causa. No one ought to be harassed with proceedings twice, if it appears to the court that it is for one and the same cause.

Nemo est haeres viventis. No one can be the heir of a person who is still living.

Nexus. Connection; bond.

Nisi. Unless; (also used of a decree or order which will later be made absolute 'unless' good cause be shown to the contrary); provisional.

Nisi prius. Cases which were directed to be tried at Westminster only if the justices of assize should 'not' have tried them in the country 'previously'.

Nocumenta infinita sunt. There is no limit to the types of situations which constitute nuisances.

Nomen collectivum. A collective name, noun or description; a word descriptive of a class.

Non compos mentis. Not of sound mind and understanding.

Non constat. It is not certain.

Non est factum. That the document in question was not his deed.

Non haec in foedera veni. This is not the agreement which I came to sign.

Non omnibus dormio. I do not turn a blind eye on every instance of misconduct.

Non sequitur. It does not follow; an inconsistent statement.

Noscitur a sociis. The meaning of a word is known from the company it keeps (ie from its context).

Nova causa interveniens. An independent cause which intervenes between the alleged wrong and the damage in question.

Novus actus interveniens. A fresh act of someone other than the defendant which intervenes between the alleged wrong and the damage in question.

Nudum pactum. A bare agreement (unsupported by consideration).

Nullius filius. No man's son; a bastard.

Obiter dictum (dicta). Thing(s) said by the way; opinions expressed by judges in passing, on issues not essential for the decision in the case.

Obligatio quasi ex contractu. An obligation arising out of an act or event, as if from a contract, but independently of the consent of the person bound.

Omnia praesumuntur contra spoliatorem. Every presumption is raised against a wrongdoer.

Omnia praesumuntur rite et solemniter esse acta donec probetur in contrarium. All things are presumed to have been performed with all due formalities until it is proved to the contrary.

Omnis ratihabitio retrotrahitur et mandato priori aequiparatur. Every ratification of a previous act is carried back and made equivalent to a previous command to do it.

Onus probandi. The burden of proving.

Op. cit. (opere citato). In the book referred to previously.

Orse. Otherwise.

Par delictum. Equal fault.

Parens patriae. Parent of the nation.

Pari materia. With equal substance.

Pari passu. On an equal footing; equally; in step with.

Pari ratione. By an equivalent process of reasoning.

Parol. By word of mouth, or unsealed document.

Participes criminis. Accomplices in the crime.

Pater est quem nuptiae demonstrant. He is the father whom the marriage indicates to be so.

Passim. Generally; referred to throughout the book or source in question.

Patrimonium. Beneficial ownership.

Pendente lite. While a law suit is pending.

Per. By; through; in the opinion of a judge.

Per capita. Divided equally between all the persons filling the description.

Per curiam. In the opinion of the court.

Per formam doni. Through the form of wording of the gift or deed.

Per incuriam. Through carelessness or oversight.

Per quod. By reason of which.

Per quod consortium et servitium amisit. By reason of which he has lost the benefit of her company and services.

Per quod servitium amisit. By reason of which he has lost the benefit of his service.

Per se. By itself.

Persona(e) designata(e). A person(s) specified as an individual(s), not identified as a member(s) of a class nor as fulfilling a particular qualification.

Per stirpes. According to the stocks of descent; one share for each line of descendants; where the descendants of a deceased person (however many they may be) inherit between them only the one share which the deceased would have taken if alive.

Per subsequens matrimonium. Legitimation of a child 'by subsequent marriage' of the parents.

Plene administravit. A plea by an executor 'that he has fully administered' all the assets which have come into his hands and that

no assets remain out of which the plaintiff's claim could be satisfied.

Plus quam tolerabile. More than can be endured.

Post. After; mentioned in a subsequent passage or page.

Post mortem. After death.

Post nuptial. Made after marriage.

Post obit bond. Agreement or bond by which a borrower agrees to pay the lender a sum larger than the loan on or after the death of a person on whose death he expects to inherit property.

Post obitum. After the death of a specified person.

Pour autrui. On behalf of another.

Prima facie. At first sight.

Primae impressionis. Of first impression.

Pro bono publico. For the public good.

Profit a prendre. The right to enter the land of another and take part of its produce.

Pro hac vice. For this occasion.

Pro privato commodo. For private benefit.

Pro rata. In proportion.

Pro rata itineris. At the same rate per mile as was agreed for the whole journey.

Pro tanto. So far; to that extent.

Pro tempore. For the time being.

Publici juris. Of public right.

Puisne. Inferior; lower in rank; not secured by deposit of deeds; of the High Court.

Punctum temporis. Moment, or point of time.

Pour autre vie. During the life of another person.

q.v. (quod vide). Which see.

Qua. As; in the capacity of.

Quaere. Consider whether it is correct.

Quaeritur. The question is raised.

Quantum. Amount; how much.

Quantum meruit. As much as he has earned.

Quantum valebant. As much as they were worth.

Quare clausum fregit. Because he broke into the plaintiff's enclosure.

Quasi. As if; seemingly.

Quasi ex contractu. *See* OBLIGATIO.

Quatenus. How far; in so far as; since.

Quia timet. Because he fears what he will suffer in the future.

Quicquid plantatur solo solo cedit. Whatever is planted in the soil belongs to the soil.

Quid pro quo. Something for something; consideration.

Qui facit per alium facit per se. He who employs another person to do something does it himself.

Qui prior est tempore potior est jure. He who is earlier in point of time is in the stronger position in law.

Quoad. Until; as far as; as to.

Quoad hoc. As far as this matter is concerned.

Quo animo. With what intention.

Quot judices tot sententiae. There were as many different opinions as there were judges.

Quousque. Until the time when.

Ratio decidendi. The reason for a decision; the principle on which a decision is based.

Ratione domicilii. By reason of a person's domicile.

Re. In the matter of; by the thing or transaction.

Renvoi. Reference to or application of the rules of a foreign legal system in a different country's courts.

Res. Thing; affair; matter; circumstance.

Res extincta. The thing which was intended to be the subject matter of a contract but had previously been destroyed.

Res gestae. Things done; the transaction.

Res integra. A point not covered by the authority of a decided case which must therefore be decided upon principle alone.

Res inter alios acta alteri nocere non debet. A man ought not to be prejudiced by what has taken place between other persons.

Res ipsa loquitur. The thing speaks for itself, i.e. is evidence of negligence in the absence of an explanation by the defendant.

Res judicata. A matter on which a court has previously reached a binding decision; a matter which cannot be questioned.

Res nova. A matter which has not previously been decided.

Res nullius. Nobody's property.

Respondeat superior. A principal must answer for the acts of his subordinates.

Res sua. Something which a man believes to belong to another when it in fact is 'his own property'.

Restitutio in integrum. Restoration of a party to his original position; full restitution.

Res vendita. The article which was sold.

Rex est procurator fatuorum. The King is the protector of the simple minded.

Rigor aequitatis. The inflexibility of equity.

Sc. *See* SCILICET.

Sciens. Knowing.

Scienter. Knowingly; with knowledge of an animal's dangerous disposition.

Scienti non fit injuria. A man who is aware of the existence of a danger has no remedy if it materialises.

Scilicet. To wit; namely; that is to say.

Scintilla. A spark; trace; or moment.

Scire facias. A writ; that you cause to know.

Scriptum praedictum non est factum suum. A plea that the aforesaid document is not his deed.

Secundum formam doni. In accordance with the form of wording in the gift or deed.

Secus. It is otherwise; the legal position is different.

Sed. But.

Sed quaere. But inquire; look into the matter; consider whether the statement is correct.

Semble. It appears; apparently.

Sentit commodum et periculum rei. He both enjoys the benefit of the thing and bears the risk of its loss.

Seriatim. In series; one by one; point by point.

Serivitium. Service.

Sic. So; in such a manner; (also used to emphasise wording copied or quoted from another source: 'such was the expression used in the original source').

Sic utere tuo ut alienum non laedas. So use your own property as not to injure the property of your neighbour.

Similiter. Similarly; in like manner.

Simplex commendatio non obligat. Mere praise of goods by the seller imposes no liability upon him.

Simpliciter. Simply; merely; alone; without any further action; without qualification.

Sine animo revertendi. Without the intention of returning.

Sine die. Without a day being appointed; indefinitely.

Solatium. Consolation; relief; compensation.

Sotto volce. In an undertone.

Specificatio. The making of a new article out of the chattel of one person by the labour of another.

Spes successionis. The hope of inheriting property on the death of another.

Spondes peritiam artis. If skill is inherent in your profession, you guarantee that you will display it.

Stare decisis. To stand by what has been dedided.

Status quo (ante). The previous position; the position in which things were before; unchanged position.

Stet. Let it stand; do not delete.

Stricto sensu. In the strict sense.

Sub colore officii. Under pretext of someone's official position.

Sub modo. Within limits; to a limited extent.

Sub nom. (sub nomine). Under the name of.

Sub silentio. In silence.

Sub tit. (sub titulo). Under the title of.

Suggestio falsi. The suggestion of something which is untrue.

Sui generis. Of its own special kind; unique.

Sui juris. Of his own right; possessed of full legal capacity.

Sup. *See* SUPRA.

Suppressio veri. The suppression of the truth.

Supra. (Sup.) Above; referred to higher up the page; previously.

Talis qualis. Such as it is.

Tam ... quam. As well ... as.

Toties quoties. As often as occasion shall require; as often as something happens.

Transit in rem judicatam. A right of action merges in the judgment recovered upon it.

Turpis causa. Immoral conduct which constitutes the subject matter of an action.

Uberrima fides. Most abundant good faith.

Ubi jus ibi remedium. Where there is a legally recognised right there is also a remedy.

Ubi supra. In the passage or reference mentioned previously.

Ultimus heres. The ultimate heir who is last in order of priority of those who may be entitled to claim the estate of an intestate.

Ultra vires. Outside the powers recognised by law as belonging to the person or body in question.

Uno flatu. With one breath; at the same moment.

Ut res magis valeat quam pereat. Words must be construed so as to support the validity of the contract rather than to destroy it.

v. (versus). Against.

Verba fortius accipiuntur contra proferentem. Ambiguous wording is construed adversely against the party who introduced it into the document.

Vera copula. True sexual unity.

Verbatim. Word by word; exactly; word for word.

Vice versa. The other way round; in turn.

Vide. See.

Vi et armis (et contra pacem domini regis). By force of arms (and in breach of the King's peace).

Vigilantibus et non dormientibus jura subveniunt (or jus succurrit). The law(s) assist(s) those who are vigilant, not those who doze over their rights.

Vinculum juris. Legal tie; that which binds the parties with mutual obligations.

Virgo intacta. A virgin with hymen intact.

Virtute officii. By virtue of a person's official position.

Vis-a-vis. Face to face; opposite to.

Vis major. Irresistible force.

Viva voce. Orally; oral examination.

Viz. (videlicet). Namely; that is to say.

Voir dire. Examination of a witness before he gives evidence, to ascertain whether he is competent to tell the truth on oath; trial within a trial.

Volens. Willing.

Volenti non fit injuria. In law no wrong is done to a man who consents to undergo it.

Index

Act of Parliament. *See* STATUTE
Act of State,   89, 112, 116, 200
Affray,   432
Agent provocateur,   159
Alien,   89
Armed forces,
    provisions relating to   448–449
Arrest. *See also* CRIMINAL LAW,
    POLICE,
    bail after,   387
    citizen's,   174
    entry and search after,   359
    entry for purpose of,   359
    force, use of,   292, 413
    general conditions,   366
    information to be given on,   369
    preserved powers,   416
    search upon,   373
    serious arrestable offence,   412
    unlawful,   1, 36, 66, 97, 209
    warrant, without,   97, 174, 201,
    365
Assemblies,
    public,   443
    trespassory,   444–446
Asylum,   501–506

Blasphemy,   22
    definition,   147
Borstals,
    duty of care,   84
Boundary Commission,
    discretion of,   133
Breach of the peace,
    binding-over,   207
By-law. *See under* LOCAL
    AUTHORITY

Canada,
    Canada Act , 1982 ... 106
    constitution,   180
Certiorari,   15, 21, 78, 110, 140,
    149, 151, 164, 165
Colony,
    legislatures, power of,   16

Compulsory purchase,
    confirmation, limitation of action,
    193
    jurisdiction,   206
    local authority, unauthorised
    purpose,   196
Confessions,   403
    handicapped, by,   404
Confidentiality,   13
Constitution,
    amendment or repeal,   26
Consultation,
    industrial training boards,   3
Contempt of Court. *See under*
    COURTS
Council. *See* LOCAL AUTHORITY
Courts. *See also* HABEAS CORPUS
    contempt of –
        Act, 1981, ... 320–334
        criminal,   11
        strict liability,   320
Criminal injuries,
    compensation,   137
Criminal law,
    Criminal Law Act, 1967 ... 292
Crown. *See also* PREROGATIVE,
    armed forces –
        dispersal and ordering of,   35
        liability in tort,   2, 257
    compensation, liability,   10, 31
    contract –
        breach of liability for,   41,
        43, 111, 179
        employment of,   63, 64, 185
    jurisdiction and procedure,   258
    levying money,   214
    meaning,   198
    Ministers of, Act,   314–317
    payment, right to,   38
    right to sue,   23, 255
    satisfaction of orders against,
    259
    tortious liability,   62, 256, 448
Crown liability. *See* CROWN

Damages,
  excessive award,   178
Declaration,   65
Defamation,
  privilege,   81
  House of Commons –
    books published by order of,
    194
Delegated powers. *See also*
DELEGATED LEGISLATION, LOCAL
AUTHORITY, MAGISTRATES,
STATUTORY POWER,
  validity,   17
Deportation. *See* IMMIGRATION
Detention. *See also* HABEAS
CORPUS, MARTIAL LAW,
  access to legal advice,   394
  after charge,   386
  continued authorisation,   382
  custody officers,   376–379
  further,   383, 384
  limitation on,   374, 381
  minimum period,   167
  review of,   380
  unlawful,   39
Discovery of documents,   4, 32,
46, 59, 260
  companies,   179
Discretion,
  local authority,   184
  minister, exercise by,   93, 98,
  115
  natural justice and,   29
  unfettered,   108
Dispensing power,   212
Dominions. *See also*
COMMONWEALTH
  extra-territorial legislation,   243
  laws, validity of,   242
  meaning,   241
  Parliament of the UK, legislation
  by,   244
  Statute of Westminster, 1931 ...
  240–244

Ecclesiastical courts, 213
Elections,
  freedom of,   218
  peer, of, to House of Commons,
  117
  Representation of the People Act,
  1949 ... 56, 73
  Representation of the People Act,
  1981 ... 318–319
  Representation of the People Act,
  1983 ... 337–342

Emergency powers,
  Emergency Powers Act, 1920 ...
  236, 237
  proclamations, issue of,   236
  regulations,   237
Estoppel,   203
European communities,
  Act of, 1993 ... 507–513
  Article 12,   113
  effect of Directive,   107
  equal pay,   101, 123
  European Communities Act, 1972
  ... 305–307
  failure to implement Directive,
  74
  national law, and,   172
  part-time workers,   160
  precedent of law,   49, 58, 77
  scope of Treaty of Rome,   199
  treaties, implementation of,   306
**European Convention for the
Protection of Human Rights and
Fundamental Freedoms, 1950** ...
530–547
  ultra vires, and,   166
Evidence,
  confessions,   403–404
  unfair,   159, 405

Fear or provocation of violence,
433, 436
Fingerprinting,   368, 398, 399
Foreign compensation,
  determinations,   6

Gaming licences,
  natural justice,   141

Habeas corpus,
  Courts, jurisdiction to inquire into
  order,   155
Harassment, alarm or distress,
434–436
Highway,
  reasonable use,   8
House of Commons. *See under*
PARLIAMENT
House of Lords. *See under*
PARLIAMENT
Human rights,   530–547

Immigration,
  appeals –
    conditions, against,   301
    deportation orders, in respect
    of,   302

Immigration, appeals (continued)
determination by adjudicators,
303
exclusion from the UK,
against, 300
Tribunal, to, 304
burden of proof, 83
community rights, 452
control –
administration of, 296
general provisions for, 295
decision to deport, 170
deportation –
appeals against orders, 451
exemptions from, 299
procedure for, 297
recommendations for, 298
hearing, 15
Immigration Act, 1971 ... 293–304
polygamy, and, 450
principles, general, 293
Refugee Convention, and,
502–506
regulation, general provisions for,
295
right of abode, statement of,
294
tribunal, appeal from, 505
Injunction,
restraining persons from acting,
335
Inquiry. *See also* TRIBUNALS AND
INQUIRIES
natural justice, conducted with,
75
Interception of communications,
418–424

Judge,
interest in company, 54
Judicial review,
application for, 336
Jockey Club, 138
locus standi, 146, 161
Minister, and, 100
prerogative, and, 50
prisoners, 114
public law, and, 188
Jury, 221
bias, 142
Justices of the Peace. *See*
MAGISTRATES

Legal advice,
access to, 158, 394

Legal representation,
right of, 69, 120, 121
Libel. *See* DEFAMATION
Licensing justices. *See*
MAGISTRATES
Local authority,
bad faith, 204
by-law, validity, reasonable, 92
decision-making, 42, 48
defamation, privilege, whether,
53
discretion, 148
expenditure, 12
duty of care, 61
interests of ratepayers, 30
ultra vires, 9, 52, 68, 80, 109,
124, 126, 129, 132

Magistrates,
bias, 132, 157, 176
clerk, improper conduct, 176
***Mandamus*,** 119, 136, 145, 152,
153, 185
Meetings. *See* UNLAWFUL
MEETINGS
Minister,
decision of, 164
discretion of, 33, 161, 168
duty of care, 187
power to transfer functions, 314

Natural justice,
bias, 88, 132
breach of, 7
discretion and, 45, 189
duty to act fairly, 94
hearing, right to, 71, 79, 99,
103, 129, 178
legal representation, 69, 120,
121
notice, giving, 44
ousting of, 76
university students, 34
Negligence,
Department of Employment, 90
Northern Ireland,
valid regulation, 102
Notice,
validity, 5

Obscene publications, 262–265,
273–274
Official Secrets Act, 1911 ... 234,
235
Official Secrets Act, 1920 ... 238,
239

Official Secrets Act, 1989 ...
476–487

Panel on take-overs and mergers,
judicial review, and,   153
Parliament,
Act of. *See* STATUTE
Boundary Commission,   81, 426,
427, 429
constituencies,   425
Dominions, power to legislate for,
82
duration of,   233
future, no power to bind, by
statute,   67
House of Commons –
contempt of,   191
licensing laws,   143
privilege,   118
defamation. *See*
DEFAMATION
Select Committee,   55
Speaker, certificate of,   229
House of Commons
Disqualification Act, 1957 ...
308–313
House of Lords –
Life Peerages Act, 1958 ... 261
peeress, not eligible to sit in,
181
powers as to Money Bills
227
privilege of Member at all
times,   195
restriction of powers,   228
Parliamentary Commissioner,
complaint, provisions,   281
consultations,   287
discretion,   154
evidence,   283
investigation, authorities and
departments subject to,   279
subject to,   280
procedure,   282
Parliamentary Commissioner Act,
1967 ... 276–291
report by,   285
Passport,
refusal of application,   162
Peerage,
disclaimer,   266–268
Irish,   270
Life, creation of,   261
Scottish,   269
woman,   271

Planning permission,
valid,   95
Police,
assaults on,   272
breach of the peace, and,   197
Codes of Practice,   401, 402
complaints and discipline,
407–411
fingerprinting,   395, 399
intimate samples,   396, 399
local authority, not servants of,
72
obstruction of,   181
office under Crown, whether,
96
powers of entry, search and
seizure,   349–364, 521, 523
questioning and treatment by,
390–400
refusal of access to solicitor,   158
searches,   390–392
special procedure,   415
records,   345
road checks,   346
stop and search, power of,   343,
344, 466, 519
voluntary attendance at police
station,   370
**Police and Criminal Evidence Act,
1984 ...** 343–417
Policy,
continuing,   173
Prerogative. *See also* CROWN
judicial review, and,   50
keeping the peace,   169
law, and,   127, 128
levying of money,   86
limitation of scope,   161, 163
mercy,   144
restriction of, Dominion statute,
28
salpetre,   225
treaty-making powers,   20
Prevention of terrorism,
453–475
Prison,
mutiny,   171
Privacy,
right to,   105
Privilege. *See also* CROWN,
PARLIAMENT
defamation,   18, 40, 47, 125
Public assemblies,   443
Public interest immunity,   135
Public law,
meaning,   139

Public law (continued)
 private law, and, 202
Public order. *See also* PUBLIC
 MEETINGS, RIOT, UNLAWFUL
 MEETINGS
 political uniforms, 245
 Public Order Act,1936 ... 245–246
 Public Order Act 1986, 430–447
 quasi-military organisations,
 246
Public processions, 440–442
Public Worship Act, 1874,
 time limit for complaint, 85

Race relations
 anti-apartheid policy, 205
Raves,
 police powers, 522, 524
 sound equipment, 525–526
Regulations,
 ultra vires, 14
Rhodesia,
 lawful government, 104
Riot, 30, 436, 439

Search warrants, 134
 execution, 357
 safeguards, 356
Secretary of State,
 changes in departments or
 functions, 315
Seizure of documents, 70
Ship money,
 case of, 192
Silence,
 account, failure to, 516, 517
 facts, failure to mention, 514
 trial, at, 515
Solicitor,
 access to, 158, 394
Standing army, 216
Statute,
 legality of, 122
Statutory instruments,
 annulment, subject to, 251
 definition, 247
 numbering and printing, 248
 Parliament, laying before, 250
 drafts, 252
 publication and citation, 248,
 249
 regulations, 254

Statutory instruments (continued)
 validity, 175, 208
Suspending power,
 illegal, 211

Taxation. *See also* INCOME TAX,
 PREROGATIVE, SHIP MONEY
 amnesty 87
 immunity from, 27
 nuclear weapons, and, 37
 ultra vires, 51
Terrorism,
 prevention, 453–475
Ticket touts, 529
Trade unions,
 natural justice, 25
Trespass,
 aggravated, 527–528
Trespassers. *See also* ASSEMBLIES
 removal of, 520
Tribunals and inquiries. *See also*
 DOMESTIC TRIBUNAL, NATURAL
 JUSTICE
 appeals from, 497, 505
 chairmen of, 492
 Council on Tribunals, 488–491
 error on face of record, 150
 members of, 491
 procedural rules, 494–495
 reasons for decisions, 496
 removal of members, 493
 Scottish Committee, 489
 statutory inquiries, 495
 superior courts, supervisory
 powers of, 498

Ultra vires. *See* DELEGATED
 LEGISLATION, DELEGATED
 POWERS, DOMESTIC TRIBUNAL,
 LEGAL REPRESENTATION, LOCAL
 AUTHORITY, MAGISTRATES,
 NATURAL JUSTICE, REGULATIONS
Unlawful meetings,
 breach of the peace, likelihood of,
 19

Violent disorder, 431

War damage,
 compensation, abolition of rights
 to, 275